Cambridge Monographs on the History of Medicine

Health, medicine and mortality
in the sixteenth century

VICTORIA.

IVSTICIA.   PRVDENTIA.

DIEV ET MON DROYT.

COMPENDIOSA
totius Anatomie delineatio, ære
exarata: per Thomam Geminum.
LONDINI.

Health, medicine and mortality in the sixteenth century

EDITED BY
CHARLES WEBSTER

READER IN THE HISTORY OF MEDICINE AND DIRECTOR OF THE WELLCOME UNIT
FOR THE HISTORY OF MEDICINE, UNIVERSITY OF OXFORD

CAMBRIDGE UNIVERSITY PRESS
CAMBRIDGE
LONDON · NEW YORK · MELBOURNE

Published by the Syndics of the Cambridge University Press
The Pitt Building, Trumpington Street, Cambridge CB2 1RP
Bentley House, 200 Euston Road, London NW1 2DB
32 East 57th Street, New York, NY 10022, USA
296 Beaconsfield Parade, Middle Park, Melbourne 3206, Australia

© Cambridge University Press 1979

First published 1979

Printed in Great Britain at the University Press, Cambridge

Library of Congress Cataloguing in Publication Data

Main entry under title:
Health, medicine and mortality in the sixteenth
century.

Includes index.
1. Medicine–England–History–16th century.
2. Public health–England–History–16th century.
3. Mortality–England–History–16th century.
I. Webster, Charles. [DNLM: 1. History of Medicine,
16th century–England. 2. Mortality–History–England.
WZ70 FE5 H4]
R487.H42 610′.942 78–73234
ISBN 0 521 22643 0

TO THE MEMORY OF
SANFORD VINCENT LARKEY

CONTENTS

ILLUSTRATIONS

CONTRIBUTORS

PATRICIA ALLDERIDGE
Bethlem Royal Hospital, Monks Orchard Road, Beckenham, Kent
BR3 3BX

ANDREW B. APPLEBY
Department of History, San Diego State University, San Diego,
California 92182, USA

JEROME J. BYLEBYL
Institute of the History of Medicine, The Johns Hopkins University,
1900 East Monument Street, Baltimore, Maryland 21205, USA

ALLAN CHAPMAN
86A Banbury Road, Oxford

THOMAS R. FORBES
Section of Gross Anatomy, Department of Surgery, Yale University
School of Medicine, New Haven, Connecticut 06510, USA

MARGARET PELLING
Wellcome Unit for the History of Medicine, 47 Banbury Road,
Oxford OX2 6PE

ROGER SCHOFIELD
Cambridge Group for the History of Population and Social Structure,
27 Trumpington Street, Cambridge CB2 1QA

PAUL SLACK
Exeter College, Oxford

CHARLES WEBSTER
Wellcome Unit for the History of Medicine, 47 Banbury Road,
Oxford OX2 6PE

E. A. WRIGLEY
Cambridge Group for the History of Population and Social Structure,
27 Trumpington Street, Cambridge CB2 1QA

FOREWORD

The first Master of Pembroke College, Oxford, had been Regius Professor of Medicine. So had my predecessor, Sir George Pickering, in whose time the idea of this volume was conceived. Sir Thomas Browne, author of *Religio Medici*, was a member of the College at the time of its foundation; and Sanford V. Larkey, to whose memory this book is dedicated, was at Pembroke from 1925 to 1928.

It is therefore fitting that the College should act as midwife to this collection of essays on medicine in the sixteenth century. The College is grateful to all those who have contributed to this volume, and above all to Dr Charles Webster, who first had the idea, and without whom nothing could have been done. But the original impulse came from Dr Larkey's widow, Mrs Geraldine Henderson of Santa Barbara, California, whose generosity to the College has made possible the publication of this book as the most fitting tribute to the memory of Sanford V. Larkey.

Pembroke College　　　　　　　　　　　GEOFFREY ARTHUR
Oxford　　　　　　　　　　　　　　　　MASTER

ACKNOWLEDGEMENTS

The successful completion of the present collaborative volume is the result of a multiplicity of factors. The editor is particularly grateful to colleagues in Britain and America for agreeing so readily to make available for this study the results of recently completed researches. In the case of Patricia Allderidge a contribution was supplied at exceptionally short notice. The Master and Fellows of Pembroke College, and Mrs Geraldine Henderson, have consistently given the editor and contributors encouragement and support, and have provided generous financial aid both for the volume, and for the handlist of S. V. Larkey's papers prepared by Mr M. A. L. Cooke.

The staff of the library of the Wellcome Institute for the History of Medicine, London, have given frequent and prompt assistance to the editor and contributors. Many other institutions to which thanks are due are acknowledged where appropriate in the text.

From the time of its conception to the completion of work on the volume, the editor has received invaluable assistance from Margaret Pelling of the Wellcome Unit, Oxford. The index was prepared by Paul Weindling, also of the Oxford Unit. Indispensable typing assistance has been provided throughout by Mrs Irene Ashton of Sheffield.

DNB   *Dictionary of National Biography*, ed. L. Stephen and S. Lee (63 vols., 1885–1900)

P.R.O.   London, Public Record Office

STC A   A. W. Pollard and G. R. Redgrave, *A Short-Title Catalogue of Books Printed in England, Scotland and Ireland, and of English Books Printed Abroad, 1475–1640* (Oxford, 1926)

STC B   *A Short-Title Catalogue*, etc., 2nd edn, II (I to Z), revised and enlarged by W. A. Jackson, F. S. Ferguson and K. F. Pantzer (London, 1976); vol. I forthcoming

STC   collective reference to *STC* A and *STC* B

Venn   J. Venn and J. A. Venn, *Alumni Cantabrigienses. Part I. From the Earliest Times to 1751* (4 vols., Cambridge, 1922–7)

Modern spelling, capitalization and punctuation have been adopted for all except extended quotations, and for works mentioned in the text. Original spelling, but not capitalization, is given for the first citation of a work in each chapter's notes.

The place of publication of works published before 1900 is London unless otherwise stated.

Introduction

CHARLES WEBSTER

It is fitting that the completion of the present collaborative study of health, medicine and mortality in the sixteenth century should coincide with the four hundredth anniversary of the birth of the physician William Harvey, and the three hundred and fiftieth anniversary of the publication of his *De motu cordis*. The important subject of the life and work of William Harvey stands out as one of the few areas in the history of medicine to have been subjected to intensive historical scrutiny. In the present context it is interesting to note that Harvey was the subject of one of Sir William Osler's best-known lectures, 'The Growth of Truth as Illustrated by the Discovery of the Circulation of the Blood'.[1] In this Harveian Oration, as in his equally distinguished lectures on Sir Thomas Browne (1905) and Thomas Linacre (1908), Osler convincingly argued for the study of medical history as a contribution to medical humanism. He believed that biographical studies of the great medical thinkers of the past would contribute to a definitive 'biography of the mind of man'. Such a programme, calling for the integrated application of the skills of the humanities and the sciences, was seen as an essential constituent of a medical humanism continuing into the present age of scientific medicine.

Sanford Vincent Larkey, like Osler, was connected with the Johns Hopkins Medical School. Among its many innovations, Osler's medical school established one of the first university institutes for the history of medicine in the English-speaking world. Larkey was associated with this institute from its creation. He inherited Osler's conviction that the creation of collections of historical sources, and the compilation of professionally competent bibliographies, were essential pre-requisites for the development of the history of medicine. Larkey also shared Osler's commitment to the value of medical humanism. However,

---

[1] Harveian Oration, 1906. Published London, 1907; also in *Selected Writings of Sir William Osler* (London, 1951), pp. 205–36.

Larkey's conception of humanism differed significantly from that of Osler. Larkey's writings contain relatively little reference to such major figures as Harvey. Indeed his massive collection of bibliographical notes bypasses almost completely the names which are regarded as those of the founders of modern scientific medicine. Larkey subtly changed the emphasis of medical humanism, in accordance with what he regarded as the intellectual needs of the medical profession and the public, during a period of rapid advance in medical science coinciding with the upheavals caused by the Second World War.

In the context of the ever-widening horizons of modern medicine, Larkey believed that it was essential to subject the medical system to historical analysis. His programme for medical humanism entailed the maintenance of a close relationship between medicine, history and the social sciences. By this means elements of arbitrary selectivity and distortion would be removed, and through 'greater co-ordination between the history of medicine and political, social and economic history', we would come to an 'examination of the past in the light of its own intellectual and social milieu'.[2] As the quotation aptly cited at the head of the paper by Thomas Forbes in this volume indicates, Larkey's views were shared by Henry Sigerist, the Director of the Johns Hopkins Institute, who drew attention to the limitations of a history of medicine restricted entirely to the 'history of great doctors and the books they wrote'. Sigerist, himself author of *Grosse Arzte* (1932), called for a 'social history' of medicine, which would be concerned with 'the history of the patient in society, that of the physician and the history of the relations between physician and patient'.[3] In elevating the patient to an integral place in the history of medicine, Larkey and Sigerist underlined the degree to which patients provide a necessary pre-requisite for the existence of medicine.

Sanford Larkey was as faithful as any of his distinguished colleagues at Johns Hopkins in following the maxims of the social history of medicine. To be consistent, this new approach demanded a much finer degree of specialization than was traditionally to the liking of medical historians. Larkey opted for the study of medicine in Tudor England. This subject recommended itself by the obvious freshness and vitality of English post-reformation culture. This period was also characterized by

[2] S. V. Larkey, 'Thoughts on medical history and libraries – 1847 and 1947', *Bulletin of the New York Academy of Medicine*, 2nd ser., XXV (1949), 65–83; p. 75.

[3] H. Sigerist, 'The social history of medicine', *Western Journal of Surgery, Obstetrics and Gynecology*, XLVIII (1940), 715–22; p. 716.

the richness of its vernacular medical literature. Of the areas of enquiry not susceptible to organization in terms of the exegesis of great works, or major scientific innovations, none could be more conspicuously deserving of study than Tudor medicine. In exploring this area, Larkey found ready allies and collaborators in such scholars as F. R. Johnson, whose interest in medicine was awakened by an appreciation of the relevance of popular science to the understanding of Tudor literature. Universal fascination with all aspects of the 'Age of Shakespeare' guaranteed Larkey a receptive audience for his work.

Despite its intrinsic attractions, however, Tudor medicine turned out to be a subject bristling with technical difficulties. The vernacular literature upon which Larkey worked included a large number of editions of the greatest rarity, presenting problems of bibliographical variation, authorship, and provenance of texts. But Larkey recognized that any balanced interpretation of Tudor medicine necessitated a great deal of painstaking and relatively unglamorous bibliographical work across the entire field of this literature. It was also clear that the faithful reconstruction of Tudor medicine required a diligent search into a much wider body of writing relating to other aspects of the sciences, and to subjects such as witchcraft and religion. I personally came fully to appreciate the high quality of Larkey's bibliographical work when asked to undertake the updating of his 1941 contribution on science, medicine, and related subjects included in volume 1 of the *Cambridge Bibliography of English Literature*. This selective but extensive bibliography displayed excellent judgment and great accuracy over its whole range, with respect to both primary and secondary sources. It became established as the definitive guide to the scientific and medical sources which were likely to have been utilized by contemporary literary figures. Because of Larkey's diligence, revision proved to be a straightforward exercise.

The full scope of Larkey's work is described in detail in the essay and bibliography compiled by Margaret Pelling for the present volume. As she indicates, Larkey's research publications significantly added to the range and accuracy of our knowledge of Tudor medicine. His work included some notable discoveries relating to the English influence of Copernicus, Vesalius and Columbo. But in the main Larkey was concerned to increase our knowledge of aspects of medicine which were of primary interest to contemporaries; hence his conclusive researches on the bibliographical maze surrounding the first English *Herbal*, and his edition of an early ophthalmological treatise. He brought into focus a whole spectrum of minor figures such as Geminus, Udall, Surphlet and

Hunton, as well as adding to our awareness of major vernacular writers like Banister and Clowes.

Throughout his career Larkey continued to amass materials in connection with various projects relating to Tudor medicine. His exhaustive collection of bibliographical notes now deposited in Pembroke College, Oxford, contains data essential for any definitive study of this subject. Regrettably, Larkey's many other scholarly, medical and public service commitments precluded him from bringing his project on Tudor medicine to final fruition. Nevertheless his published writings stand as an invaluable asset and a constant source of reference for present-day students of Tudor medicine.

The Master and Fellows of Pembroke College decided that it would be appropriate to commemorate Sanford Larkey by sponsoring a collaborative volume on Tudor medicine, containing studies on themes with which Larkey was concerned, and adopting a scope which was consistent with his ideas on the social history of medicine. The direction taken by current research thoroughly vindicates Larkey's judgment as to profitable areas of research in the history of medicine. Subjects upon which he wrote many years ago, such as childbirth, or astrology and politics, now attract a keen following. Almost every subject discussed in this volume finds a point of reference in Larkey's published work or in his unpublished notes. It was felt that besides offering an opportunity for comment on health, disease and medicine from various vantage points within the social sciences, the present project would provide an ideal pretext for a collaboration between specialists whose work is too rarely gathered into a single volume. The full exploration of the resources of the history of medicine is only made practicable by exploiting the skills of authors whose contributions are normally dispersed through journals concerned with social history, economic history, demography, epidemiology, the various branches of medicine, as well as the history of science and medicine. It is a reflection of the high level of activity and enthusiasm among students of the topics covered in this volume that little difficulty was encountered in persuading colleagues to participate in the project. We are also fortunate in having been offered contributions which in the main reflect the results of very recent and hitherto unpublished researches.

The boundaries of the various studies have not been rigidly defined. The sixteenth century provides a focal point, but on many occasions it has been found essential to draw comparisons with late medieval contexts, and more especially to carry over the investigation into the early Stuart period. In order to attain an adequate depth of detailed analysis, and to provide a sense of unity and continuity, most of the text is concerned with England. However, besides collectively providing a model appropriate for comparison with other localized surveys, most of these English case studies have involved cross-reference to the continental situation. In the case of essays based on literary sources, or relating to intellectual traditions, questions of continental influence acquire central importance. The significance of continental precedent is emphasized by the paper of Jerome Bylebyl on the highly cosmopolitan medical school of Padua.

The present volume makes no claim to deal with every aspect of health, disease and medicine in sixteenth-century England. Such an attempt at comprehensive coverage would have led to an unacceptable degree of diffuseness in a volume of the present permitted length. Consequently we have preferred to include detailed investigations on important issues spanning the whole range of the subject.

While scholars such as Larkey pioneered the study of the vernacular literature, recent research has led to the exploitation of even less accessible sources. Contributions in the present volume are hence heavily reliant on unpublished material such as parish records, wills, probate inventories, personal papers and institutional records. The use of such sources has permitted a much greater degree of quantification on the many issues which can only be effectively resolved in quantitative terms. This facet of our work has greatly benefited from data gathered under the aegis of the Cambridge Group for the History of Population and Social Structure.

The volume divides fairly evenly into two major sections, the first concerned primarily with prevailing levels of health, and problems of disease, the second with agencies of health care. The contributions of Andrew Appleby and Paul Slack deal with the assessment of the changing pattern of health, with particular reference to the impact of epidemics and dearth. Their work enables us to establish more precisely the extent to which England was affected by crises of health and subsistence in the sixteenth century. Roger Schofield and E. A. Wrigley discuss the problem of mortality with respect to age-specific mortality rates, concentrating on infants and children as the most vulnerable age groups. Each of these early age groups is found to possess its characteristic mortality profile, amenable to explanation in terms of the changing balance of endogenous and exogenous factors. For the early modern period direct information defining causes of death is rarely available. Thomas Forbes discusses this problem with respect to a group of London parishes for which bills of mortality taken together with supplementary evidence are sufficient to enable us to obtain a colourful impression of the hazards to life facing a large urban community.

London also figures prominently in the second section of this volume, as a publishing centre, as a city with a complex structure of medical practice, as a city with a group of major hospitals, and as a focal point for innovation and dissent. Patricia Allderidge explores for the first time archival records relating to Bethlem Hospital, the most neglected of the major London hospitals, but one which has particular historical interest in view of the institutionalization of lunacy.

The structure of medical practice is discussed by Margaret Pelling and myself in relation to London, and East Anglia. The place of the university in the education and licensing of medical practitioners is considered by taking the medical faculty of Cambridge University. This section of our study offers many points of contrast with the medical school at Padua as described by Jerome Bylebyl. Paul Slack's survey of the vernacular medical literature draws attention to the wide demand for medical knowledge among educated laymen. The best of the more original medical writings bear favourable comparison with vernacular works produced elsewhere in Europe. The work of authors like Elyot, Turner, Clowes and Woodall is of major importance. The main service of the medical writers was as compilers and translators, making available to the English public an amazingly wide spectrum of the most successful continental works. Particular attention is drawn in this volume to the widespread following for astrological and alchemical medicine. Neither of these facets of medicine showed signs of losing its broad popular appeal in the course of the sixteenth century. Indeed the rise of neo-Platonism and Paracelsianism served if anything to increase their intellectual appeal.

Contributors to the collaborative volume appreciate that technical limitations have prevented the proper discussion of certain key problems relating to health and disease in the period in question. In many cases we are at the stage where further progress is hindered by the absence of evidence. Even on questions of mortality, as Paul Slack points out, we must be careful not to fall back on conclusions which are merely aberrations determined by the uneven survival of data. It has been possible to make rapid strides in the field of demography on the basis of the survival of extensive parish record evidence relating to mortality. It is much more difficult to make assessments about the changing pattern of morbidity, or about the general quality of life, and prevailing customs relating to such elements as diet, personal hygiene, sexual behaviour, lactation and the rearing of infants. These subjects are not on the whole susceptible to statistical investigation, or analysis utilizing any single source material. The important problems lying at the interface of human biology and social history are particularly unamenable to straightforward assessment. In respect of belief systems, we have access to ample sources describing the medical knowledge of the literate classes. Perceptions of disease and the medical lore transmitted orally among the classes forming the major part of the population, are subjects still far from being understood. It is by no means obvious that what is often represented as 'popular medicine' genuinely coincides with the values and practices of the non-literate classes.

Despite the acknowledged incompleteness of the present survey of health, medicine and mortality in the sixteenth century, it is hoped that our work will provide a useful foundation for further exploration of the many difficult and neglected aspects of this subject which remain to be resolved. The gradual expansion of this work will contribute a valuable element towards the understanding of early modern western society.

I

Mortality crises and epidemic disease in England 1485–1610

PAUL SLACK

Visitations of pestilence of one kind or another were familiar, inescapable features of the environment in Tudor England, regular reminders of the insecurity of life and the imminence of death. They produced years of exceptionally high mortality, when death rates in villages and towns doubled or trebled and the normal life of local communities was totally and tragically disrupted. Although these crises were of short duration, rarely lasting more than a year, and demographic and economic recovery was often rapid afterwards, they were memorable events, important landmarks in the annals of local societies. Their effects were recorded in diaries and chronicles, and each successive 'great plague' or 'great pestilence' was used as a natural point of reference until its place was usurped by the next epidemic year.[1] These crises were the spectacular features of the social and demographic, as well as the medical, landscape of early modern England.

One purpose of this essay is to ask how frequent and how serious these years of high mortality were. That they were a characteristic part of the demographic structure of pre-industrial western Europe is well known. A recent analysis of their decline by M. W. Flinn indicates that the 'stabilisation of mortality' largely occurred in the eighteenth century. Sudden and large increases in mortality were much more common in the first three quarters of the seventeenth century than later, and Flinn suggests that mortality may well have fluctuated even more violently in the sixteenth than in the seventeenth century.[2] The examples which follow provide confirmation for this suggestion as far as England is concerned. Unfortunately, it has not been possible to present quantitative data precisely comparable with those given by Professor

---

[1] See for example A. E. Hudd (ed.), 'Two Bristol calendars', *Transactions of the Bristol and Gloucestershire Archaeological Society*, XIX (1894), 134, 140–1; and for more personal reflections, *The Autobiography of Thomas Whythorne*, ed. J. M. Osborn (Oxford, 1961), pp.141ff.

[2] M. W. Flinn, 'The stabilisation of mortality in pre-industrial Western Europe', *Journal of European Economic History*, III (1974), 285–318.

Flinn, since the sources for the earlier period are less complete and more variable in quality. In particular, it has been necessary here to adopt a slightly different definition of crisis. Professor Flinn has taken a 50 per cent excess of mortality over and above the normal as a minimum requirement for a crisis in a single parish or town; but in this survey most cases in which mortality rose by less than 100 per cent in a single year have been excluded, in order to avoid doubtful cases and to reduce the size of the subject. Even so, the number of occasions on which mortality rates doubled in individual towns and villages is very large, a strong indication that the instability of mortality behaviour was at least as great in the sixteenth as in the seventeenth century.

A second purpose of this paper is to enquire into the causes of these crises. The epidemic diseases, the plagues and pestilences which produced them, seemed to contemporaries unpredictable strokes of fate. They did not think them unrelated to other features of the environment. For they were one symptom of disorder in the universe, and as such they were inevitably connected with other disorders. They might be a consequence of astrological disturbance or political division, of war or famine, of bad hygiene or personal excess. But their timing and incidence were determined by divine providence and their first cause was supernatural: epidemics were God's punishment for man's sin. While abandoning supernatural interpretations, historians have continued to look for connections between mortality crises and other changes in the environment. They have sought to relate them above all to the state of the harvest, to problems of subsistence and the pressure of population on food supplies. However, while some increases in mortality undoubtedly did coincide with periods of near-famine, many more did not, and the relative importance of diseases associated with malnutrition is not yet established. Consequently, although many historians have adopted a neo-Malthusian approach to fluctuations in mortality, others have seen major epidemics as essentially exogenous, if not completely fortuitous, events. Professor Chambers, for example, has been able to stress with some force that epidemic disease was a largely 'autonomous' influence on mortality in pre-industrial England.[3] Perhaps the most urgent, and certainly the most difficult task for the historian of crisis mortality is to analyse these interactions between

[3] J. D. Chambers, *Population, Economy and Society in Pre-Industrial England* (Oxford, 1972), chapter 4. See also R. Lee, 'Population in pre-industrial England: an econometric analysis', *Quarterly Journal of Economics*, LXXXVII (1973), 581–607; and for a general statement of the contrary view, stressing the importance of standards of living, T. McKeown, *The Modern Rise of Population* (London, 1976), especially pp.134–6.

disease and other features of society. Was pestilence as capricious and independent a stroke of fortune in past societies as it seemed?

It will quickly become apparent that there are no simple or certain answers to these problems. The forms taken by mortality crises are perplexing in their variety, and exceptions can readily be found to almost any generalization. The student of past epidemics needs no instruction in the manifold variations which occur in the relationship between biological and social change, and the study of particular instances needs to be advanced much further before there can be any approach to a satisfactory study of historical epidemiology. The aim of this essay is therefore to raise some of the questions which have emerged from work so far completed, and to suggest patterns and hypotheses which may help to stimulate further enquiry.

I

Not the least of the historian's problems arise from the unevenness of the source materials for mortality in the sixteenth century, and these demand some initial consideration. There are two relevant sorts of record: parish registers and wills. The virtues and vices of parish registers are already well known, and it is unnecessary to describe them at length here.[4] The parochial registration of burials, along with baptisms and marriages, was first ordered in 1538. But registers do not survive in any large number before the reign of Elizabeth, and many Elizabethan registers are parchment copies made at the very end of the reign, which may or may not be accurate transcripts of paper originals. Even the best-kept registers are not complete records of mortality. They record burials in the churchyard, not deaths in the parish, and they are subject to the errors and inefficiency of the parish clerks who compiled them. They are particularly liable to understate the number of deaths during a mortality crisis and sometimes in these circumstances registration broke down altogether. Parish registers are also limited by the small areas which they cover. It requires considerable effort to reconstruct from them a picture of mortality trends over a whole region. Nevertheless, these limitations have corresponding advantages. The problem of under-registration means that registers are unlikely to exaggerate the severity of the crises analysed here, and we shall see that their local coverage makes them excellent sources for measuring variations in the incidence of high

---

4 See E. A. Wrigley (ed.), *An Introduction to English Historical Demography* (London, 1966), especially pp.106–9; J. C. Cox, *The Parish Registers of England* (London, 1910), chapters 1 and 2.

mortality over small areas, particularly within large towns. With all their faults parish registers are indispensable.

For the period before 1538 and for many areas of the country before 1560, we have to turn to a more questionable source: testamentary records. The number of wills proved from year to year in the various ecclesiastical courts ought in theory to reflect changes in the level of mortality in the dioceses or archdeaconries covered by them. Probate records, unlike parish registers, should thus provide a guide to fluctuations in mortality over large areas of the country. They have been used for this purpose in a study of the great epidemic of 1557–9 by F. J. Fisher, who argues that a large rise in the number of wills proved, followed by a similar or larger fall, 'is as good a measure of an epidemic as one is likely to find'.[5] It is in fact the only readily available indicator of changes in mortality before the advent of parish registers.[6] Yet one needs to be cautious in drawing firm conclusions from these sources since they have major limitations. Not everyone made a will, and the proportion that did was not constant. Changes in testamentary habits may thus affect the total number of wills proved over any given space of time. In most ecclesiastical courts, for example, the number of wills proved was rising rapidly in the first three quarters of the sixteenth century, and it is often difficult to disentangle the effects of short-term crises from this long-term trend.

Testamentary habits may equally have varied a good deal from one part of the country to another, so that wills in different ecclesiastical courts record the mortality experience of different samples of the population. A search for the wills of people entered in the burial registers of different parishes often reveals marked variations. In the market town of Banbury between 1558 and 1570, for example, at least 1 in 16 of those buried had made a will; in one of the central parishes in the city of London, St Michael Cornhill, the proportion was 1 in 25; but in the London parish of St Botolph Bishopsgate, a few yards away, it was only 1 in 40 in the period 1559–70.[7] Such differences were no doubt to a large

---

[5] F. J. Fisher, 'Influenza and inflation in Tudor England', *Economic History Review*, 2nd ser., XVIII (1965), 126. See also T. H. Hollingsworth, *Historical Demography* (London, 1969), pp.237–40.

[6] Manor Court rolls are another source which might reveal serious mortality crises, but they are less comprehensive in their geographical coverage.

[7] Figures calculated from *Baptism and Burial Register of Banbury, Oxfordshire I*, 1558–1653, ed. J. S. W. Gibson, Banbury Historical Society, no.7 (Oxford, 1965–6), and from a comparison of *The Parish Registers of St Michael Cornhill*, ed. J. L. Chester, Harleian Society (1882) and *The Register of St Botolph Bishopsgate, London*, transcr. A. W. C. Hallen (n.pl., 1889), with the index of testamentary records cited in note 8.

degree determined by the social composition of the populations of the parishes. St Botolph, for example, was a much poorer parish than St Michael, and fewer of its inhabitants had property to bequeath. It is the unrepresentative nature of this will-making minority which provides the most serious limitation to testamentary records. Not only were those who left wills people of some property; they were also usually adult (and as a rule male) householders. Consequently the number of wills proved in ecclesiastical courts cannot be expected to reflect changes in mortality among the poor or young people. This is a major drawback if one is searching for evidence of an epidemic disease like bubonic plague which affected both these groups disproportionately.

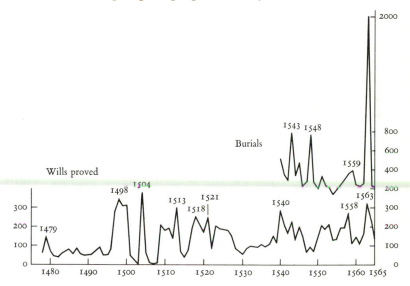

Fig. 1.   Wills proved in the Commissary Court (London division) 1478–1565 and burials in eighteen city parishes of London 1540–1565. Sources: see notes 8 and 10.

The point can be illustrated by a comparison of mortality statistics drawn from parish registers and testamentary records for the same locality. The lower half of Fig. 1 shows the number of wills proved between 1478 and 1565 in the Commissary Court of London (London division), which covered a large part of the city of London and some of the parishes around it.[8] Apart from the one or two years, especially in the

---

[8]   The source of Fig. 1 is *Testamentary Records in the Commissary Court of London*, I: 1374–1488, British Record Society, Index Library, vol.82 (London and Chichester, 1969); II: 1489–1570, vol.86 (1974).

first decade of the sixteenth century, when suspiciously few wills were proved, they appear to give a persuasive picture of periods of unusually high mortality. There is literary evidence to show that all the peak years were years of disease and pestilence in the capital, from the plague of 1479 through to that of 1563.[9] However, when we put alongside this line the aggregated burials from eighteen parishes in the city of London between 1540 and 1565, some differences emerge.[10] It is reassuring to find that the peak years coincide. But the relative sizes of the peaks suggest that the probate records understate the rise in mortality in 1543, 1548 and above all 1563, all of them years when bubonic plague struck the capital. Admittedly, we are not quite comparing like with like. The burial statistics come from the central part of the city; the wills are drawn from a larger area, including parts of the Home Counties which were no doubt less severely affected by plague than inner London itself. Nevertheless, two thirds of the wills were made by people living in the built-up area of the city. They might have been expected to show the impact of plague more clearly if they faithfully reflected the mortality experience of the whole population. A similar comparison of numbers of wills proved and burials registered in Norwich also suggests that testamentary records, because of their selective social coverage, constitute relatively poor indices of the violence of mortality in epidemics of plague.[11] The probate evidence can be used to identify crisis years, but it is not as precise an indicator of changes in the level of mortality in whole populations as the record of burials in parish registers.

II

In spite of their limitations, however, the available sources do enable us to establish a chronology of years of high mortality in Tudor England. Testamentary records from other parts of England can be used to furnish a picture of major fluctuations in mortality in the first half of the sixteenth century not inconsistent with the evidence for London displayed in Fig. 1. The numbers of wills proved in seven dioceses or

9 C. Creighton, *A History of Epidemics in Britain* (2 vols., Cambridge, 1891–4), I, 232, 282–304.

10 The parishes concerned are: Allhallows Bread St, SS Antholin, Clement Eastcheap, Dionis Backchurch, Lawrence Jewry, Mary le Bow, Michael Bassishaw and Peter Cornhill, whose registers have been published by the Harleian Society; and SS Andrew Hubbard, Lawrence Pountney, Martin Ludgate, Martin Pomeroy, Mary Bothaw, Mary Woolnoth, Michael Crooked Lane, Nicholas Cole Abbey, Olave Jewry and Stephen Coleman Street, whose registers have been consulted in the Guildhall Library, London.

11 P. A. Slack, 'Some aspects of epidemics in England 1485–1640' (University of Oxford D.Phil. thesis, 1972), pp.156–7 (hereafter Slack, thesis).

archdeaconries have been counted, and the notable peak years before 1560 are shown in Table 1.[12] Some peaks were more pronounced than others. In every case except that of London the later 1550s were wholly exceptional, with the number of wills rising to well over twice the annual average for two or more years in succession. The increases in earlier years were generally rather less violent, though still suggesting mortality rates in the will-making class 100 per cent above the norm. Where the number of wills did not quite reach twice the annual average for the previous decade, the dates have been given in brackets. While making every allowance for the quality of the data, it would seem that mortality crises hit many parts of the country in the 1520s and 1540s and were of unusual severity in the later 1550s. In the south-east at least, they were apparently not uncommon between 1498 and 1518. Only the 1530s appear as a decade of relative stability in mortality.

Table 1. *Years of high mortality 1485–1560*

Area											
Essex (1479–)	1504	1518					1540			(1550)	1557–8
Berkshire (1508–)			1521		1529		1540–1	1545		(1550)	1557–9
Worcester diocese (1509–)					1527–9		1538	1545			1557–9
Leicestershire (1510–)		1517	1521	(1526)				(1543)			1557–8
Lichfield diocese (1516–)				1524	1527	1530	(1540)	(1546)		(1551)	1557–9
Exeter diocese (1532–)								1546	1551		1557–8
East Sussex (1540–)								1545			1557–8

Source: probate records. See note 12.

The early parish registers confirm parts of this picture and permit its extension beyond 1560. The most comprehensive information appears in the recently published graph of burials, baptisms and marriages in the 400 parishes scattered across England whose registers have been analysed by the Cambridge Group for the History of Population and Social Structure.[13] This shows small peaks in the number of burials at the beginning and in the middle of the 1540s, and a major crisis when burials far exceeded baptisms between 1557 and 1559. After 1560 the reign of Elizabeth seems on the evidence of these registers to have been generally

[12] The sources for Table 1 are the calendars of wills published by the British Record Society, Index Library, vols. 7, 8, 24, 27, 31, 39, 46, 78, 79 (1892–1960). The Exeter series used is that for the Consistory Court because this provides the longest continuous series; and the date after each area is that when an apparently reliable series of registrations begins. As far as possible duplicate entries in the calendars have been excluded. Sometimes the date of the will has been used where there is no date of proof, but since most wills were made close to the time of death, this should not result in serious distortion.

[13] D. C. Coleman, *The Economy of England 1450–1750* (Oxford, 1977), fig.1, p.16. At the time of writing, the Cambridge Group's full study of these registers has yet to be published.

healthy, and the testamentary records also fail to reveal crises after 1560 as severe as those of the first half of the century.[14] There was an increase in burials in the later 1580s and early 1590s, but it was not until 1597 that the number of burials again greatly exceeded the number of baptisms.

Other work on groups of parish registers leads to similar conclusions. Besides the statistics gathered by Thomas Short in 1750 from a selection of unspecified country parishes and market towns, studies have been made of a number of parishes in the West Riding of Yorkshire, in Cumbria and in Staffordshire;[15] and the present author has investigated the surviving registers of Essex and Devon.[16] All these analyses of parish registers agree on the fact that there was an unusually large number of burials over much of England between 1557 and 1559, and again between 1596 and 1598, and that there was a lesser crisis in the years between 1586 and 1588. The evidence for mortality over large areas of England suggests that the frequent crises of the early and mid-sixteenth century were separated from those of the last decades by a long period of stability in the quarter-century after 1560.

One immediately striking feature of this chronology is its apparent relationship with changes in the quality of the harvest. Not only were the 1530s and the years from 1566 to 1585 periods of good harvests as well as of stable mortality, but the majority of the crisis years already noted coincided with or followed immediately after a dearth. Bad or disastrous harvests occurred in 1520–1, 1527–8, 1545, 1550–1, 1555–6, 1586 and 1594–7.[17] Not every crisis followed a dearth: there were occasional years of high mortality in the middle of a run of good

[14] Only in the case of Exeter Consistory Court were there years when the number of wills proved reached double the average after 1560, and these cases seem to have been the consequence of regular changes in the administration of the court. In Berkshire and in Worcester diocese, however, the number of wills rose 50 per cent above its normal level in 1587, as it did also in Berkshire in 1597.

[15] Thomas Short, *New Observations on City, Town and Country Bills of Mortality* (1750), pp.85–6; M. Drake, 'An elementary exercise in parish register demography', *Economic History Review*, 2nd ser., XIV (1961–2), 427–45; W. G. Howson, 'Plague, poverty and population in parts of North-West England 1580–1720', *Transactions of the Historic Society of Lancashire and Cheshire*, CXII (1960), 29–55; A. B. Appleby, 'Disease or famine? Mortality in Cumberland and Westmorland 1580–1640', *Economic History Review*, 2nd ser., XXVI (1973), 403–32; D. Palliser, 'Dearth and disease in Staffordshire, 1540–1670', in C. W. Chalklin and M. A. Havinden (eds.), *Rural Change and Urban Growth 1500–1800: Essays in Honour of W. G. Hoskins* (London, 1974), pp.54–75.

[16] Slack, thesis, chapter 2, and see the discussion below.

[17] W. G. Hoskins, 'Harvest fluctuations and English economic history, 1480–1619', *Agricultural History Review*, XII (1964), 44–6. Professor Hoskins's analysis is based on the price of wheat. A review of other grain prices affects the assessment of some years, though not of the major harvest failures: C. J. Harrison, 'Grain price analysis and harvest qualities, 1465–1634', ibid., XIX (1971), 135–55.

harvests, in 1517–18 and 1539–40 for example. But virtually every bad harvest appears to have been followed by a period of high mortality. If we define a bad harvest as one which raised the average price of all grains to a level more than 25 per cent above the norm, there was only one obvious exception to this rule between 1485 and 1610 – the harvest of 1600.[18] There is strong *prima facie* evidence here that conditions of food scarcity and high death rates were connected.

The picture changes, however, if we shift our focus from dioceses, archdeaconries and whole counties to smaller individual communities. Studies of aggregate mortality over a large geographical area inevitably minimize, and sometimes completely conceal, crises of a localized nature. Conversely, the smaller the geographical unit studied, the more frequent and more severe are the fluctuations in mortality revealed by the records. Even small villages might suffer from a devastating epidemic disease while their neighbours escaped. But large towns, the major centres of population and communication, were especially vulnerable to infectious diseases, which regularly removed 10 per cent or even more of their populations. This is illustrated by the information presented in Table 2, which shows the years in which there was increased mortality and presumably also epidemic disease in fourteen English towns spread across the country from London to Newcastle and from Norwich to Exeter.[19] Any year in which the number of burials in a large proportion of parishes in the town rose to more than twice the average of the previous decade has been included. So have years in which only a small part of the town was seriously affected, and years in which an epidemic disease afflicted most of the town without raising mortality rates by 100 per cent: but in both these cases the dates are given in brackets. Where parish registers are not available, for all towns before

18 Variations in the price of all grains are given in Harrison, 'Grain price analysis'.
19 Table 2 is based on detailed research in the parochial and corporation records of the towns of London, Norwich, Bristol, Exeter, Lincoln, Reading and Salisbury, supplemented by information for other towns drawn from: Creighton, *History of Epidemics;* J. F. D. Shrewsbury, *A History of Bubonic Plague in the British Isles* (Cambridge, 1970); A. D. Dyer, *The City of Worcester in the Sixteenth Century* (Leicester, 1973); *The Register of St Chad's Shrewsbury*, ed. W. G. D. Fletcher, Shropshire Parish Register Society, Lichfield diocese, xvi (n.pl., 1913) and *The Parish Register of Shrewsbury St Mary*, ed. G. W. S. Sparrow, Shropshire Parish Register Society, Lichfield dioceses xii (n.pl., 1911); J. E. O. Wilshere, 'Plague in Leicester 1558–1665', *Transactions of the Leicestershire Archaeological and Historical Society*, xliv (1968–9), 45–69, and Leicester Corporation Archives, registers of All Saints, St Martin's and St Nicholas's parishes; *Victoria History of the County of York: East Riding I* [Hull], pp.154–7; D. M. Palliser, 'Epidemics in Tudor York', *Northern History*, viii (1973), 45–63; R. H. Morris, *Chester in the Plantagenet and Tudor Reigns* (Chester, 1893), pp.78–9, and *The Parish Register of the Holy and Undivided Trinity, Chester*, ed. L. M. Farrall (Chester, 1914); G. B. Richardson, *Plague and Pestilence in the North of England* (Newcastle, 1852).

Table 2. *Epidemic years in fourteen English towns 1485–1610*

	(1485)	1498–1500 +1504	1513 +1518	1521	(1535–6)	1543	1548	1558	1563	(1569–70)	(1574–5)	1578–9	1582	1592–3	(1597)	1603+ (1606–10)
London	(1485)	1498–1500 +1504	1513 +1518	1521	(1535–6)	1543	1548	1558	1563	(1569–70)	(1574–5)	1578–9	1582	1592–3	(1597)	1603+ (1606–10)
Reading					1537	1543–4		1558	1564						1596–7	1606–8
Salisbury						1546		1558	1563–4	(1570–1)		1579–80			1596–7	1604
Bristol					1535	1544–5, 1546–7	1551–2	1557–8	1565				(1586–7)		1597	1603
Exeter		1503–4			1537	1545		1557–8	(1563–5)	1570	1575		1587	1590–1	1596–7	(1603–5)
Worcester		1502		1528			1553	1558	(1563–4)				1587	1593–4	1597–9	1609–10
Shrewsbury					1536–7		(1551)								1597	1604–5
Chester		1506	1518				(1551)	1558			1575–6				(1597–9)	1603–5 +1608
Norwich	(1485)	1500 +1503–4	1513–14	1520		1544–5	1554–5	1557–9			1574	1579–80	1584–5	1589–92		1603–4
Leicester								1559	(1564)				1586–7	1593–4		1610–11
Lincoln						1546	(1550–1)	(1557–8)					1582	1590–1	(1597)	(1610–11)
Hull					1537						1575–6		1582		(1597–8)	1602–3
York	(1485–6) +1493	1501+ 1505–6		(1521)	1538–41		1550–2	1558–9			1576					1604
Newcastle						1544–5				1570–1		1579		1588–9	1596–7	1604–10

Sources: see note 19.

1538 and for some even later, identifications are more tentative and have been based on literary references in local records to plague, pestilence or high mortality. However, where the evidence is slight the dates have again been enclosed in brackets. And the major epidemics, those in which the level of mortality in one year appears to have been three times the normal, are printed in italics.

This table supports some of the conclusions drawn from wills and from the studies of burial registers for large numbers of neighbouring parishes. It shows that the early and middle years of Elizabeth's reign were comparatively, though not invariably, healthy; and it suggests that there was high mortality over much of England in the opening years of the sixteenth century and again in the 1540s, the 1550s and the 1590s. Yet in many towns these were far from the worst demographic crises of the period, and there were numerous other years in which several towns suffered from high death rates. In Exeter, for example, the greatest mortalities occurred in 1570 and 1590, and in Norwich in 1579, 1584, 1589 and 1603, not in 1558 or 1597. Most of these urban crises did not coincide with bad harvests; they had no connection with famine. But virtually all of them were attributed by contemporaries to 'plague'. The most important occurred in the period from 1603 to 1611, when the disease spread from London throughout the country and affected every single one of the fourteen towns. 'Then were all the shires in England grievously visited', commented a contemporary observer, 'Note the work of God'.[20] There appears to have been a comparable gradual movement of bubonic plague from London to other towns in and after 1535, 1543, 1563 and 1592.

Plague therefore played an important role in mortality behaviour in towns, and it is the characteristic epidemiology of the disease which largely explains why many of these urban epidemics were not reflected in the mortality statistics for whole regions considered earlier. Partly this was because the disease was always worse in towns than in the countryside, although small villages were not unaffected, as we shall see later. Partly it was because plague spread slowly from town to town, and town to village, and its impact on regional mortality was hence distributed over several years, not concentrated in one or two. It was unlikely to have a simultaneous effect on death rates across a wide area. But the history of the larger towns shows that some communities were regularly subjected to severe mortality crises. In these fourteen towns

[20] MS. note in a seventeenth-century hand in Oxford, Bodleian Library, Gough London 154.

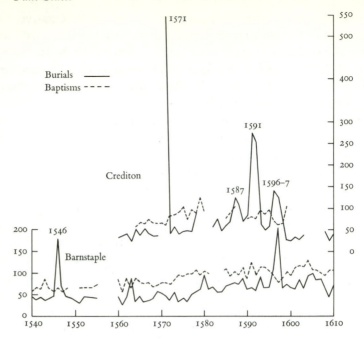

Fig. 2   Burials and baptisms in two Devon towns 1540–1610. Sources: see
note 21.

they occurred on average once every sixteen years between 1485 and
1610.

This, like all averages, conceals as much as it reveals, however. Some
settlements, even urban ones, could escape the worst consequences of
epidemic disease for decades, as Table 2 shows. The absence of crises in
York for most of Elizabeth's reign contrasts sharply with their regularity
in Norwich. In general, ports were more at risk than inland towns, and
London's vulnerability to disease was as exceptional as its size. Yet there
were also marked variations between towns of similar size in the same
part of the country. The two small Devonshire towns of Crediton and
Barnstaple provide an instructive contrast in this respect. The burial
statistics presented in Fig. 2 show that both suffered in 1597. While this
was the only major crisis in Elizabethan Barnstaple, however, there were
three others, two of them caused by outbreaks of plague, in Crediton.[21]

---

[21] The sources for Fig. 2 are a transcript of the parish register of Crediton in the library of the
      Devon and Cornwall Record Society, Exeter, and *Barnstaple Parish Register 1538–1812*, ed. T.
      Wainwright (Exeter, 1903).

Conclusions about the chronology and frequency of violent fluctuations in mortality thus depend on the standpoint adopted, on whether it is that of a single locality or of a whole region or country. On the one hand there were crises of wide geographical distribution when mortality rates over large regions of the country may have doubled. These often followed a failure of the harvest and they were apparently more common before 1560 than after. On the other hand there were local crises, often unrelated to changes in the quality of the harvest, which raised the number of burials in a town or village to double or treble its normal level. They occurred at different times in different places, but were so common that it would be difficult to find a period of five years after 1538 when there was not a devastating epidemic somewhere in England.

Such variations, as well as the inadequacy of the sources before 1560, make precise comparisons between mortality crises in the sixteenth century and other periods impossible. All the evidence suggests, however, that the crises of 1557–9 and 1597–8 were more serious on a national scale than any which occurred in the seventeenth or eighteenth centuries. It shows too that in most towns the epidemics of the sixteenth century were at least as severe and as frequent as those in the seventeenth century, and on occasion more so.[22] Whatever may have been the case in the fifteenth century, the dark ages of demographic history,[23] disastrous increases in mortality were familiar hazards of life in Tudor England.

III

If we are to explore the character and impact of these mortalities, we must enquire more closely into their causes. It will already be clear that there were several different kinds of crisis, and various typologies for classifying them have been suggested, principally by historians of *ancien régime* France.[24] Three categories would in fact have been familiar to contemporaries, who were accustomed to discuss the relative savagery of

[22] In the case of plague, for example, the only epidemic waves to affect the majority of large English towns after 1610 occurred in 1625–7 and 1636–8.

[23] For a recent survey of this period see J. Hatcher, *Plague, Population and the English Economy 1348–1530* (London, 1977).

[24] See the discussion in *Problèmes de mortalité*, ed. P. Harsin and E. Helin, Congrès et Colloques de l'Université de Liège, xxxiii (Liège, 1965); J. Meuvret, 'Demographic crisis in France from the sixteenth to the eighteenth century', in *Population in History*, ed. D. V. Glass and D. E. C. Eversley (London, 1965), pp.507–22; P. Goubert, *Beauvais et le beauvaisis de 1600 à 1730* (Paris, 1960), pp.45–59.

War, Famine and Pestilence.[25] The group of mortality crises associated with the first of these, those brought about by the epidemic diseases which accompanied sieges and followed in the wake of armies, played little part in sixteenth-century England, thanks to the Tudor peace. There were movements of disease consequent upon English involvement in military activity abroad. In 1563 and 1589, for example, it is likely that virulent infections were brought to England by ships and men returning from continental expeditions.[26] But these, like other epidemics, can be included in one or other of the two remaining types of crisis which predominated.

In the first category were crises in which bad harvests and high mortality more or less coincided, and in which it is probable that there was a direct relationship between the two. Some of the increased number of deaths were no doubt caused by simple starvation, but the majority were the result of malnutrition lowering resistance to one or more infectious diseases.[27] As has already been indicated, however, these 'famine' crises, or crises of subsistence as French historians term them, were not the only ones of importance. It is plain that there was no long-term correlation between the movement of food prices and fluctuations in mortality. In localities where the two can be compared in detail, in the towns of Exeter, London and Lincoln, for which we have local series of grain or bread prices, high prices and high mortality occasionally coincided, but major increases in death rates also occurred when prices were low.[28] A second category of crisis therefore consists of those in which high mortality was caused by epidemic disease alone, whether by bubonic plague or some other apparently 'autonomous' infection. These two groups are readily distinguishable.

There is also, however, a possible third category: a category of 'mixed' crises in which there were both bad harvests, and hence no doubt

---

[25] See for example Dekker's 'Dialogue betweene warre, famine and the pestilence', in *The Plague Pamphlets of Thomas Dekker*, ed. F. P. Wilson (Oxford, 1925), pp.107–12; William Gouge, *Gods three arrowes: plague, famine, sword* (1631).

[26] Shrewsbury, *History of Bubonic Plague*, p.200; *Tudor Royal Proclamations*, ed. P. L. Hughes and J. F. Larkin (3 vols., New Haven, Conn., 1964–9), II, no.510; J. J. Keevil, *Medicine and the Navy I, 1200–1649* (Edinburgh and London, 1957), pp.77–9.

[27] See the stimulating discussion in J. D. Post, 'Famine, mortality and epidemic disease in the process of modernization', *Economic History Review*, 2nd ser., XXIX (1976), 14–37; and for a modern medical discussion of the problem, N. S. Scrimshaw, C. E. Taylor and J. E. Gordon, *Interactions of Nutrition and Infection*, WHO Monograph Series, no.57 (Geneva, 1968).

[28] For Exeter and London, see Chambers, *Population, Economy and Society*, pp.94–6 (on the period 1660–1760, but similar conclusions apply to the later sixteenth century); A. B. Appleby, 'Nutrition and disease: the case of London 1550–1750', *Journal of Inter-disciplinary History*, VI (1975), 1–22. Grain prices in Lincoln, which can be compared with the information in Table 2, are given in J. W. F. Hill, *Tudor and Stuart Lincoln* (Cambridge, 1956), pp.222–6.

widespread malnutrition, and also epidemics of diseases which are not known to be aggravated by simple inanition or by particular protein or vitamin deficiencies. Such diseases probably include some of the virus infections and, most important of all, bubonic plague. These cases present the most difficult problems for historical analysis. For although there may be no direct biological relationship between malnutrition and disease in these instances, no clear evidence that resistance to the infection is reduced by food shortage, there may yet be important indirect connections when the two coincide. The large-scale shipment of grain from country to country or locality to locality in years of dearth might aid the movement of rodents carrying disease; equally the migration of individuals, of vagrants and beggars, in search of food or charity, which commonly increased when harvests failed, might serve to disseminate an epidemic. In these ways the economic and social circumstances consequent upon bad harvests could facilitate exposure to infection and accelerate the spread of disease.[29] It would be naive to suppose that the progress and effects of any epidemic were not influenced by such an environment. However, for purposes of analysis of the sixteenth-century evidence it is convenient to distinguish this third category from the simpler 'famine' crises in the first.

In order to identify these three types of crisis accurately, we need more than the simple mortality and price statistics already referred to. We require some indication of the diseases which produced so many casualties. At this distance in time any precise medical diagnosis is, of course, impossible, but something can be learned both from contemporary descriptions and from the seasonal incidence of disease revealed by the chronological distribution of burials in parish registers. Although very few burial registers regularly provide information on the cause of death,[30] many refer in one or two years or individual cases to 'the sweat' or 'the plague', to 'flux' or 'the spotted fever'. The reliability of these descriptions can often be questioned. Even 'plague' might still occasionally be employed to mean any stroke of ill fortune, and 'pestilence' could refer to almost any epidemic disease. Thus the town of Sandwich was said to be suffering in 1562 from 'a threefold plague – pestilence, want of money, dearth of victuals'.[31] By the second half of the sixteenth century, however, it seems that both terms were being

[29] Post, 'Famine, mortality and disease', pp.31–4.
[30] An exception is the parish register of St Botolph Aldgate, on which see T. R. Forbes, *Chronicle from Aldgate* (New Haven, Conn., 1971).
[31] Kent Archives Office, Sa/ZB6, Sandwich Annals under 1562. See note 113 below for a similar quotation relating to London.

more often used, usually with the definite article, to describe a specific disease, bubonic plague, and to distinguish it from others. In Shropshire in the 1580s, for example, an epidemic might be described as 'much like the plague but... not the plague'. The early bills of mortality which separated plague deaths from the rest similarly reflect contemporary concern to isolate this particular disease, and efforts were made by local as well as medical authorities to avoid confusion between plague and a disease with somewhat similar symptoms, the 'spotted fever' or typhus.[32] In a period when the definition of separate disease entities was just beginning, local descriptions of the major epidemics must be treated cautiously, but they need not be rejected out of hand. Moreover in the case of the most spectacular of epidemic diseases, bubonic plague, contemporary descriptions usually receive support from the seasonal distribution of burials in the parish register: there is a rapid rise in the number of entries in the summer and a more gradual decline in the late autumn or winter of the year. Thus a combination of literary and parish register evidence often indicates at the very least whether or not high mortality is likely to have been the result of bubonic plague.

It is on indications such as these that the following account must necessarily rely. It will be based largely on evidence drawn from selected areas of the country, from the counties of Devon and Essex and from the towns of Exeter, Bristol, Norwich and London. An attempt has been made to see as many as possible of the surviving burial registers of these localities.[33] All major increases in mortality have been noted, and their

32   Shrewsbury, *History of Bubonic Plague*, p.236; F. P. Wilson, *The Plague in Shakespeare's London* (Oxford, paperback edn, 1963), pp.189ff.; Hull Corporation Records, Bench Book 5, fol. 213v.; Norfolk and Norwich Record Office, Norwich Court Book 1624–34, fol. 279v. For a discussion of early modern perceptions of the distinction between diseases see L. G. Stevenson, '"New diseases" in the seventeenth century', *Bulletin of the History of Medicine*, XXXIX (1965), 1–21; *Problèmes de mortalité*, p.460.

33   Some 300 parish registers have been examined, either in the original or in transcript form. Those relating to Norwich, Exeter, Bristol, Essex and Devon (defined by their sixteenth-century boundaries in each case) are listed in the bibliography to Slack, thesis, and comprise: transcripts in the Library of the Society of Genealogists (16 registers) and the Library of the Devon and Cornwall Record Society (77); 20 published registers; and registers in the Bristol Archives Office (9), St Mary Redcliffe Church Bristol (2), Exeter City Muniments (2), East Devon Record Office (6), Norfolk and Norwich Record Office (14, mostly microfilms of Norwich registers), and Essex Record Office (92). The last are among those described in *Catalogue of Essex Parish Records 1240–1894*, Essex County Council, 2nd edn (Chelmsford, 1966). For London, 25 registers published by the Harleian Society, 20 registers of city parishes in the Guildhall Library, the register of St Saviour Southwark in the Greater London Record Office, and the following published registers have been examined: *Allhallows London Wall* (n.pl., 1878), *St Botolph Bishopsgate* (n.pl., 1889), *St Christopher le Stocks* (London, 1882), *St Margaret's Westminster* (London, 1914), *St Mary Woolnoth and Mary Woolchurch Haw* (1886), *St Nicholas Acons* (Leeds, 1890).

violence has been measured, not by actual death rates (which cannot be calculated in the absence of figures for total populations), but by a 'crisis mortality ratio' drawn from the burial registers themselves. The number of burials in the twelve months when mortality was greatest has been divided by the 'normal' annual average in the parish, usually calculated for the previous decade. Thus where the number buried in an epidemic year was 26 and the previous average 13, the crisis mortality ratio is 2.0. Other signs of epidemic disease have also been noticed, whether in the form of specific references to cause of death, or as clusters of burials occurring within a few days or within a few families. These may demonstrate the presence of an epidemic even when annual mortality statistics were scarcely affected.

There is no lack of material of this kind and only a selection of it will be used here. But the vast majority of it comes from the second half of the sixteenth century. The crises of the early Tudor period are not documented in comparable detail. Consideration of them will therefore be postponed until they can be discussed in the light of the fuller evidence for the later sixteenth century. There is, however, one necessary exception. The fame of the 'sweating sickness' which afflicted early Tudor England gives it a claim to first place in any account of epidemics in the sixteenth century. It should also be dealt with first because, in spite of its virtual monopoly of contemporary attention, its role as a major cause of high mortality can seriously be questioned.

The dates of the successive outbreaks of the sweat, 1485, 1507–8, 1517, 1528 and 1551, suggest that it may have been responsible for some of the early years of high mortality in Tables 1 and 2. The exact nature of the disease remains mysterious and has been the subject of some controversy, though it was probably a viral infection of some kind.[34] But a strong element of myth as well as of mystery has surrounded the sweat, and has almost certainly attracted to it more historical attention than it warrants. It impressed contemporaries because it was spectacular. It killed within twenty-four hours. It attacked a community suddenly and then was gone. In particular it struck the eminent and the famous:[35] the sons of the Duke of Suffolk in 1551, the King's Latin Secretary and

---

[34] See the debate between A. Patrick and R. S. Roberts, 'A consideration of the nature of the English sweating sickness', *Medical History*, IX (1965), 272–9, 385–9; Shrewsbury, *History of Bubonic Plague*, p.185n.

[35] Creighton, *History of Epidemics*, I, chapter 5; *The Records of the City of Norwich*, ed. W. Hudson and J. C. Tingey (2 vols., Norwich and London, 1906–10), II, p.cxxiv; *Parish Register of Holy . . . Trinity Chester*, p.72.

Wolsey himself in 1517. At a more provincial level, the mayors and aldermen of towns like Norwich and Chester, as well as of London, died of it. It was given dramatic names like 'The New Acquittance, alias Stoop! Knave and know thy master'; and it was greeted abroad as the 'English sweat'.[36] Small wonder that Caius dedicated to it the first original medical work in English on a specific disease.[37]

Yet where we have precise evidence of its demographic effects, in the last outbreak of 1551, this is not impressive. The sweating sickness ran through a parish in the space of a few days, a fortnight at most, and the deaths in this period were seldom sufficient to produce a major increase in the annual total of burials. Crisis mortality ratios as high as 2.0 for 1551 are few and far between. In London, for example, the disease struck between 4 and 19 July.[38] It is named in three of the thirty surviving parish registers, and its effects can be inferred from an unusual number of deaths in these two weeks in twelve other parishes, but in none of them did the burial total for the whole year rise by as much as 100 per cent. One of the most unfortunate was St Peter Cornhill, where thirty-six burials were recorded in 1551, nineteen of them between 4 and 13 July, as against an annual average of twenty. At the end of the month the epidemic spread to Essex, where it hit a smaller proportion of parishes than in the crowded metropolis but had a more serious impact on mortality in infected villages. Its effects can be observed in seven of the thirty-two surviving parish registers of the county, and in five of them the number of burials over the whole year reached twice the average. In Devon the picture was similar. The sweating sickness arrived there in the middle of August, and it affected only nine of the thirty-three parishes with surviving registers, three of them severely. The worst outbreak was in the village of Uffculme, just off the main Taunton to Exeter road, where twenty-seven people were buried in the month of August, compared with a normal *annual* average of nine. Although the number of wills proved in Exeter Consistory Court at this time might appear to

---

[36] Entry in the Loughborough parish register (information from Mr R. A. McKinley; the entry has been misread by J. Nichols, *The History and Antiquities of the County of Leicester* (4 vols., 1795–1815), III, p.891, and later historians have followed him); F. Henschen, *The History of Diseases* (London, 1966), p.62; J. F. C. Hecker, *The Epidemics of the Middle Ages* (1844), pp.248–9.

[37] *A boke or counseill against the disease commonly called the sweate or sweatyng sicknesse* (1552), printed in *The Works of John Caius*, ed. E. S. Roberts (Cambridge, 1912).

[38] Machyn dated the epidemic from 8 July, but the registers suggest that it may have begun earlier: *The Diary of Henry Machyn*, ed. J. G. Nichols, Camden Society, old ser., XLII (1848), p.8. See also Caius, *A boke or counseill* in *Works*, ed. Roberts, p.11.

suggest the contrary, Uffculme was the exception rather than the rule.[39]

It is possible that earlier epidemics of the sweating sickness had been more serious than that of 1551, but there is no convincing evidence of this. Their coincidence with some of the years of high mortality in Tables 1 and 2 seems persuasive until one finds that these were also years of bubonic plague. It is likely that there was plague as well as the sweating sickness in York and Norwich in 1485–6, and in 1517 the former disease was again present in various parts of the country. Certainly in 1551 and 1552 it was bubonic plague not the sweat which was largely responsible for high death rates in York and Bristol, as it may have been in Lincoln too.[40] It seems probable that the sweating sickness caused high morbidity, especially noticeable among the social elite, that it was a serious scourge in a few scattered rural parishes, but that it had only a minor effect in larger communities. The major causes of fluctuations in mortality in Tudor England must be looked for elsewhere, and they can best be identified in the second half of the sixteenth century.

IV

If the sweating sickness is something of a diversion in this enquiry, it had at least one permanent effect. It established itself as part of contemporary medical vocabulary, and the term was applied to later outbreaks of what were probably viral diseases. It was especially revived by some observers to describe the fevers which swept across the whole country between 1557 and 1559.[41] Unlike the sweating sickness, however, these infections were responsible for the greatest mortality crisis of the sixteenth century. This had more than one component, and it was, in the terminology suggested earlier, a 'mixed' crisis.

It is difficult to measure its dimensions with precision, since the religious changes of 1558–9, as well as the epidemics themselves,

---

[39] Cf. W. G. Hoskins, 'Epidemics in Tudor Devon', in idem, *Old Devon* (Newton Abbot, 1966), p.142. For the incidence of the sweat elsewhere, see N. Griffin, 'Epidemics in Loughborough 1539–1640', *Transactions of the Leicestershire Archaeological and Historical Society*, XLIII (1967), 24–6; Drake, 'An elementary exercise', p.434; Cox, *Parish Registers*, pp.143–4; R. Sharpe France, 'A history of plague in Lancashire', *Transactions of the Historic Society of Lancashire and Cheshire*, XC (1938), 30.

[40] Palliser, 'Epidemics in Tudor York', pp.46, 49–51; Creighton, *History of Epidemics*, I, pp.290–1; John More, *A table from the beginning of the world to this day* (Cambridge, 1593), p.209; *Adams' Chronicle of Bristol*, ed. F. F. Fox (Bristol, 1910), p.100; Bristol Archives Office, parish register of St Nicholas's.

[41] John Jones, *A diall for all agues* (1566), sig. IIv; William Bullein, *A newe boke entituled the governement of healthe* (1558), fol. xliiv.

disrupted the registration of burials in many parishes. The testamentary evidence for the crisis is impressive, as we have seen, but there are limits to the quantitative conclusions which can be drawn from it. Professor Fisher's calculations from probate records suggest that over the five-year period 1556–60 death rates were 150 per cent above the norm, and that the country's population may have fallen by as much as 20 per cent.[42] This would be so if mortality rates among the section of the population not making wills rose by the same ratio as among the sample who did. There is reason to suppose that this was not the case, however. The testimony of contemporary chronicles led John Strype to conclude that the fevers of 1557–9 'killed an exceeding great number of all sorts of men, but especially gentlemen, and men of great wealth'.[43] One need not infer that these epidemics hit the rich more than the poor. That seems unlikely. But mortality rates were normally higher than average in the poorer sections of the population. If they were more uniform across the social spectrum in 1557–9 than in earlier years, then the increase above the norm would have been greater in the will-making class than elsewhere. This would explain some otherwise incomprehensible discrepancies in the local evidence. It would account, for example, for the fact that in Norwich the number of wills proved quadrupled in 1558, while the number of registered burials only doubled.[44]

Although the number of wills proved probably exaggerates the violence of the crisis in the later 1550s, the parish registers, where they survive, leave no room for doubt that it was unique both in its geographical spread and in its persistence for several years in succession. The Cambridge Group's analysis of 400 parish registers suggests that the number of burials was almost twice the average for the three years 1557–9, and if mortality rates were normally around 30 per thousand, an extra 9 or 10 per cent of the population may have died.[45] Equally important in its long-term demographic implications was the fall in baptisms which accompanied the rise in mortality. It appears that fertility may have been declining as early as 1556, even before the worst effects of disease manifested themselves. If mortality rates were not as

---

[42] Fisher, 'Influenza and inflation', p.127.
[43] Ibid., p.125.
[44] The number of wills of Norwich citizens has been calculated from *Index to Wills Proved in the Consistory Court of Norwich*, ed. M. A. Farrow, British Record Society, Index Library, vol.73 (London and Chichester, 1950), and burial totals from eight city parish registers in the Norfolk and Norwich Record Office.
[45] Coleman, *Economy of England*, fig.1, p.16.

high in the later 1550s as has sometimes been supposed, they were sufficient, combined with a decline in fertility, to impose a major check on population growth.

Closer inspection of parish registers in different localities reveals no simple or uniform pattern in this crisis which might indicate a single cause of death. The timing and extent of mortality varied from place to place. Often burials rose first in 1556, then again in the summer of 1557, and jumped to even greater heights in the winters of 1557–8 and 1558–9. But some parishes might be affected by only one part of this sequence, or by none. Despite the wide geographical impact of the crisis, some counties were worse affected than others. In both Devon and Essex one third of the surviving registers reveal high burial totals in the later 1550s, but the fluctuations were greater in Essex than in the West. It was only in the eastern part of Devon, in parishes like Colyton and Broadhembury, that the number of burials more than doubled for two or three years in succession. Increases of this magnitude were much more common in Essex, where this was much the worst crisis in the period. In some of the smallest parishes, in White Roothing and Little Waltham, for example, the number of burials was four times the annual average in two successive years, usually in 1557 and 1558. A similar increase was recorded in Ardleigh over three years, from the summer of 1556 to the summer of 1559. In larger centres of population the crisis was less prolonged, though still on occasion severe. Thus in the small town of Saffron Walden the crisis mortality ratio between November 1558 and October 1559 was 3.3.

In general, however, it would appear that towns suffered less than the countryside at this time, and were affected later. Worcester is the only town in Table 2 in which this crisis inflicted losses comparable with those suffered in the major epidemics of bubonic plague which will be considered later. In Bristol and Exeter, for example, the number of burials rose by less than 100 per cent in most of the parishes with surviving registers. The same was true in London. The registers of thirty-two, nearly one third, of the parishes of London have been examined for these years, and although there are signs of an unusually large number of burials in all of them, in only fourteen did the total approach twice the average. In the majority of cases 1559, not 1557 or 1558, was the peak year. The exceptions to this generalization lay not in the city itself but on its less prosperous fringes: the parishes of St Saviour Southwark, St Margaret Westminster, and St Martin-in-the-Fields, where the crisis apparently started earlier, in 1557, and lasted longer.

Something of the complexity of this prolonged crisis can therefore be seen from the profile of its development in St Martin-in-the-Fields, shown in Fig. 3.[46] Burials have been plotted on a quarterly basis for each calendar year, starting with January to March, and 'conceptions' have been calculated by counting back nine months from baptisms, so that mortality and fertility changes can be synchronized.[47] The two successive and mounting peaks to the crisis were characteristic of its impact in other parts of the country, though they sometimes occurred in different months. Characteristic too was the fall in conceptions, though it occurred in this parish later than in others.

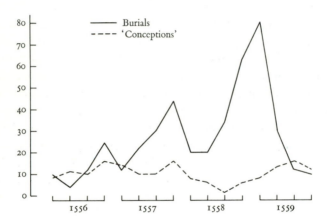

Fig. 3.   Burials and 'conceptions' in St Martin-in-the-Fields 1556–9. Sources: see note 46.

Unfortunately the parish clerk of St Martin left little indication of the cause of death. Only four casualties were attributed to plague ('peste') and the chronological distribution of burials shows that this cannot have been the chief culprit. More numerous, and perhaps more suggestive, are the clerk's references to the social status of the deceased. Of the 108 people buried in 1557, 19 were described as paupers, 3 of them dying 'in the street'. In 1558, however, there were only 4 paupers among the 137 burials. The difference is not a large one, but it is not inconsistent with other literary evidence which indicates that the character of the diseases involved in this crisis changed towards the end of 1557.

46   The source for Fig. 3 is *A Register of Baptisms, Marriages and Burials in the Parish of St Martin in the Fields 1550–1619*, ed. T. Mason, Harleian Society (1898).
47   It should be stressed that this method of calculating fertility measures at best only successfully completed conceptions.

Strype's summary of contemporary chronicles refers to 'hot burning fevers and other strange diseases', which began 'in the great dearth 1556' and increased in the two following years. At the end of 1557 there were also, he says, 'quartan agues', which returned in the summer of 1558 and the winter of 1558–9.[48] The elasticity of the terms 'fever' and 'ague' does not make for diagnostic clarity. In the earlier years, however, in 1556 and 1557, references tend to be to 'burning' and 'spotted' fevers, terms which seem at other times (in the context of gaol fevers, for example) to refer to typhus. Thus there were 'great burning fevers' in Sandwich in 1556. Typhus is one of the classic famine diseases, and its presence would not be surprising after the disastrous harvests of 1555 and 1556 which brought famine to much of northern Europe.[49] By 1558, on the other hand, in York and Essex as well as elsewhere, all the talk was of 'the new ague' or 'new disease', which has plausibly been taken to refer to a virulent viral infection, a variety of influenza. This would explain the speed with which the disease spread, its winter incidence in many parishes, and references like that in the Annals of the College of Physicians in 1558 to tertian, double tertian and continuous tertian fevers in town and country.[50] It would explain too why high mortality continued and even grew worse after the good harvests of 1557 and 1558.

The dual origins of the crisis are suggested also by the notes in the register of St Margaret Westminster, the parish next to St Martin-in-the-Fields, in 1557. Registration broke down altogether between November 1557 and October 1558, and the full profile of mortality cannot be reconstructed. But between May and November 1557 the clerk recorded the cause of death of most of those buried in the parish.[51] Out of 269 entries, 15 deaths were attributed simply to famine; 4 to 'penury' or 'very poverty'; 14 to the 'flux' or 'bloody flux', that is dysentery; and 33 to the 'pining sickness', a term which sounds as if it may well have been applied to tuberculosis. All these 66 deaths can be interpreted as the consequence of starvation or of infections which

---

48 Quoted in Fisher, 'Influenza and inflation', pp.125–6.

49 Kent Archives Office, Sa/ZB6, under 1556; Hoskins, 'Harvest fluctuations', p.36. On burning fever and gaol fever, see Thomas Cogan, *The haven of health* (1584), p.282, and on typhus, W. MacArthur, 'Medical history of the famine' in R. Dudley Edwards and T. D. Williams (eds.), *The Great Famine* (London, 1956), pp.263–315.

50 *York Civic Records*, v, ed. A. Raine, Yorkshire Archaeological Society, Record Series, cx (n.pl., 1944), p.189; London, Royal College of Physicians, Annals 1 1518–72, fol. 17v. See also Essex Record Office, Calendar of Queen's Bench Indictments, 604 I 94, 604 II 97; Hecker, *Epidemics of the Middle Ages*, pp.221–2.

51 *Memorials of St Margaret's Church, Westminster*, ed. A. M. Burke (London, 1914), pp.398–400.

have a synergistic relationship with malnutrition.[52] Three-quarters of them occurred before the end of September 1557, before the good harvest of that year brought food prices down. In addition, 80 deaths were attributed to agues or fevers. Before October 1557 there were 41 of these, many of them probably cases of typhus since several people died of a 'burning ague' and one of an ague with 'god's marks' or spots. Between October and November 1557 there were 39 further cases, but the majority were now attributed to the 'new ague' or 'new sickness', and it was no doubt this disease which was still raging in the parish when registration resumed in the winter of 1558–9.

It seems legitimate, therefore, to classify this as a 'mixed' crisis. The increase in mortality which affected several rural parishes and some of the poorer sections of London's population between the summer of 1556 and the autumn of 1557 was the result of typhus or of other infections aggravated by malnutrition. Early falls in fertility may also have been the product of near-famine conditions.[53] But the crisis was considerably worsened and extended by a virulent virus infection between 1557 and 1559 which brought high death rates to more prosperous sections of the population and which by 1559 had affected most towns. This second element in the crisis was probably not directly dependent on the first. For whether or not malnutrition reduces resistance to viral infections, and there is as yet no clear experimental evidence that it invariably does,[54] the presumed influenza of the later 1550s raged most strongly as conditions of subsistence improved. It was the rapid succession of 'famine' and more 'autonomous' diseases which made the later 1550s exceptional years in the demographic history of Tudor England.

V

Partly because of its exceptional features, the crisis of 1556–9 illustrates to an extreme degree the difficulties involved in determining the relationship between disease and its social environment in the past. After 1560, however, the pattern of crises becomes both simpler and clearer. A straightforward distinction can be made between 'famine' crises on the one hand and those caused by more 'autonomous' epidemics, all of them in fact outbreaks of bubonic plague, on the other. They usually occurred

---

[52] See Scrimshaw, Taylor and Gordon, *Nutrition and Infection*, especially pp.11–16, 63–5.
[53] On the relationship between malnutrition and falls in fertility, see E. Le Roy Ladurie, 'L'aménorrhée de famine (XVIIe siècles)', *Annales: Économies, Sociétés, Civilisations*, XXIV (1969), 1589–1601.
[54] Scrimshaw, Taylor and Gordon, *Nutrition and Infection*, pp.137, 262.

on separate occasions and they had different characteristics. This neat division can be observed also in the seventeenth century, until plague finally disappeared from England after the epidemic of 1665–6. Since the division was no temporary phenomenon it is convenient to examine famine crises and plague epidemics in Elizabethan England, before turning back to the less well-documented period before 1560 to ask whether the same patterns obtained then.

Famine crises were the less numerous and may be considered first. There were only two of them of any severity between 1560 and 1610. The first was in the eighteen months following the bad harvest of 1586, which pushed grain prices to levels unknown since 1556. The second occurred in the years from 1596 to 1598, at the end of the longest run of harvest failures of the century. There were poor harvests in 1594 and 1595, a dearth as catastrophic as that of 1556 after the harvest of 1596, and a further bad harvest in 1597. The average price of all grains was 84 per cent above the norm in the harvest-year 1596–7, and the cost of peas and beans, which might have been alternative foodstuffs for the poor, also reached unprecedented heights.[55] Food riots in many parts of the country and panic legislation in parliament on enclosure and poor relief testify to the existence of distress on a scale unknown earlier in the century.[56]

Its demographic consequences have been analysed in greatest detail in a study of the parishes of Cumbria by A. B. Appleby.[57] His investigations reveal circumstances in the North-West fully comparable with those crises of subsistence which historians have found in seventeenth-century France. The crisis of 1587–8 was less serious than that of 1596–8, although it was evident across the whole region. Burials rose during the winter in several parishes, sometimes to double or treble their usual number, and the winter incidence of the disease and the large number of adults buried point to typhus as the main cause of death. This epidemic was probably aggravated by malnutrition following the dearth of 1586, although there is evidence that grain prices may have eased in the autumn of 1587. In some parishes there was also a fall of a third or more in the number of conceptions, suggesting that disease or malnutrition or both produced amenorrhea and hence a decline in

55 Harrison, 'Grain price analysis', p.154; Hoskins, 'Harvest fluctuations', p.38; *The Agrarian History of England and Wales IV, 1500–1640*, ed. J. Thirsk (Cambridge, 1967), p.820.

56 E. P. Cheyney, *A History of England from the Defeat of the Armada to the Death of Elizabeth* (2 vols., London, 1914–26), II, pp.3–36; P. Clark, 'Popular protest and disturbance in Kent 1558–1640', *Economic History Review*, 2nd ser., XXIX (1976), 365–81.

57 Appleby, 'Disease or famine?'.

fertility. The crisis ten years later was even more severe. The level of mortality was high from 1 597 to 1 599, with burials in 1 597 often three or four times the norm; and conceptions again fell in several parishes by between a third and a half. But the proportion of adults among burials was now not unusual, and casualties were spread throughout the year. In the absence of direct evidence of typhus or another epidemic disease, Appleby is led to the conclusion that simple starvation was probably a common cause of death in 1 597–9.

There is thus no reason to doubt reports from northern England in 1 597 that people were 'starving and dying in our streets and in the fields for lack of bread'.[58] The question that remains is whether these conditions were confined to the North. Appleby is inclined to think that they were, arguing that there were 'two Englands' in this respect, one more vulnerable to subsistence crises than the other. Yet there is in fact evidence of the adverse demographic effects of harvest failure in many places further south. It is true that mortality rates in the South often fluctuated less violently than in the North-West, and that these fluctuations were most apparent, as we shall see, in areas where the local economy was in one respect or another similar to that of Cumbria. It is true also that the crisis of 1 586–7 was by no means general. It affected, for example, only a small minority of parishes in Devon and Essex, some of them close to Exeter and Colchester where outbreaks of gaol fever in county prisons may have started a chain of typhus infection.[59] The crisis of 1 597, however, had a much wider impact. It was undoubtedly a national rather than a purely localized phenomenon.

It is not perhaps surprising that there should be ample evidence for its effects in Devon, since that county, like the North-West, was a part of the highland zone. Between the summer of 1 596 and the end of 1 597 the number of burials more than doubled in one third of the Devonshire parishes for which registers survive, and crisis mortality ratios occasionally reached 4.0. The geographical distribution of the affected parishes is revealing. Most of them were in the northern half of the county, places like Rose Ash, Witheridge, Molland, Oakford and Clayhanger in the foothills of Exmoor, Ilsington, Dean Prior and South Tawton on the edges of Dartmoor, and a belt of parishes across the Culm Measures from Holsworthy to Crediton. Notably unaffected were

58 Quoted ibid., p.419.
59 Essex Record Office, Calendar of Queen's Bench Indictments, 668 II 272–9, 670 I 81, 88–92; Raphael Holinshed, *Chronicles* (3 vols., 1 587), III, pp.1 547–8; F. Willcocks, 'The Black Assizes in the West', *Transactions of the Devonshire Association,* XVI (1 884), 597–9.

parishes in the mixed-farming lowlands in the south of the county, especially those in the fertile South Hams region between Exeter and Plymouth. As in Cumbria, therefore, the vulnerable settlements were in pastoral country, producing little corn even when harvests were good, and many of them had large sections of their populations dependent on by-employments in the cloth industry.[60] Theirs was a precarious farming economy, doubly vulnerable when the harvest failed. Not only did the cost of food rise: there was a consequent contraction in demand for textiles and a fall in the price of wool which cut incomes and employment in pastoral areas, and which could prolong the economic consequences of bad harvests even after the harvest itself improved.[61]

Such precarious local economies were most common in the highland zone of England, but they were not confined to it. Rural industry and pasture farming went hand in hand in parts of the lowlands and their susceptibility to harvest crises was reflected in a rise in mortality in the later 1590s. In Essex the number of burials doubled or trebled in a period of twelve months between 1596 and 1598 in no less than a quarter of the parishes with surviving registers. Most of these parishes were in the north and west, the most densely populated parts of the county. They included villages like Ardleigh in the north-east, a region where the poor were said in 1597 to be 'chiefly relying on the clothiers' for their income; and parishes in the north, like Toppesfield, which were described in 1595 as 'pasture towns and little or no tilling used by them, the occasion whereof at this present dearth of grain hath caused a great and lamentable cry of the poor'.[62] While crisis mortality ratios were in general lower than in Devon, rarely exceeding 3.5, the economic circumstances which defined communities prone to harvest crisis were very similar.

These same circumstances, a shortage of locally grown grain and dependence on employment in the textile industry, were equally apparent in many of the towns of southern England; and they had comparable consequences in the later 1590s. There were twice the usual number of burials in Chelmsford and Saffron Walden in 1597–8, for example. Conditions were worse in Crediton and Barnstaple, towns on

---

[60] *The Agrarian History of England and Wales*, ed. Thirsk, pp.72–3; W. G. Hoskins, *Devon* (London, 1954), pp.125–8. Cf. J. Thirsk, 'Industries in the countryside', in *Essays in the Economic and Social History of Tudor and Stuart England*, ed. F. J. Fisher (Cambridge, 1961), pp.81–2.

[61] As perhaps in 1587. Cf. Appleby, 'Disease or famine?', pp.429–30; *The Agrarian History of England and Wales*, ed. Thirsk, pp.629–30.

[62] Essex Record Office, Q/SR 129/66, 66a; F. Hull, 'Agriculture and rural society in Essex 1560–1640' (University of London Ph.D. thesis, 1950), pp.123, 471, 472, 483.

either side of the vulnerable area of Devon, as Fig. 2 shows. In Crediton the crisis mortality ratio was 3.3 in 1596–7, and it had been 2.5 in 1587; at least 7 per cent of the population of a little over 2,000 died on each occasion. In Barnstaple the crisis of 1597 appears more spectacular than in Crediton because no other epidemic can be found to rival it after 1546, but the crisis mortality ratio was 3.0, 202 people out of a population of around 3,000 died in one year, and the number of conceptions fell by a third.[63] These were the results of an urban situation in which, it was reported, there was little 'corn brought to market . . . and such snatching and catching for that little and such a cry that like never was heard'.[64]

Local research would no doubt reveal many similar crises in other small towns of southern England, especially textile towns. In two of the three parishes of Reading, for example, the total number of burials between August 1596 and July 1597 was 166, compared with a previous annual average for the two parishes of 45.[65] In Salisbury, a larger city of more than 6,000 people, the increase in mortality was smaller. The number of burials did not quite reach twice the average, but the number of conceptions fell by a third and there was no doubt about the distress in the town. A contraction in consumer demand in 1597 hit a cloth industry already in decline, the unemployed population was further swollen by an influx of rural vagrants, and in one parish in that year 78 of the 230 people buried were specifically described as paupers.[66]

The largest English towns with their rich mercantile elites, their charitable resources and poor-relief institutions were, however, normally much better placed than smaller centres to withstand the effects of dearth. Their aldermen and councillors often purchased corn from the Baltic in 1596 and 1597 for sale at reduced prices to the poor, and while it would be difficult to argue that these purchases had a major impact on standards of nutrition, they were one manifestation of the economic resources which could be drawn on when grain prices rose.[67] Consequently, in none of the larger English cities, with the possible

---

[63] Total populations for Crediton and Barnstaple have been roughly calculated from the annual average number of baptisms, using a multiplier of 30.

[64] J. B. Gribble, *Memorials of Barnstaple* (Barnstaple, 1830), pp.625–6.

[65] *The Register of the Parish of St Mary, Reading*, ed. G. P. Crawfurd (Reading, 1892); Berkshire Record Office, register of St Giles's parish, Reading.

[66] P. Slack, 'Poverty and politics in Salisbury 1597–1666', in *Crisis and Order in English Towns 1500–1700*, ed. P. Clark and P. Slack (London, 1972), pp.169, 196.

[67] E.g., Bristol Archives Office, Mayors' Audits 1595–6; *Adams' Chronicle of Bristol*, pp.149, 153; Exeter City Muniments, Act Book 5, fols. 163r, 178r, 187r. Such measures and resources seem not to have significantly delayed the impact of the crisis in the way that has been noticed in Nantes: A. Croix, *Nantes et le pays nantais au XVIe siècle* (Paris, 1974), pp. 133–6.

exception of Newcastle,[68] did the total number of burials in 1597 reach twice the average. That is not to say, however, that the more impoverished sections of these large urban populations did not find themselves in the same critical situation in 1597 as some of their rural neighbours. In fact a topographical breakdown of mortality, which is made possible by the large number of parishes in the major cities, shows clearly that they did so.

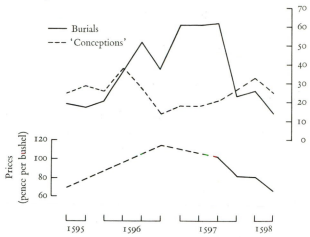

Fig. 4.   Burials and 'conceptions' in five Exeter parishes July 1595 – June 1598, with wheat prices. Note that no prices are recorded for October 1595 – September 1596 or January to June 1597. Sources: see notes 72 and 73.

The citizens of London were most fortunate. There was a small increase in mortality but it was not serious across the city as a whole. In 1597 the total number of burials in fifty-two parishes was 40 per cent above the annual average for the decade. Nevertheless death rates were higher in some parishes than in others. In Allhallows London Wall, St Botolph Bishopsgate, St Botolph Aldgate and St Mary Somerset, all of them among the poorer parishes in the city,[69] crisis mortality ratios ranged between 1.6 and 2.0, rather above the ratios elsewhere. There were similar small differences between different quarters of Norwich. Although the corporation imported 4,600 quarters of rye from Amsterdam,[70] the number of burials in St Peter Permentergate, one of

---

[68]   Unfortunately I have been unable to discover Newcastle parish registers with entries for the sixteenth century.

[69]   Their poverty is suggested by the subsidy assessments referred to in note 105 below.

[70]   Norfolk and Norwich Record Office, Court Book 1595–1603, pp.93. 157; Clavors' Accounts 1555–1646, fol. 76r.

the more impoverished areas of the city, rose to almost twice the average. In the two large towns of western England, Bristol and Exeter, the social incidence of the crisis was still more striking. The corporation of Bristol reported the town to be 'greatly burdened with many poor people' in 1596, and in the following year, while registered burials in the prosperous central parishes of the town remained at their usual level, they multiplied threefold in four poor suburban parishes.[71] The incidence of the crisis was determined by the social geography of the town.

Poverty, malnutrition and death also went hand in hand on the fringes of Exeter. Between October 1596 and September 1597 the total number of burials was twice the annual average and the total number of conceptions fell by 40 per cent over five parishes, all of them the poorer quarters of the town, close to its walls, and one of them the notorious slum district of St Sidwell.[72] The development of the crisis in these parishes is illustrated in Fig. 4. It shows the close correlation between mortality among the poor, and local fluctuations in the price of wheat, which was registered in the Mayor's Court.[73] There are some gaps in the record, but it is clear that prices, which were already high in Exeter in 1595, reached a fresh peak towards the end of 1596 as the number of burials rose and conceptions fell in the suburbs. The vital statistics did not return to normal levels until the final quarter of 1597 when prices were beginning to fall.

In both town and country therefore the localities most seriously affected by the crisis of the later 1590s had distinct social and economic features. Together with the simple chronological coincidence of high food prices and rising death rates, which is so evident in Exeter, they leave no doubt that high mortality was directly connected with an environment of poverty and food scarcity. It does not follow that simple starvation was always the connecting link. Malnutrition reduces resistance to a host of infections which might do the job equally well.

71   Bristol Archives Office, Vetus Liber Ordinacionium, fol. 64r. The four parishes were St John, St Mary Redcliffe, Temple and SS Philip and Jacob.
72   The five parishes are those of St David, St Thomas, St Sidwell, St Mary Major and Holy Trinity, transcripts of whose registers are in the Devon and Cornwall Record Society Library, Exeter. On the social geography of Exeter, see W. T. MacCaffrey, *Exeter 1540–1640* (Cambridge, Mass., 1958), pp.112–13; *Exeter in the Seventeenth Century*, ed. W. G. Hoskins, Devon and Cornwall Record Society, new ser., II (Exeter, 1955), pp.xvii–xix, and note 101 below. Burials in the parishes of Exeter are usefully summarized in R. Pickard, *The Population and Epidemics of Exeter in Pre-Census Times* (Exeter, 1947), but where my calculations from the register transcripts differ from Pickard's, I have preferred my own figures.
73   Average prices have been calculated from Exeter City Muniments, Dr R. C. Easterling's transcript of wheat prices recorded in the Mayor's Court Rolls.

Typhus was no doubt one disease involved, for there are probable references to it in the later 1590s,[74] but it was not alone. As in the North-West there was seldom an obvious prevalence of adults among those buried[75] and mortality was often heavy in the summer of 1597 as well as in the previous and succeeding winters. Other diseases known to be aggravated by malnutrition added to the toll of death in southern England. Dysentery in particular was common in the summer of 1597. In Great Coggeshall, Essex, for example, there was an 'extraordinary bloody flux' which 'the more the physicians laboured to cure, the more sharp and vehement it grew'.[76] There may have been pulmonary ailments too, if the references to consumption as well as to flux and fever in the registers of the London parishes of Allhallows London Wall and St Botolph Aldgate can be relied upon.[77] But typhus and dysentery between them might well be sufficient to account for the prolonged high mortality, without any marked age or seasonal incidence, of 1597. An Oxfordshire doctor appears to have thought so: he described the diseases in the 'pestilential sickness' of 1597 as sometimes flux without fever, sometimes fever without flux, and sometimes both at once.[78]

Whatever the diagnoses of this doctor's modern counterpart might be, however, the important historical fact is that malnutrition made the decisive contribution to high death rates in town and country in 1596–8. Epidemic diseases like bubonic plague, which might produce similarly heavy mortality independently of conditions of food shortage, were not widespread at this time. Although plague was present in a few parishes in the later 1590s,[79] it was emphatically not the main cause of death in the

---

[74] See, for example, the number of deaths from 'ague' in Forbes, *Chronicle from Aldgate*, pp.104–5.

[75] See for example the ages of those buried in one London parish: *The Registers of the Parish of Allhallows London Wall*, ed. E. B. Jupp and R. Hovenden (n.pl., 1878), pp.118ff. The percentage of adults buried in 1597 was no larger than in more normal years.

[76] Essex Record Office, Great Coggeshall parish register; Palliser, 'Dearth and disease in Staffordshire', p.62. Dysentery was a major scourge in northern Germany in 1599: E. Woehlkens, *Pest und Ruhr im 16. und 17. Jahrhundert* (Hanover, 1954), pp.75–8, diagrams xiv, xv.

[77] *Registers of Allhallows London Wall*, pp.131–4; Forbes, *Chronicle from Aldgate*, pp.102, 104.

[78] Oxford, Bodleian Library, Rawlinson MS A369, fol. 35. The presence of diseases such as these leads me to doubt the general applicability of A. B. Appleby's conclusion that stark starvation was a common cause of death in 1597: 'Disease or famine?', p.424. In fact the question in his title – disease *or* famine – presents too simple and misleading an alternative. It evades the crucial issue of the nature of the disease involved: whether it was directly connected with malnutrition or not.

[79] E.g., possibly in parts of Kent: Kent Archives Office, transcript of Cranbrook parish register under 1597 and Sa/Ac 6, fol. 240r; and in Ludlow: Shrewsbury, *History of Bubonic Plague*, p.177. There were some cases of plague reported in London and Norwich also, but it was not the main cause of increased mortality: *The Economic Writings of Sir William Petty*, ed. C. H. Hull (2 vols., Cambridge, 1899), II, p.433; Norfolk and Norwich Record Office, reports of burials in Norwich Court Book 1595–1603.

localities we have examined. The diseases which killed the poor and the malnourished in 1596–8, and which were no doubt carried from place to place by vagrants tramping into towns such as Salisbury, were rightly summed up by one observer as 'great sickness by famine'.[80]

VI

Outbreaks of bubonic plague in the second half of the sixteenth century stand in sharp contrast to the famine crisis of 1596–8.[81] Because of the unusually long run of bad harvests which caused it, the latter was in many respects an exceptional, if not a unique event in the country after 1560. Although harvest failures and epidemic diseases coincided on several later occasions, in 1623–4 for example, and even once or twice in the eighteenth century, the consequent fluctuations in mortality were less violent.[82] Plague epidemics, on the other hand, as Table 2 suggests, were more frequent phenomena. They swept across the country in the early 1560s, 1590s and 1600s, and there were several more localized outbreaks in the intervening years.

Plague epidemics were also more severe than harvest crises in the communities they affected. Fig. 2 shows this to be the case in Crediton, where crisis mortality ratios of 10.6 and 7.4 were recorded in the plagues of 1571 and 1591–2 respectively; and in Barnstaple the plague of 1546 was much more devastating than the crisis of 1597, its effect on burials being understated in the figure because registration broke down at the height of the epidemic. If the number of burials in harvest crises was sometimes three or four times higher than usual, in epidemics of plague the ratio was typically between 4 and 12. Even in the North-West plague had a more violent effect on mortality in the parishes it affected than the famine of 1597. In Penrith in 1598 it pushed the number of burials to 12.9 times the average.[83] It is rarely possible to translate such ratios into mortality rates, but where estimates can be made they tell a tragic story. It would seem that the epidemics of 1571 and 1591–2 in

---

[80] J. Hall, *A History of the Town and Parish of Nantwich* (Nantwich, 1883), pp.112–13.

[81] I hope to analyse plague epidemics at greater length than is possible here in a forthcoming book, *The Impact of Plague in Tudor and Stuart England*.

[82] Flinn, 'Stabilisation of mortality', pp.300–2; A. Gooder, 'The population crisis of 1727–30 in Warwickshire', *Midland History*, I, no.4 (1972), 1–22; J. A. Johnston, 'The impact of the epidemic of 1727–30 in South-West Worcestershire', *Medical History*, xv (1971), 278–92; Chambers, *Population, Economy and Society*, pp.92–3.

[83] Appleby, 'Disease or famine?', p.422; cf. J. Hughes, 'The plague in Carlisle 1597/8', *Transactions of the Cumberland and Westmorland Antiquarian and Archaeological Society*, new ser., LXXI (1971), 51–63.

Plate 1. London weekly bill of mortality (1603)

Bill of mortality for the week ending 20 October 1603: one of the earliest preserved weekly printed bills, including a detailed statement of fatalities occasioned by the 1603 plague epidemic. Reproduced by permission of the Guildhall Library, City of London.

1602.   1603.

A true Report of all the Burials and Christnings within the Citie of
London and the Liberties thereof, from the 23. of December, 1602. to the 22. of
December, 1603. Whereunto is added the number of euery seuerall Parish, from the 14. of
July, to the 22. of December, aswell within the Citie of London and the Liberties thereof,
as in other Parishes in the Skirts of the Citie and out of the Freedome, adioyning to
the Citie: According to the Report made to the KINGS most
Excellent Maiestie, by the Company of Parish
Clearkes of the same Citie.

	Buried in all	Of the Plague	Christnings
December 23	83	3	69
January 6	78	0	97
January 13	83	1	114
January 20	80	0	105
January 27	82	4	128
February 3	104	1	102
February 10	76	0	108
February 17	96	3	109
February 24	85	0	108
March 3	82	3	110
March 10	101	2	110
March 17	103	3	106
March 24	60	2	106
March 31	78	6	59
Aprill 7	66	4	143
Aprill 14	79	4	86
Aprill 21	98	8	84
Aprill 28	109	10	85
May 5	50	11	78
May 12	112	18	103
May 19	122	22	81
May 26	122	32	98
June 2	114	30	82
June 9	111	43	110
June 16	144	59	90
June 23	182	72	95
June 30	267	158	82
July 7	445	263	89
July 14	612	424	88

This Weeke was the Out-Parishes
brought in to bee ioyned with the
Citie and Liberties.

	Buried in all	Of the Plague	Christnings
July 21	1186	917	50
July 28	1728	1396	138
August 4	2256	1922	115
August 11	2077	1745	110
August 18	3054	2713	95
August 25	2853	2539	127
September 1	3385	3035	97
September 8	3078	2724	105
September 15	3129	2818	89
September 22	2456	2195	90
September 29	1961	1732	81
October 6	1831	1641	71
October 13	1312	1146	73
October 20	766	642	67
October 27	625	508	75
November 3	737	594	70
November 10	585	442	65
November 17	384	251	64
November 24	198	105	58
December 1	223	102	64
December 8	163	55	72
December 15	200	96	71
December 22	168	74	70

The totall of all that hath beene
buried this yeere —————— 38244
Whereof of the Plague ————— 30578
Christning: —————————— 4789

Parish	Buried in all	Of the Plague
Albones in Woodstreet	183	164
Alhallowes Lumbardstreet	109	98
Alhallowes the great	286	230
Alhallowes the lesse	227	182
Alhallowes Breadstreet	33	27
Alhallowes Stayninges	123	103
Alhallowes the Wall	216	174
Alhallowes Hony-lane	12	5
Alhallowes Barking	390	339
Alphage Cripplegate	175	132
Andrewes by the Wardrobe	290	256
Andrewes Eastcheape	114	108
Andrewes Vndershaft	165	142
Annes at Aldersgate	146	125
Annes Black Fryers	235	226
Antholines Parish	32	27
Austines Parish	92	78
Barthol. at the Exchange	93	83
Bennets at Pauls Wharfe	199	136
Bennets Grace-Church	40	30
Bennets Finck	95	78
Bennets Sherhog	26	24
Botolph Billinsgate	91	73
Christ Church Parish	334	271
Christophers Parish	41	35
Clements by Eastcheape	48	40
Dionis Backchurch	112	88
Dunstanes in the East	227	197
Edmunds in Lumbardstreet	78	67
Ethelborow within Bishopsg.	163	134
Saint Faithes	115	96
Saint Fosters in Fosterlane	91	81
Gabriel Fanchurch	67	56
George Botolphlane	36	30
Gregories by Paules	272	227
Hellens within Bishopsgate	98	83
Iames by Garlickhithe	141	110
Iohn Euangelist	9	5
Iohn Zacharies	131	118
Iohns in the Walbrooke	136	122
Katherines Cree-Church	400	337
Katherine Coleman	190	167
Lawrence in the Iewry	88	71
Lawrence Pountney	161	134
Leonards Fosterlane	232	210
Leonards Eastcheape	34	39
Magnus Parish by the Bridge	109	76
Margrets New-fishstreet	83	61

Parish	Buried in all	Of the Plague
Margarets Pattons	54	44
Margarets Moses	70	60
Margarets Lothbery	96	88
Martins in the Vintry	218	190
Martins Orgars	90	77
Martins Iremonger lane	27	19
Martins at Ludgate	199	161
Martins Outwich	39	32
Mary le Bow	26	24
Mary Bothaw	35	31
Mary at the Hill	142	120
Mary Abchurch	124	110
Mary Woolchurch	52	37
Mary Colchurch	10	8
Mary Woolneth	99	91
Mary Aldermary	80	68
Mary Aldermanbery	81	70
Mary Stayninges	49	57
Mary Mounthaw	51	41
Mary Sommersets	197	177
Matthew Fridaystreet	16	13
Maudlins in Milkstreet	33	30
Maudlins by Oldfishstreet	128	104
Michael Basishaw	141	109
Michael Cornhill	130	91
Michael in Woodstreet	156	137
Michael in the Riall	100	79
Michael in the Querne	61	46
Michael Queenhithe	138	105
Michael Crooked Lane	110	97
Mildreds Poultry	84	62
Mildreds Breadstreet	43	33
Nicholas Acons	41	32
Nicholas Cole Abbay	147	103
Nicholas Olaues	83	69
Olaues in the Iury	41	33
Olaues in Hartstreet	201	171
Olaues in Siluer-street	115	92
Pancras by Soperlane	20	16
Peters in Cornhill	141	80
Peters in Cheape	55	37
Peters the poore in broadstr.	44	30
Peters at Pauls Wharfe	97	88
Steuens in Colmanstreet	361	315
Steuens in the Walbrooke	24	20
Swithins at Londonstone	120	89
Thomas Apostle	86	64
Trinitie Parish	116	108

Parish	Buried in all	Of the Plague	
Andrewes in Holborne	1191	1125	
Bartho. the lesse Smithfield	86	74	
Bart.the great Smithfield	195	165	
Brides Parish	913	805	
Botolph Algate	1413	1280	
Bridewell Precinct	108	103	
Botolph Bishopsgate	1228	1094	
Botolphs without Aldersg.	576	508	
Dunstanes in the West	510	412
Georges in Southwarke	915	804
Giles without Creeplegate	2408	1745
Olaues in Southwarke	2541	2383
Sauiours in Southwarke	1914	1773
Sepulchres Parish	2223	1861
Thomas in Southwarke	249	221
Trinitie in the Minories	40	35
Clements Templebarre	662	502	Martins in the Fields 505 405
Giles in the Fields	456	402	Mary White-chappel 1539 1352
Iames at Clarkenwell	725	619	Magdalens in Bermondsey street 597 562
Katherines by the Tower	653	585	At the Pest-house 115 115
Leonards in Shorditch	878	740	

Buried in all within these 23. Weekes —————— 33681
Whereof, of the Plague ——————————————— 29083
London, Printed by William Stansby.

Plate 2. London annual bill of mortality [1625]

Bill of mortality for the year 1602–3, providing a comparative account
of fatalities in the parishes of London. The final entry demonstrates
that the Pest-house was in operation at this time. Reproduced by
permission of the Guildhall Library, City of London.

Crediton removed respectively a quarter and a fifth of the population. The plagues of 1563, 1593 and 1603 in London are estimated to have killed, respectively, of the order of 23, 13 and 20 per cent of the city's population.[84] In both Exeter and Bristol more than 14 per cent of the population died on two occasions in the last forty years of the sixteenth century. In Norwich at least 30 per cent of the population died during the great plague of 1579, the first of a string of epidemics in the city and the worst so far recorded in any large English town in the sixteenth century.[85]

The speed with which plague cut down so many victims also distinguished it from other epidemic diseases. There were cases in which it spread slowly through a town, lasting for more than a year and producing relatively few casualties. But the major epidemics usually ran their course within six to eight months, rapidly reaching a peak in the late summer or early autumn and declining more slowly through the winter: a seasonal pattern determined by the warm climatic conditions necessary to produce a large number of insect vectors for the disease.[86] The vast majority of deaths therefore took place within a very short space of time. In Norwich during the plague of 1579, for example, more than 3,000 people were buried in the three months from August to October. Less severe epidemics lasted rather longer, but they were still over within a year. Fig. 5 shows the quarterly totals of burials during the plague of 1590–1 in the five Exeter parishes whose experience in 1595–8 is recorded in Fig. 4. The epidemic produced no sharp drop in conceptions; it was accompanied by a fall rather than an increase in wheat prices; but its effect on mortality was violent. The contrast between the profiles of the different sorts of crisis recorded in Figs. 3, 4

[84] Conclusions based on the calculations in I. Sutherland, 'When was the Great Plague? Mortality in London 1563–1665', in *Population and Social Change,* ed. D. V. Glass and R. Revelle (London, 1972), pp.287–320. See Plates 1 and 2.

[85] Estimates for Exeter based on the parish registers and on indications of total population in MacCaffrey, *Exeter 1540–1640*, pp.11–13, and in Exeter City Muniments, Subsidy Assessments, nos. 2 and 3, and London, House of Lords Record Office, Main Papers, Protestation Returns, BC9–29. For Bristol and Norwich, see P. Slack, 'The local incidence of epidemic disease: the case of Bristol 1540–1650', in *The Plague Reconsidered,* Local Population Studies Supplement no.4 (Cambridge, 1977), p.51; *Records of the City of Norwich,* II, pp.cxxvi–cxxvii; Slack, thesis, pp.127–8, 135–6, 166–7.

[86] The standard work on the epidemiology of bubonic plague is R. Pollitzer, *Plague* (Geneva, 1954). See also L. F. Hirst, *The Conquest of Plague* (Oxford, 1953), pp.260–80, and for historical epidemics, J-N. Biraben, *Les hommes et la peste en France et dans les pays européens et méditerranéens* (2 vols., Paris, 1975–6), I. The latter's consideration of the role of climate (pp.13–15, 134–9) stresses the importance of humidity as well as warmth in providing favourable conditions for fleas and hence for epidemics.

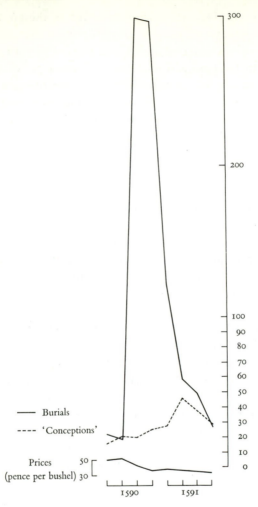

Fig. 5. Burials and 'conceptions' in five Exeter parishes 1590–1, with wheat prices. Sources: see notes 72 and 73.

and 5 demonstrates the unusually sharp and sudden disaster which was the distinctive result of an epidemic of bubonic plague.

Plague was distinctive also in its method of transmission and hence in its geographical incidence. Dependent as it was on both rodent and insect vectors, it did not spread as rapidly or as far as the virus infections of 1558–9. Neither did it reach as many remote villages as were affected by the harvest crisis of 1597. It was concentrated in settlements where large numbers of rodents and men were in closest contact, that is in towns; and it reached smaller communities more haphazardly as rats or fleas were transported along the main routes of communication by water and land.[87] An epidemic wave like that of 1563–8 or 1603–10 usually began with the importation of a virulent strain of the disease into the ports of the South or the South-East from the continent. Its immediate movement to the main centres of communication, the larger towns like London and Norwich, was virtually inevitable, and there it took hold first in the rodent and then in the human population. It might be carried also to scattered villages, especially those on main roads and rivers, before winter conditions temporarily slowed its progress. In the spring the disease sometimes revived and the process of transmission began again. Thus in Essex the places most often infected by plague were the ports of Harwich and Maldon, the towns of Colchester and Chelmsford, and one or two villages close to the main London to Harwich road like Terling.[88] Many more isolated rural settlements entirely escaped.

In Devon the plague region was even more clearly delineated. The disease normally arrived in Plymouth, Dartmouth or Exeter by sea and it was always concentrated in the southern half of the county, especially in the South Hams region where a warm climate and a relatively densely settled population provided ideal conditions for its transmission.[89] Here a small hamlet like Bridford, close to Exeter, could suffer as frequently and as severely as a market-town like Newton Abbot. But plague rarely affected the villages of the northern half of the county which were especially vulnerable during the harvest crisis of 1597. The plague epidemic of 1589–93 in Devon, though somewhat unusual in the extent of its dispersal across the county, provides a typical example of the patterns of diffusion which might occur. Plague was brought into the county, probably with other diseases, by the fleet which returned to Plymouth from Portugal on 1 July 1589.[90] Immediately the number of burials rose in Plymouth and shortly afterwards in Dartmouth, and the

[87] Shrewsbury, *History of Bubonic Plague*, pp.3, 29; Pollitzer, *Plague*, pp.386–90.

[88] On Colchester, see I. G. Doolittle, 'The plague in Colchester 1579–1666', *Transactions of the Essex Archaeological Society*, IV (1972), 134–45. I am grateful to Dr W. J. Petchey for providing me with information on mortality in Maldon.

[89] The density of population in southern Devon appears both from the muster roll of 1569 (figures kindly supplied by Professor W. G. Hoskins) and from the subsidies for the 1520s: see the map in J. Sheail, 'The distribution of taxable population and wealth in England during the early sixteenth century', *Transactions of the Institute of British Geographers*, LV (1972), 120. It is interesting to note that the same area of Devon was seriously affected in 1348–9: Shrewsbury, *History of Bubonic Plague*, p.61.

[90] Keevil, *Medicine and the Navy*, pp.77–9. On plague in northern Spain in 1589, see J. Nadal and E. Giralt, *La population catalane de 1553 à 1717* (Paris, 1960), pp.39–40.

infection spread from there to many parishes between the two ports.[91] Carew reported that 'the diseases which the soldiers brought home with them' proved to be 'the very pestilence' and 'did grow more grievous as they carried the same farther into the land'.[92] Civilians might be equally responsible for spreading infection. Plague reached Totnes in 1590, and the first to die was 'Marjorie the daughter of Mr Wyke of Dartmouth'. In the same year it struck Exeter, which then became another centre of infection. One of the first victims in Dean Prior, for example, was 'Richard Budmore of Exon, found dead in the way'. In East Devon Feniton, Honiton, Offwell and Widworthy were all infected in 1591, and Sidmouth and Colyton in 1592 and 1593. By then it is probable that fifty-five of the eighty-nine parishes or towns with surviving registers had suffered to some degree from bubonic plague.[93] All the larger towns in the county, save Barnstaple, were among them, and the vast majority of the infected parishes were in southern or eastern Devon.

Even so, the movement of the disease cannot have appeared as orderly to contemporaries as it does to the historian. Some northern villages like Littleham were infected: one or two places in the south like Paignton may have escaped. Moreover the precise routes of infection could not be foreseen, and some parishes may well have been the victims of two separate waves of infection. The clerk of Wolborough parish, which included the market town of Newton Abbot, noted one epidemic of plague beginning on 2 August 1590 and ending on 20 February 1591, and a second beginning in September 1592. The presence of plague was noted in the register of Crediton in September 1590, when the disease was perhaps imported from Exeter, but in August 1591 a more serious epidemic started when a man who 'took the infection by lodging one of Torrington' and a Torrington inhabitant 'who died in the highway' were among the first burials. Small wonder therefore that supernatural omens were sometimes sought to explain the incidence and timing of the disease. The first victims of plague in Newton Ferrars in 1589 fell sick, it was asserted, after they had seen 'a vision of a corpse or a dead body carried to the parish [church] there to be buried'.[94]

The severity of the disease was even more unpredictable than its local

---

[91] See R. M. S. McConaghey, 'Dartmouth medical records', *Medical History*, IV (1960), 98.

[92] *Richard Carew of Antony: The Survey of Cornwall*, ed. F. E. Halliday (London, 1953), p.85.

[93] The fifty-five localities include not only parishes in which the number of burials doubled, but also parishes with smaller increases in mortality but where there was either a reference to 'plague' or an obvious concentration of burials in a few families – often an indicator of the presence of plague.

[94] Exeter City Muniments, Commonplace Book of John Hooker, fol. 363v, under 1588–9.

incidence. In total the urban population of Devon suffered a higher death rate than the rural, because several villages were free from infection. But there was no consistent relationship between the level of mortality and the size of the communities which were infected.[95] If we measure the crisis mortality ratios for each of the fifty-five parishes visited by plague in 1589–93, we find ratios of more than 5.0 in eleven parishes, of between 3.0 and 5.0 in twelve parishes, and of between 2.0 and 3.0 in thirteen parishes. The remainder were less seriously affected. One of the larger towns in the county, Crediton (ratio 7.4), was among the places devastated, but these also included smaller settlements like Dean Prior (ratio 9.3) and Stoke-in-Teignhead (ratio 7.6). Variations in mortality depended rather on a multitude of more immediate factors. Casualties might be few if fleas from an infected newcomer to a village transmitted plague only to members of one household and not to the local rodent populations, or if the infection arrived too late in the year for a major epidemic to develop. Thus there were cases like that reported from Barnstaple in November 1604 when 'the plague entered into this town: few died'.[96] Such chance elements in the epidemiology of bubonic plague were crucial in determining its effects on any single occasion, and they overlaid and to a considerable extent obscured the fundamental continuing regularities in the incidence of the disease: its dependence on established communication networks and its regular urban incidence.

A final point of contrast between epidemics of plague and 'famine' crises in the later sixteenth century lies in their timing. We have noticed already that plague epidemics did not follow harvest failures, and there is no reason why they should have done. They were the result of the slow march of infection across the continent, from the Levant through the Mediterranean to the maritime countries of north-western Europe.[97] There might be chance coincidences of the two phenomena. The plague of 1598 in parts of northern England, for example, entered the country from Scotland at the end of a harvest crisis. But such conjunctions, which could have serious demographic consequences, were extremely rare in England after 1560.[98] The plagues which coincided with harvest

[95] A similar conclusion is reached in Biraben, *Les hommes et la peste*, I, pp.298–302; J-N. Biraben, 'Certain demographic characteristics of the plague epidemic in France, 1720–22', *Daedalus*, Spring 1968, pp.536–45.

[96] J. R. Chanter, *Sketches of the Literary History of Barnstaple* (Barnstaple, 1866), p.113.

[97] Biraben, *Les hommes et la peste*, I, pp.118–29.

[98] The major exception was the plague of 1630–1, which was particularly severe in northern England: Sharpe France, 'History of plague in Lancashire', pp.59–80.

failure in parts of France and Spain in 1587 and 1597–9, for example,[99] did not reach southern England until 1589 and 1602 respectively, by which time harvests were good. In this respect, as in its apparently random fluctuations in mortality, bubonic plague was an 'autonomous' determinant of demographic crises.

It would, however, be absurd to conclude from this that environmental factors were of little importance in the impact of plague. We have noted the role of transport facilities and of towns in its carriage and persistence. One further regularity in the incidence of plague in the later sixteenth century deserves mention. Within towns plague, like famine, was particularly severe in the poorer suburbs. This was a natural consequence of the epidemiology of the disease. If it was not aggravated by malnutrition, plague was closely associated with bad housing and poor hygiene, with an environment in which rats, fleas and men lived in closest proximity. Contemporaries had no doubt that the disease flourished in 'narrow lanes, alleys and other pestered and noisome corners where families of poor people are thronged together as men use to pack wool sacks one upon another'.[100] There was an observed correlation between plague and poverty. It was visible no doubt even in villages, although it can seldom be reconstructed from the historical record. But its prevalence in towns can be measured by the sort of parochial breakdown of mortality employed earlier in our discussion of the crisis of 1597.

The epidemic in Exeter in 1590–1 may be taken as an example. The subsidy assessments of 1544 and 1602 can be used to range the eleven parishes with surviving registers in order of wealth, from the rich quarters of St Petrock, St Martin, and St Mary Arches, with their many tax-paying merchants, in the centre of the town, to the much poorer and more populous extra-mural suburbs of St David, Holy Trinity and St Sidwell.[101] Plague was not entirely absent from the central areas. Although the number of burials did not rise above the norm in St Mary, the ratio of epidemic to normal burials in St Petrock between August 1590 and July 1591 was 4.7 and in St Martin 2.9. In the suburbs,

99 Glass and Eversley (eds.), *Population in History*, p.465; P. Deyon, *Amiens, capitale provinciale* (Paris, 1967), pp.17–18; Nadal and Giralt, *La population catalane*, pp.39–40; B. Bennassar, *Recherches sur les grandes épidémies dans le nord de l'Espagne à la fin du XVIe siècle* (Paris, 1969), pp.60–6.

100 Francis Herring, *A modest defence of the caveat given to the wearers of impoisoned amulets* (1604), sig. B1.

101 The subsidy assessments in P.R.O., E179/98/247, and *Exeter in the Seventeenth Century*, pp.1–6, 123, have been used to calculate the taxable wealth per acre in each parish. The full figures are in Slack, thesis, p.118.

however, the crisis mortality ratios were much higher: 6.3 in St David, 7.0 in St Sidwell, 9.2 in Holy Trinity. Since mortality rates were probably higher in the suburbs even in more normal years, the proportion of the population dying in the extra-mural parishes in 1590–1 must have been at least twice as great as that in the central parishes, perhaps 20 per cent as against less than 10 per cent. The incidence of plague, like that of harvest crises, reflected and substantially reinforced the existing imbalance of health between rich and poor.

Similar patterns have been found in epidemics in other large towns in the later sixteenth and early seventeenth centuries. They were as marked in London and Bristol as in Exeter, and in the case of some of the richer parishes in those cities it can be shown that social distinctions were as important in determining the distribution of mortality within parishes as between them. In Christ Church parish, Bristol, in 1603, for example, plague was concentrated in the narrow alley of the Pithay, not along the main thoroughfares of Wine Street and Broad Street.[102] In Norwich as in some other eastern towns the importance of the social and economic environment was demonstrated in a further way. Plague disproportionately affected the large foreign immigrant community of Dutch and Walloon refugees. In the plague of 1603 death rates among the immigrant community may well have been twice as high as among the English, and their heavy losses in 1579 provoked complaints that the foreigners' 'corrupt keeping of their houses and necessaries' helped to spread contagion. Even earlier, in 1563, Bishop Grindal noted the distress in the 'back lanes and alleys of London, and amongst the poor strangers; for these are the sorest visited'.[103] Conditions of overcrowding and bad housing, the usual circumstances of recent immigrants, determined the local incidence of epidemic disease.

Bubonic plague was thus not so completely autonomous an influence on mortality as it might at first seem. The capricious nature of its timing, its uneven rural distribution and its variable severity in any afflicted community justified contemporary attribution of it to divine providence. Yet its urban, and especially its suburban, incidence was equally obvious and testified to its interaction with historical and social circumstances.

[102] Slack, 'The local incidence of epidemic disease', pp.55–7. For London, see Shrewsbury, *History of Bubonic Plague*, pp.227–8, 326; *The Vestry Minute Book of the Parish of St Bartholomew Exchange*, ed. E. Freshfield (1890), pp.xlv–xlix.

[103] Norfolk and Norwich Record Office, reports of alien and native burials entered in the Norwich Court Books; *The Records of the City of Norwich*, II, p.335; *The Remains of Edmund Grindal*, ed. W. Nicholson, Parker Society (Cambridge, 1843), p.259.

VII

Having discussed famine and plague crises during the reign of Elizabeth, we can now turn back to the decades before 1560. These require separate consideration not only because the sources are less full, but also because, inadequate though they are, they show that the epidemic picture in the early sixteenth century was in several respects less clearly defined than that which obtained later. In particular some of the regularities evident in Elizabethan epidemics of plague appear to have been less pronounced earlier.

The first point of contrast lies in the distribution of plague in urban communities. There is some evidence to suggest that mortality rates were more uniform in different parts of towns in the epidemics of the 1540s and 1550s than in those of the later sixteenth century. The number of deaths was not necessarily any greater as a proportion of the population, but it was more evenly spread across the town. Unfortunately the earlier the epidemic considered, the fewer the surviving registers and the more likely it is that high mortality rates in some suburban parishes escape analysis. Thus, for example, only two registers survive for the plague of 1546–7 in Exeter, both of them from parishes in the centre of the town, St Petrock and St Mary Arches. It may be significant nevertheless that they show this to have been the most serious epidemic in these two parishes in the century. Similarly in Bristol, the plague of 1544–5 was unusually severe in the parishes of Christ Church and St Ewen in the heart of the town. A somewhat wider sample of evidence is available for Norwich in the plague of the same year. There mortality was as heavy in the central parishes of St George Tombland, St Peter Mancroft and St Simon and St Jude, as it was in St Giles and St Peter Permentergate, parishes which were considerably less prosperous. In the plague of 1579 and its successors, on the other hand, the balance of health was decisively tilted against the latter parishes and in favour of the former.[104]

A preliminary survey of the parish registers of London indicates comparable changes in the distribution of plague mortality in the capital. The plagues of 1543 and 1548 affected the eighteen city parishes whose burials are shown in Fig. 1 no less severely than the outer parishes of St Saviour Southwark and St Margaret Westminster, which were among those bearing the brunt of plague mortality from the middle of Elizabeth's reign onwards. In 1563 plague was still relatively evenly

---

[104] Slack, 'The local incidence of epidemic disease', pp.51, 59; Slack, thesis, p.159. I hope to consider this point at length in the work cited in note 81.

distributed across the city as compared with the later epidemics. Using the Tudor subsidy assessments we can select a sample of nine rich and seven poor parishes in the city with surviving registers, and compare their experience in the plagues of 1563 and 1593.[105] The prosperous parishes, all of them in the centre of the city, reveal a crisis mortality ratio of 6.6 in 1563. There was little difference from the poor parishes along the river-bank and close to the walls, where the ratio was 5.8. In 1593, however, the ratio of epidemic to normal burials was only 3.2 in the richer parishes but 5.7 in the poorer. Although this analysis needs to be developed in more detail than is possible here, it suggests that plague was becoming more concentrated in the outer London parishes in the later sixteenth century.

The reasons for this development, if it were to be established, also require further investigation. The most likely explanation is that the social geography of towns was changing, that with urban growth – most remarkable in London – the suburbs were increasingly impoverished areas and the central parishes more exclusively middle-class quarters. Thus the socially selective incidence of plague was probably not new in the later sixteenth century; it simply became more visible on the ground. A polarization in residential patterns made the differences in mortality in different social classes observable in the form of parochial variations. There may also have been some real improvement in standards of hygiene in the central areas of towns, as their residents acquired more changes· of clothing and built new houses, and as corporations began to develop more efficient machinery for cleaning the streets.[106] It is possible finally that there was a growing propensity

---

[105] The rich parishes are: Allhallows Honey Lane, Allhallows Bread Street, SS Antholin, Mary le Bow, Mary Woolnoth, Matthew Friday Street, Michael Bassishaw, Mildred Poultry, Stephen Walbrook. The poor are: Allhallows London Wall, SS Andrew Hubbard, Andrew by the Wardrobe, Botolph Aldgate, Botolph Bishopsgate, Mary Magdalen Old Fish Street, Mary Somerset. They have been identified from the assessments in P.R.O., E179/251/15B (1523–4); Guildhall Library, MS. 2942 (1572). The social differences between the two groups were evident also in the seventeenth century: see D. V. Glass, *London Inhabitants Within the Walls 1695*, London Record Society, II (London, 1966), map p.xxiii; R. W. Herlan, 'Social articulation and the configuration of parochial poverty in London on the eve of the Restoration', *Guildhall Studies in London History*, II (1976), 43–53.

[106] The urban environment in the sixteenth century needs more attention than it has hitherto received. For evidence of improvement in the centre of towns, as well as of suburban building, from the mid-century, see Dyer, *Worcester*, pp.157–64; W. G. Hoskins, 'The Elizabethan merchants of Exeter', in *Elizabethan Government and Society: Essays presented to Sir John Neale*, ed. S. T. Bindoff, J. Hurstfield and C. H. Williams (London, 1961), pp.178–9; *Historic Towns*, II, ed. M. D. Lobel (London, 1975), 'Bristol', pp.17–19. In Norwich, however, much rebuilding may have already been completed by 1525: ibid., 'Norwich', p.17. Regulations for street cleaning are surveyed in J. H. Thomas, *Town Government in the Sixteenth Century* (London, 1933), chapter 6.

among the better-off to flee from towns as plague approached and seek safety in the countryside, leaving central parishes virtually empty; but it would be difficult to show that flight was a more common habit at the end of the sixteenth century than at the beginning. Whatever the precise combination of factors involved, however, these are all environmental changes which may have decisively affected the geographical distribution of plague.

A second possible change in the patterns described by plague in the sixteenth century is even more difficult to establish with certainty and much less easy to account for. It is possible that plague was more widely and more evenly dispersed across rural areas as well as across towns before 1550 than after. The increasing volume of evidence for local outbreaks of plague makes precise comparison between the two parts of the century difficult, and it is impossible to reach any conclusions about the period before 1538. In Essex therefore we cannot know whether it was plague which affected the number of wills proved in 1504 and 1518 (though the presence of the disease in London suggests that it may have been),[107] nor how widely it was spread. Certainly by the time registration began, plagues in Essex were by no means widely dispersed. The surviving registers suggest, on the contrary, that the epidemics of the early seventeenth century covered a larger area than those of the sixteenth. The evidence for Devon, however, points decisively the other way. There the plague of 1546–7 was undoubtedly the most widespread crisis of the whole century between 1540 and 1640. It affected twenty-six out of the thirty-three parishes with surviving registers, many of them small villages, and in twenty of these the number of burials more than doubled.[108] No later epidemic produced a similar increase in mortality in more than thirteen of these parishes.

One cannot generalize from a single case. More county studies will be needed to show whether or not Devon was exceptional. But it should serve as a corrective to the impression, too often given by historians mesmerized by the increasing volume of evidence, that plague was more widespread in the later sixteenth and early seventeenth centuries than earlier.[109] It would also, if it were confirmed by other studies, be consistent with the hypothesis that plague epidemics in the later Middle

[107] Creighton, *History of Epidemics*, I, pp.288, 290–1.
[108] For some local details, see Hoskins, 'Epidemics in Tudor Devon', pp.134–42.
[109] Biraben's graphs of the number of places affected by plague are especially vulnerable to this criticism: *Les hommes et la peste*, I, pp.115–20.

Ages were more pervasive than those which followed.[110] It is possible, to put it more strongly, that the plague of 1546–7 in Devon is a late example of generalized outbreaks of plague which had once been common but which were absent from most of England after 1538. Amidst the many uncertainties which surround the history of plague, however, the reasons for its gradual decline from a well-nigh universal to an increasingly urban phenomenon are the most puzzling. It is tempting to suppose that secular changes in climate, the onset of the 'Little Ice Age' in the later sixteenth century, had something to do with it; but the history of climate is scarcely less contentious than the history of plague.[111] The problem is complicated further by the fact that changes in the diffusion of the disease were not accompanied by a decline in its virulence. Plague continued to produce violent increases in mortality in the places it affected. For whatever reason, however, the distribution of plague grew narrower after its first appearance in the fourteenth century, and the case of Devon suggests that the process of change may not have been completed by 1538, still less by 1500.

A third distinction between epidemics of plague in the early and later sixteenth century is indicated by another feature of the 1546–7 epidemic in Devon. It followed a disastrous harvest failure in the West in 1545. Wheat prices reached the highest level ever known in Exeter in the early months of 1546 when the movement of plague across the county was about to begin.[112] There are other instances which show that the timing of plague epidemics had not always been so clearly divorced from that of harvest crises as it was in the last century of the disease in England. It has been noticed that the great plague of 1563 in London was unlike later epidemics in that it followed immediately after a bad harvest in 1562.[113] Although the price of bread did not rise as high as in the later 1580s and

---

[110] See Hatcher, *Plague, Population and the English Economy*, especially pp.15–17, 57, for arguments that plague may have been more widespread in the fifteenth century than earlier work, based on selective evidence from chronicles, has suggested.

[111] See E. Le Roy Ladurie, *Times of Feast, Times of Famine: A History of Climate since the Year 1000* (London, 1972), pp.225–43. Biraben's findings indicate the need for caution: *Les hommes et la peste*, I, pp.134–9. The quarantine measures practised by local authorities are still less likely to have affected the diffusion of plague at this early date; they were not widely adopted in England until the very end of the sixteenth century, and even then they were not effectively enforced, as I hope to show elsewhere.

[112] Hoskins, 'Harvest fluctuations', p.35. The harvest of 1546 was, by contrast, good, but plague had already begun in Exeter and several other parishes before the autumn of 1546.

[113] Appleby, 'Nutrition and disease', p.8. Cf. John Stowe's comment that 'the poor citizens of London were this year plagued with a terrible plague, as with the pestilence, scarcity of money and dearth of victuals: the misery whereof were too long here to write. No doubt the poor remember it': *A summarie of Englyshe chronicles* (1565), fol. 244v.

1590s, partly because other cereals were less scarce than wheat,[114] there was at least one recorded death from 'famine', in St Margaret Westminster at the end of July 1563, just as the number of plague deaths was reaching its crescendo. When this epidemic reached other parts of the country, in 1564 and 1565, however, harvests were good and prices low. Earlier in the century it was sometimes the provinces which suffered plague and food-shortage simultaneously. The plagues which began in London in 1543 and 1548 attacked other towns and counties when the bad harvests of 1545 and 1550–1 had raised prices and severely reduced food supplies. In Lincoln, for example, plague in 1551 coincided with conditions in which 'even horsebread' was scarce, 'to the great famishing and destruction of the whole people of this city', and there was a serious shortage of corn in Bristol in December 1550, shortly before an epidemic of plague began.[115]

There may well have been similar sequences leading to 'mixed' crises in the years before the beginning of parish registers. It is not unlikely that in 1501 and 1502, in 1520 and 1521, and in 1527 and 1528 crisis mortalities were the product both of plague, to which there are references in some parts of the country, and of harvest failure.[116] Such a combination probably accounts for the demographic disaster which Mr Phythian-Adams has uncovered in Coventry in the early 1520s, and which left a quarter of the town's houses empty.[117] This is not to argue that malnutrition, when it preceded plague mortality, contributed directly to it. Inanition does not lower resistance to infection from the plague bacillus.[118] However, quite apart from the addition of deaths from typhus or other diseases to the casualties caused by plague, the movement of vagrants and rodents in search of food may have helped to spread plague more widely and more quickly, and to bring rats and men more often into contact, than would have been the case in years of good

---

[114] Harrison, 'Grain price analysis', p.153; *The Agrarian History of England and Wales*, ed. Thirsk, p.819.
[115] Lincolnshire Record Office, Lincoln Entries of Common Council, 1541–64, fols. 79, 89v; London, British Library, Lansdowne MS. 2, fol. 91.
[116] Shrewsbury, *History of Bubonic Plague*, pp.159, 163, 167; Creighton, *History of Epidemics*, I, pp.287–8, 292. See Biraben, *Les hommes et la peste*, I, pp.125, 148, for continental epidemics in these years.
[117] C. Phythian-Adams, 'Coventry and the problem of urban decay in the later Middle Ages' (unpublished paper submitted to the 1971 Urban History conference); I am greatly indebted to Mr Phythian-Adams for discussing his findings with me. For evidence of sickness in Beverley in 1521, see Beverley Corporation Records, Keepers' Account Rolls, 1520–1, 1522–3.
[118] Scrimshaw, Taylor and Gordon, *Nutrition and Infection*, pp.70, 177–82; Biraben, *Les hommes et la peste*, I, pp.147–54.

harvest. This might help to explain, for example, the broad diffusion of plague across Devon in 1546–7.

There is thus evidence to suggest that neither the urban incidence of plague nor its distinction from harvest crises was as evident in the early as in the later sixteenth century. The reasons for these contrasts are obscure and the range of possibilities is wide, from changes in the urban environment or in climate, to fortuitous events like a decline in the frequency of coincidence between plague and harvest failure. Neither is the evidence itself conclusive. It comes from perhaps exceptional, and certainly unusually well-documented instances, as in Devon in the 1540s and Coventry in the 1520s. It would, however, support the further hypothesis that in some respects mortality crises were becoming more 'stable' in the course of the sixteenth century – more clearly defined in their incidence, and less 'mixed' in their causation.

Such a change would have important implications outside the scope of this survey. It might affect our picture of demographic change. Although we noted earlier that the crises revealed in testamentary records in the early sixteenth century seemed from their chronology to be caused by periods of dearth, we can now see that 'exogenous' diseases, influenza in the later 1550s, plague on earlier occasions, may have been equally if not more important. Did the two together help to keep population low in the early sixteenth century, and was their increasing differentiation one of the factors permitting rapid population growth after 1560? This sort of stabilization might also explain some changes in attitude in the course of our period. It could account for the growing habit of distinguishing plague from other diseases, for example, but equally for the persistence into the seventeenth century, when it no longer applied to English circumstances, of the assumption that plague and famine were invariably associated.[119] The implications of this suggested change in the pattern of crises make it all the more regrettable that its character is concealed by the inadequate evidence for fluctuations in mortality in early Tudor England.

VIII

We have tried in this essay to illustrate the different influences which determined the nature of mortality crises in Tudor England, as well as to

---

[119] The Caroline Privy Council for example thought that plague was 'the ordinary effect' of famine: *Acts of the Privy Council of England 1630–1* (London, 1964), p.113.

examine such features as they had in common. It will be evident that the former are as striking as the latter, and that epidemiological history provides few certainties, least of all about the secular changes in the impact of a disease like bubonic plague. Nevertheless it is possible to arrive at some broad answers to the two questions raised at the beginning of this enquiry.

It is clear in the first place that many, perhaps most, mortality crises in Tudor England were not the direct result of food shortage or deteriorating standards of living. The probate evidence and the regional studies of parish registers described earlier suggest a striking correlation between widespread high mortality and high prices. But investigation of individual localities shows that famine crises in the later sixteenth century were neither so frequent, nor so violent in the communities they affected, as outbreaks of bubonic plague. If they appear more common and more serious in the decades before 1560, that may be because those were in fact 'mixed' crises, in which a major part was taken by diseases which had no direct connection with malnutrition. Influenza filled this role in 1558–9, and plague, it seems probable, in some earlier years. Admittedly the diffusion of these diseases may have been indirectly assisted by conditions of dearth, though less perhaps in the case of a viral infection like influenza than in that of a normally slow-spreading disease like plague. Yet it can scarcely be doubted that these epidemics would have been the cause of serious demographic crises even without earlier bad harvests. Mortality crises in this period cannot be interpreted simply as Malthusian phenomena.

Neither, however, were they wholly autonomous, independent of the social and economic environment in which they occurred. Many major epidemics might have their origins outside the country or even the continent, and to that extent be exogenous influences on its demography, but their local manifestations were affected, often decisively, by local circumstances. Although the timing of plague epidemics, for example, was the consequence of waves of infection developing far from England, and was subject to seasonal changes in climate, their incidence was determined by factors such as facility of transmission, rodent densities, and conditions of hygiene, some of them affected by social and economic changes. The neo-Malthusian, and the exogenous interpretations of mortality crises are no doubt useful hypotheses for discussion. They can also be applied with some accuracy to one or two individual cases: the first to the famine fevers of 1597, the second to the viral infections of 1558–9. But they are rough and inadequate tools if one wishes to account for the majority of crises which fell between these two extremes.

The second question posed at the outset concerned the frequency of mortality crises in Tudor England. As we have seen, the national picture suggests a succession of crises in the first half of the period, and another at its close, separated by more healthy years in the middle of Elizabeth's reign. An alternative approach, and one more representative of contemporary experience, is to ask how frequently any given community might expect to suffer a crisis in which the death rate doubled or more than doubled. In the large towns such crises occurred regularly, once every sixteen years on average in the towns shown in Table 2. In smaller places they were less frequent, though still not uncommon. The registers of 165 villages and 27 market towns in Devon and Essex have been examined, some of them beginning only in the 1560s and 1570s.[120] Yet of the 27 market towns only 2 had no epidemic which doubled the mortality level before 1610, and 13, one half, suffered twice or more often. Some of the 165 villages were rather more fortunate. One third of them, 56 in all, had no epidemic of this severity before 1610. But no less than 40, a quarter, had more than one.

We can measure the average frequency of crises for all these communities more precisely if we divide the aggregate number of years in which the parishes were under observation before 1610, by the number of occasions on which there were crisis mortality ratios of 2 or more. We find that on average, market towns suffered serious mortality once every thirty-seven years, and smaller communities once every sixty-three years. Since the later sixteenth century is more heavily represented in these averages than the decades before 1560, they may well understate the crisis experience of small settlements over the whole century. They also conceal the sort of local variations which have been noted earlier. But they suggest that a Tudor Englishman might expect to experience one serious mortality crisis in his life-time, and they show once more that it was towns, and in towns plague, which played the leading role in the history of crisis mortality in the sixteenth century.

This account has been concerned almost wholly with mortality, the final effect of epidemic disease, and with its dryly quantitative aspect. It should not be concluded, however, without acknowledging that this is

---

[120] Market towns have been identified from the lists in *The Agrarian History of England and Wales*, ed. Thirsk, pp.471, 474. Parish registers beginning later than 1585, and those with large gaps in registration, have been excluded from the sample discussed here, though some of them have been drawn on for evidence of the individual crises considered earlier.

only part of the history of epidemics, and that it was not necessarily their most obvious or disturbing feature for contemporaries. No less important, but less easily measured, is morbidity. In plague epidemics case-mortality rates were probably in the region of 50–70 per cent, in which case almost twice as many people may have been infected by plague as died of it.[121] When the number of burials trebled in a parish, implying a death rate of roughly 9 per cent, it would not be unreasonable to suppose that one in seven of the inhabitants fell victim to the disease. In the epidemic of 1604, for example, the corporation of Salisbury found that it had to support 411 different households, containing one fifth of the population of the town, less than half of whom actually died of plague.[122] The effects of harvest crises should equally be visualized in terms of sickness as well as death, as the widespread falls in fertility demonstrate. The impact of disease was much wider than the number of burials might lead one to suppose.

Some epidemics no doubt had a small effect on mortality but incapacitated large numbers. The sweating sickness is a probable example, and there were undoubtedly others which have escaped our parish register net. There was malaria in parts of East Anglia and the Fens.[123] There were periodic epidemics of influenza, the most notable after 1558 occurring in 1580. It was reported from Berwick on Tweed in that year that there was a

new disease, whereof three or four thousand at once in Edinburgh were suddenly sick. The same sickness reigneth generally in this town, beginning with pains in the head or eyes, sores in the throat and breast, in nature of a cold. None have died thereof as yet in this town and very few in Edinburgh, notwithstanding that all the inhabitants in manner were visited.[124]

If this was the case in two towns in 1580, the similar fevers of the later 1550s must have been as universal as Strype thought:

---

[121] Shrewsbury, *History of Bubonic Plague*, p.5; Hollingsworth, *Historical Demography*, pp.357, 365. There were no doubt numerous local variations, however, of the kind noted by Pollitzer, *Plague*, p.32. Biraben (*Les hommes et la peste*, I, p.303) cites examples at the higher end of this range, but some English references in the early seventeenth century suggest that half those who caught plague escaped: P.R.O., SP 16/349/70, 13/200/14.

[122] Slack, 'Poverty and politics', p.170; the names of the householders have been compared with burial entries in the registers of St Edmund's, St Thomas's and St Martin's parishes. The first of these registers is in the Salisbury Diocesan Record Office; the two latter are still in the parish churches, and I am grateful to the incumbents for permission to consult them.

[123] W. P. MacArthur, 'A brief history of English malaria', *British Medical Bulletin*, VII (1951), 76–7; John Norden, *An Historical and Chorographical Description of the County of Essex*, Camden Society, old ser., IX (1840), p.7. There are signs of regular epidemics of malaria in the registers of Bradwell on Sea, Dengie and Beaumont-cum-Moze, Essex.

[124] *The Correspondence of Robert Bowes*, Surtees Society, XIV (1842), pp.84–5.

If the people of the realm had been divided into four parts, certainly three parts of those four should have been found sick ... And hereby so great a scarcity of harvestmen, that those which remained took twelve pence for that which was wont to be done for three pence... Divers places were left void of ancient justices and men of worship to govern the country ... In most men's houses, the master, dame, and servants were all sick, in such sort, that one could not help another.[125]

The economic and social costs of sickness in pre-industrial England, some of which are indicated in this description, are subjects which await historical investigation. During epidemics families pawned their household goods or spent their meagre savings. Local authorities raised extra poor rates to support the sick. Unemployment increased and production fell disastrously. In the worst plagues the normal bustle of urban life virtually ceased. 'Grass grew in the streets' was an observation repeated in accounts of plague in chronicle after chronicle, but it was not necessarily inaccurate for all that.[126] In this survey of mortality crises we have touched only the tip of the iceberg of the stresses imposed on past societies by epidemic disease.

[125] Quoted in Fisher, 'Influenza and inflation', pp.125–6.
[126] See for example Oxford, Bodleian Library, Rawlinson MS. B282, fol. 77v; T. Gent, *Annales regioduni Hullini* (York, 1735), p.39; R. Simpson, *A Collection of Fragments Illustrative of the History ... of Derby* (2 vols., Derby, 1826), I, 109.

2

Infant and child mortality in England in the late Tudor and early Stuart period

ROGER SCHOFIELD AND E. A. WRIGLEY

One of the most striking features of the improvement in expectation of life at birth which has occurred since Tudor times has been a massive change in the relative numbers of deaths early and late in life. If, for the sake of simplicity, we consider model life tables constructed for stationary populations, we find that in a 'modern' population with an expectation of life of, say, 75 years, about one half (48.4 per cent) of all deaths are of people aged 80 and above, whereas the proportion of deaths occurring under age 10 is only 2.4 per cent. In a 'pre-industrial' population, on the other hand, with an expectation of life of, say, 37.5 years, the position is almost reversed; the over-80s account for only 6.7 per cent of the deaths while the under-10s contribute 34.4 per cent.[1] At modest rates of population growth the contrasts are even more striking, as may be seen in Table 1, in which the percentages dying at the two extremes of the life span are shown both for stationary populations and those growing at 1 per cent per annum.

Table 1. *Percentages of total female deaths in different age groups (Model North life tables)*

Age group	Stationary population		Population growing at 1 per cent p.a.	
	e_0		e_0	
	37.5	75.0	37.5	75.0
0—9	34.4	2.4	46.7	4.9
80 and over	6.7	48.4	4.1	42.1

Source: Coale and Demeny, *Regional Model Life Tables*.

[1] These percentages are taken from the Model North life tables in A. J. Coale and P. Demeny, *Regional Model Life Tables* (Princeton, 1966). They are for female populations. The percentages for male deaths under comparable mortality conditions are similar.

The doubling of expectation of life (e_o) from 37.5 to 75 years produces such a dramatic change because it was brought about by the virtual elimination of deaths from exogenous causes, while progress in combating endogenous causes of death has been rather limited. Since young life was once lost on a very large scale to infectious disease whereas endogenous causes of death have always accounted for the bulk of deaths at advanced ages, mortality rates early in life are now at a trivial level when compared with the early modern period whereas death rates late in life have not fallen greatly. For example, as Table 2 shows, death rates in early childhood where $e_o = 75$ are less than 3 per cent of their level where $e_o = 37.5$, whereas in the age group 75–9 the comparable figure is 50 per cent. At still higher ages there is even less difference. Infant mortality rates show a less marked fall than early childhood death rates because there is a substantial endogenous component in infant mortality.

Table 2. *The relative levels of female life table death rates ($1000q_x$) at $e_o = 75$ and $e_o = 37.5$*

Age group	Death rates		(2) as % of (1)
	$e_o = 37.5$	$e_o = 75.0$	
	(1)	(2)	
0–1	171.6	18.2	10.6
1–4	152.0	4.0	2.6
5–9	65.4	1.9	2.9
75–9	493.6	247.8	50.2

Source: Coale and Demeny, *Regional Model Life Tables.*

Model life tables are valuable indicators of the pattern and main characteristics of mortality rates in early modern Europe, but, since they are derived from modern data and extrapolations from modern data, it would be premature to assume that they are a safe guide to the mortality experience of the past. England is unusually well provided with sources which allow an investigation of this question, since the standard of parochial registration was already high in the sixteenth and early seventeenth centuries. Indeed the coverage of vital events was probably better then than at any later period because Nonconformity was negligible and baptism normally took place within a week of birth. This meant few children died before baptism (in contrast with the later eighteenth century when this was common), and even when a child died before baptism it appears to have been usual to record its burial (in many registers the burial of still–born children or abortive births is recorded).[2] Elsewhere in Europe, in contrast, good parochial registration coverage of vital events is rare until the late seventeenth or eighteenth centuries, either because no comprehensive registration system had been created, as in Sweden, or because the coverage of events was incomplete. In France, for example, burial registers were normally either too incomplete in coverage or too uninformative about age and parentage to sustain adequate mortality studies until the later seventeenth or early eighteenth centuries.[3]

Registers which begin before 1600 survive for about 4,000 out of the total of 10,000 ancient parishes of England. Of these, many are unsuitable for any serious demographic study because of breaks in registration, and others are useful only for aggregative tabulations because the form of entry lacks the detail necessary for nominative work which depends upon drawing together information covering the whole or a part of the life cycle of individuals and their families. There still remain, however, several hundred registers good enough to permit an adequate study of infant and child mortality. In this essay we shall describe findings drawn from family reconstitution studies of eight parishes: Alcester, Warwickshire; Aldenham, Hertfordshire; Banbury, Oxfordshire; Colyton, Devon; Gainsborough, Lincolnshire; Gedling, Nottinghamshire; Hartland, Devon; and Terling, Essex.[4]

These eight parishes do not, of course, represent the full range of the mortality experience of Tudor and early Stuart England. But they differ sufficiently in size, location and economic type to make the common characteristics they display suggestive. In the absence of census data

[2] See E. A. Wrigley, 'Births and baptisms: the use of Anglican baptism registers as a source of information about numbers of births in England before the beginning of civil registration', *Population Studies*, XXXI (1977), 281–312.

[3] M. Fleury and L. Henry, *Nouveau manuel de dépouillement et d'exploitation de l'état civil ancien* (Paris, 1965), pp.23–6.

[4] We owe much to those who have undertaken reconstitution work in association with the Cambridge Group. In this essay we have drawn upon the work of the following: Mrs L. Clarke (Gainsborough); Mrs P. Ford (Alcester); Dr D. Levine (Terling); Mr W. Newman Brown (Aldenham); Mrs S. Stewart (Banbury, Hartland); Mrs J. Young (Gedling).

The reconstitutions cover a much longer period than is covered in this essay. In most cases they run through to 1837 when civil registration began. They form part of a larger group of reconstitution studies which will be fully described in a forthcoming book in which we hope to present our findings about fertility and nuptiality as well as mortality. The book will also contain details of the computer programs used in analysing the body of reconstitution data.

A description of the technique of reconstitution may be found in E. A. Wrigley, 'Family reconstitution', in E. A. Wrigley (ed.), *An introduction to English historical demography* (London, 1966), pp.96–159. For a general discussion of the nature of the historical evidence of population change, see R. S. Schofield, 'Historical demography: some possibilities and some limitations', *Transactions of the Royal Historical Society*, 5th ser., XXI (1971), 119–32.

estimates of population size are inevitably subject to substantial margins of error. If, however, we assume that crude birth rates normally fall within the range 25–40 per 1,000, the populations of the eight parishes may be estimated to have been, about the year 1600, approximately as shown in Table 3. The two largest, Gainsborough and Banbury, were

Table 3. *Approximate populations of the reconstitution parishes c. 1600 (see text)*

Alcester	1,225 ± 250
Aldenham	1,160 ± 230
Banbury	2,500 ± 500
Colyton	1,650 ± 330
Gainsborough	2,200 ± 440
Gedling	550 ± 100
Hartland	1,200 ± 240
Terling	600 ± 120

Source: aggregative tabulations of the listed parishes.

substantial market towns where the bulk of the population made a living from handicraft and service occupations. In the others, agriculture was the dominant source of income and employment, but some, like Terling and Aldenham, were close to London and increasingly affected by the demands of the London food market, while others, notably Hartland, were remote and inevitably largely confined to production for local needs by the difficulty and high cost of transport. Colyton in this period had a substantial woollen industry.

We may begin by considering the general pattern of infant and child mortality. Table 4 shows the life table male and female death rates (q_x) for the ages 0, 1–4 and 5–9 for the eight parishes. Rates are shown for the half-centuries 1550–99 and 1600–49 separately, and for the whole period 1550–1649.[5] The mass of information is not easy to digest when presented *in extenso* but it is useful to set it out in full initially to make it apparent that the death rates 1–4, and still more 5–9, are based on very small absolute numbers of deaths in the smaller parishes. In some cases

[5] The data are cohorted by date of birth, so that a small proportion of the deaths for the period 1550–99 will have taken place after 1600 and for the period 1600–49 after 1650. Reconstitution could begin before 1550 in the cases of Colyton and Terling and therefore covers the whole period 1550–99 in these parishes, but for the other parishes reconstitution was begun later (the earliest baptisms are to be found in each register at the following dates: 1558 Banbury, Gedling, Hartland; 1559 Aldenham; 1561 Alcester; 1564 Gainsborough).

Table 4. *Infants and children at risk and dying, with mortality rates* ($1000q_x$)

	MALE							FEMALE						
	1550–99			1600–49			1550–1649	1550–99			1600–49			1550–1649
	Risk	Dying	Rate	Risk	Dying	Rate	Rate	Risk	Dying	Rate	Risk	Dying	Rate	Rate
Infants														
Alcester	441	77	175	846	129	152	160	387	60	155	802	91	113	127
Aldenham	598	78	130	666	79	119	124	543	68	125	633	71	112	118
Banbury	1,162	200	172	1,690	279	165	168	1,070	147	137	1,607	239	149	144
Colyton	833	117	140	1,204	109	91	111	730	86	118	1,204	107	89	100
Gainsborough	1,008	176	175	1,832	445	243	219	940	148	157	1,841	376	204	188
Gedling	267	24	90	416	42	101	97	231	18	78	435	39	90	86
Hartland	677	60	89	701	70	100	94	654	62	95	644	45	70	82
Terling	335	45	134	354	40	113	123	313	37	118	335	37	110	114
Children 1–4														
Alcester	280	25	89	562	52	93	91	256	23	90	567	70	123	113
Aldenham	411	30	73	462	34	74	73	373	27	72	429	25	58	65
Banbury	743	57	77	1,070	123	115	99	733	62	85	1,062	101	95	91
Colyton	560	46	82	845	66	78	80	526	33	63	870	79	91	80
Gainsborough	632	60	95	1,090	127	117	109	616	67	109	1,141	171	150	135
Gedling	208	11	53	315	29	92	76	182	7	38	313	14	45	42
Hartland	492	19	39	506	21	42	40	455	17	37	468	26	56	47
Terling	216	14	65	221	27	122	94	196	10	51	207	16	77	65
Children 5–9														
Alcester	170	6	35	356	18	51	46	163	6	37	366	10	27	30
Aldenham	269	6	22	306	9	29	26	245	6	24	296	10	34	30
Banbury	477	22	46	672	31	46	46	457	30	66	671	33	49	56
Colyton	364	12	33	583	15	26	29	375	6	16	560	29	52	37
Gainsborough	393	12	31	694	43	62	51	360	9	25	702	48	68	54
Gedling	162	2	12	225	11	49	34	142	3	21	242	4	17	18
Hartland	330	10	30	380	8	21	25	305	4	13	335	13	39	27
Terling	125	6	48	121	6	50	49	119	3	25	107	4	37	31

Source: reconstitution tabulations.

chance events – an accident with a cart, a drowning at the ford, a severe bout of illness in a single family – might make a large difference to the rates, especially in Gedling or Terling in the 5–9 age group.

Table 5. *Infant and child mortality rates (1000q$_x$)*

	MALE			FEMALE		
	1550–99	1600–49	1550–1649	1550–99	1600–49	1550–1649
Infants						
Alcester	175	152	160	155	113	127
Aldenham	130	119	124	125	112	118
Banbury	172	165	168	137	149	144
Colyton	140	91	111	118	89	100
Gainsborough	175	243	219	157	204	188
Gedling	90	101	97	78	90	86
Hartland	89	100	94	95	70	82
Terling	134	113	123	118	110	114
Mean	138	136	137	123	117	120
Children 1–4						
Alcester	89	93	91	90	123	113
Aldenham	73	74	73	72	58	65
Banbury	77	115	99	85	95	91
Colyton	82	78	80	63	91	80
Gainsborough	95	117	109	109	150	135
Gedling	53	92	76	38	45	42
Hartland	39	42	40	37	56	47
Terling	65	122	94	51	77	65
Mean	72	92	83	68	87	80
Children 5–9						
Alcester	35	51	46	37	27	30
Aldenham	22	29	26	24	34	30
Banbury	46	46	46	66	49	56
Colyton	33	26	29	16	52	37
Gainsborough	31	62	51	25	68	54
Gedling	12	49	34	21	17	18
Hartland	30	21	25	13	39	27
Terling	48	50	49	25	37	31
Mean	32	42	38	28	40	35

Source: reconstitution tabulations.

In Table 5 the same information is recapitulated but this time showing the rates alone. Since the section of the table dealing with infant mortality shows two parishes, Gedling and Hartland, in which both the male and female rates were under 100 for the period 1550–1649 as a whole, it is perhaps convenient to begin by considering the question of the reliability of the results presented. An infant mortality rate of under 100 is very low for any period before the twentieth century, and it is entirely reasonable to be deeply suspicious of rates as low as this. Are they not what might be expected if children who died soon after birth escaped registration, a phenomenon that is known to have become widespread by the eighteenth century?[6]

The dependability of the results may be tested both by considering the relationship between infant death rates and those later in childhood, and by examining the distribution of deaths within the first year of life. If it were true that the deaths of very young children tended to escape registration, infant death rates would tend to be too low relative to death rates 1–4, and, within the first year of life, there would be a more marked under-registration of infant deaths in the first month of life than later. As it happens, tackling this issue is also a convenient way of presenting some of the more interesting substantive features of mortality early in life in Tudor and early Stuart times. We may therefore turn to the question of the relative levels of infant and child mortality in this period, clearly a question of interest in its own right since, whereas the average level of infant mortality in the eight parishes fell slightly between 1550–99 and 1600–49, the level of child mortality 1–4 rose sharply, and mortality 5–9 rose even more sharply.

Here the regional model life tables of Coale and Demeny can be very helpful in affording some insight into both the plausibility of the data, and the nature of the changes taking place. In Table 6 the information given in Table 5 is re-expressed in terms of the levels contained in the Model West and Model North life tables. Low levels in the Coale and Demeny tables imply high mortality and vice versa. For females level 1 is equivalent to an expectation of life at birth of 20 years. Expectation of life rises by $2\frac{1}{2}$ years for each higher level (thus level 3 yields an expectation of life at birth of 25 years, and so on). Male expectation of life is slightly lower at each level.

For simplicity and also to minimize the problems caused by the small numbers, the level shown for each age group is the average of the male and female levels. The levels are those within each life table set which have rates nearest to the rates shown in Table 5. Thus in Table 5 the male and female infant mortality rates for Banbury in 1550–99 are 172 and 137 respectively. In the Model North tables the level which gives the rate nearest to these two rates is in each case level 10. The rates 1–4 are 77 and 85. These are nearest to level 14 and level 13 in Model North. The average of the two levels is 13.5. Hence the figure in Table 6. The rates

---

[6] See Wrigley, 'Births and baptisms'.

Table 6. *Mortality expressed in terms of model life table levels (all levels based on Table 5 data)*

		North		West	
		1550–99	1600–49	1550–99	1600–49
Alcester					
Age group:	0	9	11.5	10.5	12.5
	1–4	13	11.5	11	10
	5–9	13.5	13	8	7.5
Aldenham					
Age group:	0	12	12.5	13	13.5
	1–4	14	14.5	13	13.5
	5–9	16.5	14.5	12.5	9.5
Banbury					
Age group:	0	10	10	11.5	11
	1–4	13.5	11.5	12.5	10
	5–9	10	11.5	3.5	5
Colyton					
Age group:	0	12	15.5	13	16
	1–4	14.5	13.5	13	11.5
	5–9	16	13	12	8
Gainsborough					
Age group:	0	9	6	10.5	7
	1–4	12	9.5	10.5	8
	5–9	15	8.5	10.5	2
Gedling					
Age group:	0	16	14.5	16.5	15.5
	1–4	17	15	15.5	13.5
	5–9	18	14	15	9.5
Hartland					
Age group:	0	15	16	16	16.5
	1–4	18	16.5	16	15
	5–9	17	15	13	10
Terling					
Age group:	0	12	13.5	13	14.5
	1–4	15.5	12.5	14.5	11
	5–9	13	12	8.5	6
Mean of 8 parishes					
Age group:	0	11.5	12	13	13
	1–4	14	13	13	11.5
	5–9	14.5	12	10	6.5

Sources: Coale and Demeny, *Regional Model Life Tables*; rates in Table 5.

5–9 are 46 and 66; the nearest levels are 12 and 8 for males and females respectively, and the figure shown in Table 6 is 10, the average of the two levels.

First let us consider the overall position shown in the levels based on the mean mortality rates for the eight parishes. In 1550–99 the Model North and Model West levels suggest different conclusions. To judge by Model North the rates 1–4 and 5–9 agree well with each other, but the infant mortality rates are substantially too high. The Model West system on the other hand suggests an excellent agreement between the infant rate and the rate 1–4 but mortality at age 5–9 is higher than would be suggested by this Model. By 1600–49 the position has changed. Now all three rates agree well with each other in the Model North system, but there is a substantial disagreement between the infant rate and the rate 1–4 to judge by Model West, and a truly massive disagreement between the rates 1–4 and 5–9. If Model West were taken as the criterion it would be reasonable to conclude that both infant and early childhood deaths were seriously under-recorded. If the rates in Table 5 are largely accurate in both half-centuries, then the period as a whole saw the transition from a set of infant and child death rates indeterminate in pattern between the North and West Models, to a set which was very clearly North in character. The change occurred because child death rates rose while the infant rate hardly changed.

There are two general reasons for believing that the pattern of change is genuine. First, this was the period during which increased contact with extra-European areas probably led to the population's being exposed to new kinds of infectious disease to which there had not yet been time to adjust genetically or immunologically.[7] If this were so, it is to be expected that it would affect children above the age of weaning relatively more severely than those who were still fed at the breast. Further evidence bearing on this point is presented below.[8] Second, it is very clear that in the mid-nineteenth century when William Farr constructed the third English life table, using civil registration data from the first seventeen years of registration 1838–54, the pattern of relationships between death rates early in life was of the Model North type. The rates, converted in the same manner as those used in Table 6, are shown in Table 7.

---

[7] On this point see J. D. Durand, 'The modern expansion of world population', *Proceedings of the American Philosophical Society*, CXI (1967), 136–59, and more generally, W. H. McNeill, *Plagues and Peoples* (New York, 1976).

[8] See below, p.90.

The mean rates for the eight parishes shown in Table 6 are not necessarily a guide to the overall national situation. They might even be a poor guide to change in the individual parishes, if the mean mortality rates used were produced by averaging rates of parishes with strongly contrasting mortality structures and trends. We therefore turn next to

Table 7. *The third English life table (1838–54) expressed in terms of model life table levels (male and female levels averaged as in Table 6)*

	North	West
Age group: 0	10.5	11.5
1–4	9.5	8
5–9	11	5.5

Sources: Coale and Demeny, *Regional Model Life Tables*; W. Farr, *English Life Table* (1864).

consider the degree of homogeneity in the experience of the eight parishes. The absolute mortality levels varied quite widely. Were their relative movements similar? Table 8 represents an attempt to capture the most important evidence from Table 6 which bears on this point. It shows the average of the differences between paired levels in each parish both ignoring sign and taking it into account. For example, the figure of 2.8 on the first line of the Model North section of the table is the average of the differences between the mortality levels shown in Table 6 for ages 0 and 1–4 in the individual parishes (4 in the case of Alcester where the two levels were 9 and 13, 2 in the case of Aldenham where the levels were 12 and 14, and so on). The fact that the figure is also 2.8 when sign is ignored shows that in every parish the life table level for the 1–4 year olds was higher than the infant level. Since low life table levels imply high mortality, in Model North terms infant mortality in these parishes was invariably relatively higher than mortality at ages 1–4. On the other hand, Table 8 shows an excellent agreement between infant mortality and mortality at ages 1–4 in terms of Model West in the later sixteenth century, since the average absolute difference in level is as low as 0.5, while taking sign into account the figure is only 0.3.

The most striking feature of Table 8 is the evidence for a close conformity to a Model North pattern in the first half of the seventeenth century. All the average differences are very low. The absolute differences in the three paired age group comparisons range between 0.8 and 1.6. When sign is taken into account the average differences are negligibly small. In contrast, Model West does not capture the mortality pattern in this period at all well. The differences in level are large and are all of the same sign. Average differences of 6.1 levels between infant

Table 8. *Average differences between levels for pairs of age groups for the eight parishes (see text)*

Model North Age group	1550–99		1600–49	
	A	B	A	B
0/1–4	2.8	2.8	0.6	1.4
1–4/5–9	0.2	2.1	−0.3	0.8
0/5–9	3.0	3.0	0.3	1.6
Model West Age group	1550–99		1600–49	
0/1–4	0.3	0.5	−1.8	2.0
1–4/5–9	−2.9	2.9	−4.4	4.4
0/5–9	−2.6	2.6	−6.1	6.1

Source: Table 6.

A: average difference (recognizing sign).
B: average absolute difference (ignoring sign).

mortality and mortality at ages 5–9 (compared with 2.6 levels in 1550–99) show how far the mortality pattern was at variance with Model West. In the later sixteenth century the mortality pattern conformed neither to Model North nor Model West, for although the early childhood rates (1–4/5–9) conformed well to Model North, neither of these age groups conformed well with Model North infant mortality, while the good fit of infant rates with rates at ages 1–4 within the Model West system is not paralleled when later childhood is considered. But in the following half-century, the rise in mortality at ages above 1 pushed all eight parishes towards a consistent Model North pattern of infant and child mortality rates.

It may be noted, incidentally, that in Gedling and Hartland, the two parishes with exceptionally low infant mortality rates, the patterns are the same as in the parishes with higher infant mortality. In both,

CAPVT II.

De mixtura vtriusque sexus seminis, eiusque substantia & forma.

P Ostquam autem vterus, quod genitale fœminei sexus membrum est, viri genituram conceperit, suum quoque semen illi admiscet,

C 3   ita

Plate 3. Childbirth as depicted in 1554
From Jacob Rueff, *De conceptu et generationis* (1554). It will be noted that in addition to midwives and nurses, astrologers are portrayed in the childbirth scene. Geminus (see Frontispiece) was the publisher and engraver of a translation of the other major illustrated handbook on midwifery, by Roesslin. Reproduced by permission of the Curators of the Bodleian Library.

according to the Model North pattern, infant mortality was relatively *high* compared with rates later in childhood in 1550–99. In both, the infant rates are exactly what might be expected in view of the rates at ages 1–4 in this period by Model West standards. And in both, by 1600–49 the pattern of rates generally conforms very well to a Model North standard. If infant rates were too low in these parishes, therefore, the factor of under-registration must have affected deaths later in life as severely as infant deaths. This is intrinsically improbable, but there is, as we shall see, additional reason to give credence to the infant mortality rates, low as they are, and therefore also to the whole pattern of infant and child death rates shown in Table 6. The evidence to support this assertion comes from the biometric analysis of infant mortality, which allows a subdivision of total infant mortality into exogenous and endogenous causes of death.

Biometric analysis of infant mortality is possible wherever the distribution of age at death within the first year of life is known. The method was developed by Bourgeois-Pichat, and has been widely used both on historical and on contemporary data.[9] Its purpose is to enable a division to be made between deaths due to infectious ailments and those arising from birth trauma, congenital defect and functional inadequacy. It rests upon the fact that very few, if any, endogenous deaths occurred beyond the first month of life, and the empirical discovery that the cumulative total of deaths between the end of the first and the end of the twelfth month usually conforms closely to a straight line, if plotted on an axis representing the number of days since birth which has been logarithmically transformed so that the distance of any point on the axis from the origin is proportional to $\log^3(d+1)$ where d represents age in days.[10] By projecting the line of cumulative deaths between months 1 and 12 to the left until it cuts the vertical axis, an estimate can be made of the proportion of deaths due to endogenous rather than exogenous causes. In Fig. 1, for example, the *a–b* interval represents the endogenous mortality rate in the rural counties of England in 1905 (22 per 1,000), while *b–c* (17 per 1,000) represents the exogenous rate in the first month of life. Total exogenous mortality is 85 per 1,000 (107 total less 22 endogenous).

It is an important feature of the biometric analysis of infant mortality

---

[9] J. Bourgeois-Pichat, 'La mesure de la mortalité infantile', *Population*, VI (1951), 233–48 and 459–80.

[10] The application of this technique to English parish register material is more fully discussed in Wrigley, 'Births and baptisms'.

that the estimate of endogenous mortality is, in effect, a residual. If, for example, many infant deaths in the first month of life were missed, the whole loss would be taken from the total of endogenous deaths. If there were serious under-registration early in the first year but a steeply rising curve representing deaths above one month, it would be quite possible for the line representing exogenous deaths to cut the vertical axis below the point of origin (this would happen in Fig. 1 if sufficient early deaths

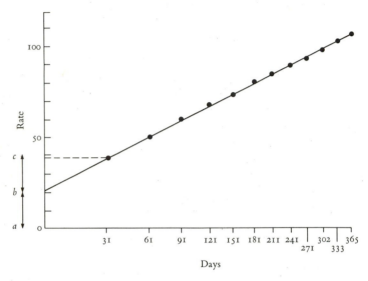

Fig. 1.   Infant mortality per 1000 live births in rural counties of England 1905. Source: *Sixty-eight Annual Report of the Register General* (London, 1907), pp. cxxx–cxxxi.

were missed to lower the total rate for the first month from 39 per 1,000 to 16 or fewer). If, therefore, infant deaths were failing to be registered it is likely that the endogenous rate would fall to improbably low levels while leaving the exogenous rate unaffected.

Table 9 gives some details of the distribution of deaths within the first year of life in each of the eight reconstitution parishes, and includes the mean rates of the group as a whole. The data are for the whole period 1550–1649. Both the cumulative totals of deaths and the cumulative rates are shown.

The data of Table 9 are drawn from tabulations different from those of Table 5. It will be apparent that the infant mortality rates of Table 9 are higher than those of Table 5. For example, the infant mortality rate of both sexes combined for Alcester in Table 5 is 144 per 1,000 (allowance having been made for the sex ratio at birth), whereas in Table 9 the rate is 149. Similarly, the implied rate for the mean of the eight parishes is 129 in Table 5, but 139 in Table 9. The reason for the difference between the rates in the two tables is that in most parishes the burials of some children are recorded in such a way that their sex is not known ('the infant child of', *et sim.*). These were children who had died shortly after birth and before baptism. They form part of a larger class of infant burials which cannot be directly linked to a preceding baptism because death occurred very early in life. Strictly, of course, the levels shown in Table 6 should

Table 9. *Deaths and death rates (per 1000) within the first year of life 1550–1649. Cumulative totals up to and including certain days*

	Day							Total of related
	0	6	29	59	89	179	364	births (baptisms)
Alcester								
Deaths	81	146	228	263	292	337	379	2,541
Rate	32	57	90	104	115	133	149	
Aldenham								
Deaths	86	126	194	219	233	278	327	2,489
Rate	35	51	78	88	94	112	131	
Banbury								
Deaths	229	437	621	683	728	845	939	5,697
Rate	40	77	109	120	128	148	165	
Colyton								
Deaths	95	141	213	275	309	372	437	4,078
Rate	23	35	52	67	76	91	107	
Gainsborough								
Deaths	465	716	933	1,004	1,062	1,176	1,334	6,005
Rate	77	119	155	167	177	196	222	
Gedling								
Deaths	68	90	120	132	135	145	157	1,396
Rate	49	64	86	95	97	104	112	
Hartland								
Deaths	53	79	124	150	172	221	244	2,719
Rate	19	29	46	55	63	81	90	
Terling								
Deaths	70	88	119	137	152	168	187	1,400
Rate	50	63	85	98	109	120	134	
Mean of 8 parishes								
Rate	41	62	88	99	107	123	139	

Source: reconstitution tabulations.

be adjusted to reflect this additional mortality, and this would reduce model life table levels by about one half-level in most cases. However, this would not have affected the conclusions based on Table 6 (and in one parish, as we shall see, there is reason to fear that infant mortality is overstated in the new tabulation by the inclusion of some still-born

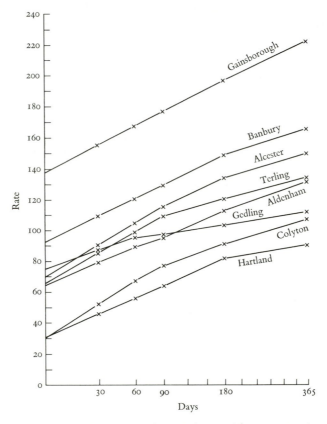

Fig. 2.   Infant mortality rates for eight parishes 1550–1649. Source: reconstitution tabulations (Table 9).

children). All deaths of infants dying unbaptized are treated as if they had occurred in the first day of life and consequently appear in the first column of Table 9.[11]

Fig. 2 shows the same data as in Table 9, converted into graphical form

[11] See Wrigley, 'Births and baptisms' for a more complete discussion of the issues touched upon in this paragraph.

to enable endogenous and exogenous mortality to be distinguished, while in Fig. 3 the curves representing the mean experience of the eight parishes for the two half-centuries are shown separately. As might be expected the curves in Fig. 2 which relate to large parishes, such as Gainsborough or Banbury, exhibit a markedly regular shape, whereas in

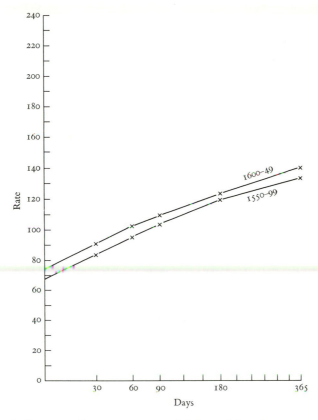

Fig. 3. Infant mortality rates: mean of eight parishes. Source: reconstitution tabulations.

the small parishes, such as Gedling, very few deaths occurred in some of the age divisions so that the rates are more subject to random effects. The tendency for the curves to be convex on their upper surface (seen clearly in Fig. 3) is very frequently found in biometric analysis of English infant mortality in this period and later. It has also been found in some French studies, and Blayo and Henry attribute it to excess mortality early in the first year of life associated with lung and chest infections and marked by a winter peak in mortality.[12]

Perhaps the most striking feature of Fig. 2 is the marked tendency for exogenous mortality to vary less than endogenous mortality (the slopes of the curves, with the exception of Gedling, are notably similar). The rates are set out in Table 10. The sample standard deviation in the exogenous rates is 14.6 compared with 34.3 for the endogenous rates. The uniformity in the exogenous rates is, indeed, very remarkable given the very different locations and sizes of the parishes. Gedling is the only parish seriously out of line with the rest, and it is quite possible that the very low exogenous rate in the parish is misleadingly low, an effect of random variation where small numbers are involved.

Table 10. *Endogenous and exogenous infant mortality rates per 1000, 1550–1649*

	Endogenous	Exogenous	Total
Alcester	70	79	149
Aldenham	76	66	131
Banbury	93	72	165
Colyton	31	76	107
Gainsborough	138	84	222
Gedling	75	37	112
Hartland	31	59	90
Terling	66	68	134
Mean	71	68	139
Standard deviation	34.3	14.6	

Source: reconstitution tabulations.

A comparison of these rates with those prevailing somewhat later on the continent is instructive. In general, European exogenous infant mortality rates were higher than in England, but the variation was very great, and some very low rates occurred. Henry, in the most famous of all parish reconstitution studies, that of Crulai in Normandy, estimated that exogenous infant mortality in the period 1672–1742 was 65–70 per 1,000. Only two of the eight parishes fall below this range.[13] Most similar

---

[12]   Y. Blayo and L. Henry, 'Données démographiques sur la Bretagne et l'Anjou de 1740 à 1829', *Annales de démographie historique* (1967), 142.

[13]   E. Gautier and L. Henry, *La population de Crulai* (Paris, 1958), p.170. See also the summary of data drawn from French studies of endogenous and exogenous infant mortality reported in Wrigley, 'Births and baptisms'.

continental studies, however, produce higher rates than those observed in the eight parishes. Mortality in early life in Tudor and early Stuart England was very modest by the standard of the pre-industrial world generally.

Exogenous mortality under 1 arises, of course, from the same range of diseases which continues to claim victims among young children in later years, so that parishes with relatively high exogenous infant mortality might be expected also to show high death rates in early childhood. Details of the pattern of rates in the eight parishes in the century 1550–1649 are set out in Table 11. The consistency of the pattern linking

Table 11. *Rates of exogenous infant mortality and of mortality in early childhood 1550–1649 (1000q_x)*

	Age 0 (exog.)	1	2	3	4	1–4	Rank 0 (exog.)	1–4
Alcester	79	41	28	16	18	102	2	2
Aldenham	66	34	15	15	11	69	6	6
Banbury	72	36	28	28	16	95	4	3
Colyton	76	33	23	18	13	80	3	5
Gainsborough	84	57	33	24	17	122	1	1
Gedling	37	26	26	5	8	60	8	7
Hartland	59	14	13	8	8	43	7	8
Terling	68	33	27	11	15	81	5	4
Mean	68	34	24	14	13	82		

Source: reconstitution tabulations.

exogenous infant mortality and mortality in the next four years of life is evident. The ranking of the parishes shows little change between the two age groups, with Gainsborough first and Alcester second in both lists. Three parishes have the same ranking, four move up or down only one place, while Colyton moves two places.

The level of endogenous infant mortality varied very widely among the eight parishes, that is, by a factor of four between Colyton and Hartland at one extreme, and Gainsborough at the other, where the rate reached an extraordinarily high level. At 138 per 1,000 it implies that about one child in seven died soon after birth from endogenous causes. Very few rates as high as this have been found in comparable studies of pre-industrial European parishes, and where such rates have been reported there has usually been evidence of the inclusion of still-born children among recorded deaths.[14] The average level of endogenous rates in the eight parishes is 71 per 1,000 (62 if Gainsborough is excluded). This is an average very similar to those found in studies of seventeenth- and eighteenth-century France, whereas the average level of exogenous infant mortality in the same studies was 75 per cent higher than in the eight parishes of Table 10.[15]

There can be very little doubt, given the method employed in the biometric analysis of infant deaths, that any tendency to under-register deaths would depress endogenous rather than exogenous rates. Since the endogenous rates of the eight parishes are as high as those found elsewhere even though exogenous rates are lower, suspicion that infant and child death rates in the eight parishes are understated is allayed. This does not, of course, exclude the possibility that registration was defective in individual parishes, but it is unlikely that there was any general defect in this regard. Nor is it justifiable to assume that the endogenous rates in Hartland and Colyton, the two Devon parishes, at 31 per 1,000 are the least dependable because they are the lowest. There is much nineteenth-century evidence to sustain the view that endogenous rates as low as 20 per 1,000 were widespread even in places with much higher overall

[14] It is very probable that this happened in Gainsborough. In the first half of the period, 1550–99, the endogenous rate was 100 per 1,000 but in the second half, 1600–49, it rose abruptly to 157 per 1,000. The number of events in Gainsborough was so large that random fluctuation can be ruled out as an explanation of the change, but an examination of the distribution of death in the first days of life suggests that many registered burials were of still-born children. The death rate in the first day of life increased by 46 per 1,000 from 47 to 93 per 1,000. The former rate, though higher than in the other seven parishes, was of the same order of magnitude as those found elsewhere, but the latter was much higher than in any of the other seven in 1600–49. It also accounts for the great bulk of the rise in endogenous mortality in the eight parishes taken together.

In all parishes in both half-centuries a substantial proportion of the deaths in the first day of life arise from the creation of 'dummy' birth entries to match burials which cannot be linked to preceding baptisms but which clearly belong to given families. When this happens there is usually a break in the sequence of baptisms in the family and the 'dummy' birth fits into the gap. Sometimes the child when buried is explicitly termed still-born and where this happens the burial is, of course, excluded from all infant mortality calculations, but sometimes a burial (in the form 'the sons of', *et sim.*) may refer to a still birth without making the fact explicit. It may be noted, incidentally, that although some early deaths may have been treated, because of the 'dummy' birth procedure, as occurring on the first day of life when they were actually a day or two older, this is offset by the fact that a child baptized and dying on the day of its birth was sometimes not buried on that day but a day or two later. Since age is perforce measured as the difference between the date of baptism and the date of burial, this would cause age at death to be overstated. The spread of deaths in the first week of life in Ludlow 1577–1619 probably reflects the tendency for delay in burial to reduce the degree of skewness in the distribution which might be expected from the inclusion of deaths associated with 'dummy' births.

Ludlow 1577–1619

Day	0	1	2	3	4	5	6
	64	60	32	23	28	24	28

[15] See Wrigley, 'Births and baptisms' for details of the French rates.

infant mortality, and well before it is reasonable to suppose that medical care had made any progress in reducing endogenous rates.[16]

Parishes with high endogenous infant mortality rates do not necessarily also have high exogenous rates, although Gainsborough is highest in both. Colyton and Gedling in particular show marked discrepancies in their ranking in the two lists. Indeed the overall fit between the rankings for endogenous and exogenous mortality is less good than that between the rankings for exogenous infant mortality and mortality in early childhood (Table 11).

So far we have been discussing the endogenous and exogenous infant mortality rates for the whole period 1550–1649. If the period is divided into two half-centuries and separate estimates are made of the levels of the two rates in each parish, the fluctuations in rates are in general minor, and are hardly worth reproducing in full. It will be clear from Fig. 3 that the average overall infant rate rose between 1550–99 and 1600–49 from 134 to 142 per 1,000. The endogenous rate rose from 68 to 73 and the exogenous from 66 to 69. In the parishes taken individually, the average change in exogenous rates was only 11 per 1,000. The comparable figure for endogenous rates was rather higher, at 18 per 1,000, almost entirely due to the fact that the rate at Gainsborough rose very sharply from 100 to 157 (the exogenous rate over the same period rose only slightly from 75 to 91). But we have already noted that this rise was probably spurious, or largely so.[17]

In view of the tendency, shown clearly in Table 11, for exogenous infant mortality rates and those for children aged 1–4 to conform to a common pattern in absolute levels, it is of interest to consider jointly their change over time. It is to be expected that mortality in the second half of the first year of life would tend to show the greatest similarity to mortality in the next few years because by then any protective effect from breast feeding is more likely either to have ceased or to have been much reduced. Table 12 compares mortality levels in the two half-centuries using the average rates of the eight parishes for each age interval. While the changes in the ratio of the rates in the two half-centuries are not entirely regular, they are suggestive. The rate for the second quarter of the first year (3–5 months) did not change significantly between the late sixteenth and early seventeenth centuries. The rate for the second half of the first year rose by about a quarter. The rise was less marked in the second year but thereafter became more pronounced

---

[16] The point is examined in some detail in Wrigley, 'Births and baptisms'.
[17] See above, note 14.

Table 12. *Comparison of early childhood mortality rates between 3 months and 5 years 1550–99 and 1600–49 (averages for the eight parishes)*

	Months		Years					
							Age	
	3–5	6–11	1	2	3	4	1–4	5–9
1550–99	16.3	13.5	31.1	19.6	11.4	10.3	70.0	30.3
1600–49	15.6	17.1	36.3	27.3	16.5	15.8	89.4	40.8
Ratio								
(1600–49)/(1550–99)	0.96	1.27	1.17	1.39	1.45	1.53	1.28	1.35

Source: reconstitution tabulations.

through to the fifth year of life, though it appears to have moderated thereafter since the ratio 5–9 is lower than the comparable ratios for the third, fourth and fifth years. Too much must not be made of this pattern in view of the small number of parishes involved and the instability of the rates in the smaller parishes, but it is consonant with the hypothesis that the major infectious diseases of childhood were taking a markedly heavier toll in the seventeenth century (mortality rates 1–4 rose still further in the second half of the seventeenth century).

Although there is solid ground for supposing that the infant and child mortality rates in the eight reconstitution parishes are substantially accurate, it does not follow, of course, that they were typical. Probably they are a little lower than those for the country as a whole. A study of sixteen parishes undertaken for a different purpose showed an average infant mortality level of 149 per 1,000 in the 1580s and 157 per 1,000 in the 1630s (compared with rates of 134 and 142 per 1,000 for the eight parishes in 1550–99 and 1600–49).[18] The sixteen included three parishes in large cities, and the results for this group of parishes may well be closer to the national average than those for the eight parishes described in this chapter.[19]

Ludlow was one of the parishes in the group of sixteen just

[18] The endogenous and exogenous rates in the sixteen parishes were approximately 68 and 81 per 1,000 in the 1580s, and 75 and 82 per 1,000 respectively in the 1630s. See Wrigley, 'Births and baptisms' for details of this study.

[19] The sixteen are: Barton-under-Needwood (Staffs.); Bromfield (Salop); Bruton (Somerset); Dymock (Glos.); Eastham (Worcs.); Farnham (Yorks., W.R.); Ludlow (Salop); St Martin, Coney St (York City); St Michael Cornhill (Middx.); Middleton (Lancs.); Ottery St Mary (Devon); Tatenhill (Staffs.); St Vedast (Middx.); Wedmore (Somerset); Wem (Salop); Widecombe-in-the-moor (Devon).

mentioned. Like Gainsborough and Banbury it was a settlement of some size, and like them experienced rather high rates of infant mortality. No full reconstitution of Ludlow has been carried out, but an *ad hoc* study of mortality has been undertaken covering the years 1577–1619 (the register first becomes suitable for this purpose in 1577), and involving a total of 3,431 burials. Although the results of full reconstitution studies are far more comprehensive and may be slightly more accurate, some points of interest emerged in the course of the special study of mortality in Ludlow. They throw further light on the characteristics of mortality in this period, though without further work it would be premature to assume that the patterns found in Ludlow will be mirrored elsewhere. In particular, the contrast between the stability of overall mortality patterns based on long time periods, and the great volatility of mortality

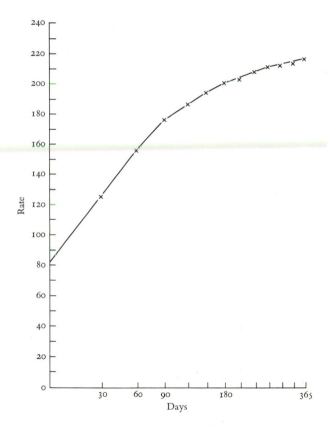

Fig. 4. Infant mortality rate in Ludlow 1577–1619. Source: *Ludlow Parish Register.*

patterns in the short run is striking. The seasonal incidence of mortality also displays interesting features.

The overall level of infant mortality in Ludlow 1577–1619 was 215 per 1,000 (endogenous rate 81, exogenous 134). The graphical representation of the cumulative rate is shown in Fig. 4. The exogenous rate is much higher than in any of the eight reconstitution parishes discussed earlier in the chapter, and the convexity of the upper surface of the curve on the graph is much more pronounced, so pronounced indeed that although the total exogenous rate is almost twice the average of the eight parishes, the rate in the second half of the first year of life (16 per 1,000) is only equal to the average for the eight parishes (see Table 12).

Infant deaths were just over a fifth of all deaths in Ludlow at this period (721 out of 3,431), a comparatively modest fraction given the high level of infant mortality. There is, however, nothing to occasion much surprise in this aspect of infant mortality in Ludlow. More surprising, perhaps, is the absence of a common pattern of annual fluctuation between infant deaths and deaths at other ages, as may be seen in Table 13. In the three years of highest mortality (1587, 1597 and 1609) the number of infant burials was only 13, 19 and 11 respectively, a total of 43, which is even less than might be expected in three ordinary years with an annual average of infant burials of 17. Equally, years in which there were exceptional numbers of infant burials were not years in which mortality at other ages was at a high level. The three years with the highest total of infant deaths were 1582 (27), 1589 (29) and 1617 (25). Yet other deaths in these three years were only 48, 47 and 54 respectively as against an annual average of 63.

If infant deaths are subtracted from total deaths the epidemic peaks stand out much more vividly. For example, burials in the three crisis years of 1587, 1597 and 1609, if indexed to the base 100, where 100 equals the average number of burials per annum excluding the three crisis years, were at a level of 259, 180 and 206 respectively. A parallel calculation made after excluding infant burials from the totals produces figures of 313, 200 and 248. The relative 'height' of crisis peaks is considerably accentuated by the elimination of a class of deaths whose timing appears random in relation to mortality later in life. If this pattern proves to be generally found, and given also the high percentage of all deaths which were infant deaths, it would suggest that relatively modest increases in the gross burial totals may indicate considerable surges in mortality, when allowance is made for infant deaths. It may be noted

Table 13. *Annual burial totals in Ludlow by age 1577–1619*

	Total	Infant	'Child'	'Adult'
1577	50	12	7	31
1578	58	14	16	28
1579	55	14	11	30
1580	92	20	23	49
1581	53	10	17	26
1582	75	27	19	29
1583	59	21	10	28
1584	82	24	17	41
1585	84	22	18	44
1586	94	21	18	55
1587	191	13	27	151
1588	97	12	8	77
1589	76	29	13	34
1590	53	12	12	29
1591	95	12	14	69
1592	78	16	12	50
1593	88	22	9	57
1594	67	14	16	37
1595	109	22	41	46
1596	79	19	16	44
1597	133	19	36	78
1598	54	8	11	35
1599	69	19	14	36
1600	64	20	12	32
1601	79	16	20	43
1602	69	12	15	42
1603	62	18	11	33
1604	75	12	12	51
1605	54	12	6	36
1606	70	12	16	42
1607	86	20	33	33
1608	63	18	12	33
1609	152	11	49	92
1610	58	16	5	37
1611	69	15	12	42
1612	73	17	15	41
1613	100	18	16	66
1614	92	12	19	61
1615	66	8	16	42
1616	74	23	6	45
1617	79	25	9	45
1618	76	20	11	45
1619	79	13	19	47
Mean	80	17	16	47

Source: *Ludlow Parish Register*, Shropshire Parish Register Society, XIII (1912).

that the peak of burials in 1609 was due to an outbreak of plague in Ludlow. In the period from 22 December 1608 until 23 December 1609, 103 burials are marked with a cross in the register to indicate a plague death. Of the eleven infant deaths which occurred in this period only two were attributed to plague, the children in question dying at 4 and 5 months. However this may be an exceptional result; infant mortality rates were often very high in plague periods.[20]

It is also possible, though with less precision, to subdivide the deaths of those above the age of 1 year into 'children' and 'adults' by treating as the former all those who when buried were described as 'son of' or 'daughter of' the head of the family. Although anyone living at home unmarried might be described in this way, including some who were in their twenties or thirties, it is safe to assume that the overwhelming bulk of those so described were young children under 10, both because above that age children left parental households to go into service or to marry,[21] and because death rates 1–9 were so much higher than those in adolescence and early adulthood.

Table 14. *Years of high mortality by age category in rank order, Ludlow 1577–1619*

Rank	Total deaths	Infant deaths	'Child' deaths	'Adult' deaths
1	1587	1589	1609	1587
2	1609	1582	1595	1609
3	1597	1617	1597	1597
4	1595	1584	1607	1588
5	1613	1616	1587	1591

Source: *Ludlow Parish Register.*

It is noticeable that infant, 'child' and 'adult' deaths tended to move independently of each other. The years of highest mortalities in the three categories are shown in Table 14. No year on the infant list appears in either the 'child' or 'adult' list, and although there are three years

[20] See R. S. Schofield, 'An anatomy of an epidemic', in *The Plague Reconsidered*, Local Population Studies Supplement no. 4 (Cambridge, 1977); and M. and T. H. Hollingsworth, 'Plague mortality rates by age and sex in the parish of St Botolph's without Bishopsgate, London, 1603', *Population Studies*, XXV (1971), 131–46.

[21] The loss of children from the parental household into service, however, did not become pronounced until a rather later age, perhaps about 14, while marriage came much later. Marriage under the age of 20 was very uncommon, and the mean age of marriage for both sexes was in the mid-twenties.

common to the 'child' and 'adult' list (1609, 1597, 1587), the agreement between these two is not close. The year of heaviest 'adult' mortality is fifth on the 'child' list, and the second highest year on the 'child' list, 1595, was a year of only average 'adult' mortality. The years 1595 and 1607 are unusually interesting since in these two years both infant and 'child' mortality was high, but 'adult' mortality was either average, as in 1595, or unusually low, as in 1607. On the other hand, there were years, notably 1616, in which adults were far more severely affected than children. Both infant and 'child' mortalities in that year were at average levels, but the number of 'adult' burials was the sixth highest in the whole series.

The epidemic which killed so many children in 1595 occurred from June to September. In those four months there were 5, 17, 9 and 4 'child' burials, a total of 35, which accounts for the whole of the excess child mortality in that year. It is interesting to note that the disease also attacked the older group amongst children under 1. In the same four late summer months there were 8 infant deaths, all except one being of children aged above 3 months, an age period during which mortality was usually very modest.

Table 15. *Relative severity of years of high mortality in Ludlow (100 = average annual burial frequency excluding 1587, 1597 and 1609)*

Year	(1)	(2)	(3)
1587	259	313	357
1609	206	248	218
1597	180	200	185

(1): All burials.
(2): Burials minus infant burials.
(3): 'Adult' burials.

The age-specific impact of crisis mortality can also be considered in relation to 'adult' deaths. The three years of highest 'adult' deaths (1587, 1609 and 1597) are the same as the three highest years over all, but, as may be seen in Table 15, the relative severity of the peaks varies according to the degree to which 'adult' deaths are isolated from total deaths. The year 1587 was one of long drawn-out crisis. Indeed every month from November 1586 to February 1588 produced burials well above the average with particularly severe mortality during the last eight months of the period. Yet infants were not in the least affected by the epidemic, and children only comparatively mildly, so that the mortality peak becomes more and more pronounced as the index becomes increasingly a measure of adult mortality alone. This was not the case, however, in 1609 and 1597. The plague of 1609 did not increase infant mortality, but there were 49 'child' deaths, so that the 'adult' index figure of 218 is very little different from the crude general index, although the intermediate index from which only infant deaths were excluded was at a much higher level. Much the same is true of 1597. The worst mortality of the year was concentrated in the three months August–October when 61 burials were recorded. Children were severely affected. Of the 36 'child' deaths in the year, 22 occurred in these three months (there were 34 'adult' deaths out of the annual total of 78). Only the infant population was untroubled by the outbreak. Earlier in the year there had been 16 deaths in March, but this was largely an adult phenomenon.

Table 16. *Seasonal distribution of burials in Ludlow 1577–1619* (100 = equal distribution of annual total amongst months, corrected for number of days in the month)

	J	F	M	A	M	J	J	A	S	O	N	D	Total burials
All burials													
All ages	98	104	118	111	106	103	83	100	96	90	93	99	3,431
Infant	127	128	106	98	96	93	73	83	94	85	108	119	721
'Child'	71	84	109	101	121	125	103	162	110	69	64	79	699
'Adult'	97	103	125	122	104	99	80	84	92	99	98	98	2,011
Same expressed as three-month moving means													
All ages	100	107	111	112	107	97	95	93	95	93	94	97	
Infant	125	120	111	100	96	87	83	83	87	96	104	118	
'Child'	78	88	98	110	116	116	130	125	114	81	71	71	
'Adult'	99	108	117	117	108	94	88	85	92	96	98	98	
Burials excluding the crisis years 1587, 1597 and 1609													
All ages	107	108	120	113	110	102	80	94	86	86	93	102	2,955
Infant	127	129	104	90	97	92	73	85	95	82	111	118	678
'Child'	78	84	114	106	126	131	110	156	89	64	62	76	587
'Adult'	109	108	129	125	110	96	73	75	81	96	96	104	1,690
Same expressed as three-month moving means													
All ages	106	112	114	114	108	97	92	87	89	88	94	101	
Infant	125	120	108	97	93	87	83	84	87	96	104	119	
'Child'	79	92	101	115	121	122	132	118	103	72	67	72	
'Adult'	107	115	121	121	110	93	81	76	84	91	99	103	

Source: Ludlow Parish Register.

Just as there were marked differences in the annual fluctuations in the number of deaths in different age categories in Ludlow, so there were also marked differences in the seasonal incidence of death by age. Table 16 shows the seasonal distribution of all Ludlow burials and of the three age divisions. They are shown for the whole period 1577–1619 both including the three years with severe epidemics, and with these years excluded. The two series are also shown as three-month moving means to enable the overall trends to be picked out more easily, and in Fig. 5 the information from the moving means without the crisis years is recapitulated graphically. The index figures for each month are calculated in such a way that if the deaths were evenly spread throughout the year, taking the different number of days in the months into account, the figure for each month would be 100.

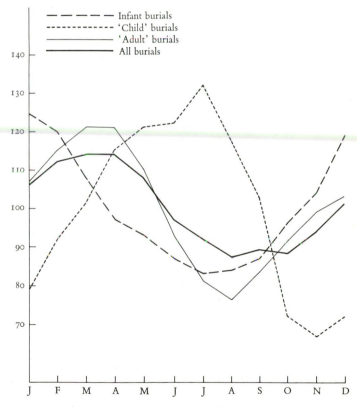

Fig. 5.   The seasonal pattern of mortality in Ludlow 1577–1619: three (month moving means of indexed totals. Source: *Ludlow Parish Register* (Table 16).

The three seasonal curves, representing infant, 'child' and 'adult' burials, describe very different paths in Fig. 5. The pattern of infant mortality shows a marked tendency to peak in midwinter (December–February), and is very low during the summer months. In part this simply reflects the seasonal pattern of births. Given that a very high proportion of infant deaths occurs in the first month of life (58 per cent in Ludlow during this period), it is to be expected that the timing of births during the year would affect that of infant deaths. Most deaths in the first month were due to endogenous causes and these are unlikely to be greatly affected by seasonal influences. Table 17 shows that there is firm evidence to support this view, since deaths under 1 month show a seasonal distribution closely similar to the distribution of baptisms, whereas deaths in the later months of the first year of life peak strongly in the winter months.

Table 17. *The seasonal distribution of baptisms and infant deaths (three-month moving means of indexed totals)*

	J	F	M	A	M	J	J	A	S	O	N	D	Total
(1) Baptisms	106	111	107	104	95	89	86	90	99	105	104	106	3,360
(2) Infant deaths 0 months	117	120	113	99	89	85	89	89	96	98	100	104	417
(3) Infant deaths 1–11 months	136	120	99	94	96	90	80	76	76	91	109	136	304
Difference (1) – (2)	−11	−9	−6	+5	+6	+4	−3	+1	+3	+7	+4	+2	
Difference (1) – (3)	−30	−9	+8	+10	−1	−1	+6	+14	+23	+14	−5	−30	

Source: Ludlow Parish Register.

In contrast to infant mortality, 'child' mortality peaked markedly in the summer, and especially in August, but was at a low ebb during the winter, a pattern which suggests the high incidence of diseases such as dysentery which may become prevalent in hot summers. The contrast between the seasonal patterns of infant and 'child' burials is especially clear in Fig. 5 where they appear almost as mirror images of each other. The peak is almost as marked even when the three major crisis years are excluded from the tabulation. The complete divorce between the childhood pattern and that for infants, especially the older infants who survived the first month, may suggest that weaning occurred late, so that children were not greatly exposed to infections from contaminated food or drink until they had passed their first birthday.

'Adult' burials, especially when crisis years are excluded, reached a maximum in the late spring and were at their lowest point during the summer, which suggests that respiratory infections may have been a major cause of death amongst 'adults'. Because 'adult' burials were the largest single category of burials, and also because the seasonal patterns of infant and 'child' deaths tended to offset one another, the overall pattern of seasonal mortality tended to follow the 'adult' pattern, though with reduced amplitude of fluctuation.

How far the seasonal mortality patterns visible in Ludlow were to be found elsewhere in England will repay further investigation. The overall monthly pattern in Ludlow is not very different from that in the country as a whole. Table 18 shows the pattern found in a very large

Table 18. *Seasonal distribution of burials (indexed totals)*

	J	F	M	A	M	J	J	A	S	O	N	D	Total
England (404 parishes)	111	120	119	118	101	86	81	85	92	92	96	99	161,203
Ludlow	98	104	118	111	106	103	83	100	96	90	93	99	3,431
Ludlow (excl. 3 crisis years)	107	108	120	113	110	102	80	94	86	86	93	102	2,955

Sources: Cambridge Group aggregative tabulations of 404 parishes; *Ludlow Register*.

sample of 404 parishes during the period 1580–1619. The differences between Ludlow and the national sample are not very marked, though it does not, of course, follow that the seasonal pattern of infant, 'child' and 'adult' mortality was also the same in England as a whole. Tabulations of the seasonal distribution of infant mortality have been made for five of the eight reconstitution parishes. For each of them an indexed monthly distribution was calculated for the two half-centuries 1550–99 and 1600–49. In the smaller parishes the monthly infant burial totals were, of course, rather small so that the index numbers are liable to fluctuate rather wildly in a small parish. If, however, the index numbers for each of the five parishes are averaged (there are, of course, two for each month for each parish, or ten in all for each month) a more stable pattern emerges, shown in Table 19 in the form of a three-month moving mean. The similarity between this and the comparable set of figures for Ludlow suggests that the seasonal pattern of infant mortality observed in Ludlow may have been widespread.

The comparable distributions of deaths at ages 1–4 and 5–9 are even more subject to wild fluctuations because of small numbers in the small parishes (in both age groups there may be zero values in particular months). In the two largest parishes, Gainsborough and Banbury, this problem is less acute, however, and in Table 20 three-month moving means are shown. They were derived, like those in Table 19, by

Table 19. *Seasonal distribution of infant burials (three-month moving means of indexed totals)*

	J	F	M	A	M	J	J	A	S	O	N	D
Five reconstitution parishes	117	120	109	103	90	83	86	91	93	93	100	114
Ludlow	125	120	111	100	96	87	83	83	87	96	104	118

Sources: reconstitution tabulations; *Ludlow Parish Register*.

Note: The five reconstitution parishes are Banbury, Gainsborough, Gedling, Hartland and Terling.

averaging the index numbers for each parish for the two half-centuries 1550–99 and 1600–49. The pattern for the deaths 1–4 is similar to that in Ludlow, though the summer maximum and winter minimum are less pronounced. In the 5–9 age group the burials are much less numerous. They, too, show a summer peak, but only in the late summer, and the peak extends through the autumn and into the winter. The numbers on which the indexes were constructed in the first half-century (63 in Banbury, 37 in Gainsborough) are very small, however, and it would be unwise to assume that the seasonal pattern of child mortality is firmly established. Indeed there may well have been marked differences between different parishes according to the prevalence of local diseases.

Table 20. *Seasonal distribution of child deaths in Banbury and Gainsborough (three-month moving means of indexed totals: see text)*

Age	J	F	M	A	M	J	J	A	S	O	N	D
1–4	99	95	93	93	100	101	112	117	111	93	88	95
5–9	114	91	92	91	85	88	94	123	119	101	102	102

Source: reconstitution tabulations

Although the subject of this essay has been infant and child mortality in Tudor and early Stuart England, it may improve its balance to make a brief reference in conclusion to adult mortality. The estimation of adult mortality by family reconstitution is a complex operation. The estimates are based on the married population alone and they are necessarily imprecise because some people migrate out of the parish after marriage and their dates of burial are unknown. A convenient way of setting bounds to this indeterminacy is to make two fairly extreme sets of assumptions about the mortality experience of the group which passes out of observation, and then in each case to combine the results with those obtained for the group remaining behind whose mortality history is known. This procedure yields two estimates of the adult mortality of the married population as a whole, between which the true figure will almost certainly lie.[22]

Table 21. *Expectation of life at age 30 (e_{30})*

	Range (years)		Model life table level nearest to centre point of range			
	Male	Female	North		West	
			M	F	M	F
Alcester	27.3–29.9	28.4–31.9	6	6	8	7
Banbury	25.7–28.4	27.6–31.0	5	5	6	6
Colyton	27.6–29.9	28.7–31.3	6	6	8	7
Gainsborough	23.8–25.8	26.6–29.7	3	4	4	5
Gedling	31.0–32.4	28.7–30.7	9	5	11	6
Hartland	30.9–33.3	30.7–33.4	10	8	11	9
Terling	27.3–31.0	26.9–30.8	7	5	8	6

Source: reconstitution tabulations.

Note: The figures given in the first two columns are the averages of data for the two marriage cohorts of 1550–99 and 1600–49. The differences between the two cohorts were slight in all the parishes and there was no general tendency to rise or fall. The figures for Aldenham were not available when this table was made up.

The ranges quoted in Table 21 are not the full range from the pessimistic to the optimistic extremes, but the range from the average of the two figures to the optimistic figure. There are strong grounds for

[22] The detailed algorithm is too complex to be described here. A very similar method of estimating adult mortality is described in E. A. Wrigley, 'Mortality in pre-industrial England; the example of Colyton, Devon, over three centuries', in D. V. Glass and D. E. C. Eversley (eds.), *Population and Social Change* (London, 1972), pp.546–80. We intend to describe the present method in a forthcoming volume devoted to the presentation of the result of reconstitution studies of about fifteen parishes.

believing that the true figure lies in this range. It is beyond the scope of this chapter to explore this point in full, but it may be noted that the pessimistic figure incorporates the assumption that from the moment of passage out of observation those whose date of burial is not known were subject to mortality rates consonant with an expectation of life at birth of only 20 years. Not only is this an extreme assumption in regard to mortality level, it is also improbable on general grounds since a long life may in many cases have increased the likelihood of dying outside the parish in which the marriage took place.

The agreement between the male and female figures in Table 21 is good on the evidence of the model life table equivalents except in the case of Gedling and, to a lesser degree, Terling, but as these are the two smallest parishes it is probable that the discrepancies are caused by the relatively small number of available observations.

Table 22. *Model West mortality levels based on* $_5q_5$ *and* e_{30}

	$_5q_5$	e_{30}
Alcester	7.5	7.5
Banbury	5	6
Colyton	8	7.5
Gainsborough	2	4.5
Gedling	9.5	8.5
Hartland	10	10
Terling	6	7

Source: Tables 6 and 21.

The agreement between the life table levels in Table 21 and those in Table 6, on the other hand, is at first sight very poor. In Model North terms adult mortality is radically worse than infant and child mortality (by an average of about six levels). Nor does the agreement with the Model West levels in the two tables initially seem impressive. If, however, we concentrate solely on later childhood mortality 5–9 ($_5q_5$) in 1600–49, and the Model West levels in Table 21, there is an excellent fit. Table 22 shows this clearly.

Thus, although mortality rates between birth and age 5 or age 10 corresponded well with those of model life tables, as did the rates from age 5 upwards, the model tables concerned were different in level or type. The shape of mortality in early modern England was therefore distinctive, a mixture of Model North and Model West characteristics, with adult mortality relatively much higher than mortality in the first years of life. Taken together, the infant, child and adult mortality rates in Tudor and Stuart England suggest an expectation of life at birth in the range 35–40 years, an unusually high level by the general standards of early modern Europe.[23] This was largely due to the relatively low infant and child mortality rates, an advantage which remained despite the sharp rise in child mortality between the late sixteenth and early seventeenth centuries.

---

[23] By 'splicing' a life table which describes infant and child mortality to a life table which appears to capture mortality experience later in life, it is, of course, easily possible to calculate an expectation of life at birth for English populations at this period. For example, if we assume that for the eight parishes their mean mortality experience is best reflected by Model North level 12 to age 10 and thereafter by Model West level 7 (see Tables 6 and 22), expectation of life at birth (e_0) is 38.8 for men, 41.3 for women and 40.0 for the sexes combined. We have seen, however, that there is some reason to think that mortality in the eight parishes was less severe than in the country generally. The infant mortality level in the eight, for example, was 15 per 1,000 lower than in a larger sample of parishes (see above, p.82). This is equivalent to about one level in the Princeton regional model life table series, and would suggest an expectation of life at birth 2 or 3 years lower than that found in the eight parishes. It may be noted that estimates of expectation of life at birth can also be made for individual parishes using the method just described. They range between 31.7 years (e_0) in Gainsborough and 48.3 years in Hartland (sexes combined in both cases).

3

Diet in sixteenth-century England: sources, problems, possibilities

ANDREW B. APPLEBY

I think it could be plausibly argued that changes of diet are more important than changes of dynasty or even of religion.

George Orwell, *The Road to Wigan Pier*

Diet may be more important than dynasties or religion, as Orwell suggested. But, like it or not, we know a great deal more about the monarchs and religious reformers of history than we do about the diet – the food – eaten by the majority of people in the past, however important food may have been.[1] In this essay I shall indicate what little is known about diet in sixteenth-century England, mention some of the problems with the available evidence, and propose some subjects that might benefit from further research. I shall also suggest that the social distribution of food in Tudor England had some resemblance to the social distribution of food in the world today. In our affluent industrial societies the major nutritional problems seem to be that we eat too much and that what we eat has too high a proportion of meat and of animal fats. Malnutrition is the product of plenty. Parts of the Third World, however, have diets very low in animal fats and proteins, hunger is common, and starvation is not unknown. Malnutrition is the product of want. The same dietary problems can be found in sixteenth-century England. The wealthy ate vast amounts of meat, prepared in increasingly elaborate ways and served with growing ostentation. At the same time the poor became more dependent on a monotonous fare of basic food grains. Towards the end of the century the very poor fell below the level of subsistence into starvation. Perhaps I should add that throughout this essay the word 'diet' is used in its modern sense, as food. It does not have its sixteenth-century connotation of a regimen of health,

---

[1] Peter Laslett has complained that until recently historians have not even bothered to ask whether or not everyone had enough to eat in early modern England. See *The World We Have Lost* (London, 1965), p.127.

incorporating all aspects of medicine, food and self-discipline in one balanced whole.

By all accounts the food of the well-to-do was both varied and plentiful through the sixteenth century, probably becoming somewhat richer and more elaborate towards the end of the century. The nobility ate great quantities of meat; every day, William Harrison wrote, they have 'beef, mutton, veal, lamb, kid, pork, cony, capon, pig, or so many of these as the season yieldeth'.[2] On feast days the nobility provided themselves, their guests and servants with an astounding array of dishes. On the feast of Epiphany in 1508 the household and guests of Edward Stafford, Duke of Buckingham – a total of 459 persons – ate 678 loaves of bread, 36 'rounds' of beef, 12 mutton carcases, 2 calves, 4 pigs, 6 sucking pigs, 1 lamb, numerous chickens and rabbits, as well as oysters, ling, cod, sturgeon, flounder, lamprey, large eels, plaice, a conger eel, roach (small freshwater fish), dogfish, tench (freshwater fish similar to carp), a salmon, swans, geese, capons, peacocks, herons, mallards, widgeons, teals, woodcocks, snipes, unspecified great and little birds, larks, quails, eggs, butter, milk, and 6d worth of herbs. All this was washed down with Gascon and other wine and 259 flagons of ale.[3] Clearly, this was a diet composed primarily of meat, fowl, fish, bread, wine and beer. At this feast the vegetables, shown as 'herbs', cost a paltry 6d, although other vegetables, such as onions, may have been eaten but were too insignificant from a cost standpoint to include in the account books of the household. Epiphany falls in early January and fruit and vegetables may have played a more prominent role in menus at other times of the year and, perhaps, at less sumptuous dinners.

It is not entirely clear whether vegetables were readily available in the early sixteenth century and, if available, to what extent they were consumed in the typical better-off English household. Some fifty different types of 'herbs' – a catch-all rubric – were known in the late fifteenth century, including cabbage, leeks, sorrel, lettuce and endive.[4] Onions were available throughout the century.[5] Writing in 1578, however, Harrison said that little use had been made of vegetables until the reign of Henry VIII; 'they remained either unknown or supposed as

[2] William Harrison, *The Description of England*, ed. G. Edelen (Ithaca, NY, 1968), p.126.
[3] J. Burnett, *A History of the Cost of Living* (Harmondsworth, 1969), p.80.
[4] A. L. Simon, *The Star Chamber Dinner Accounts* (London, 1959), p.24. See also the list of vegetables in Andrew Boorde, *A compendyous regyment or a dyetary of helth*, ed. F. J. Furnivall (1870), pp.278–81.
[5] J. C. Drummond and A. Wilbraham, *The Englishman's Food: A History of Five Centuries of English Diet* (London, 1958), p.22.

food more meet for hogs and savage beasts to feed upon than mankind'. As the century wore on vegetables became a more usual part of the diet, not only of the poor but of the wealthy. Harrison commented that by the time he was writing melons, pumpkins, gourds, cucumbers, radishes, skirrets (a water parsnip), parsnips, carrots, cabbages, turnips and salad greens were 'fed upon as dainty dishes at the tables of delicate merchants, gentlemen, and the nobility'. The wealthy, Harrison noted with distaste, had even taken to eating such unnatural foods as mushrooms and aubergines.[6]

The dinner accounts of the court of Star Chamber reflect the emphasis on meat, fowl and fish. The lords of the Star Chamber were served ten pounds of beef per lord per dinner, but presumably much of this went to their attendants, servants and guards. Even in Elizabethan England ten pounds of beef was surely too much for one man at one sitting.[7] In addition the lords ate mutton, lamb and veal, and brawn, a sort of preserved paste made from the foreparts of a fattened boar.[8] Aside from brawn the lords did not eat pork, perhaps because it was thought to be a lower-class meat. All manner of poultry was consumed at the Star Chamber dinners: cocks, hens, pullets, capons, geese, pigeons (cooked in pies), ducks, pheasants, partridges, quails, snipes, woodcocks, plovers, gulls (which were netted and then fed on beef to rid them of their fishy taste), curlews, herons, blackbirds and larks. Rabbits and conies were provided on most flesh days.[9] Beginning in 1563, Wednesday, Friday, Saturday, and certain other days were fish days, amounting in all to some 153 days in the year. On those days the lords made do with cod, turbot, sole, herring, mullet, plaice, flounder, smelt, dory, gurnard, conger eel, salmon, trout, lamprey, eel, crayfish, carp, pike, perch, bream, barbel, chub and loach.[10] Porpoises were served to the lords on at least two occasions, and at one dinner in 1590 a lobster was served. Perhaps surprisingly, lobster was relatively much more expensive then than now; this one lobster cost as much as thirty-two pounds of beef.[11] Oysters were served at most dinners in the winter, on meat days as well

[6] Harrison, *Description of England*, p.264.
[7] Simon, *Star Chamber Accounts*, p.3.
[8] Ibid., p.5; Harrison, *Description of England*, p.314.
[9] Simon, *Star Chamber Accounts*, pp.6–14.
[10] Ibid., pp.15–23; Harrison, *Description of England*, editor's note, p.126n.
[11] Simon, *Star Chamber Accounts*, p.18. I think Simon mistakes the weight of a stone of beef in London, thinking that it was six pounds when it was eight pounds, according to Harrison, *Description of England*, p.457, and R. E. Zupko, *A Dictionary of English Weights and Measures* (Madison, Wisconsin, 1968).

as fish days. Prawns, shrimps, crabs, whelks and cockles also found their way to the Star Chamber table.[12]

Only one of the 'herbs' known at the end of the fifteenth century – spinach – appears in the list of foods for the Star Chamber, but others may have been included under the general heading of 'herbs and onions'. Other vegetables eaten included globe artichokes, cauliflower and peas, and carrots, which seem to have been something of a novelty when they were listed in the accounts for 1567.[13] Fruits of various sorts appeared on the accounts; apples were served at all dinners and pears when they were in season. Peaches were mentioned as well as gooseberries, barberries, quinces, imported prunes, and oranges and lemons, which also were imported. When they were available these fruits would have supplied vitamin C and it would seem that the economically advantaged would not have suffered from vitamin C deficiency. These examples, of course, are drawn from Westminster and do not necessarily reflect the availability of either fruits or vegetables in other parts of the realm. Certainly apples, pears, plums and cherries were grown in many parts of England and wild berries could be gathered elsewhere.[14] Towards the end of the century fruits and vegetables were brought to the most remote corners of the realm, for those who had the money to pay for them. The German copper miners at Keswick, deep in the heart of the Cumbrians, had artichokes and oranges shipped to them from London by way of Newcastle. The price of the oranges was surprisingly reasonable, considering the distance: 100 oranges cost only 2s in February 1569. Six artichokes cost the same amount.[15] Early in the next century Lord William Howard bought 'artichoke roots' for his garden at Naworth Castle, Cumberland, although the records do not indicate whether or not these plants flourished in the bleak Cumberland climate. The Howard household books also show the purchase of quantities of cherries, plums, apples, pears and imported oranges.[16]

The lords of the Star Chamber supplemented the foods mentioned above with white bread, probably the 'manchet' bread spoken of by Harrison,[17] and with spices of various sorts, including mustard, pepper,

[12] Simon, *Star Chamber Accounts*, pp.18–19.
[13] Ibid., p.24.
[14] Drummond and Wilbraham, *The Englisman's Food*, p.22; Boorde, *A compendyous regyment*, pp.282–4; C. Williams, *Thomas Platter's Travels in England 1599* (London, 1937), p.184.
[15] W. G. Collingwood, *Elizabethan Keswick* (Kendal, 1912), pp.32–4.
[16] *Selections from the Household Books of the Lord William Howard of Naworth Castle*, ed. G. Ornsby, Surtees Society, LXVIII (1878), p.92 and passim.
[17] Harrison, *Description of England*, pp.133–4.

ginger, cloves, nutmeg, cinnamon and saffron. Salads were dressed with red or white vinegar and olive oil.[18] Predictably, the lords drank quantities of ale, beer and wine. The usual wine was claret (a term applied then to a light red Bordeaux), which was drunk young, less than eighteen months old. Both Bordeaux reds and whites were also drunk.[19]

There is no need here to add other examples of the foodstuffs eaten by the rich. It is, I think, clear that they enjoyed a varied diet, with adequate amounts of fruit and, at least by the end of the century, vegetables. Their food, however, was perhaps too heavily weighted towards meat, fowl, fish, wine and beer – and they perhaps ate too much for their own good. Harrison complained that many of the nobility and gentry overate, remaining at the dinner table from eleven in the morning until two or three in the afternoon.[20] Philip Stubbes deplored the elaborate dishes that had become common by 1585, noting that 'every dish [has] a several sauce appropriate to his kind'.[21] Perhaps this new enthusiasm for sauces could be traced to the 'musical-headed Frenchmen' that the nobility had begun to employ as cooks.[22]

All these fine foods and elaborate preparations could be ruinously expensive; more than one nobleman 'sent all his revenues down the privy house'.[23] They could also be unhealthy. Lawrence Stone thinks there was a connection between the aristocratic diet and the very common incidence of calculi.[24] It is also likely that the diet was excessively high in animal fats, which may have contributed to cholesterol build-up and hardening of the arteries. The animals of the sixteenth century were not fattened in the methodical manner that we follow today, but any diet with so much meat in it must have had a high proportion of fat. Stone notes that butter – a major source of animal fat – was not a major item in the diet, but the Star Chamber accounts indicate that considerable quantities of both table butter and cooking butter were bought. Fish were all fried in butter.[25] It is conjecture, of course, but the fats in the diet may have been at a dangerously high level. Perhaps it made little difference to the rich in terms of longevity; the arterial problems that come from a fatty diet would have appeared only

---

[18] Simon, *Star Chamber Accounts*, pp.34–5.
[19] Ibid., pp.37–8.
[20] Harrison, *Description of England*, pp.141–4.
[21] Quoted in Burnett, *Cost of Living*, p.80.
[22] Harrison, *Description of England*, p.126.
[23] Quoted in Lawrence Stone, *The Crisis of the Aristocracy* (Oxford, 1965), p.562.
[24] Ibid.
[25] Simon, *Star Chamber Accounts*, p.32.

in middle age or later. Also the sixteenth-century aristocrat was physically more active than the sedentary businessman of today and his activity may have reduced the risk of arterial or coronary disease.

The account books and household books kept by the nobility provide copious evidence about their diet or, at least, those foods they purchased for their tables. As we move down the economic hierarchy, however, our sources become much less satisfactory. Between the nobility at the top and the poor at the bottom of the social pyramid lay the great mass of English men and women. And, unfortunately, little is known about their diet. An occasional account book for a prosperous farmer survives, usually from the seventeenth century rather than the sixteenth. It seems that the Loder household and the Best household ate well – and fed their servants and labourers well.[26] Eric Kerridge has argued that the diet of the farm servants in these households, and of the labourers dependent on the latter, was superior to that of the average fifteenth-century husbandman, with adequate amounts of fats, calories, vitamins and minerals.[27] His rosy picture of rural life agrees with the accounts left by foreign travellers in England. By continental standards the food eaten by the English was plentiful, with far more meat than was customary across the Channel. Emmanuel van Meteren, an Antwerp merchant who lived for many years in Elizabethan London, noted that the English 'eat a great deal of meat: and as the Germans pass the bounds of sobriety in drinking, these do the same in eating'.[28] Lupold von Wedel on his visit in 1584–5 commented that 'the peasants and citizens [of England] are on the average rich people', adding that 'I have seen peasants presenting themselves statelier in manner, and keeping a more sumptuous table than some noblemen do in Germany. That is a poor peasant who has no silver-gilt salt-cellars, silver cups, and spoons'.[29] Other examples could be given; to foreign eyes England was a prosperous country, with a substantial, well-fed peasantry and citizenry. It should be kept in mind that the foreign visitors saw only the well-off peasants, not the very poor. Nevertheless, as Joan Thirsk points out, it is noteworthy that

---

[26] Henry Best, *Rural Economy in Yorkshire in 1641*, ed. C. B. Robinson, Surtees Society, XXXIII (1857); G. E. Fussell, *Robert Loder's Farm Accounts, 1610–20*, Camden Society, 3rd ser., LIII (1936).

[27] See E. Kerridge, *The Agricultural Revolution* (New York, 1968), pp.333–4, and idem, *The Farmers of Old England* (Totowa, New Jersey, 1973), pp.158–60.

[28] W. B. Rye, *England as Seen by Foreigners in the Days of Elizabeth and James the First* (1865), p.70. See also p.110 for a similar observation by Paul Hentzner, a native of Brandenburg.

[29] G. von Bulow (transl.), 'Journey through England and Scotland made by Lupold von Wedel in the years 1584 and 1585'. *Transactions of the Royal Historical Society*, new ser., IX (1895), 268.

foreigners did not find poverty so pervasive in England as to warrant comment.[30]

Aside from the tales of travellers and the occasional farmer's account book, the most promising source for information about the diet of this middling group is the probate inventories, those lists of the goods a person owned at his or her death. These sometimes go into great detail, noting items worth as little as a penny or two. In addition to indicating the wealth of the deceased, an inventory can give some clues to the diet, as the following examples show. At his death in 1600, Thomas Stoddart of Aikton, Cumberland, left one cow, five sheep, two bushels of barley and five and one-half bushels of oats. John Atkinson, of Crosby, in Cumberland, left in 1565 one mare, four bushels of barley, three bushels of rye and six bushels of oats. Robert Brown of Wigton, Cumberland, at his death in 1570 owned three oxen, six cows, two sheep and one 'old nag', as well as fourteen bushels of oats and eight of barley.[31] Richard Askew, of the parish of St John Beckermet, on the west coast of Cumberland, left in 1588 five cows, one horse, five sheep, unspecified quantities of oats and barley, two pigs, three geese, an unspecified number of hens and three bee hives.[32] These examples are fairly typical of the inventories of modest husbandmen of Cumberland in the later sixteenth century.

What can these inventories tell us about the diet of these men and their families? First, it seems that Stoddart, Brown and Askew ate oats and barley as their bread grains. No other grain appears in their inventories and it is unlikely that they purchased wheat or rye. An analysis of many other inventories testifies that the commonest grain in this region was oats, followed by barley. But what about Atkinson? His inventory lists rye; does this show that he ate rye? Not necessarily. Both wheat and rye appear infrequently on the inventories and were apparently eaten primarily by the more prosperous yeomen and the gentry. Atkinson was quite poor – his estate came to only £3 – and he may have grown the rye as a 'cash' crop, to sell, rather than to consume himself. This example highlights one major shortcoming of the inventories: it is impossible to say what items were intended for sale and what for home consumption.

[30] J. Thirsk, 'Introduction', in J. Thirsk (ed.), *The Agrarian History of England and Wales IV: 1500–1640* (Cambridge, 1967), p.xxxvi.
[31] Probate inventories for the diocese of Carlisle are in the Cumbria Record Office, boxed by year and arranged alphabetically.
[32] Inventories for the diocese of Chester, deaconry of Copeland, are in the Lancashire Record Office.

The same problem arises in determining the role of animals in the diet of these husbandmen. Askew had pigs, geese and hens; instead of eating them he may have sold them at some nearby market to gain money for rent. Even the eggs laid by the hens and the honey produced by his bees may have been sold rather than eaten by his family. The cows and sheep owned by these men may also have been sold. In other words, the inventories tell us what grains and animals a person owned at his death, but they do not separate these goods into what was intended for sale and what was to be consumed. Therefore, it is almost impossible to calculate the amount of animal protein in the diet of these people.

Nor do the inventories in Cumberland and Westmorland – the region I know best – list vegetables or fruit. Of course, that does not mean that the husbandman did not eat an occasional cabbage, some onions, or berries; small quantities of these may have been of too little value to include in the inventories. But we remain as ignorant about the vegetables eaten by these people as we are about their consumption of meat or dairy products. With our limited knowledge it is very difficult to say whether these people had a qualitatively adequate diet. Did they, for example, eat enough fruits, vegetables, or seasoning herbs that contained vitamin C, to ward off scurvy? It is impossible to say. Both rickets and scurvy were reported as 'new' diseases in the seventeenth century but they may have been present earlier and not differentiated from other ailments.[33] An additional problem that we face in analysing the diet of this group – and indeed it is a problem with any historical study of diet – is that bacteria in the human intestinal tract can change over time and permit the body to adapt to diets that would not maintain health in a modern European or American. The natives of New Guinea, for example, thrive on a diet largely made up of sweet potatoes, a diet that would quickly cause malnutrition in an Englishman today. In short, we cannot impose our own nutritional standards on these early modern English men and women because we know very little about their utilization of their food.

Although I have stressed the problems posed by the probate inventories, I should add that they are useful for determining in broad outline the food eaten in a region. They indicate what grains were grown and consumed; oats and barley predominated in the north-west, but rye was more common in the north-east, wheat in the south, barley

---

[33] John Pechey, *A general treatise of the diseases of infants and children* (1697), p.148; S. X. Radbill, 'Pediatrics', in A. G. Debus (ed.), *Medicine in Seventeenth Century England* (Berkeley and Los Angeles, 1974), pp.263, 267.

in East Anglia and the west, and so forth.[34] The inventories also give some idea of the variety of foodstuffs that were grown. In Cumberland and Westmorland relatively few small husbandmen kept pigs or poultry, compared to other regions, and few grew peas or beans, which would have provided another valuable source of vegetable protein to complement the vegetable proteins of the ubiquitous oats and barley. In Leicestershire, by contrast, peas and beans were an important crop.[35] Their cultivation may have given a degree of insurance against hunger when the grain harvest was poor. These broad regional differences are important and the inventories provide useful insights into these differences, although they do not permit precise analysis of the diets of individuals.

To this point, I have discussed the diet of the rich and the diet of what I have rather arbitrarily called the 'middling' group, who range in wealth from the prosperous large landholder down to the modest husbandman. In general, members of this middling group raised their own food rather than buying it on the market. If we move once more down the economic scale we find another large group of rural people without the means always to feed themselves in the sixteenth century. And there was a sizeable group of city and town workers whose economic condition worsened throughout the century. These groups at the bottom of the economic hierarchy, I shall argue, saw a steady deterioration of their diet throughout the sixteenth century, until by the end of the century they suffered malnutrition and, in the 1590s, famine. These were the people without a secure 'place' in society: the landless labourer, the town worker, the cottager, the vagabond.

Before we look at the diet of this disadvantaged group, perhaps it would be helpful to provide some demographic and economic background. During the sixteenth century England had a great increase in population, from some 2.3 million persons in 1522–5 to 3.75 million in 1603.[36] Where did these additional people, these extra mouths, go? London absorbed some but others stayed on the land. Of those who stayed in the rural areas, some inherited a part of the family holding and became small farmers alongside their brothers. In areas where partible inheritance was practised, family holdings were progressively broken

34 The predominant crops can be traced conveniently in J. Thirsk, 'The farming regions of England', in Thirsk (ed.), *The Agrarian History of England and Wales*, pp.1–112.

35 W. G. Hoskins, *The Midland Peasant* (London, 1965), pp.154–6.

36 J. Cornwall, 'English population in the early sixteenth century', *Economic History Review*, 2nd ser., XXIII (1970), 44. See also E. A. Wrigley, *Population and History* (London, 1969), pp.77–8.

up, to give each son a piece of the parental land. In 1507, for example, there were 72 customary holdings in the Forest of Rossendale in Lancashire. By 1527 these had been fractured into 101; these in turn were broken into 200 by 1608.[37] This does not mean that the 200 holdings of 1608 were necessarily the same total size as the 72 holdings of 1507; additional small parcels of forest land may have been enclosed and added to the holdings. But it does mean – in this example and many others that could be given – that the size of the average holding shrank, sometimes to the point where it could no longer support a family. Not everywhere, of course, was there partible inheritance and the breaking up of holdings. In those areas of peasant impartible inheritance, the sons who did not inherit the parental land had to seek land elsewhere. In many instances, particularly in the uplands and the forests, these landless men became squatters, carving out small bits of land on which they built huts and planted grain. Often these encroachments were miniscule, too small to maintain a family unless the members of the family had some form of other employment, either as farm labourers or as spinners or weavers of cloth. In Rossendale a commission to enquire into encroachments of forest land in 1616 unearthed fifty-nine such encroachments by otherwise landless squatters. The combined area of all fifty-nine was less than six and one-half statute acres.[38] This example is no doubt extreme, but similar encroachments occurred widely in sixteenth-century England. Elizabeth's government became sufficiently alarmed over the increase in poor cottagers to pass a statute in 1589 forbidding the erection of cottages with less than four acres of land.[39] These two processes – the breaking up of established holdings and the squatting on the common pastures and in the forests – created a body of poor smallholders who were vulnerable to harvest failure and depression in the clothing trade. When the harvest failed they had to pay more for the grain they needed to buy to supplement the inadequate yield of their own tiny plots of ground. At the same time that food prices rose they often found themselves without employment: farm labourers would be less in demand because a smaller crop needs less labour to harvest it, and as

[37] G. H. Tupling, *The Economic History of Rossendale*, Chetham Society, new ser., LXXXVI (1927), pp.76, 235. See other examples in A. B. Appleby, *Famine in Tudor and Stuart England*, forthcoming from Stanford University Press, chapter 4.

[38] Tupling, *Rossendale*, pp.66, 232–3. In Lancashire the customary acre was 1.6 times the statute acre; the commission's figures have been converted to statute acres. For other examples of squatting see Appleby, *Famine in Tudor and Stuart England*, chapter 4.

[39] J. Thirsk, 'Enclosing and engrossing', in Thirsk (ed.), *The Agrarian History of England and Wales*, pp.227–8.

people spent more money on food they could spend less on clothes, thus producing a decline in the clothing trade. In addition to these two groups of rural poor there is some indication of another shadowy group of marginal smallholders: sub-tenants who took short leases, usually for one year or less, from more established landholders.[40] Little is known about the sub-tenants but they probably faced the same difficulties as the other smallholders. Population growth had created a large impoverished group at the very bottom of rural society, a group that may have always been at subsistence level and was certainly pushed towards starvation at the end of the century. Put simply, there were too many people in rural England at the end of the sixteenth century to be fed, given the inequitable distribution of land and the existing agricultural technology. This is not to say that agricultural output remained constant during the century; new land was brought into cultivation, certain new crops were grown, improvements were undertaken, but either agricultural output did not expand as rapidly as population or the benefits of increased production went to the better-off, not to the rural poor.[41]

Paradoxically, we know more about the diet of the poor than the diet of the independent, subsistence husbandmen who stood above them in the economic hierarchy. The poor bought food, which the independent husbandmen usually did not, and price movements during the century tell us something of changes in their diet. It would be misleading to imply that all those who bought food rather than growing it themselves were somehow poor. In many instances the price series that survive are drawn from institutions like colleges, that could hardly be characterized as poor. And of course wealthy London merchants, doctors and lawyers also bought their food on the market. But the prices that these institutions and these people paid were to some degree determined by prices on the larger market, prices set by all purchasers, including the poor.

The poor also appear, as the better-off do not, in great numbers in the parish burial registers towards the end of the century when famine swept many of them away. The very poor also left the occasional inventory, but this has the drawbacks common to all inventories mentioned earlier.

Let us look first at the long-term price movements that took place during the sixteenth century, and attempt to relate these to the diet of the

[40] Thirsk, 'The farming regions of England', in Thirsk (ed.), *The Agrarian History of England and Wales*, p.88.
[41] For improvements in agriculture see Kerridge, *The Agricultural Revolution*, passim.

poor. Judging by the controls and regulations that authorities throughout western Europe set to cover virtually every transaction, grain was the core of the diet of the poor, and we shall begin with grain price movements. The price series prepared by Peter Bowden indicate that the price of wheat rose during the sixteenth century by × 4.6, comparing the average price of wheat for the decade 1500–9 to that of 1590–9.[42] Barley rose by × 5.6 during the same period, oats by × 6.0 and the price of peas and beans by × 4.7. Price information for rye is not complete for the first decade but the rise was of the order of × 5.3. Thus the increase in wheat prices was the least dramatic, followed by peas and beans, rye, barley, and finally oats. Wheat was always the most expensive grain, followed usually by rye, barley and oats. The long-term price movements suggest that the cheaper grains moved somewhat closer in price to wheat. This, in turn, suggests that buying pressure by the poor was forcing up the price of the less desirable grains, or that the poor were switching away from wheat, as all grain prices rose, and consuming cheaper grain alternatives. If this hypothesis is correct, relatively more people were eating inferior grains at the end of the century than at the beginning. In a word, their diet had deteriorated, at least from the standpoint of preference. The change from wheat to another bread grain, however, was probably not important from a health standpoint. All the grains were important sources of carbohydrates, proteins, vitamins and minerals, although there is marginally more protein in today's wheat than in other grains. Of course, the protein content of the strains of grain grown in the sixteenth century is not known.

It is interesting that peas and beans did not increase in price as much as oats or barley. They were an important supplemental food of the poor, especially during the dearth, and one would expect them to have increased in price strongly, similarly to oats, the cheapest bread grain. But perhaps there was strong resistance to eating peas and beans, which were normally fed only to animals. Or it may be that their price rise was moderated simply because they were animal food, not always under buying pressure by the poor, as were oats.

The amount of meat eaten by the poor in the early sixteenth century is not known but relative price movements suggest that the *per capita* consumption of meat declined during the century. The price of all

---

[42] All the following price and wage data, unless otherwise indicated, are from P. Bowden, 'Statistical appendix', in Thirsk (ed.), *The Agrarian History of England and Wales*, pp.814–70.

livestock rose, but not as rapidly as the price of grain. Employing the same opening and closing decadal prices as before, we find that the price of sheep rose by × 5.0, cattle by × 4.5, pigs by × 3.6, and poultry and rabbits by × 2.8. Sheep prices rose more than wheat but less than the inferior grains, and no other livestock increased in price as much as wheat. If – as I have suggested – buying pressure by the poorer segments of society explains the differential price rise between wheat and the inferior grains, it seems that the poor put little pressure on the price of livestock. They appear to have spent their pennies on the cheaper bread grains, not on meat. The relative strength of sheep prices, it should be mentioned, was not due only to the use of sheep as food. Throughout the century they were valuable as a source of wool and Bowden suggests that in the first half of the century wool prices were rising more rapidly than grain prices.[43] This, in part, helps account for the steep increase in sheep prices.

These conclusions about meat consumption agree with the findings of Alan Everitt's study of the probate inventories of farm labourers. Although few labourers kept pigs, bacon was fairly common and Everitt concludes that it was purchased from local farmers who had pigs. Beef was rarely mentioned in the inventories and mutton never. These labourers may have on occasion killed and eaten a hen, duck or even a goose, but poultry appears too infrequently on the inventories to have been a regular item in the labourer's diet.[44] It should be added that considerable regional variation existed; in the extreme north-west labourers and other cottagers did not possess poultry, nor have I found any mention of bacon in the inventories of the poor in the sixteenth century. Towards the end of the seventeenth century, however, these began to appear as the rural standard of living improved somewhat.

The prices of other items that occasionally figured in the diet of the poor – milk, cheese and butter – are difficult to trace because of gaps in the price series, but they seem to have increased by about × 3.4 during the century, somewhat less than grain prices. This implies that the poor were eating less of these as time went on, but it may be that most dairy products, at least in the country, never reached market. Many of the poorest farm labourers and cottagers had a beast or two, even though they did not have enough arable land to supply themselves with grain,

[43] P. Bowden, 'Movements in wool prices, 1490–1610', *Yorkshire Bulletin of Economic and Social Research*, IV (1952), 118–24.
[44] A. Everitt, 'Farm labourers', in Thirsk (ed.), *The Agrarian History of England and Wales*, pp.450–3.

and they probably ate and drank the milk products of these animals. One of the difficulties facing the student of diet in the sixteenth century is that one does not know how important the market was for many goods. If the market was very thin for milk and butter in the countryside because most people, even the poor, produced their own, the price series we have may not faithfully reflect consumption patterns. The poor bought at least a part of their grain and were involved in the grain market to some extent. However, they may not have bought any other foodstuffs. Part of the food eaten in sixteenth-century England was sold on the market – and appears in price movements – but part was raised for subsistence and one cannot always determine where the line dividing the two lay.

With this qualification, I think price data give a general picture of an erosion in the diet throughout the sixteenth century. Apparently there was a switch away from wheat to the lower-priced and less-desired grains. A larger proportion of the population was eating barley and oats at the end of the century than at the beginning. And meat consumption had relatively declined as well, as inflation forced the poorer people to spend more of their income on grains rather than meat. This may also have been the case with dairy products, although it is not certain.

This suggested decay in the diet accords with the trend of real wages during the century. Wage rates for agricultural labourers rose by × 2.7 between the century's first and last decades but this increase certainly did not match the rise in the price of foodstuffs. Peter Bowden has calculated the fall in real wages for labourers and concludes that they fell by half.[45] His findings apply to wage rates; actual real income may have fallen even more because regular work may have been hard to get late in the century when there was a surplus of farm labourers. With shrinking incomes, it is understandable that the poor changed their eating habits and consumed more cheap grains – which provided the most calories per penny – and cut back on all other foodstuffs.

These comments on the diet of the poor have centred on the rural poor rather than the urban poor. The same dietary deterioration apparently took place in the towns and cities. It may, indeed, have been somewhat worse. The fall in real wages was comparable: the purchasing power of the wages of building craftsmen fell by just over half.[46] But it

---

[45] Bowden, 'Statistical appendix', p.864. Labourers' wages were also at times supplemented by various food or fuel allowances; see the judicious discussion by Everitt, 'Farm labourers', especially pp.435–42.

[46] Bowden, 'Statistical appendix', p.865. See also E. H. Phelps-Brown and S. V. Hopkins, 'Seven centuries of the prices of consumables, compared with builders' wage-rates', in E. M. Carus-Wilson (ed.), *Essays in Economic History* (London, 1962), II, pp.179–96.

CERTAINE PHILOSOPHICAL

Preparations of Foode and Beuerage for Sea-men, in their long voyages : with some necessary, approoued, and Her-

meticall medicines and Antidotes, fit to be had in readinesse at sea, for preuention or cure of diuers diseases.

And first for Foode. A cheape, fresh and lasting victuall, called by the name of *Macaroni* amongst the Italians, and not vnlike (taue onely in forme) to the *Cuscus in Barbary,* may be vpon reasonable warning prouided in any sufficient quantity, to serue either for change and variety of meat, or in the want of fresh victuall. With this, the Author furnished Sir *Francis Drake* and Sir *Iohn Hawkins,* in their last voyage.

2 Any broth or *Colase,* that will stand cleare and liquid, and not gellie or grow thicke when it is cold, may also be preserued by this fire of Nature from all mouldinaile, fowrenesse, or corruption, to any reasonable period of time that shalbe desired. A necessary secret for all sicke and weake persons at sea, when no fresh meate can be had, to strengthen or comfort them.

3 Now for Beuerage: All the water, which to that purpose shall bee thought needefull to be caried to sea, wil bee warranted to last sweete, good, and without any mention to putrefaction, for 2, 3, or 4 yeeres together. This is performed by a Philosophicall fire, being of a sympatheticall nature with all plants and Animals. In the space of one moneth, the Author wil prepare so many Tunnes thereof, as shall be reasonably required at his hands.

4 By this meanes also both Wine, Perrie, Sider, Beere, Ale, and Vineger, may be safely kept at sea, for any long voyage, without feare of growing dead, sowre or mustie.

5 And, as for Medicine, if any Nobleman, Gentleman, or Merchant, shall by his Physition be aduised to cary any speciall distilled waters, decoctions, or iuyces of any plant or any other liquid vegetable or animall body whatsoeuer with him in any long voyage, this Author will so prepare the same onely by fortifying it with his owne fire of kinde, that he may be assured of the lasting and durabilitie thereof, euen at his owne pleasure.

6 Here I may not omit the preparation of the iuice of Limons with this fire: because it hath of late been found by that worthy Knight Sir *Iames Lancaster,* to be an assured remedy in the scurby. And though their iuice will, by naturall working and fermenting, in the end so spirituaize it selfe, as that it will keepe and last either simply of it selfe, or by the help of a sweete oliue oyle *supernatant:* yet this Author is not ignorant, that it hath lost much of his first manifest nature, which it had whilest it was conteined within his owne pulp and fruit: (as is euident in the like example of wine, after it hath wrought long , which differeth exceedingly both in taste and nature from the grape out of which it was expressed) whereas being strengthened with this philosophicall fire , it retaineth still both the naturall taste, race, and verdure, that it had in the first expression : and so likewise of the Orange.

7 There is also a specificall powder for Agues *Quotidian,* and *Tertian* : and sometimes it helpeth *Quartans.* Halfe a dramme is sufficient for a man : and a quarter of a dramme for a child. It is taken in white Wine Beere, or Ale. It cureth sometimes at the first taking, often at the second , and seldome or neuer faileth at the third time. It is not offensiue to the taste. It expelleth the disease, without any euacuation or weakening of the Patient.

8 A sweete Paste, for the head-ache : which commonly giueth ease, in one houres space, either vpon the first or second taking, because it is specificall. The dose is the weight of 6.d.

9 A safe, generall & gentle purging powder, to be taken in white wine , working easily without any conuulsion, or other offence to

the stomacke. It is pleasant, and hath not any common or knowen purgatiue therein. It weakeneth not the Patient, neither doeth the body grow costiue after it: which is vsuall in most of the common purgatiues. There haue been so many trials made vpon all sorts of complexions with this powder , as that it may well deserue the name of a generall purge : yet I can least commend it in Cholericke bodies. The dose is two drammes and an halfe at a time. This being taken in warme weather for three dayes together, in the Spring and Fall, will preuent both the Gowte and Dropsie, and most of those diseases that spring from rheumaticke causes : and if it cure them in eight or ten dayes , take it for aduantage. It cureth the Pockes newly taken in hue or sixe dayes : and in tenne or twelue dayes, at the most, it cureth a deepe rooted Pocke.

10 And if the plague, burning Feauer, or small Pockes, or Meazels happen to infect any of the Souldiers or Mariners , or others in the ship: then it, within sixe or eight houres after infection, a dose of my Antidotary powder (whereof eight graines are sufficient) be taken, it commonly preuenteth the rage and violence of the Plague, by mastering the poyson, seldome suffering any sore to arise : and it disperseth and conquereth the matter of the small Pockes and Meazels: whereby in a few houres it vanisheth, without making the Patient heart-sicke. And, in the cure of any kind of poyson , no Vnicornes horne , no *Bezoar* stone, no *Terra Lemnia* or *Sigillata,* no Mithridate &c. is able to match the same, though taken in a double proportion. It is an excellent remedie against swooning, or any sodaine passion of the heart.

11 There is also a medicine, which I will commend for the sea (being a notable astringent powder) which stayeth any flux of blood in a short time , and often cureth the Piles and Emerrhoides.

12 The Essences of spices and floures (as of Cinnamom, Cloues, Mace, Nutmegs, Rosemary, Sage, &c) being in the forme of powders, may with lesse danger be caried at sea, are more apt to be mixed and incorporated with Syrups, Iuleps or Conserues, are more pleasing to nature, and are more familiarly taken , and with better successe then the chymicall oyles themselues, drawen by limbecke : their effects are answerable to the nature of the oyles.

Thus much I am bold to offer and publish for the benefit of seafaring men, who for the most part are destitute both of learned Physitions and skilfull Apothecaries : and therefore haue more neede then others to cary their owne defensatiues and medicines about them. Which if it shall receiue entertainment according to the worth thereof and my iust expectation , I may happily be encouraged to prie a little further into Natures Cabinet , and so to disperse some of her most secret Iewels , which she hath long time so carefully kept, onely for the vse of her dearest children: otherwise, finding no speedy or good acceptance of this my proffer (but rather crossed by malice or incredulity) I doe here free and enlarge my selfe from mine owne fetters : purposing to content my spirits, with such priuate and pleasing practises , as may better sort with my place and dignitie, and in likelyhood prooue also more profitable in the ende , then if I had thanklessely deuoted my selfe to *Bonum Publicum.* In which course, happy men are sometimes rewarded with good words: but few or none, in these dayes, with any reall recompense.

Ut Deus per Naturam, sic Natura per ignem Philosophicum.

H. P. *Miles.*

seems reasonable to suppose that the rural poor had better access to vegetables or wild berries, perhaps to game, or fish, than did the poor of London or the larger regional cities. I think it is also reasonable to suppose that the urban poor ate fewer dairy products than the country cottager with a cow or a couple of sheep pastured on the village common. The urban worker, however, badly and monotonously fed as he was, had one advantage over the poor countryman. The cities had charities which could blunt the effects of harvest failure. The cottager usually had no such charities to fall back on in the sixteenth century.

To this point, I have indicated some of the probable long-term changes in the diet of the poor but I have not discussed the short-term effects of harvest failure on the diet. When the harvest failed, and grain prices shot upward, the same dietary decay that took place over the long term was compressed into months or at most a few years. Harvests in the sixteenth century varied considerably from one year to the next depending on the vagaries of the weather, but W. G. Hoskins found six years of 'dearth' in the century, defining dearth as a harvest year when the price of wheat rose 50 per cent or more above the 31-year moving average price of wheat. These years were 1520, 1527, 1555, 1556, 1596 and 1597. Hoskins analysed only wheat prices in detail but he found that the price of other, cheaper grains moved up at the same time as wheat prices.[47] These years, then, indicate years of dearth for the grains – oats and barley – eaten by the poor as well as for wheat. Hoskins does not maintain that the price increases of all grains were the same but merely that they tended to move together. Of the six years identified as dearth years, four were paired: 1556–7 and 1596–7. Hoskins remarked on the tendency of good or bad harvests to run in series. One bad year often followed another because the hungry husbandmen had eaten some of the seed corn needed for the following year's planting.

The short-term price movements during periods of dearth do not seem to indicate a switch away from wheat to a cheaper substitute as occurred over the long term. In the dearth year of 1596 wheat prices rose 132 per cent, using wheat prices for 1584–93 as a comparative base.[48] Barley increased only 101 per cent and oats 127 per cent. Certainly all grains were very dear but the price of wheat rose relatively more than

[47] W. G. Hoskins, 'Harvest fluctuations and English economic history, 1480–1619', *Agricultural History Review*, XII (1964), 28–46. See also the critical essay by C. J. Harrison, 'Grain price analysis and harvest qualities, 1465–1634', ibid., XIX (1971), 135–55. Mr Harrison recognizes, however, that in years of high prices, all grain prices rise, although not all to the same extent.

[48] I have returned here to the prices in Bowden, 'Statistical appendix'.

the price of oats or barley, and also more than the prices of peas and beans, which respectively increased 94 and 105 per cent. The harvest failure of 1596 was caused by heavy summer and autumn rains. It may be, of course, that these rains were for some reason more destructive of wheat than of the other foodstuffs mentioned. However, I would suggest that the more likely explanation is that the purchasing power of the poor simply ran out, while the better-off, who bought wheat, continued to buy and forced further increases in the price of wheat.[49] The terrible harvest of 1596 came on the heels of the deficient harvests of 1594 and 1595, and by the harvest year of 1596 the resources of the poor may have been totally exhausted, thereby putting less pressure on the cheaper foods as compared to wheat. The dearth continued in 1597 and prices that year lend support to this hypothesis. Wheat rose 113 per cent above the base price, while barley increased only 62 per cent and oats 42 per cent. When Harrison wrote that in times of high grain prices the 'artificer and the poor labouring man' were forced to live on 'horse corn, I mean, beans, peason, oats, tares, and lentils', he was not referring to periods of dearth as severe as 1596–7, when the poor could not even afford 'horse corn', and had little or nothing to eat.[50]

To some extent these conclusions depend on the choice of base years used for price comparisons. If 1593 alone is used as the base to compare with 1596 and 1597, a different picture unfolds: in 1596 wheat prices rose 109 per cent above the 1593 price, barley 156 per cent, oats 175 per cent, peas 145 per cent and beans 120 per cent. But 1593 was a year of unusually low prices and I think comparison with the longer base period is preferable.

This analysis of price movements suggests, in short, that the diet of the poor changed for the worse during the sixteenth century as they ate more cheap grains and less wheat. Perhaps it would be more precise to say that there were more people eating cheap grains at the end of the century than at the beginning. The price figures may reveal the increase of the poor rather than any actual changes in their eating habits. But considered either way, more English men and women ate oats and barley in the 1590s than in the first decade of the century. The price analysis also suggests that in times of prolonged dearth, such as 1596–7, even the cheapest food was unavailable at a price the poor could afford.

---

[49] My general argument here owes much to P. Bowden, 'Agricultural prices, farm profits, and rents', in Thirsk (ed.), *The Agrarian History of England and Wales*, particularly pp. 601–5, but I am not sure I agree with his argument about short-term price movements, p.626.

[50] Harrison, *Description of England*, p.133.

This latter conclusion is confirmed by the burials listed in the parish registers. In 1597, the year in which the effects of the harvest failure of 1596 were felt, thousands starved to death or died of diseases brought on by malnutrition. This year brought a nasty end to the long century of rising food prices and falling real wages. A sample of 382 rural parish registers collected by the Cambridge Group for the History of Population and Social Structure from all across England shows that burials in 1597 rose 52 per cent above the average number for the years 1592–6 and 1598–1602. At the same time the number of baptisms fell by 19 per cent, as compared to the average for the other years, and England's population declined as burials exceeded baptisms.[51] The Cambridge Group's sample is somewhat weighted towards the south of England and does not truly reflect the killing power of famine in the north in 1597. In the parishes of Cumberland and Westmorland burials were three or four times the normal number; famine carried off perhaps one-tenth of the population. In these counties there is no evidence of any epidemic disease and the deaths appear to have been caused by simple starvation.[52] In the West Riding of Yorkshire mortality was very high, probably also because of starvation.[53] Although the north suffered more than the south, the Cambridge Group's sample indicates that it was a national crisis. Recent studies have also found localities in the south where the burials more than doubled.[54] In London, where John Graunt a half-century later would write that not one person in four thousand died of starvation, the number of deaths increased significantly in 1597, to almost double the number in years of low mortality.[55] The effect of the famine on London deserves further study; possibly the heightened mortality was the result of some epidemic disease unrelated to harvest failure, although it was not a plague year. London, and many other towns, had charities that were lacking in the countryside and over-all, I think, indigenous urban mortality was less than rural mortality. I use the word indigenous because the poor often flocked to the cities in hope of charitable relief, died there, and swelled the cities' burial figures. Philip

[51] I am indebted to the Cambridge Group for these data.

[52] A. B. Appleby, 'Disease or famine? Mortality in Cumberland and Westmorland 1580–1640', *Economic History Review*, 2nd ser., XXVI (1973), 408n.

[53] M. Drake, 'An elementary exercise in parish register demography', *Economic History Review*, 2nd ser., XIV (1961–2), 435–6.

[54] See D. Palliser, 'Dearth and disease in Staffordshire, 1540–1670', in C. W. Chalklin and M. A. Havinden (eds.), *Rural Change and Urban Growth 1500–1800* (London, 1974), pp. 54–75 and, for a crisis in the early seventeenth century, C. D. Rogers, *The Lancashire Population Crisis of 1623* (Manchester, 1975).

[55] See Appleby, *Famine in Tudor and Stuart England*, chapter 9.

Stubbes left a graphic account of the wanderings of the poor in times of want:

[They] die, some in ditches, some in holes, some in caves and dens, some in fields . . . rather like dogs than christian people . . . yet they are forced to walke the countries from place to place to seeke their releefe at every mans doore, except they wil sterve or famish at home . . . . Yea, in such troups doe they flocke, and in such swarmes doe they flowe, that you can lightlie go any way, and you shall see numbers of them at everie door, in everie lane, and in everie poor cave.[56]

Starvation was obviously an extreme case of dietary deprivation, an instance when the quantitative food needs of the poor were not even minimally met. The records are surprisingly silent about the suffering that took place in 1597 and it is only fairly recently that historians have argued that the poor actually starved. Perhaps emaciated beggars were too common, too 'normal' a sight to comment on. Perhaps the foreign visitors were struck by the wealth of the prosperous peasants but did not think the poor worth a comment, for the continent had also seen a great increase in the number of poor through the century.

As I indicated, the terrible harvest years of 1596 and 1597, coming together, caused death by famine. Was there also starvation in 1555 and 1556, when two other years of dearth fell together? This question deserves further study but, from the little now known, it does not seem so. The years 1557–9 were ones of terrible mortality, usually blamed on influenza, but the peak of the mortality came in 1558, more than one full year – and one plentiful harvest – after the harvest failure of 1556 had its impact.[57] Perhaps – but I am sceptical of this explanation – the epidemics of 1557–9 were unusually deadly because the resistance of the people had been lowered by the earlier food shortage.

In this essay I have argued that the diets of the rich and poor in a sense diverged during the sixteenth century. I do not mean that the poor ever ate the same food as the rich but that in the course of the century the food of the rich became increasingly luxurious while the food eaten by the poor became more heavily weighted towards cheap bread grains. When the tables of the rich groaned with meat of all kinds, the poor were eating less meat than formerly. Finally, at the end of the century – if not before – harvest failure brought starvation to many of the poor. Beyond this broad outline little is known about the diet of, or its effect on, the

[56]   Philip Stubbes, *The second part of the anatomie of abuses*, ed. F. J. Furnivall (1882), p.43.
[57]   Wrigley, *Population and History*, pp.74–5.

daily life of, the sixteenth-century English man or woman. Were the poor so chronically underfed that they were incapable of doing a hard day's work? One recent study has suggested that the inadequate diet limited the amount of work that could be done in early modern England and argues that only when food became more plentiful was it possible to work the long hours necessary for the industrial revolution.[58] The problem is, however, that we do not know what the caloric intake was, except during times of famine when it was clearly insufficient. Nor can we be sure how people adapted to their diet. Without more evidence it is difficult to make a convincing case for this theory. Were the malnourished poor easy prey to the epidemic diseases of the period? Another recent study has discovered no clear correlation between high food prices and the incidence of epidemic disease in London, but more work should be done on this important topic.[59] One can at least hope that the problem of diet in the sixteenth century will soon receive the historical attention that heretofore has been lavished on political and religious history.

[58] H. Freudenberger and G. Cummins, 'Health, work, and leisure before the Industrial Revolution', *Explorations in Economic History*, XIII (1976), 1–12.

[59] A. Appleby, 'Nutrition and disease: the case of London, 1550–1750', *Journal of Interdisciplinary History*, VI (1975), 1–22.

4

By what disease or casualty: the changing face of death in London

THOMAS R. FORBES

If you open a textbook, any textbook, of medical history and try to find what health conditions were in rural France in the eighteenth century, or what disease meant to the family of an artisan at the same period, you will as a rule not find any information. We know much about the history of the great medical discoveries but very little on whether they were applied, or to whom they were applied.

Henry Sigerist (1940)

What Henry Sigerist called 'the social history of medicine' derives its importance from the fact that it is the collective medical history of the people of a community, or a city, or a country.[1] It is the story not of the doctor but of the patient, an account not of what contemporary medicine might do but of what it did – or, more often, did not – do. The available records, in most cases kept by laymen, are confused for us not only by the medical conceptions of the period but also by the layman's ignorance of medicine itself. Information about the mortality of English parishes and towns up to the middle of the nineteenth century must usually be derived from parish registers and the London bills of mortality; in spite of their limitations, such sources are the best surviving, and they can be invaluable (see Plates 1 and 2). Tabulations of

[1] H. E. Sigerist, 'The social history of medicine', *Western Journal of Surgery, Obstetrics and Gynecology*, XLVIII (1940), 715. See also T. McKeown, 'A sociological approach to the history of medicine', *Medical History*, XIV (1970), 342–51.

The present article is an edited version of the article of the same title published in the *Journal of the History of Medicine and Allied Sciences* in 1976. This was the published form of the Gideon De Laune Lecture, delivered 23 April 1975 to the Worshipful Society of Apothecaries of London. My best thanks are due to the Guildhall Library, Corporation of London, and to its former Keeper of Manuscripts, Dr A. E. J. Hollaender; to the Archives Department, Westminster City Library, and to its Archivist, Miss Margaret Swarbrick, for telling me of these records and for repeated and generous assistance. I am also grateful to the vicar and churchwardens of the parish of St Martin-in-the-Fields for kind permission to reproduce information from the records of that parish.

This research was supported in part by Public Health Service Grants 1-R01-LM-00019, 5-R01-LM-00570 and 5-R01-LM-01538, all from the National Library of Medicine, and by PHS 5-S01-RR-05358-09 and -10.

births and deaths by year do indicate, up to a point, the rising and falling tides of population in a parish. Such data often provide the best available vital statistics, particularly for provincial parishes, for the years before 1801.

A few exceptional parish registers and mortality books record not only the name (and hence almost always the sex) of each person who died and was buried in a parish and the date of interment, but also his or her age and the supposed cause of death. Sometimes other information was added, such as a notation that the deceased was an occupant of a workhouse, or a prison. Transcription and tabulation of such material can make possible a useful analysis. A parish record provides a sample, not a broad survey, but as the samples accumulate and are compared, a wider view appears. I shall try to show parts of such a picture drawn from the records of five London parishes (Table 1), beginning with the burials themselves.[2]

Not the least of urban sanitary problems was the interment of bodies. The parish of St Martin-in-the-Fields comprised only twenty-six acres and was one of London's smallest.[3] A report that in 1680 it had 40,000 inhabitants was probably exaggerated.[4] Yet from June 1685 to July 1687

Table 1. *Total burials in five London parishes*

St Botolph without Aldgate	1558–1626	22,731
St Martin-in-the-Fields	1685–7	3,465
St Martin-in-the-Fields	1694–1703	12,391
St Giles Cripplegate	1774–93	6,845
St Giles Cripplegate	1833–5	725
St Anne Soho	1814–28	8,039
St Bride Fleet Street	1820–49	4,513
		58,709

² See also T. R. Forbes, *Chronicle from Aldgate: Life and Death in Shakespeare's London* (New Haven, Conn., 1971), pp.39–40, 96–9, 165–8; idem, 'Mortality books for 1774–1793 and 1833–1835 from the parish of St Giles, Cripplegate, London', *Bulletin of the New York Academy of Medicine*, 2nd ser., XLVII (1971), 1524–36; idem, 'Mortality books for 1820 to 1849 from the parish of St Bride, Fleet Street, London', *Journal of the History of Medicine*, XXVII (1972), 15–29; idem, 'Sextons' day books for 1685–1687 and 1694–1703 from the Parish of St Martin-in-the-Fields, London', *Yale Journal of Biology and Medicine*, XLVI (1973), 142–50; idem, 'Burial records for the parish of St Anne Soho, London, in 1814–1828', ibid., XLVII (1974), 93–100.

³ J. Angus, 'Old and new bills of mortality; movement of the population; death and fatal diseases in London during the last fourteen years', *Journal of the Statistical Society of London*, XVII (1854), 117–42.

⁴ H. B. Wheatley, *London Past and Present* (1891), pp.477–80. See Plate 5 for a view of sixteenth-century London.

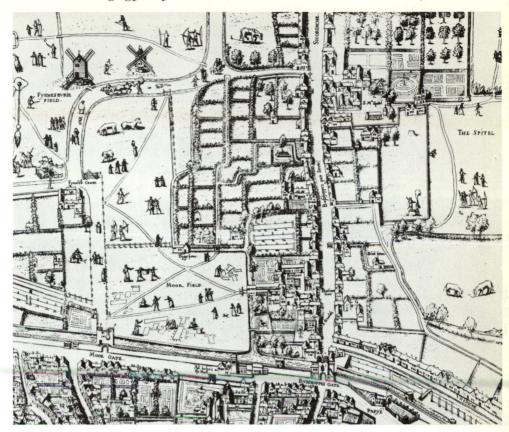

Plate 5. The Moorfields district of London in 1559
One of only two surviving sections of a detailed map of London, which formed the basis of subsequent smaller-scale maps. The Moorfields district includes the Bethlem Hospital and part of the parish of St Botolph without Bishopsgate. Reproduced by permission of the Museum of London.

and June 1694 to March 1703, the equivalent of eleven years, there were in this parish no fewer than 15,856 burials, an annual average of over 1,400. As London's population grew, the difficulties in finding space for graves became worse. In June 1842 a Select Committee of the House of Commons, appointed to investigate the problems of burial in the metropolis, published a horrifying report. Gravediggers, for example, had to employ ghoulish ingenuity to find spaces for the dead. The sexton of St Anne Soho had become notorious for his methods of making it possible to cram ever more bodies into the ground.[5] He seems to have had little choice; there were 8,039 burials in fifteen years, an average of more than 500 annually, in the church of St Anne and its graveyard.

The burial records to be described for the five London parishes included age at death, except for the parish of St Martin-in-the-Fields where individuals were classified only as men, women or children. As already mentioned, sex could almost always be determined from the given name. Information as to the 'cause' of death was supplied to the minister or clerk of the parish by searchers, an office begun in the sixteenth century which employed for a pittance old women to examine or 'view' the body. Originally their examination seems to have been for signs of plague, but later other alleged causes of death were also reported. John Graunt, London haberdasher, freeman of the Draper's Company, and vital statistician, explained how the system worked.

When anyone dies, then, either by tolling, or ringing of a bell, or by bespeaking of a grave of the sexton, the same is known to the searchers, corresponding with the said sexton. The searchers hereupon (who are antient matrons, sworn to their office) repair to the place where the dead corps lies, and by view of the same, and by other enquiries, they examine by what disease or casualty the corps died. Hereupon they make their report to the parish clerk.[6]

The searchers were not always reliable.[7] Supposedly selected for their honesty and ability, they took an oath of office and were subject to penalties for failure to perform their duties properly. Nevertheless the searchers functioned as laymen, obtaining their information by more or less casual inspection of the body and by questioning the family and neighbours. The old women were poorly paid for their unpleasant and sometimes dangerous job, and they could be bribed to report that a death actually due, for example, to the plague was instead caused by a less threatening disease. In this way the family of the deceased could escape the mandatory quarantine for plague. Finally, the searchers were ignorant. A correspondent in *The Gentleman's Magazine* complained in 1799: 'In two parishes, which I could point out, the searchers cannot write; the mistakes they make are numberless in the spelling of christian and surnames, for, they trust to memory till they get home; then, child

[5] *Report from the Select Committee on Improvement of the Health of Towns . . . Effect of Interment of Bodies in Towns*, P.P. 1842, X, p.349; J. Saunders, 'London burials', in C. Knight (ed.), *London* (6 vols., 1841–4), IV, pp.161–74.

[6] John Graunt, *Natural and political observations on the bills of mortality*, reprint of 6th edn (1759), pp.7–9, 13–14.

[7] T. R. Forbes, 'The searchers', *Bulletin of the New York Academy of Medicine*, 2nd ser., I (1974), 1031–8.

or neighbour writes what they suppose it to be.'[8]

Since the reign of Henry VIII parishes had been required to maintain records of baptisms, weddings and burials.[9] Formal reporting of this information for central registration and tabulation, however, did not begin until the Registration Act was passed in 1836 and the office of searcher became obsolete. Even then, registration was optional; it was not made obligatory until 1874.[10] Medical certification of London deaths was not required until the same year. Hence the essential role of the searchers during two and a half centuries was to record the cause of death in the absence of any other public register of deaths. Because of their manifest deficiencies, one might be tempted to dismiss the searchers as historical curiosities. But to do so would be to fail to recognize the importance of these 'antient matrons' to English vital statistics. Most of what we know about the incidence of various 'causes' of death as reported in the bills of mortality and a few parish registers came from information supplied by the searchers.

The records for St Botolph's parish are unusually full and descriptive. Indeed, the registers are almost day books for the parish. Here we are reminded that death did not always come at home. There are, for example, notations of burial services for men and women who died in the cage, a kind of small gaol or covered pen, mentioned centuries later in *Oliver Twist*:

Henrye Buxton of Aldewarke in Yorkshire who died in the cage next to Aldgate.
William Jones a vagrant whoe died in the cage in Eastsmithfield.

Death could come anywhere.

Margaritt whoe died by the towne ditch.
Grace Butcher who dyed on the heighe waye on Tower hill.
A boye that died in a hayloft att the Red Lyon.
Robert a vagrant that died in the streete.
A Poore woman being vagrant whose name was not known shee dyed in the striete under the seate before Mr. Christian Shipmans howse called the crowne without aldgate on she being in the high striete. . . . yearse xxiiij she was no parishioner with us neather cowld we learne from whence she came she dyed of the plague.
Jane Quyre, an Irish Child who dyed in the street, daughter to an Irish vagrant.
A poore man who died in a stable whose name wee could not learne.[11]

8 [Anon.], *The Gentleman's Magazine*, LXIX (1799), 657–8.
9 Forbes, *Chronicle from Aldgate*, pp.39–40.
10 C. Singer and E. A. Underwood, *A Short History of Medicine* (New York, 1962), p.714.
11 Forbes, *Chronicle from Aldgate*, pp.75–80.

Since the first census was not taken in England until 1801, we know almost nothing about 'the population at risk'. Hence we cannot determine the incidence of deaths from disease in terms of rates per thousand population. However, it is useful to calculate deaths from a given 'cause' or for a given time period as a percentage of all deaths. Also, since all the parishes are in London and all were crowded and poor, their mortality statistics may legitimately be compared. The differences and similarities that are then observed reflect changes and lack of change in the proportions of deaths from various causes in these sample parishes

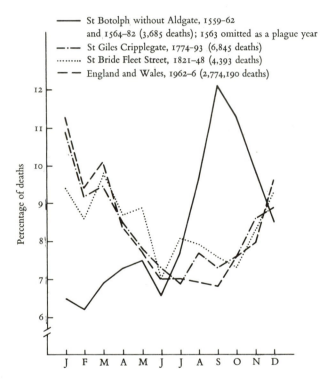

Fig. 1.   Percentage distribution of deaths by month.

during successive periods of history. Sometimes related data are not directly comparable, reminding us that until well into the nineteenth century there was little or no standardization of the recording of mortality statistics.

If the percentage of all deaths, except plague deaths, in each month is plotted graphically for three parishes and the curves are compared, that for St Botolph differs conspicuously from the others (Fig. 1). The curve for St Botolph's parish is unusual because of the relatively high proportions of deaths in August–November. For the other parishes during the seventeenth, eighteenth and nineteenth centuries, and for England and Wales for 1962–6,[12] the shape of the curves is very much the same. A curious feature of all the curves, except that for St Botolph's parish, is the modest but definite peak in March, interrupting the steady decline from January to summer. Thomas Short's study of the London bills of mortality includes data for the eighteenth century which reveal a similar spike.[13] I have found no explanation for the March peak.

In St Botolph's parish in the sixteenth century the clerk recorded 'still-born' deaths. It is likely that he was talking about what we would call 'foetal deaths', that is foetuses dying at any stage of pregnancy as well as at term. The annual totals of such deaths fluctuated greatly, probably reflecting various degrees of failure to report them. Still-born deaths in St Botolph comprised 5.8 per cent of all deaths, including those from plague. John Graunt, writing in 1662 about his findings from the bills of mortality, noted that

the abortives and stillborn are about the twentieth part [5 per cent] of those that are christned; and the numbers seemed the same thirty years ago as now, which shews there were more in proportion in those years than now; or else, that in these latter years due accounts have not been kept of the abortives, as having been buried without notice, and perhaps not in church-yards.[14]

Graunt's remark well illustrated the difficulty in obtaining reliable information concerning still-births. About a century later in St Martin's parish their proportion had dropped to 3.2 per cent. The nineteenth-century figure for St Giles's parish was 2.1 per cent, only slightly higher than the proportion of all foetal deaths in England and Wales and in Greater London in 1968.[15]

Age at death was recorded, as already mentioned, for all except St Martin's parish. If for a given parish the number of deaths in each of the standard age groups is counted, and that total is calculated as a percentage of all deaths, the results can be presented graphically (Fig. 2). When this is done for the parishes except St Martin's and also for England and Wales in 1968,[16] several facts at once are apparent. Most conspicuous is the huge proportion of parish deaths – 31 per cent to 48

[12] *The Registrar General's Statistical Review of England and Wales* (London, 1964–8), pt I, table 16.
[13] Thomas Short, *New observations, natural, moral, civil, political and medical, on city, town and country bills of mortality* (1750), pp.176, 192, 207.
[14] Graunt, *Natural and political observations*, p.16.
[15] *The Registrar General's Statistical Review of England and Wales* (London, 1970), pt I, tables E, 25.
[16] Ibid., table 14.

per cent – under the age of 5. Until the 60–9-year age group is reached, the percentages of deaths in past centuries in London, as represented by our samples, continue to exceed the modern percentages. Then, as the 1968 curve climbs to its peak at about the biblical three score years and ten, the curves for past centuries drop even lower, simply because very few people survived past 80. Except for deaths in the under-5-year groups, the curves for the four parishes are quite similar.

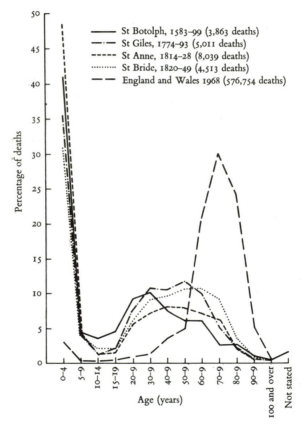

Fig. 2.   Percentage distribution of, deaths by age group.

Bearing in mind the very small percentage of under-5 deaths in modern times and the very large percentage of such deaths in the parishes, we can now observe the distribution of deaths during the first five years of life (Fig. 3). The graph makes clear that in 1968 nearly all deaths under age 5 occurred in the first twelve months; additional data, not included here, reveal that almost 50 per cent of the deaths under age

5 actually occurred in the first week. In other words, as we know, infants who now survive the first hours and days of life have a good chance of reaching maturity. In the parishes in earlier centuries, mortality continued high, diminishing only slowly during the first five years. Thomas Short mournfully concluded in 1750, 'What a fatal time is infancy and childhood to young citizens!'[17]

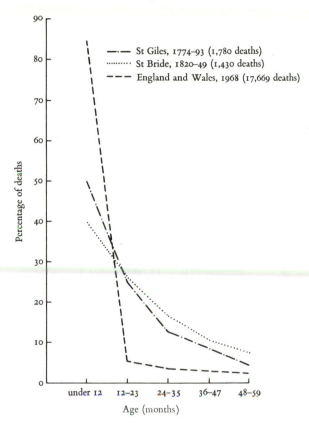

Fig. 3.   Percentage distribution of deaths under age 5.

Although plague was intermittent, no other disease caused such fearful loss of life in relatively short periods of time (Fig. 4). This graph for the parish of St Botolph shows the effects of four epidemics. In most years burials exceeded christenings in number, a deficiency made up by the steady migration of country dwellers into the city. Tuberculosis was a major threat. 'Con' in the St Botolph records stood for 'consumption',

---

[17]   Short, *Bills of mortality*, p.207.

'convulsions', or perhaps both (Table 2). Certainly tuberculosis seems to have been the leading endemic disease, particularly if we assume that 'pining', 'long sick', and 'decay' sometimes masked additional cases of this disease. Such terms, descriptive of the course rather than the nature of an illness, were frequently employed by the searchers.

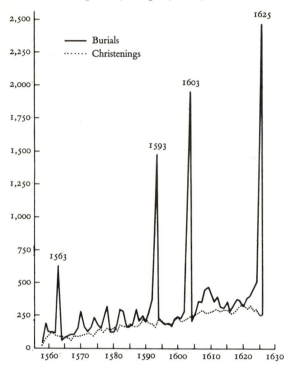

Fig. 4.   St Botolph without Aldgate: burials and christenings 1558–1626.

The St Anne and St Bride records reported many cases of 'watery head', 'water on the brain', and 'dropsy on the brain'. This was a form of hydrocephalus. Most of the victims were from 6 months to 4 years old; one of every eight deaths under age 5 was attributed to this cause. Chronic hydrocephalus is a relatively uncommon condition, but in the two parishes acute hydrocephalus, or tuberculous meningitis, was much less so. Short's review of the London bills of mortality for 1734–42 indicates that 5.1 per cent of deaths at all ages were ascribed to 'head-mould shot' or 'horseshoe head', old names that probably also referred to what we call hydrocephalus.[18] The corresponding figures for 'watery

18   Ibid., pp.176, 192.

Table 2. *Proportional mortality (per cent) from ten most common 'causes' of death*

	St Botolph	St Martin	St Giles	St Anne	St Bride
Plague	23.6				
Consumption		16.6	8.5		9.6
Convulsions	22.2	10.3	32.5	14.1	5.6
[Not stated]	14.1				4.6
Pining, decline	13.2		13.9	25.3	17.1
Ague, fever	6.1	9.5	23.7		
Flux, colic	2.5	13.3			
Smallpox	2.4	5.3	5.0	4.1	
Childbed	1.5		0.8		
Teeth	1.1	10.4			
Age		5.4	6.9	8.4	5.6
Still-born		3.2			
Rising lights		2.8			
Stoppage		2.8			
Dropsy			2.7	3.5	3.8
Lunacy			1.6		
Suddenly			1.3		
Inflammation				10.8	5.5
Whooping cough				4.6	3.3
Measles				4.6	
Watery head				4.2	4.1
Asthma				3.2	4.9
	86.7	79.6	96.9	82.8	64.1

head' in the two parishes were 4.1 per cent and 4.2 per cent. The tubercle bacillus must have been widely distributed in London. As late as 1842, according to an early *Report of the Registrar General*, 3.8 per cent of all deaths in metropolitan London were ascribed to hydrocephalus.[19] 'Convulsions', like 'dropsy', described a symptom; its cause is not revealed. Convulsions were reported as a cause of death mostly in children. In St Giles's parish more than 90 per cent of babies dying under 1 year of age were said to have succumbed to this condition.

Deaths in childbed constituted 0.8 per cent to 1.5 per cent of all deaths.

---

[19] *Sixth Annual Report of the Registrar General of Births, Deaths and Marriages in England* (1845), pp.94–5.

In St Botolph's parish there were seventy-six deaths in childbed and 3,236 christenings in the years 1583–99. This is equivalent to a maternal death rate of 23.5 per 1,000 deliveries. In St Martin's parish the proportional mortality rate, 1.3 per cent of all deaths, was roughly 100 times the 1968 rate for England and Wales. Midwifery in the sixteenth and seventeenth centuries was, with a few notable exceptions, at a very low level, and childbirth was a perilous experience.[20] There is no clue as to the specific cause of death in childbirth except for three or four instances in St Botolph's parish when it was noted that the pregnant woman also had plague, stone or colic. Deaths in childbirth constituted 0.7 per cent of all London deaths in 1842.[21]

'Teeth' or 'breeding of the teeth' was often listed as a cause of death in infants. Thomas Phaer wrote in *The Book of Children* in 1553 that 'About the seventh month, sometimes more, sometimes less, after the birth, it is natural for a child for to breed teeth, in which time many one is sore vexed, with sundry diseases and pains'.[22] Of course children did not die because they were teething, but they might succumb to a concurrent disease. Even in the eighteenth century a medical authority observed that 'above a tenth part of infants die in teething, by symptoms proceeding from the irritation of the tender nervous parts of the jaws, occasioning inflammations, fevers, convulsions, gangrenes, &c.'[23] Teething was blamed for 2 per cent of all London deaths in 1842.[24]

St Botolph's parish records ascribed three deaths to 'mother', an old name for the uterus. 'Rising lights' accounted for 2.8 per cent of all deaths in St Martin's parish; lights once meant lungs. Seventeenth-century physicians argued as to whether 'rising of the lights' was the same affliction as 'rising of the mother', 'choking of the mother', the 'hysteric passion' (hysteria), or a related malady. Sennert spoke of the rising of 'malignant vapours up through the veins and arteries to the lungs, and by communication thence to the heart, and this upon the least commotion or unusual motion of the mind or body; which being the cause also of that distemper which hath been hitherto supposed to be seated in the mother'.[25] It was only much later that someone pointed out

20 T. R. Forbes, 'The regulation of English midwives in the sixteenth and seventeenth centuries', *Medical History*, VIII (1964), 235–44.
21 *Sixth Annual Report of the Registrar General*, pp.94–5.
22 Thomas Phaer, *The boke of chyldren*, ed. A. V. Neale and H. R. E. Wallis (1553; Edinburgh, etc., 1955), pp.38–9.
23 William Buchan, *Domestic medicine* (Boston, 1793), p.377.
24 *Sixth Annual Report of the Registrar General*, pp.94–5.
25 M[archamont] N[edham], *Medela medicinae: a plea for the free profession ... of physick* (1665), pp.50–1.

that men can also become hysterical. Not unrelated was 'the vapours', a form of melancholy caused, it was believed, by gas in the stomach or intestines. 'Rising of the lights' was a term still in popular use in the nineteenth century.

Individuals sometimes died suddenly. A not unusual explanation in Shakespeare's day was that the victim had been 'taken in a planet'. Of twenty-two such incidents in St Botolph's parish, all but four took place in 1593, a plague year. Seventeen of these fatalities occurred in children. The terms are probably related to 'planet struck' and 'moon struck', that is, the victim was thought to have been suddenly smitten by the hostile influence of a planet. In *Hamlet* Marcellus speaks of the season

Wherein our Saviour's birth is celebrated,
The bird of dawning singeth all night long:
And then, they say, no spirit dare stir abroad:
The nights are wholesome; then no planets strike.[26]

Nicholas Culpeper, a seventeenth-century physician, shed light on this malady when he wrote of catalepsy:

in English it is called congelation, or taking, and by the ignorant struck with a Planet.
It is a sudden detention and taking both of body and mind, both sense and moving being lost, the sick remaining in the same figure of body wherin he was taken; whether he sit or lie, or whether his mouth and eyes were open or shut, as they are taken in the disease so they remaine.[27]

'Stroke' even now refers to the sudden onset of an illness, as in sunstroke or stroke of apoplexy.

Death from 'spleen' or from a 'thought' – 'he died of inward grief of mind or of a thought' – was reported by the clerk of St Botolph for eleven men and ten women. 'Spleen' and 'thought' seem to have referred to what we would call depression or anxiety; one is reminded of 'Take no thought for your life' and 'Take therefore no thought for the morrow' (Matt. 6:25, 31, 34, etc.) in the contemporary King James translation of the Bible. Deaths allegedly from 'lunacy', of an unspecified nature, represented 1.6 per cent of all deaths in St Giles's parish in the eighteenth and early nineteenth centuries. For a small fraction of this group a second fatal condition such as 'fever' or 'decline' was also reported.

'Inflammation', 'whooping cough' or 'chin cough', and 'measles'

---

[26] *Hamlet*, act I, scene 1.
[27] Nicholas Culpeper, *Culpeper's last legacy* (1655), p.30.

were prominent as alleged causes of death in the parishes of St Anne and St Bride, but were less conspicuous in the earlier records. Diagnosis of whooping cough and measles was probably less precise than it is now. There were 271 deaths from 'thrush' in St Martin's parish.

Many other real or imagined diseases were less frequently claimed as causes of death. 'Swine pox' is said to have been a Tudor name for what we call chicken pox. 'Tympany' colourfully described an excessive accumulation of abdominal gas or air. 'Bleach' and 'scald head' were ill-defined skin diseases. 'Purples' was probably 'purpura'. 'Haemorrhoids', 'fistulas', and 'ruptures' are mentioned. Other actual or alleged causes included 'stoppage', 'rickets', 'ulcer', 'apoplexy', 'cancer', 'impostume' (abscess), 'scurvy', 'worms', 'gangrene' and 'mortification', 'croup', 'liver grown', 'scarlet fever', 'cholera', and 'palsy'. 'Surfeit', supposedly brought on by an excess of food or drink, was not infrequently listed as a cause of death in Shakespeare's day and later. Thus in the St Botolph record for 23 February 1588: 'Peter Yeop being a stearman [steers-man] born in Skee Dam in Holland . . . being drunk at the house of George Johnson a carter dwelling in the liberty of Eastsmithfield where he ended his life of a surfeit with drink . . .'. 'Great age' was listed as the cause of death of forty-three persons in St Botolph's parish. Twelve of them allegedly lived for 100 to 110 years. The longest life was accredited to 'Agnes Sadler widow of the age of 126 years'.

Of all persons buried in St Giles's parish from 1774 to 1793, 1.8 per cent succumbed in hospitals. Fifty-six of these people died in St Bartholomew's and fifty in St Luke's; both institutions were outside the parish but lay near by. Smaller numbers ended their lives in Guy's, St Thomas's, St Margaret's, St George's, and the Smallpox and Lying-In Hospitals. The causes of death were varied but not remarkable. While 41 per cent of all parish burials during this period were those of children, only 16 per cent of those who died in hospitals were children. It was a prejudice of the nineteenth century that the mother herself should care for her child rather than send it to an institution;[28] this idea had its roots in the past. Of the hospital deaths at all ages, 60 per cent were male, 38 per cent female and the rest unidentified as to sex. One can only guess at the reasons for this imbalance.

The sextons of St Giles's parish buried a good many persons who had died in the workhouse or were classified as 'poor'. These categories constituted 6.8 per cent and 14.9 per cent, respectively, of all deaths in

---

[28] C. Dainton, *The Story of England's Hospitals* (London, 1961), pp.93, 95.

the years 1774–93 and 1833–5. About 13 per cent of the workhouse occupants and 44 per cent of the other 'poor' were children. Females in the workhouse considerably outnumbered the males, a situation reflecting the greater economic dependency of women. Of fifty deaths from cholera in the parish, thirty-five were those of workhouse inmates. No cause was recorded for nearly half of the deaths of poor persons and residents of workhouses.

The St Anne funeral day books also identified workhouse occupants. Their deaths constituted 5.1 per cent of all deaths in the parish. Fifty-seven per cent of those persons dying in the workhouse were females. If, again, this figure is taken to be proportional to the sex ratio among the living occupants of this institution, we would find further evidence for the relatively greater problems of women in finding economic support. Examination of the distribution by age of persons dying in the workhouse yields the not surprising conclusion that, compared with all persons who succumbed in the parish, proportionately fewer children and more elderly persons ended their days in this institution.

In St Bride's parish in the first part of the nineteenth century there was also a high proportion of parish deaths in the workhouse. As of May 1840 it and others of a similar nature were merged as the West London Union, an establishment that was utilized jointly by adjoining parishes. Workhouses had sunk to a low level of mismanagement, and reforms were introduced in 1834. Deplorable conditions again developed,[29] as Charles Dickens and others have made clear. Angus quotes figures from *The Registrar General's Weekly Reports* showing that in 1850 just over 1 per cent of London's inhabitants was in workhouses.[30] The fact that from 1820 to 1849 15.7 per cent of all persons buried in St Bride's parish died in the workhouse or in the West London Union would argue that this parish had more than its share of the poor. Of the 709 persons who succumbed in the workhouse or union, 53.5 per cent were female, although females constituted only 47.2 per cent of all other parish deaths. The incidence of medically certified but non-specific reasons for death – 'debility', 'decay', or 'decline' – was more than twice as high in institutions for the poor as in the rest of the parish. One wonders about the care with which death certificates for paupers were issued.

The mortality books for the parishes of St Giles and St Bride also identify individuals who ended their lives in gaols and prisons. Between

---

[29] *Encyclopaedia Britannica*, 14th edn (1929), art. 'Workhouse'.
[30] Angus, 'Old and new bills of mortality', p.139.

1774 and 1793, forty-one persons dying in the Wood Street Compter and one in the Poultry Compter were buried by the parish. These were debtors' prisons, lying just south of St Giles's parish. Close to the southern boundary of St Bride's parish and near Blackfriars Bridge stood the massive Bridewell, in the nineteenth century a house of correction until it was torn down in 1864.[31] Two persons who died there, a 9-month-old girl and a woman of 30, are listed in the St Bride mortality books.

The equally notorious Fleet Prison stood on what was originally the eastern bank of the Fleet River, later the Fleet Ditch, and eventually covered over. The prison then stood on the east side of Farringdon Street, within the ward of Farringdon Without and the parish of St Bride Fleet Street. By Act of Parliament in 1842 the prisons of the Fleet, Marshalsea and Queen's Bench were merged into the Queen's Prison, and the Fleet Prison was mercifully closed. Two years later it was purchased by the corporation of the City of London and demolished. In the nineteenth century the Fleet was mostly a prison for bankrupt persons and debtors. Its debtor population in the period 1830 to 1834 was between 700 and 884, with the amounts owed by the prisoners ranging from £2 to £18,107.[32] The mortality books of St Bride's parish record the deaths of fifty-six prisoners in the Fleet between 1820 and 1839. The ages at death of the thirty-nine males and seventeen females were from 2 days to 86 years, but thirty-two of the thirty-nine were between 30 and 68 years old when they died. Twelve of the children whose deaths in prison are noted were under the age of 9. The list of causes, except in length, is not remarkable. It should be remembered that at this period the usual time spent in prison was comparatively short. In the first quarter of 1850, for example, there were only 5,435 persons in all of London's prisons, and their average stay was fifty-three days.[33]

Fatalities from accident and violence comprised, depending on the parish, from 0.6 per cent to 1.9 per cent of all deaths. The comparable figure for England and Wales in 1968 was 3.9 per cent.[34] That the proportion of accidental and violent deaths today looms two or more times as high as in the past is undoubtedly due to our greatly lessened mortality from disease. Fatalities not caused by illness are now relatively

31 H. A. Harben, *A Dictionary of London* (London, 1918), pp.235, 368.
32 Ibid.; *Encyclopaedia Britannica*, art. 'Fleet Prison'; J. Ashton, *The Fleet* (1888), pp.1, 2, 13, 313, 318–19.
33 Angus, 'Old and new bills of mortality', p.139.
34 *Registrar General's Statistical Review* (1970), pt I, table 7.

more conspicuous. The church records did not always note the reasons for accidental and violent deaths, particularly in the parishes of St Anne and St Bride. Since about one fifth of all such deaths were for unexplained reasons, we must approach any tabulation with caution. Of the specified causes drowning led the list, constituting relatively a far greater hazard than it does now (Table 3). Nearly all drowning accidents

Table 3. *Causes of accidental death (per cent)*

	St Botolph, St Martin and St Giles combined	England and Wales, 1968
Drownings	21.2	2.5
Overlaid	19.9	
'Killed'	19.0	
Falls	13.4	30.9
Horses, vehicles	6.5	36.1
Burns, scalds	4.8	4.8
Buildings collapsed	3.9	
Crushing, blows	3.0	2.3
[Not stated]	3.0	
Guns, gunpowder	2.6	0.2
Asphyxia, gas poisoning	2.2	4.6
Poisoning by solid or fluid	0.4	2.5
Other		16.2
Total deaths	231	17,815

occurred in the Thames, and many were occupational. Boatmen were lost when their skiffs and wherries were upset, sailors fell from their ships, and labourers carrying sacks on their backs slipped from the planks that led from barges to wharves. Of course the Thames was a threat chiefly to people who lived or worked on or near it. St Botolph's parish was close by; its records list twenty-one drownings, but not all were in the river. A little girl of 3 lost her life when a chair in a privy 'whelmed backward' and she fell into the town ditch (13 October 1596). Joan Mallett, another child, 'being alone by itself playing in the Grey Hound Alley near a shallow well of a garden . . . where by chance the said child falling into the well was drowned and the coroner's [in]quest having seen and viewed the said child she was buried the xiii^th day of June anno 1592 years iii'. A hazardous condition was responsible for the death on 30 August 1598 of another girl who being a chyld abowt the age of ffyve yeares was playing with other smale children on wednesday the xxxth day of august ano 1598 in the yeard of Mr Thomas Goodman gen[tleman] neare a pond in the said yeard, being in the said parish where the said Margaret fell in the said pond neare a stable end and with the water of the said pond the said Margaret was choked and drowned whereof she dyed wch pond lying open neare the sayd stable was verie dangerous for children, wherefore it was presented by the said crowners quest.

A boy aged 7 or 8 'was drowned in Goodman's Fields in a pond, playing with other boys there and swimming' (19 May 1615). A young girl 'drowned in a pond behind her father's house . . . by mischance fetching a pail of water' (17 December 1597). A young woman 'drowned in the town ditch near the said garden stair fetching of water the xxviith day of August anno 1598 on a Tuesday at night about the hour of viii or nine of the clock'. It is a measure of sixteenth-century sanitation that the town ditch which supplied water for domestic use also served the privies.

A 26-year-old bargeman was 'washing himself in the river of the Thames where the stream [current] taking him he was drowned' (28 June 1591). A cooper employed on a lighter transporting beer from a wharf to a ship in the Pool of London died when he fell into the river 'near Limehouse' (23 May 1590). Another accident involved the deaths of several people in December 1616. One of them was Joan Moorton, wife of a sailor. 'She (with divers others) was by great misfortune drowned in the river of Thames . . . coming by water from Wandsworth and not found till this time, the Lord deliver us from such like mischance, for God knoweth, it was a sorrowful voyage to them.'

Falls were proportionately much less frequent then than now. Many were from ladders and scaffolds, on stairs, from a loft or window, or on a ship. In March 1596

Derick van Veedar a straunger being the cooke of a shipp called the Samson of Emdon . . . being in the Road before woollwich fell from the mast in to the ship whereof he dyed . . . he was a bacheler & was no parishioner with us.

Edward Frier, a Bricklayer who dwelt in the Minories street . . . died of a fall, which he had from the topp of the new Church at Wapping, where he wrought [3 November 1618].

Road traffic, then as now, was a hazard. Streets could be crowded with people of all ages and with horses and horsedrawn vehicles. Now the roads have fewer people and unending cars and lorries; street fatalities as a proportion of all deaths are more than five times what they were in earlier centuries. Perhaps the greater speed and lesser noise of the motor vehicle contribute to the difference.

For burns and scalds the figures show no change. Burns in the past nearly always involved either the old and infirm, or young children who were left unattended by adults. Evidence from some of my unpublished research indicates that in the nineteenth century, at least, many burns occurred partly because of the pinafores worn by little children. These garments were easily ignited when a toddler came close to the fireplace with its open fire, used not only for warmth but throughout the year for cooking.

In Elizabethan England guns and gunpowder were relatively new. Powder was imported from the continent until the 1560s, and the dangers of this unfamiliar mixture were not always appreciated. A gunpowder factory was permitted to conduct its dangerous operations on Fleet Lane, close to the Fleet Prison; the factory blew up during a fire on 30 June 1588. A casualty was one

ffrauncis smithe of the Borroughe of Sothworke in the countie of Surrye Saultpeter maker who beinge in fleete lane in a goon poulder house there to receive monye for sault peeter the sayde house by casualtie of fyer aboute fower yearse last past was Blowne up with goon poulder whereby he was greeviously Bourned Disfigured and maymed in Dyvers parts of his bodye aparant to be howld wherefore he hath been a long tyme sicke and in great payne spendinge and concerninge all that ever he could make in sekinge helpe for to cure him selfe.

Alms had to be provided by St Botolph's parish on 21 September 1595 for 'Edward Chilton a gun maker . . . who about six years past lost his left hand trying of a piece called a musket'. Some victims of such accidents did not escape with their lives. There was an inquest in the parish church

to enquyer howe Richard Hawkesworth a single man being a shoomaker of Blacke fryers came to his end who was hurt by mischaunce in a may game [around the May Pole] cominge throwghe Aldersgate striete wth a pece [piece, gun] one his necke and havinge serten powder in his slieve which by mischaunce he shooting of his sayd peece fyered the sayd powder hurte or burnt his arme and his syde wheareof he dyed . . . [22 June 1590].

A farrier was killed in June 1621 when he used his forge to heat a gun barrel and learned too late that it was loaded. A 'powder shop' in St Martin's parish blew up in January 1703, killing two people. There were also shootings in the parish of St Anne.

Poisoning by toxic gases overtook labourers cleaning out privies and sailors asleep in closed forecastles heated with charcoal stoves. Henry Whyte 'was smothered by the damp of a well' in 1584 at a site close to the Thames. Quite possibly the 'damp', now an obsolete term except for gases such as carbon dioxide and methane that may accumulate in coal mines, had come from rotting vegetation near the river and had settled into the well. A man, presumably a chimney sweep, was found dead in the 'funnel' of a chimney where he had suffocated. Another 'stifled to death in a house of office'.

In St Martin's parish it was recorded that no less than forty-six infants were 'overlaid', that is suffocated, when older persons lay on top of them. It was not unusual for several people, including children, to share one bed, or what passed for a bed, and for some of them to be intoxicated. Infants may not have always been 'overlaid' by accident. In the eighteenth and nineteenth centuries many unwanted babies were disposed of by exposure, starvation and violence, and some writers believe that overlying was a popular form of infanticide.[35] This form of death presumably was not restricted to St Martin's, but I have not encountered the term 'overlaid' in other records. It seems likely that such deaths in other parishes either were not recognized or were recorded in more general terms.

A good many suicides were probably not reported as such. In St Martin's parish, for example, suicides comprised only 0.1 per cent of all deaths. Since the comparable percentage for England and Wales in 1968 was eight times as much,[36] we can suspect that the parish suicides were grossly under-reported. Some deaths by drowning presumably were due to suicide or even homicide. In Tudor times and for long afterward, the taking of one's own life was a particularly abhorrent act – both a sin against the teachings of the church, and a felony.[37] In 1590, for example, a coroner's inquest met to determine the circumstances of a suicide in St Botolph's parish. One Amy Stokes had hanged herself in her chamber, fastening a cord to a beam

and putting the same with slydinge knott abowte her neck as it apeared standinge upon a three Footed stoole wch with one of her feete she had thrust from her and so hanged her selfe . . . and being fownde by the Jurie or Crowners quest that she Fallinge from god had hanged or murthered her selfe, Where upon Judgment was given . . . by the sayd crowner that she should be carried from her sayd howse to some cross way neare the townes end and theare that [she] should ha[ve a] stake dreven thorowgh her brest and so be buried with the stake to be seene for a memoryall that others goinge by seeinge the same myght take heede for committinge the lyke faite. And the sayd Amy Stokes was so buried in the crossway Beyond sparrowes corner neare to the place wheare the

35 P. E. H. Hair, 'Deaths from violence in Britain: a tentative secular survey', *Population Studies*, XXV (1971), 5–24; W. L. Langer, 'Checks on population growth: 1750–1850', *Scientific American*, CCXXVI (1972), 93–9.

36 *Registrar General's Statistical Review* (1970), pt I, table 7.

37 *Chronicle from Aldgate*, pp.165–9.

owld cross ded stand the sayd vij^th Day of September ano 1590 abowte the owere of viij or ix of the clocke at nyght she was abowte three skore yeares owld.[38]

This grim episode tells its own story. Not until 1823 was a law (4 George IV, c.52) passed that made it no longer legal for a coroner to order the burial of a *felo de se* in a public highway with a stake driven through the body. However, the statute still required that interment of a suicide

be made within twenty-four hours of the finding of the inquisition, and ... take place between the hours of nine and twelve at night.

Provided nevertheless, that nothing herein contained shall authorize the performing of any of the rites of christian burial on the interment of the remains of any such person as aforesaid; nor shall anything hereinbefore contained be taken to alter the laws or usages relating to the burial of such persons.

On the other hand, burial in a churchyard of the body of an executed criminal had been permitted for centuries.

A natural result of the harsh attitude toward the taking of one's life was a frequent attempt to mitigate or obscure suicide as a cause of death. In the eighteenth and nineteenth centuries coroners' inquests almost routinely reported that such deaths occurred while the victims were 'distracted' or 'lunatic' or 'of unsound mind' and hence, by implication, not responsible for their acts. A similar attitude prevailed toward sick persons who managed to destroy themselves while delirious. One such individual in 1624 in St Botolph's parish 'died of a wound which he gave himself in his sickness being as it were distraught and light-headed, and after the coroner's inquest had viewed him, order was appointed to have him laid in christian burial. It seemed he was ill looked unto in his sickness'.

Homicides, whether manslaughter or murder, were of diminishing relative frequency in the parishes, constituting from 0.4 per cent of all deaths in the sixteenth century to 0.2 per cent in the nineteenth. There was a more conspicuous decline in homicides when calculated as percentages of all deaths by accident and violence (Table 4). A considerable number of executed persons, nearly all males, were buried in the five parishes. In St Botolph's parish were the graves of sixteen men and one woman who had been put to death for various crimes between 1577 and 1613. While the records are not entirely explicit, it appears that thirteen of the executed men whose bodies were buried in the parish were pirates hanged at Execution Dock in Wapping, downstream from the Tower.

[38] Ibid., pp.164–5.

Thomas nicolson prisoner executed at wappinge was buried [25 April 1577].
Walter debarnell saylor executed at wappinge [4 April 1579].
Walter Wren and Charles Wakam who were executed at Waping for robing of
a spanishe shipp in the straights were buryed in this our churchyard [8 July
1580].
Phillip boyl for pyracy on the seas was executed at Waping and in this church
was buried [21 July 1580].

Table 4. *Distribution of accidental and violent deaths (per cent)*

	St Botolph, 1573–1624	St Martin, 1685–7, 1694–1703	St Giles, 1774–93, 1833–5	St Anne, 1814–28	St Bride, 1820–49	England and Wales, 1968
Accidents	49.55	74.1	50.0	66.3	56.0	78.3
Suicides	6.3	7.9	26.1	24.7	13.1	20.2
Homicides	28.85	13.4	6.5	5.6	1.2	1.5
Executions	15.3	4.6	17.4	3.4	1.2	
[Not stated]					28.6	
Total deaths	111	216	46	89	84	22,743

The four remaining executions were for murder. Thomas Guest and his
wife were hanged at Tyburn in 1613 for causing the death of their
servant, Susan Poynard. Thomas Campion, a labourer, 'for murdering
of John Donstone a bricklayer, was executed right over against the Sign
of the Blue Anchor near the highway that goeth toward Hogg Lane
within the Liberty of London' (23 May 1588). Donstone had been
murdered in the Blue Anchor, an inn. His assailant was executed close to
the scene of his crime.

One of the St Bride mortality books describes a curious death in 1831:
'A youth name unknown found packed in a deal box at the Belle
Sauvage, Ludgate Hill, brought there by the Sheffield coach.' The Belle
Sauvage was a famous coaching inn. We are given no further
information, but it is probable that the youth's body had been shipped
from outside London by a grave robber to an anatomist.

The coroner has functioned since the Middle Ages. However, except
in the volumes from St Botolph, I have found almost no mention of
coroners and inquests, even though accidental, violent, and suspicious
deaths were supposed to be investigated by these officers of the crown
and their juries. The St Bride mortality books do record 'coroner's
warrant' for twenty-four deaths without information as to cause.
'Visitation of God' appears a few times in the St Bride records and was
often invoked by coroners' juries in the nineteenth century to explain a

death from natural causes. An editorial in *The Lancet* in 1874 indicates that the phrase was a 'time-honoured verdict'.[39] A report of the medical officer of health of the town of Whitby had quoted the following well-justified statement from the *Report of the Registrar General* for 1841: 'To the question, "What is the cause of death?" such verdicts as Natural death or Visitation of God, it is scarcely necessary to say, are no answers at all, but mere evasions of the inquiry.' The coroner of Whitby, offended both by the quotation from the *Report* and by the comments of his colleague, retorted that a coroner's jury was entirely free to give such an opinion. According to *The Lancet*, the coroner of Whitby 'was happy to say that he had not yet outlived his belief in God, and he hoped it would be long before an English jury could be found that had done so'.

This survey of the common man's mortality in five London parishes from the sixteenth until well into the nineteenth centuries is based largely on the records of laymen – the searchers and the parish clerks. Their limitations and those of medicine itself oblige us to view the details with caution and sometimes with scepticism. Yet the record tells us some new facts and confirms others suggested by collateral sources.

Most striking is the appalling infant and child mortality. In Shakespeare's day, of every 100 babies born in St Botolph's parish about 70 survived to their first birthday, 48 to their fifth, and 27–30 to their fifteenth. In St Bride's parish in the early nineteenth century, one in eight of the deaths at all ages was that of an infant under 1 year.

Plague, consumption, fevers, gastro-intestinal ailments, and other infectious diseases took a heavy toll at most ages. The 'cause' of death was often masked by such non-specific terms as 'decay', 'pining', 'long sick', and 'dropsy'. Deaths in childbed occurred at about 100 times their rate in 1968. Violent and accidental deaths were relatively much less frequent than now, but this in past centuries was in large measure due to the heavy incidence of mortality from disease.

---

[39] [Anon.], 'Death by "Visitation of God"', *Lancet*, 1874 (i), p.452.

5

Management and mismanagement at Bedlam, 1547–1633

PATRICIA ALLDERIDGE

The sources for the early history of Bethlem Hospital are scattered and fragmentary, and the bulk of the evidence for even the sixteenth and seventeenth centuries is only just beginning to be seriously studied.[1] The period covered in this chapter marks, for example, what has always appeared to be a clearcut administrative reorganization – the most complete and radical to take place between the hospital's foundation in the thirteenth century and the implementation of the National Health Service Act in 1948. On closer examination, however, the process of change from a medieval to a modern system is seen to have been long drawn out, and at this stage can be only partially understood. Rather than attempt any comprehensive study, therefore, it seems preferable now to concentrate on certain isolated events which are well documented, and which give valuable insight into the life of the hospital at specific dates.

When the priory of St Mary of Bethlehem was founded in 1247 by Simon Fitzmary, on the site of his own property in Bishopsgate, the only

---

[1] The main documentary sources used for this interim study are the Repertories of the Court of Aldermen in the Corporation of London Records Office, State Papers in the Public Record Office, and the Minute Books of the Court of Governors of Bridewell and Bethlem. (The last are not normally accessible for research, but the first eight volumes, from 1559 to 1642, are now available on microfilm in the archives of the Bethlem Royal Hospital, and it is hoped eventually to obtain microfilm of the whole series.) Printed sources include *Memoranda, References and Documents Relating to the Royal Hospitals of the City of London* (1836), prepared and published by a committee of the Court of Common Council, which contains copies of many useful documents. The Charity Commissioners' *Report* for Bridewell and Bethlem, 1840, makes intelligent use of the hospitals' own records for the historical background, besides providing an excellent and detailed picture of their organization in 1837. Secondary sources for the whole history of Bethlem are generally very unreliable, whether ancient or modern, and certainly no recent study of the earlier period has made use of original sources. The only full-scale history of the hospital ever published, *The Story of Bethlehem Hospital* by the Rev. E. G. O'Donoghue (1914), is a useful reference book provided that all material is reworked from the original source: a dangerous one if this is not done. Subsequent writers have nearly all relied on O'Donoghue, and have generally chosen his more fantastical reconstructions for quotation, misquotation and reinterpretation. Nevertheless, his source references are invaluable.

specific duty laid on the canons, brethren and sisters was to celebrate mass for the souls of Fitzmary and his relations and certain named friends, and to receive the Bishop of Bethlehem and his envoys when they chanced to be in England.[2] But although no special provision was made in Fitzmary's deed of foundation, which is eloquent about the founder's devout motivation but somewhat imprecise on administrative matters, it seems possible that the eventual establishment of some kind of hospice was envisaged from the outset. The order of St Mary of Bethlehem was already running hospitals elsewhere in Europe, and it may be that design rather than underemployment first led the London house to turn its hand to similar work.

Certainly from about 1330 the name of 'hospice' or 'hospital' is found associated with it: but when it first began to specialize in the care of the insane is not yet known. Unfortunately a date has now become attached to this event, and it may be worth taking this opportunity to explain why the date 1377 does not, on present evidence, have any significance in the history of Bethlem. The only evidence of any weight at all on the subject is a statement in the Privy Council enquiry of 1632 (referred to later) that 'When [Bethlem Hospital] was first employed to the use of distracted persons, appeareth not. The first mention we find of it to be employed so, was in the beginning of the reign of Richard II'.[3] The Commissioners' source is unknown, but it may be assumed that the wording did not, at least, imply that the occupation was a particularly recent one or they would have drawn this conclusion themselves. There is also a statement by Stowe in his *Survey of London* (1603), referring to a house at Charing Cross: 'Then had ye an house wherein sometime were distraught and lunatic people, of what antiquity founded, or by whom I have not read, neither of the suppression, but it was said that sometime a king of England, not liking such a kind of people to remain so near his palace, caused them to be removed farther off, to Bethlem without Bishops gate of London, and to that hospital the said house by Charing Cross doth yet remain'. It should be noted here that when Stowe says 'it was said' rather than 'I have read', it is to acknowledge himself to be on shaky ground: also, that whoever said it may have been casting his mind back for anything up to 200 years.

Nevertheless the Reverend E. G. O'Donoghue, in *The Story of Bethlehem Hospital* (1914), added to these two statements some highly

---

[2] The original grant of land for the foundation of the priory, dated 23 October 1247, has not survived, but it was transcribed in the visitation of 1403 (see note 5 below).

[3] See note 29 below.

debatable material of his own, and came up with the conjecture that 'the king who ordered the transfer of the mad folk, was Edward III or Richard II, and that the date of the transfer was 1377, or thereabouts'.[4] The 'thereabouts' has, of course, never been seen since, and the alleged events of 1377 have now taken on the status of established fact. But even leaving aside the fact that Edward spent the first half of 1377 dying at Sheen, while Richard came to the throne in June at the age of 10, and is unlikely to have got himself sufficiently played in by the end of the year to start ordering the removal of lunatics from the neighbourhood, the evidence found by the 1632 commission would seem to suggest that the hospital was already taking insane patients by around that date, and may have been doing so for an undefined period before.

Whether or not there was ever a mass transfer from a house at Charing Cross is another matter; but the hospital certainly did own a property of some size there from a period before 1403. The 1632 Commissioners also refer to an Exchequer record of 1611/12 relating to this property, formerly called 'the Stone House', stating that it 'was sometimes employed for the harbouring of mad and distracted persons, before such time as they were moved to the now Hospital of Bethlem': but this could mean no more than that the people involved in the case had read Stowe's *Survey*, or at most that they had used with Stowe a common source of information, which cannot now be found.

The earliest primary evidence to be found today is in a record of a visitation of 1403, which enquired into the deplorable state of affairs at the hospital (the first of many such).[5] Here it is stated that there were six men '*mente capti*' and three other infirm, presumably in the hospital, though the sentence is curiously incomplete. Elsewhere the inmates are generally referred to simply as the 'poor and infirm', but there is one other reference to the 'infirm and mad', and one to a woman who had been brought there by her neighbours to recover her '*sanitas*'. Though this would normally be taken to mean soundness of body, it is in this context open to possible interpretation as soundness of mind. It is clear, therefore, that at this time the hospital was engaged in the care of the insane, and that the fact was sufficiently well known to require no special explanation; and thenceforward it has a continuous history of such employment.

[4] O'Donoghue, *Bethlehem Hospital*, chapter 8.
[5] The original document is among the Chancery Rolls in the Public Record Office. The sources used here are a nineteenth-century translation in the Bethlem archives, and the original Latin version printed in the Charity Commissioners' *Report* for Bridewell and Bethlem: 32nd *Report*, part VI (1840), pp.600–7.

Relatively little is known of its work during the fifteenth century; but around 1450 William Gregory, the chronicler and Lord Mayor of London, wrote of 'A church of Our Lady that is named Bedlam. And in that place be found many men that be fallen out of their wit. And full honestly they be kept in that place; and some be restored unto their wit and health again. And some be abiding therein for ever, for they be fallen so much out of themselves that it is incurable unto man'.[6]

Gregory may have exaggerated. 'Honesty' is not a word which springs to mind in association with Bethlem's administration or with the treatment of its patients during the first two thirds of its history, at least at any point illuminated by visitation, commission, or enquiry: and already by the fifteenth century the mastership of the hospital had become an appointment of the crown, and was used by the King to reward men whose only qualification for the post seems to have been their ability to profit by it. Some of them certainly profited to the great prejudice of the hospital and its charitable work; but nevertheless it managed to survive and to continue in business, and at the time of the Dissolution the mastership of Bethlem Hospital appears to have been still regarded as a desirable office, as indicated by a remark of a certain Dr Barnes in 1536 that he would sooner have it than a bishopric.[7] By the early part of the sixteenth century, Bethlem was thus a small but reasonably well-established hospital of fluctuating fortunes, still officially a monastic institution, but apparently by now completely secularized in its management. It was firmly identified with the care of the insane, and its name was already becoming part of the vocabulary. Sir Thomas More, who lived nearby in Bishopsgate, was familiar with its inmates, and wrote, 'For thou shalt in Bedlam see one laugh at the knocking of his own head against a post, and yet there is little pleasure therein':[8] and John Skelton could castigate Wolsey as 'such a mad bedleme/For to rule this realm',[9] with apparently every chance of being understood.

The building itself still stood on the site of Fitzmary's property in Bishopsgate, approximately where the south-east corner of Liverpool

6 [J. Gairdner (ed.), *The Historical Collections of a Citizen of London in the Fifteenth Century*, Camden Society (1876), 'III: William Gregory's chronicle of London'.] Though this is almost certainly the source, the extract was copied several years ago and the most rigorous searching has so far failed to re-locate it.

7 Apparently Dr Robert Barnes (1495–1540), protestant divine. The story is told in O'Donoghue, *Bethlehem Hospital*, p.110, with circumstantial-sounding detail, but the sources are not given.

8 Sir Thomas More, *The Four Last Things*, ed. D. O'Connor (London, 1935), p.6.

9 John Skelton, *The Poetical Works*, ed. A. Dyce (2 vols., 1843), II, 'Why come ye nat to Courte?', ll. 652–3.

Street station now stands. The earliest picture of it dates from *c*.1559 (Plate 5), when it appeared on a large-scale survey of London of which the original copperplate for the Moorfields section has survived. Unlike the better known 'exact survey' of Wenceslaus Hollar, made after the Great Fire in 1667, this depiction correlates very well with a groundplan of the building which is annexed to a building lease of 1677 in the Bethlem archives (Plate 6). If the priory had indeed been intended for a hospice from the outset, the 'Hospital House' may have been custom-built, though nothing more conclusive can be said on this score. From the plan and lease of 1677 it can be deduced that the long building running from east to west in the *c*.1559 map is the hospital proper, apparently including the small north/south wing at the west end. Taken together with the two tenements at the east end (which by then were occupied by the steward and porter respectively), the whole measured 200 feet in length in 1677, and was 51 feet wide at the west end. It is not likely that these measurements would have altered materially even if parts of the original structure had been rebuilt; but there is no reason to suppose that this had happened, except possibly in respect of the two tenements.

In 1632, according to an entry in 'the muniment book' quoted by the Charity Commissioners in the nineteenth century, the old house contained 'below stairs a parlour, a kitchen, two larders, a long entry throughout the house, and 21 rooms wherein the poor distracted people lie, and above the stairs eight rooms more for servants and the poor to lie in'.[10] Beyond this it is uncertain how much comprised current or recent alterations: but it seems unlikely that the arrangements described here would have changed much since the early sixteenth century; and the accommodation provided by the hospital was probably for about fifteen to twenty patients throughout the period with which we are concerned (except for overcrowding in the 1620s, which will be mentioned later). Elsewhere on the site stood tenements which were leased out, and the small church shown in the courtyard in *c*.1559 was demolished shortly after the map was made and replaced by more tenements. The hospital also owned property at Charing Cross, as has been mentioned, but most of its rents came from leases of the buildings within the Bethlem precincts. The hospital's site was bounded by Bishopsgate itself on the east and 'Deep Ditch' on the west, though precisely where its northern and southern boundaries are to be found on the *c*.1559 map has not yet

---

10   Charity Commissioners' *Report*, p.500.

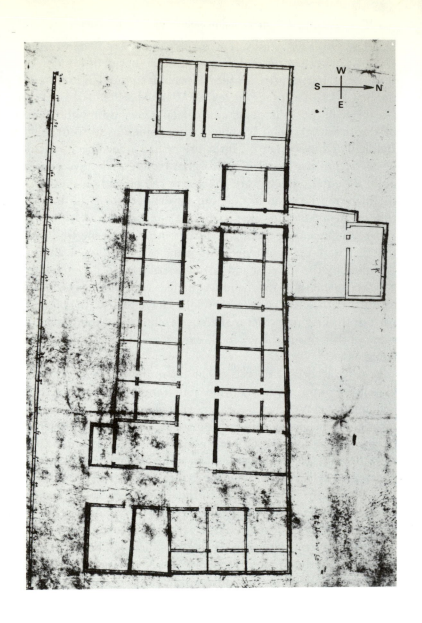

Plate 6. Groundplan of Bethlem Hospital, 1677
The only surviving groundplan of the original hospital, annexed to a
1677 building lease. Reproduced by permission of the Board of
Governors of The Bethlem Royal Hospital and The Maudsley
Hospital. For a depiction of the hospital as it stood in 1559, see Plate 5.

been established. There is evidence of considerable carelessness in the management of its properties, some of which had actually gone astray by this time, and the total rental in 1555 amounted to only £34 13s 4d per annum.

That Bethlem was still an asset, whether as a hospital or as a source of revenue from its lands, is shown by the determination of the City of London from an early date to obtain control of it. The means whereby the crown had acquired the patronage is still very unclear, but it is certainly a factor which adds much confusion to the administrative scene in the sixteenth and early seventeenth centuries. By 1406 it was being claimed that Bethlem was a foundation of the King's forebears, and the King's appointment of the master continued unbroken until 1536: but for a short time in the fourteenth century the City of London had actually made the appointment, and had only given up after a struggle when their own nominee of 1381 was finally ousted by the King's chaplain. The details of the City's claim in the sixteenth century have so far been only partially uncovered: but the subject can be found running through the records of the Court of Aldermen throughout the first three decades of the century. In 1504, for example, the court ordered 'that against the [next court] all records concerning Bedlem and the patronage thereof may be prepared and showed the court the same day'.[11] The City evidently already had a degree of supervision over the hospital, sufficient to give access to certain of its records, but the exact relationship at this period is far from clear. Two aldermen were later appointed to 'view all evidences concerning the foundation of Bethelem and the patronage of the same', but the outcome is unrecorded.

In 1514 a more determined effort was made, when various people were deputed to search the muniments concerning 'the title of the City for the patronage of the place of Bethlem': but it is not until 1537 that we find the City sufficiently advanced in its claim to be attempting to buy off the King's last nominee, Sir Peter Mewtys, who appears to have agreed 'upon reasonable sum to be paid to him [to] restore the possession of the patronage of Bedlem which of right belongeth to this City'. What became of this promising deal is unknown, for by 1542 the records were once more being searched 'with all speed' and it was not until July 1546 that the mayor reported decisively to the court that he had, for £100 paid to Sir Peter Mewtys, and 20 marks to one Thomas Scopeham,

---

[11] Quotations in this and the following paragraph are from the Repertories of the Court of Aldermen, Corporation of London Records Office. As the Repertories have a good descriptive index it has not been thought necessary to give a precise reference to each.

mercer, 'clearly purchased and bought to the use of the commonalty of this city the whole interest, title and right of the said Messrs Mewtas and Scopeham of and in the hospital of Bethelem and all the lands and tenements thereunto belonging'. The background to the latter part of these negotiations is the suppression by Henry VIII of the religious houses and the seizure of their lands and buildings, and the City's efforts to get back its lost hospitals 'for the aid and comfort of the poor, sick, blind, aged and impotent persons, being not able to help themselves nor having any place certain wherein they may be lodged, cherished and refreshed till they be cured and holpen of their diseases and sickness'.[12] The petition from which these words are taken was submitted in 1538 in respect of St Thomas's, St Bartholomew's, and two other former religious houses in London: but Bethlem was omitted, presumably on the grounds that it already belonged to the City (if only the King could be convinced of this).

In 1546 the City achieved part of its objective with a covenant from the King granting the hospital of St Bartholomew and all its lands, to be followed in January 1547 by a solemn and substantial charter to the same effect.[13] Into these two lengthy documents the 'house and hospital called Bethelem' is suddenly and surprisingly introduced, only to be dismissed in a few lines. The wording, however, is significant, and suggests that the City did not achieve all it might have liked. The mayor, commonalty and citizens were granted only the 'custody, order and government' of the hospital and its lands, and were appointed 'masters, keepers and governors' of the same, to hold to the uses and purposes ordained in the foundation or thereafter to be ordained by the King or his successors. By contrast the freehold of St Bartholomew's and all its estates, specified in great detail, was granted outright. Thus the City became the governor, but not the possessor, of Bethlem, a position which was confirmed in a charter of Charles I in 1638. It has been repeatedly said that £113 16s 8d was paid to the crown for the patronage of Bethlem but though this sum was reimbursed in 1549 to the then mayor, Sir Martin Bowes, in respect of the purchase of Bethlem, it is the exact amount which he had paid to Sir Peter Mewtys and Thomas Scopeham two years earlier, and is therefore obviously no more than a repayment of this expenditure.

---

[12] Original in the Journals of the Court of Common Council, Corporation of London Records Office. Quoted here from *Memoranda Relating to the Royal Hospitals*, appendix I, p.1.

[13] The original charter is in the archives of St Bartholomew's Hospital: there is no indication that Bethlem ever had a copy. It and the preceding covenant are printed in *Memoranda Relating to the Royal Hospitals*, appendix IV, p.9 and appendix V, p.22.

In 1553 another charter granted to the citizens of London the hospitals of St Thomas, Christ and Bridewell, and thereafter the rulers of the City settled down to sorting out the administration and finances of what came to be known as the Royal Hospitals. Bethlem's different position is apparent, however, throughout the period. Reference to 'The City's Hospitals' invariably means only St Thomas's, St Bartholomew's, Christ's and Bridewell, for which a system of electing governors from amongst the Court of Aldermen was soon established. Having got custody of Bethlem at last, the City seems to have been able to think of nothing better than to continue the traditional practice of farming it out to a master, or, as he came to be called, a keeper; though the keeper was now made theoretically accountable for the revenues to specially appointed surveyors. No governors as such were appointed for Bethlem; but after a brief period of oversight by the governors of Christ's Hospital, the management of its affairs was placed in 1557 in the hands of the governors of Bridewell, thus setting up what eventually developed into a joint administration lasting until 1948. However, during the early stages these governors took little interest in the supervision of Bethlem, over which they had, in any case, no real control.

The appointment of the keeper was made in the Court of Aldermen, and there seems to have been little to choose between those appointed by the crown and those by the City: and if the King had previously rewarded his friends and servants with the patronage of Bethlem, it is hard to see any different motives at work in the City's administration. In 1561 the 'reversion and next avoidance of the office of the keepership of Bethlem with all fees, profits and advantages thereunto justly belonging' was, at the request of the Lord Mayor, granted to Richard Munnes, his Lordship's porter.[14] Munnes (or Munes), a draper, had some difficulty in getting possession of his office because his predecessor Edward Alyn would not give it up; but within four years he had himself vacated it 'with most hearty thanks', whereupon the court appointed Edward Rest, a grocer. On Rest's death in 1571, 'at the request of my Lord Mayor and for his sake', the keepership was given to John Mell, whose occupation is unspecified but whose suitability for the office may be assessed from the fact that in June 1578, the governors of Bridewell gave him notice to 'provide him another place' by Michaelmas. He was said to have received various legacies 'and cancelled them', and to have

---

[14] Repertories of the Court of Aldermen.

abused the governors, those who gave money to the poor, and the poor themselves.[15] In July of the following year he was still there and was again dismissed, having by now also abused the surveyors, and committed other disorders jointly with his wife. Mell replied that he had been appointed by the mayor and aldermen, and would go if they disliked his behaviour: but his death in December freed the post without further controversy and it was given to Roland Sleford, a clothworker. In 1598 Sleford surrendered the keepership, apparently of his own accord: but the appalling state into which the hospital had been allowed to fall during his tenure of the office was discovered two months later by the governors of Bridewell who were appointed to 'view and peruse the defaults' there.[16]

It seems fairly clear that if there had been any truth in William Gregory's impression of the hospital in the mid-fifteenth century, it had suffered a marked decline in standards by the mid-sixteenth, and the new administration did nothing to improve matters. So far as the internal management and treatment of patients is concerned, there is little information until the 1598 survey, because this important facet of hospital life seems to have been left entirely in the hands of the keeper; but there is evidence that from time to time the aldermen did extend their interest in the institution beyond the mere tracking down of its rents and revenues. Occasionally they admitted patients directly themselves, for example, as in 1551 when they ordered that 'one William Brady, merchant, being frantic as it is reported for his railing and other condign causes shall be committed to Bedlem there to be closely kept and chained that no man speak with him'; or in 1554 when they agreed to keep the wife of John Kemp of Norwich so long as he continued to pay 26s 8d a year for her, and no longer; or in 1575 when they ordered that Widow Hallywell, 'lately become lunatic, and distraught of her wits', be committed to Bedlam and there kept.[17] They also on one occasion, in 1554, appointed four of their number to examine whether certain poor persons sent from St Bartholomew's were distraught or not, and if not, to put them out of the house. In 1567 they ordered that unlawful coal sacks taken in the City were to be washed and stuffed with straw and made into pallets at the City's expense, and delivered to the poor distraught people in Bethlem to lie on, 'for that divers of them do now lie upon the bare boards'. On the

---

[15] Court Books of Bridewell and Bethlem, vol. 1576–1579, fol.322.
[16] See note 18 below.
[17] Repertories of the Court of Aldermen.

whole, however, the Court of Aldermen were chiefly concerned during the sixteenth century with such matters as trying to lease out the chapel, removing the altar to St Thomas's, appointing keepers, and looking into the revenues.

The governors of Bridewell, ostensibly responsible for Bethlem too, seem to have been almost totally unconcerned with all Bethlem matters, except those which were forced upon them, until near the end of the century, though they did periodically send along patients. The affairs of Bridewell (which almost immediately became a prison, despite the laudable aims of its founders that it should provide rehabilitative work for the willing poor and the unwilling vagabond), occupied almost the whole of their numerous court meetings. These took place in the former royal palace of Bridewell itself, a more salubrious setting than an ancient monastic slum in Bishopsgate. And the business of Bridewell was more interesting than that of Bethlem, being mostly taken up with the examination and punishment of harlots and other lewd persons, rounded off with a few whippings. The patients of Bethlem were therefore left largely to the mercy of the keeper, and it is significant that even when they are mentioned in the records they are referred to as 'prisoners', their status being evidently indistinguishable in the governors' minds from that of their more familiar charges at Bridewell.

Late in 1598, however, something reminded the Bridewell governors of their other, if supposedly inferior, responsibilities, and on 2 December a committee was chosen 'to view the house at Bethalem where the lunatic people are kept on Monday morning next and to meet at eight of the clock at the Exchange and to make a certificate to Mr Alderman Ryder of the same'.[18] The wording may be significant: there may have been people present who did not know where Bethlem was: or more likely, it may simply have been necessary to identify the hospital building proper, as opposed to the various tenements within the precincts which feature more often in the records at this date than the hospital itself. The committee was certainly prompt in its action, and reported back two days later. This record is quoted *in extenso* from the Bridewell Court Books, and presents a simple and graphic picture of the misery and neglect which might be suffered for up to twenty-five years at a stretch, by patients as varied as the near-anonymous 'Welsh Elizabeth' (passed on by St Bartholomew's), a fellow of Pembroke College, Cambridge, and a member of the Chapel Royal.

[18]   Court Books of Bridewell and Bethlem, vol. 1597/8–1604, fol.50v.

The Fowerth daye of December 1598
A view of Bethalem [in margin]
Whereas it was ordered at a Court holden the Second daye of this instant December before the governors of this Hospitall that certayne of the sayd governors should view and p[er]use the default[es] and want of rep[ar]ac[i]ons in Bethalem where the lunatick people are kept Whereuppon we whose names are heerunder subscrybed have accordinglye viewed and p[er]used the default[es] and want of rep[ar]ac[i]ons in the sayd howse and we do fynd as followeth

Inprimis the flower over head in the Keepers lodge must be trused higher wth a long peece of tymber to gecrosse over thwart the lodge and a post to be sett at one end of it to barre upp the crosse peece and a ground plate to be layed crosse the lodge toward[es] the street syde thorowghout the whole frame and the seeling and walls are to be repayred.

Item the sinck in the Kitchen is stopped by reason of a garden wch ioyneth to it wch one Mrs. Colte or her assignes holdeth of the Cittye and by that meanes there is no sinck to passe the water awaye wch hath bine heertofore used for that the water did passe thorowgh the garden to the com[m]on sewer the [blank] in the sayd Kitchen over head is broken in sonder and is to be taken downe and a new to be putt in.

Item a new reason peece [*sic*] is to be putt in the romes over the lodge for that the old is rotten and readye to fall.

Item the great vault is to be emptyed for that it is full.

Item the tyling thorowghout is to be repayred

We do also fynd in the sayd house theis prisoners heerunder named sent in as well by this Hospitall as by other men whereof the Keeper doth receive the profittes

Salvado Mendes about three yeares past
Neme Barker about Fyve & twenty yeres past
Elizabeth Androwes about Tenn yeares past
JoneBromfeild about A yeare past
Rose Bromfeild in January last
Henrye Richardes in November last

   theis were sent in by this Hospitall

Elizabeth Dicons sent in by Mr. Oliver Skinner Salter at the request of the parishioners of East Ham in Essex and the sayd parishe doth allow for her.

Elizabeth Kempe Widdow who was taken in by Mr. Sleford tenn yeares past and doth still continew there.

Anne Claye sometyme dwelling in Aldermary parish Widdow sent in by warrant from the Lord Mayor who hath remayned there about Thirten Yeares and Mrs. Wood her sister is bound to pay fower poundes yearly towardes her maintaynaunce.

Johan Brockehurst Widdow sent in by S^r. Wolsey Dixey L. Mayor at the request of the Company of Skinners and hath allowance of xvi^d. A weeke.

Barbara Heron sent in by the Ladye Stafford who hath remayned there some viii or ix yeares and is allowed for by her

John Somerskall sent in by Mr Swaldell when he was Treasorer at the request of the Benchers of Grayes Inn about three yeares past and is allowed for by them.

Barwick Constable sent in by S[r] John Hart about two yeares now past and is maintayned by Xtopher Willoby gentleman dwelling in Kent.

Welch Elizabeth sent in from S[t] Bartholomewes Hospitall about A yeare now past the sayd Hospitall alloweth Twenty pence A weeke

Anthoney Greene fellow of Penbrooke Hall in Cambridge sent in by the L: of Canterbury about half A yeare now past and Doctor Androwes paieth Twenty nobles A yeare for him.

James Cliterbooke sent in by Mr. Mannsfeild dwelling by Maydenhead about half A yeare now past and he maintayneth him.

Hawnce A Dutchman sent in by the governors of the Dutch church about fower monthes past and they maintayne him.

Rosse an Almeswoman sent in [by] Mr. Bromeskill Vyntner dwelling at S[t] Mary Hill about fower monthes past and is maintayned by the Company of Vyntners.

John Dalton sent in by the Lord Admirall in October last and his Honor maintayneth him.

Edmond Browne one of the Queenes Chappell sent in by the L. Chamb[er]leyn in October last and his wages wch he hath of the Queene payeth his chardges.

We do fynd divers other default[es] in the sayd house in such sorte that it is not fitt for anye man to dwell in wch was left by the Keeper for that it is so loathsomly and filthely kept not fitt for anye man to come into the sayd howse

Thomas Box Thresorer	John Pollard
Florens Caldwall	George Southake
Thomas Harding	Symon Bowrman
James Austen[19]	

The wording is ambiguous, but it seems from this and other sources that the keeper was paid out of the revenues of the hospital for those patients who had been sent by the governors of Bridewell, but directly by their friends or relatives, or by the parish, for the rest; and possibly it was left to him to make the best bargain he could. Whatever he used the profits for, it is evident that not much went on household management, though the governors of Bridewell or the Court of Aldermen must be held responsible for allowing the building to fall into such a state of disrepair, even if the keeper had done little to bring it to their attention. Even leaving aside any obligation to make regular inspections, they did visit the area from time to time in connection with the leasehold properties. Six of the governors had been at Bethlem only the previous April, for example, to view a tenement whose fabric appeared to have been largely destroyed or sold off by its tenant; and it should not have been beyond their powers of observation, if they had chosen to look round, to see at least that the roof was falling in.

---

19 Ibid., fols. 51–2.

After the discoveries of 1598 the Bridewell governors did begin to visit the hospital more often, though scarcely with sufficient frequency to do more than put right some of the wrongs which had been allowed to accumulate. In 1607, for example, they opened the poor box, and finding in it 24s 2½d, promptly gave to the steward ten shillings towards buying vessels and other necessaries for the use of the poor.[20] On the same visit they 'there and then' ordered shirts and smocks to be allowed to ten 'prisoners', who had presumably been waiting for an indeterminate time in the state of dire and obvious necessity which prompted this precipitate action. The still further deterioration in standards is shown by the list of those who were to receive these benevolences: seven out of the ten are now identifiable only by their forenames or nicknames – 'Black Will', 'Welsh Harry', 'Old Madam', 'Joan of the Hospital', 'Abraham'. The governors did, however, just before this visit, order that the steward must bring to the court at Bridewell details of every patient admitted to Bethlem within a week of admission (the terminology is actually 'every prisoner committed'), but there is no very strong evidence that this order was ever carried out.

Apparently feeling a little guilty on the whole subject of their supervision of Bethlem, the governors did, at the court on 2 December 1598, resolve to find out whether the gift of the keepership of Bethlem was 'in the right of the governors of this hospital only or in the right of the Lord Mayor'. By that time, however, the Court of Aldermen had already given it to John Parrott, draper, and continued to give it to men of no apparent suitability who continued to abuse their position, until the appointment of Dr Helkiah Crooke in 1619. This event raised the office to new heights of respectability, and also of exploitation, and moreover reintroduced the element of royal patronage to a confused scene. In this case, neither the governors of Bridewell nor the Court of Aldermen can be held directly responsible for what happened, at least at the outset.

All the problems associated with Bethlem's management at this period reached their zenith under Crooke's keepership, culminating in an enquiry proportionate to the rank of the parties involved. The record of this episode is worth looking at in some detail, as it throws considerable light on the running of the hospital: and since it seems unlikely that Crooke's depredations would have differed much in quality, if they did in quantity, from those of previous keepers, or that

[20]   Court Books of Bridewell and Bethlem, vol. 1604–1610, fol.197v.

the ordering of the hospital's business would have changed much over the preceding two or three decades, the state of affairs which emerges from the enquiry may be supposed (in the absence of better evidence) to be similar in pattern to that of the previous century. Moreover, Crooke was the last of the old-style keepers from the medieval mould, and the end of his regime may be taken to mark the beginnings of the modern administration. It is therefore appropriate that his keepership should be looked at in the context of those of the preceding century.

Helkiah Crooke had received an MD from Leyden in 1597, and from Cambridge, an MB in 1599 and MD in 1604. A man of undoubted scholarship, he published his *Microcosmographia*, one of the first important textbooks on anatomy in English, in 1616. He was censor of the College of Physicians from 1627 to 1631: and most importantly from our point of view, was physician to James I. We first hear directly of his interest in Bethlem in 1618. Crooke had complained to the King against Thomas Jenner, the then keeper, that he was not fitted for his office and was inadequate in medical matters: and on 10 December a commission was issued by James I to the Bishop of London and twenty-three others, including judges, City aldermen and two physicians, to enquire into the complaint.[21] The Commissioners were also to enquire into the running of the hospital, and to replace anyone who was found unsuitable to be in charge – for which purpose Dr Crooke was recommended as a replacement: and Crooke was to have some allowance from the hospital revenues while the investigation was in progress. The King refers in the commission to 'my hospital', as he also refers to the grant to the City by Henry VIII of the government of 'his hospital'; and clearly he had decided to reassert his supposed rights and to make it clear to the citizens of London that they had no more than supervisory powers over a royal institution. Five months before this, however, the Court of Aldermen had already set up their own committee to hear and examine 'all the complaints made against the keeper of Bethlem and his deputy, how that house is governed, and of all other matters touching the same': and two days later they had actually committed Thomas Jenner and Edward Harper (presumably his deputy) to Newgate, until they put in sureties for good behaviour. Furthermore in October another committee had been set up to consider His Majesty's letter recommending Helkiah Crooke to be master 'under the patronage and oversight of the mayor and citizens of London of the

---

[21] P.R.O., SP.14, 104, no.19.

Hospital of Bethlem'.[22] In the light of this, the King's commission takes on a slightly more disingenuous aspect: battle had plainly been joined once more between crown and City for the control of Bethlem.

Crooke's real intentions in all this are not ascertainable from the evidence at present available, except that from the outset he intended, with the King's help, to take Jenner's place himself. The following year, probably about May, he petitioned the King in these terms:

> That whereas your Highnes Commission for the Ordination of your Hospitall of Bethlem hath now beene on foote neere halfe a yeere and is not yet ended or retourned by reason of some opposition Your Highnes would be pleased by your gratious letters to incourage the Commissioners in their zeale ... so to separate the Hospitall that it may be governed by it selfe as other Hospitalls because it not [*sic*] thriven at all under an other allmost these 100 yeares ... And because your Petitioner the now Guardian of the sayde Hospitall hath a whole yeere and more taken great paynes and beene at greate charge in the prosecution of this businesse the Commissioners should also (according to a clause in the end of your Highnes Commission) presently provide for his indempnitie in those charges out of the meanes of the House.[23]

It might not be difficult to guess who had been creating the opposition: it is more difficult to guess how far Crooke was really responsible for exposing Jenner's deficiencies in the first place, and still more, what were his motives. There is no doubt that he laid his finger with singular precision on both the cause and the symptoms of Bethlem's trouble over the preceding 100 years; and if his recommendation had been followed through and the hospital had been given its own separate administration, the history of the care of the insane over the next 200 years might have been radically different (and it could certainly have been no worse). So far, so high-minded: and if Crooke's subsequent career at Bethlem had not followed the path which it did, one might be inclined to overlook the final section of his petition as the reasonable anxiety of a man who has laid out a good deal of money, and needs his reimbursement. In retrospect, it looks more like an early warning that Bethlem was expected to pay dearly for Dr Crooke's guardianship.

Crooke had in fact already, on 13 April 1619, been installed by the governors of Bridewell as keeper.[24] As revealed in the Commissioners' report of 1633, the King had first written to the Court of Aldermen recommending Crooke in July 1618.[25] Crooke had written to the

22 Repertories of the Court of Aldermen.
23 P.R.O., SP.14, 109, no.68.
24 Court Books of Bridewell and Bethlem, vol. 1617–1626/7, fol.110.
25 See note 30 below.

governors of Bridewell, presumably recommending himself, the following January. This was followed in April by another letter of recommendation, written on the King's orders, from the Bishop of London, the Lord Chief Justice, the Recorder of London, and 'divers others' of the Commissioners in the Jenner enquiry: also in April, the president of Bridewell received a letter from the Duke of Buckingham on the same subject. 'After all which means used', as the Commissioners expressed it, the court proceeded to the election of Dr Crooke over the only other candidate, the luckless John Perie; who, whatever his qualifications may have been, can hardly be considered well-advised in his timing. (Crooke subsequently claimed that he had also had a grant of the office under the Great Seal, but as he was unable to produce any documentary evidence for this he was not believed.)

The articles to which the new keeper was required to subscribe are interesting, not only for the fact that Crooke subsequently contravened every one of them to the point of complete reversal, but because they show clearly the sort of misconduct by previous keepers that the governors were at last trying to remedy. The articles had been laid before the candidates before the election took place.

1 That who soever should be chosen should serve the same in p[er]son.
2 That he shall have no manner of interest in the land[es] or revennewes belonginge to the house of Bethlem
3 That he shalbe subiect to the direccon and controll of the Governors of this hospitall, for the time beinge and accompt to them
4 That he be chosen but to continue *Dumodo se bene gesserit.*
5 That he shall not urge any encrease of mainten[a]nce
That he shall subscribe to all theis thing[es] wth his owne hand before he be admitted, and agree to be displaced when he shall first offer to Receade from any of theis Articles. To p[er]forme all wch Articles the said suitors agreed and p[ro]mised to subscribe beinge chosen.[26]

It was also ordered at the same court that charitable gifts to Bethlem should be paid first to the treasurer, and from him to the keeper at the discretion of the governors, and not directly to the keeper. That Crooke agreed to subscribe to these articles at all may indicate that at the beginning he really did intend *se bene gerere*: but equally, in the confidence of the King's support, he may have felt that it did not matter much what he subscribed to. This is not the place to attempt to analyse Dr Crooke's motives, which must have been a great deal more complex than appears here; or even to consider his conduct towards the hospital

[26] Court Books of Bridewell and Bethlem, vol. 1617–1626/7, fol.110.

and its patients at all, except insofar as it throws light on the interior workings of the hospital itself.

Crooke's conflict with the governors of Bridewell began almost at once, over the bills for maintenance and expenses which he presented: and by May 1621, at a court meeting, he 'violently averred' that he would give no account of any of the money which he received for the poor at Bethlem. Over the next few years after his appointment the governors several times sent committees to investigate complaints about ill-treatment of patients or to look into bad conditions in general. A summary of what had been going on was presented by the Commissioners in 1632 and 1633, and will be examined below.

It may be because the keeper made his own arrangements for payment for the patients whom he admitted directly, and because he was paid a *per capita* maintenance allowance by the governors, that the hospital soon became overcrowded. At any rate, in 1624 the governors ordered that the keeper was to receive no lunatic person upon any warrant whatsoever, except those sent by themselves, and that the numbers were never to exceed twenty-five. The accommodation had not been enlarged, and previously there had been no more than twenty at the most: but when the governors went to 'view the prisoners' in 1624 they found thirty-one there, and were obliged to 'see the warrants how they were taken in, whether they be fit to be kept, and if they be found simple idiots, or recovered, to send them to the places whence they came ... for that the house is overcharged and wanteth room'.[27] The report of this 'view' gives the first full account of the patients in the hospital since that of 1598.

Hamon	John Hamon hath beene in the house theis 20 yeares att least, and is thought fitt to bee kepte. Brought from Camberwell
Whetston	Will[ia]m Whetstone hath beene there about 18 yeares & is fitt to bee kepte; was sent from the Court.
Flack	James Flack hath beene here about 6 yeares by warr^r: from Sr George Bowles Maior fitt to be kepte.
Fludd	Walter Fludd hath beene here about 18 yeares to bee kepte.
Bicknar	Will[ia]m Bicknar hath beene here about 20 yeares, to bee kepte.
Shaller	Gabriell Shaller hath beene here about 20 yeares, a simple fellowe, to bee returned to St Peters att Peters att Paulswharfe.
Hobson	Henry Hobson hath beene here about 4 yeares by warr^r: from Bridewell to bee kepte.
Burcott	Charles Burcott hath beene here about 4 yeares by warr^r: from Bridewell sonne to Burcott the shoemaker in Bedlem, not to bee

[27]   Ibid., fol.368.

kepte w[th]out mainten[a]nce from his father or the p[ar]ishe.

Teddar al[ia]s Bennett	Robert Teddar al[ia]s Bennett hath beene here about 9 yeares by warrant from Bridewell a simple fellowe to bee kepte & doth s[er]vice in the house.
Bond	John Bond hath beene here about two yeares by warr[r]: from Bridewell to bee sent to Barwick from whence hee came.

Will[ia]m Robertson hath beene there about 5 yeares by warr[r]: from S[r] Will[ia]m Cockaine Mayo[r]: was taken up in the sheet to bee sent to Hull from whence hee came./Mr Jackson a drap[er] in watheling street his brother.

Kite	Hugh Kite hath beene here about one yeare by warr[r]: from Bridewell penc[i]oner to y[e] marchanttaylors, to bee sent home to his wife, or to some other hospitall not fitt to bee kept here.
Manger	Phillip Manger hath beene here three yeares by warrant from Bridewell, hee is recov[er]ed and to bee sent to some other hospitall being onely lame of his feete.
Hackett	Thomas Hackett hathe beene there 5 monethes by warr[r]: from S[r] Martin Linnley Maior and S[r] Thomas Middleton Knight to bee sent to some other hospitall, hee came from S[t] Dunstans in the East.
Gibbins	John Gibbins hath beene here about 4 yeares borne att Barington in Oxford shire neare Burford hee hath land att the Banke side a play house, & pyke gardens Hernry Elmes in Fleetstreet did begyre him.
Felday	Will[ia]m Felday hath been there about 6 week[es] by warr[r]: from my lo: Maior & Mr Tr[easur]er. recomended by M[r] Recorder Fynch not fitt to be removed.
Pearson	Frauncis Pearson hath beene here about 4 monethes came out of the minorites & recomended hether by Captaine Milward being bound unto him as his Apprentice, & well recov[er]ed.
Denham	Tho: Denham hath beene here 14 dayes sent thether by Deputy Whitwell, and to bee kept no longer then the p[ar]ishe will pay his charg[es].

Weomen.

Browne	Jone Browne hath beene here about two yeares and a quarter by warr[r]: from Bridewell out of Hampshire qre [query] what allowance Bridewell hath for her, some say the p[ar]ishe from whence shee came doth allowe ii[s] vi[d] weekly towards her mainten[a]nce, very ill.
Ellis	Margarett Ellis hath beene here about 16 yeares from the p[ar]ishe of S[t] Mary Monnthawe London in reasonable case some course to bee taken for her remove, beinge willinge to goe unto Woodstock where shee was borne.
Royden	Anne Royden hath beene here about 3 yeares ½ by warrant from Bridewell borne att Coventrey or Lichfeild sent from S[t] Zacharies p[ar]ishe very madd.
Baylie	Phillis Baylie hath beene here two yeares by warr[r] from Bridewell dated the 25th of March 1622. a mad woman sometime a servant to the Matron of Bridewell.
Bygrave	Rebecca Bygrave hath beene here 3 yeares and ½ by warr[r]: from

Bridewell from the p[ar]ishe of S[t] Giles Criplegate very ill.

White-   Anne Whitehead hath beene here three monethes by warr[r.] from
head   Bridewell Recomended by M[r] Acourt from S[t] Martins Ludgate
            very ill.

Killing-   Katharine Killingham hath beene here about two yeares in Aprill last
ham   by warrant from Bridewell under 7 governors hand[es].

Parratt   Anne Parratt hath beene here about 14 yeares divers times putt out of
            the house and returned first by the Court of Ald[er]men. 2. by S[r]
            Will[ia]m Cockaine Maior & S[r] Rob[er]t Heath Recorder.
            something idle headed, to bee removed sister a M[r] Panters wife.

Floid   Mary Floid hath beene here about 4 yeares by warrant from
            Bridewell her husband liveth about Westminster very ill.

Rathbonn Eliz[abeth] Rathbonn hath beene here about 18 monethes by warrant
            from Bridewell shee came from S[t] Thomas Hospitall when shee was
            cured of the fowle disease and fell madd not yet fitt to goe abroade.

Hardick   Margarett Hardick hath beene here about 4 yeares and ½ sent by S[r]
            Will[ia]m Cokaine Maio[r] not knowne from whence shee came &
            must bee kepte.

Silvester   Anne Silvester hath beene here about 40 week[es] warr[t]: from
            Deputy Whitwell who is her Uncle, and lieth att the charge of the
            house fitt to bee removed.

            Mary Thompson hath beene here allmost two yeares by warr[t]: from
            Bridewell 5[th] Octobr[e] 1622. qe [query] from whence shee came,
            beinge a poore Idiot not fitt to bee kepte in this house. hir mother
            dwelleth w[th]in Bishopsgate & doth allow her 12[d] weekly towards hir
            mainten[a]nce.[28]

The governors of Bridewell never seem to have succeeded in imposing much control on Crooke, and over the latter part of his keepership seem scarcely to have been able even to attract his attention in passing. It must be supposed that King James's support kept him immune until 1625 from the apparently uncompromising terms of the articles to which he had subscribed: and it is obvious that Crooke's whole association with Bethlem is closely tied up with the complicated political relationships existing between the crown and the rich merchants who governed the City and its hospitals. After James's death in 1625, however, the governors did appoint a committee to confer about 'divers misdemeanours' of the keeper and report to the whole Court of Aldermen: but it was not until 1632 that fortune finally turned against him. A Privy Council enquiry was set up in June that year and reported in October;[29] it held further sessions in 1633, reporting again in April.[30]

[28] Ibid., fols.368–9.
[29] P.R.O., SP.16, 224, no.21.
[30] P.R.O., SP.16, 237, no.5.

The sort of 'misdemeanours' which had provoked this investigation had been recorded in the Bridewell Court minutes of 18 February 1631, when two of the governors reported that they had been to Bethlem the previous Saturday and found that the poor there had no food but some small scraps, and were likely to starve; and that on a previous Sunday they had been fed only with 4lb of cheese. Crooke had by now been absent for several years from the hospital, according to the findings of the enquiry, appearing only at quarter days to make up his bills; and had left the place in charge of a steward who himself committed various depredations, and in turn complained to the Lord Mayor that the keeper would not give him any money to feed the poor, forcing him to run into debt. (At this point Crooke replaced the steward with his own son-in-law, Thomas Bedford.)

A large part of the Commissioners' first report is taken up with assessing the property and revenues of the hospital. The rents amounted to £263 3s 4d, and would have been about £630 on a reasonable valuation, but many properties were let on long leases. There were also two annuities totalling £14 per annum. But the most interesting part of this report relates to the gifts in kind which were regularly sent in, showing how dependent an institution such as Bethlem still was on the practical actions of the charitably disposed.

Sent into the Hospitall weekely in Victualls.
From the Lo: Mayor   Of bread every Munday 6 penny loaves, besides broaken bread when they will come for it. Of beefe 2 Stone at the Least every Munday, and a pott of pottage made wth halfe a pecke of oatmeale.
From the 2 Sheriffes   Of bread, beefe, and pottage the like p[er] porton, from the one upon Wensday, from the other upon Thursday.
And For beere from the Lo: Mayor and Sheriffes they have as much when they will fetch it, as will serve the whole house.
Besides bread sent out of markets by the Lo: Mayor when it is found light, and oftentimes other p[ro]vision: And pieces of meate very often sent into them by the Chamberlaine of London.
Besides allsoe divers charitable gifts sent in weekely by some honorable, and other well disposed p[er]sons, as sometimes by the M^r of the Rolles, sometimes by the Lady Dudley, by Sr Hen: Martin, Sr Paull Pindar, and others.
Besides allsoe weekely contributons sent from the p[ar]ishes, and freinds of some of the distracted p[er]sons, and money given at the Hospitall doore by p[er]sons that come to see the House, and the prisoners.
By wch and other the like casuall meanes, wee find by the p[er]usall of some Stewards accompts, that in some weekes the expence of the distracted p[er]sons hath bene wholely defrayed.

It might be wondered, in view of all this, how the patients came to be found starving: but the Commissioners also found that 'it is a very usual and daily practice [for the steward] to sell unto the poor of the house, such bread and meat as is sent in from the Lord Mayor, Sheriffs, and out of the markets, and that at excessive rates, as ordinarily a penny loaf for a groat or 6d, and sometimes 2 pennyworth of bacon for 12d, and the poor have none of that meat that is so sent in, except they have money to buy it; and they have no money but as it is casually given them by such charitable persons as come to see them'. Any exceptionally good meat was eaten by the steward and his wife and friends, and the free beer was likewise sold to the inmates, as was cheese and butter which had already been paid for by the governors on Dr Crooke's bills. The steward complained that he scarcely received any money from Dr Crooke, and the Commissioners found that he had in fact received about £86 over the previous two years, out of £389 which had been paid to Crooke on his bills. Crooke also received direct, besides the City's allowance of 2s a week per patient (a recent increase from 1s), money from the parishes and friends of patients ranging from 1s to 6s a week each.

In the second enquiry Crooke was specifically charged with four articles, and the Commissioners held twenty meetings to hear his replies. The first three concerned his huge bills, and tiny disbursements, on behalf of the patients. The answers were long and devious, and the Commissioners' answers to Crooke's answers often longer still; but it is obvious that they were unconvinced by most of his replies, and particularly by the fact that he could produce no accounts; though he did offer to run up a 'conjectural account' to prove that, far from profiting by the position, he had in fact disbursed over the years £1,000 more than he had received. The Commissioners gave way here to a little barbed scepticism: 'Which allegation seeming to us very strange (as conceiving it a thing incredible, that he should for these 13 or 14 years with so much stiffness desire to hold such a place wherein he should not only get nothing, but disbursed yearly an 100 [pounds] at the least more than he received)'. It appeared also that besides the money which he received from the governors of Bridewell on his bills (which had increased from about £17 a quarter in 1619 to £55 or £56 by 1632), he took a fee of 10s to 20s on the admission of every patient, which had to be negotiated by the friends or parish, and he would not take in patients without this payment even if they had a warrant from the Lord Mayor or aldermen. Crooke's reply was that these fees belonged to him of right, that the governors of Bridewell and the City could not control him in this, and he could take what fees he could get and need not account for them.

In his answer to the final question Crooke revealed the true plight of the Bethlem patients. The charge was that notwithstanding the great profit he made from it, he never came near the hospital except to make out his bills, 'nor that he hath of long time used any endeavour for the curing of the distracted persons'. He replied that 'at his first coming to the place, he cured 17, and since that time, he hath not endeavoured any thing because he saith the governors of Bridewell do refuse to pay him his apothecaries' bills'.[31] Whatever the ins and outs of this particular dispute – and the Commissioners found that the governors had in fact offered him money but that he did nothing – there is no doubt who the losers were. Possibly in the light of the contemporary knowledge of insanity, a little neglect on the medical front might have done more good than harm: but the attitude summed up in this exchange was clearly not confined to the sphere of medication.

The Commissioners concluded that Crooke had broken all the conditions on which he was admitted; that notwithstanding the weekly allowance in certainties and casual gifts was nearly double that of the other hospitals, in none of them were the poor so ill ordered and provided for as in Bethlem; and that since he did nothing at all towards their cure, and would generally receive no one without such exactions as they had listed, the Lords of the Privy Council might wish to consider how fit he was to be further trusted with the government of the hospital, and how worthy to carry away the greatest part of the revenues on top of what he exacted. On 24 May 1633 it was reported in the Bridewell Court that Dr Crooke and his son-in-law Thomas Bedford were to be prosecuted by the Attorney-General for their misdemeanours, and in the meanwhile were to be sequestered from their offices, and the treasurer was ordered to oversee the government of Bethlem. Crooke was not, in the end, prosecuted; but he did not return to the hospital, and with him went the office of master or keeper. Two years later the rules were laid down whereby a resident steward became responsible for the day-to-day management of the hospital's affairs, and fully accountable to the governors of Bridewell: and if the latter could not yet be regarded as giving equal weight to both parts of the joint governorship, they certainly had the machinery for the control of Bethlem more firmly in

[31]   Despite Crooke's use of his medical qualifications as a lever to supplant Jenner in the keepership, there was no indication in the articles set out in 1619 that the provision of medical attention was in fact one of the keeper's duties. The evidence here is unclear. The dispute appears to be merely about the payment of bills for medicines, implying that the keeper *was* expected to provide, but not to pay for these: but the wording is slightly ambiguous, leaving open the possibility that Crooke was being offered money specifically to provide medical attention.

their hands than at any time since the new administration had been set up in the previous century.

It would be pleasing to be able to record that conditions actually improved for the patients under the new system, but the governors did not in fact show much more acumen in electing stewards than had their predecessors in choosing masters and keepers. Furthermore, the revenues were at this time quite inadequate for the maintenance of the hospital and its inmates, and although the friends of the patients or the parish officers were obliged to contribute towards the cost of their food, clothing and medicines, there must have been a good deal of unavoidable hardship, as well as the still more prevalent avoidable variety. Nevertheless great changes had taken place; and if nothing else was immediately gained, it must be said that throughout the following 300 years, it is at least possible to identify those who were ultimately responsible for the mismanagement of the hospital's affairs.

6

Medical practitioners

MARGARET PELLING AND CHARLES WEBSTER

The sixteenth century is a particularly significant phase in the development of the medical profession in England. At the beginning of the century England lagged far behind Italy in the organization of its medical profession, in medical education, and in general medical culture. During the century a College of Physicians on the Italian model was established in London. The humanistic physicians then became architects of a tripartite division of labour within the medical profession under which surgeons and apothecaries developed their separate professional identities. In the revitalized universities the medical faculties expanded, and medical education was established on a humanistic footing. From England there emerged some of the finest vernacular medical works in Europe. Culturally Italy remained the centre of medical humanism, but the scene was set for William Gilbert, William Harvey and their followers to gain for the English in the field of the medical sciences a reputation for versatility, originality and distinction.

It is important to place the above developments in perspective. Even at the end of the sixteenth century the College of Physicians was a small and not particularly influential organization. Medical graduates actively practising as physicians were relatively few in number. The tripartite division of labour cultivated by physicians was only imperfectly realized, even in London. Surgeons and apothecaries utilized gild organizations to establish their independence and freedom of operation. Little success was experienced in the control of unlicensed practitioners, either in London or in the provinces. Within the City of London unlicensed practitioners flourished, and in the countryside they were dominant. Thus humanistic physicians were in open competition with an array of representatives of a vigorous and evolving system of traditional medicine. Implicit in this situation were divergent attitudes respecting rational Galenic therapy and magically orientated medical beliefs. The coexistence of forms of medical practice based on rational and magical systems of belief is reminiscent of the position prevailing in developing countries at the present time.

Any balanced view of medicine in the early modern period, or in non-western societies, must take into account all practitioners involved in dispensing medical care. Hence in the present study a 'medical practitioner' is regarded as any individual whose occupation is basically concerned with the care of the sick. It may be objected that this broad definition blurs the vital distinction between the 'professional' and the empiric. Hitherto studies of English medicine have paid little attention to practitioners who were not university-educated or involved with the organized bodies of surgeons and apothecaries in London. Hence the classes of practitioner who were numerically dominant nationally have attracted little serious comment. It is important that all categories of practitioner should be taken into account if we are to work towards a quantitative and balanced assessment of medical care in the sixteenth century.

The difficulties involved in framing consistent and historically fruitful criteria for isolating responsible medical practitioners from empirics and quacks have often not been fully appreciated. Terms such as empiric tend to be used without consistency or sound historical justification. Adoption of technical criteria for the isolation of empirics based on the legal code, professional attachments, or educational attainment is practicable, but it tends to generate a trivial and unrealistically narrow conception of legitimate medical practice. Reference to more meaningful criteria related to professional efficiency, reliability and responsibility, or the ideal of service rather than pecuniary gain, is difficult to operate because of lack of evidence, but if applied objectively it is likely to reinforce the use of a broader rather than narrower conception of responsible medical practice.

In view of the above difficulties we have decided not to take at face value judgments made by contemporaries designating individuals and indeed major groups as 'quacks' or 'empirics'. This is not to deny that medicine was infiltrated by unscrupulous opportunists, or that individuals at all levels were guilty of conscious ethical misconduct. But it is important not to allow the special pleading of contemporary pressure groups to lead the historian into undervaluing the activities of arbitrarily defined sections of the medical community. A broader conception of medical practice has obvious historical merits, since it permits insight into the complexity and richness of medical provision in early modern societies.

Whenever possible in this study information relating to medical practitioners has been collected sufficiently systematically for results to be expressed numerically. This has necessitated a sampling approach. London and Norwich have been selected to represent the urban situation. London presents difficulties because of the complexity and evolutionary character of its medical organizations and the paucity of data about the lower ranks of medical practitioners. However London is of particular interest as exhibiting the medical problems of one of the largest and most rapidly expanding cities in Europe. Norwich, although a small town by comparison with London and major cities in Europe, was the second largest city in England throughout the sixteenth century (see Plates 1, 2, 5 and 9).

Norwich was regarded as a model in the organization of its poor relief; its spectrum of medical practitioners would have had much in common with that prevailing in cities like Bristol, Exeter and York. As a diocesan centre Norwich was responsible for medical licensing in one of the most populous areas of Britain. Our comments about medical practice in small towns and villages will be based on the counties of Norfolk and Suffolk. Lastly, Cambridge will be discussed with reference to its growing importance in medical education, and as a licensing centre, particularly for practitioners in East Anglia.[1]

London is the only English city ever to have established a College of Physicians of the type common in towns throughout Italy. It is not

[1] The best general survey so far undertaken of this subject is R. S. Roberts, 'The personnel and practice of medicine in Tudor and Stuart England', *Medical History*, VI (1962), 363–82; VII (1964), 217–34. For a more detailed study of legal aspects of this problem see idem, 'The London apothecaries and medical practice in Tudor and Stuart England' (unpublished London University Ph.D. dissertation, 1964). See also W. S. C. Copeman, *Doctors and Disease in Tudor England* (London, 1960); F. N. L. Poynter (ed.), *The Evolution of Medical Practice in Britain* (London, 1961). For a perspective on popular medical belief see K. Thomas, *Religion and the Decline of Magic* (London, 1971), pp.117–252.

In what follows the following general biographical sources have been used: *DNB*; C. H. Talbot and E. A. Hammond, *The Medical Practitioners in Medieval England* (London, 1965); A. B. Emden, *A Biographical Register of the University of Oxford AD 1501 to 1540* (Oxford, 1974); C.H. Cooper and T. Cooper, *Athenae Cantabrigienses (1500–1609)* (3 vols., Cambridge, 1858–1913); R. E. G. Kirk and E. F. Kirk, *Returns of Aliens Dwelling in the City and Suburbs of London* (4 vols., Aberdeen, 1900–8); J. H. Bloom and R. R. James, *Medical Practitioners in the Diocese of London 1529–1725* (Cambridge, 1935); W. Page (ed.), *Denizations and Naturalizations of Aliens in England* (Lymington, 1893). The authors are grateful to R. G. Frank Jr for allowing access to his paper, 'The institutional renaissance of English medicine', which is to appear in *Medical History*.

Because of the great variety of biographical sources utilized in the course of the present study it has not been practicable to provide detailed citations with respect to every separate point or identity. Major sources are cited at the beginning of each section; further information may be obtained from the biographical index of medical practitioners 1500–1640 currently being compiled at theWellcome Unit for the History of Medicine, Oxford.

surprising that the initiative for this development came from Thomas Linacre, the pioneer English medical humanist, who had spent thirteen years in Italy. Recurrent outbreaks of the sweat, plague and smallpox in London during the second decade of the sixteenth century provoked increasing concern about public health, thereby paving the way for the grant of the first charter to the College of Physicians of London in 1518.

The statutes of this College were closely modelled on those of sister institutions in Italy. However the London physicians suffered from certain disadvantages compared with Italian counterparts. By contrast with major centres in Italy London possessed no university or medical faculty for educating and supplying members of the College; the medical faculties at Oxford and Cambridge were poorly developed; the new College was situated in a city experiencing a rapid growth of population; and finally the College never enjoyed the full confidence of the civic authorities in London. The College was also at a disadvantage by virtue of its anomalous constitutional position as an extra-municipal corporation, lying outside the framework of the city companies, while attempting to exercise primary jurisdiction over a territory in which city companies were supreme.[2]

The College of Physicians of London in the sixteenth century is not an outstandingly impressive organization. Not only was it unable to secure the control of medical practice throughout the nation granted in the 1523 statutes, but it was slow to consolidate its position in London. The initial impetus given by Linacre was largely lost. The College contributed little to medical education and scholarship until the 1580s, and it was not more than peripherally involved in the work of the hospitals, or in public health. The Fellows showed little interest in adapting the College to the needs of the expanding metropolis. Their primary concerns related to fastidious details of internal management and the protection of their monopoly against the swelling tide of unlicensed practitioners. Although the Act of 1540 granted the College authority over both apothecaries and surgeons, both of these groups successfully resisted encroachment into their affairs.

Linacre had no choice but to constitute the College from amongst court physicians and from the higher ranks of London medical practice.

---

[2] G. Clark, *A History of the Royal College of Physicians of London* (2 vols., Oxford, 1964), I, pp.54–66; C. Webster, 'Thomas Linacre and the foundation of the College of Physicians', in F. Maddison, M. Pelling and C. Webster (eds.), *Linacre Studies* (Oxford, 1977) pp.198–222. Clark's work is the major source for the history of the College. See also W. Munk, *The Roll of the Royal College of Physicians*, 2nd edn (3 vols., 1878). The unpublished 'Annals' of the College, deposited in its library, are quoted with the kind permission of the President and Fellows.

His colleagues had respectable medical credentials, but they were no match for Linacre in scholarly standing. The position improved with the recruitment in February 1528 of the Oxford humanists John Clement and Edward Wotton, both of whom had studied in Italy and had assisted with the preparation of the Aldine *editio princeps* of Galen published in 1525 (see Plate 7).

Not until the return of John Caius from his visit to Italy, and particularly after his appointment as President in 1555, did the College advance beyond the design of Linacre. Caius regularized College affairs, instituted more exact record-keeping with his *Annales*, rationalized and strictly enforced the statutes, and elaborated the ceremonial functions of the College. It might also have been due to the influence of Caius that in 1565 the College was granted corpses for the purpose of dissection, which occasioned the establishment of an annual anatomical lecture. However, despite the glowing commentary of the College historian, there is very little evidence that in the sixteenth century this lecture was more than a mechanical exercise.[3] Caius, like Linacre, appreciated that the College would benefit from the expansion of university medical education. Thus most of his charitable resources were directed to Cambridge, where he undertook the reform of Gonville Hall with even greater care than that displayed in his administration of the College of Physicians. Despite the good management of Caius, the fortunes of the College flagged during the first part of the reign of Elizabeth, possibly owing to its anomalous political and religious position.

At its establishment there was no indication that the College would limit its membership. Although not codified in the statutes an understanding gradually emerged that full fellowship should be numerically limited to twenty. There was little need for such a limit, since before 1575 the fellowship, exclusive of foreign physicians, was rarely more than fifteen. It was not until the 1580s that numbers of suitably qualified and interested candidates increased to the point where the College needed to consider expansion. At this time the medical profession was feeling the first benefits of the general expansion of university education. At first in 1584 it was decided to maintain the fellowship at twenty, royal physicians being counted as additional *ex officio* members. This made little difference in practice since the foreign royal physicians had for some years been included as 'stranger' fellows. In 1590 the fellowship was increased to a maximum of thirty, but this

3 Clark, *History*, I, p.122; Charles Goodall, *The Royal College of Physicians* (1684), pp.34–7.

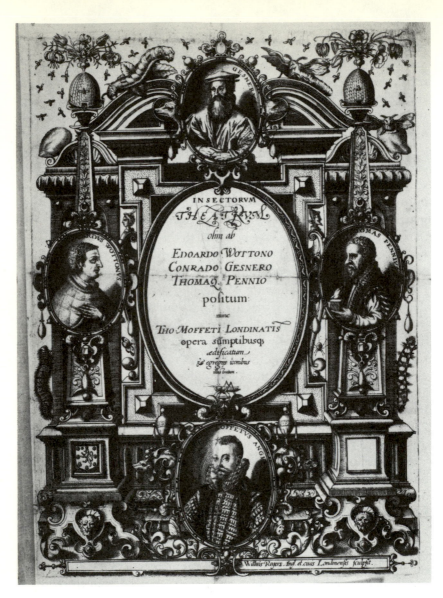

Plate 7. Title-page of Mouffet's *Theatrum insectorum* (*c.* 1590)
This title-page was prepared in connection with Mouffet's abortive
plan to publish 'Theatrum insectorum' in 1590 (MS. Sloane 4014, fol.
3). An entirely different and far less elaborate title-page was employed
in the posthumously published edition of 1634. The original engraved
title-page by William Rogers includes portraits of the celebrated
London physician-naturalists Edward Wotton, Thomas Penny and
Thomas Mouffet. Reproduced by permission of the British Library
Board.

number was to include the royal physicians.[4] The records of the College indicate that the fellowship statutorily stood at thirty in the last decade of the century. In 1585 the number of candidates was increased from six to eight, but in 1600 it was reduced again to six.[5] The above changes indicate that the College was not absolutely inflexible about its size, but also that minimal concessions tended to be made to pressure for expansion.

The statutes of the College imposed a high standard of qualification for fellowship. A doctorate in medicine was requisite for admission as a candidate. The candidate was then required to practise for four years, after which he was submitted to a four-part examination taken at three-monthly intervals.[6] The extensive list of the writings of Galen which formed the basis for these examinations was stipulated in detail in the statutes. The candidate was also tested on his knowledge of medical practice. It is doubtful whether these tests were applied in their full rigour, and short-cuts were introduced, allowing some classes of medical graduate to obtain a fellowship more rapidly. But on the whole the biographies of the Fellows suggest that admission was only given to experienced doctors of medicine.

Between 1582 and 1585 the statutes were modified to encourage the recruitment of medical graduates who had spent at least seven years as arts students and seven years in medical studies at the English universities. The more this pattern was deviated from, the more the expense and probably the delay in obtaining a fellowship.[7] These decisions suggest that the College now felt sufficiently confident about the state of the English medical schools (and, perhaps, also concerned about the ease with which medical diplomas were granted elsewhere) for it to be in order to introduce disincentives to foreign medical education.

The changing character of the College during the latter decades of the century is well illustrated by comparing the fellowship in 1572 with that of 1589. At the former date there were fourteen English fellows and four 'strangers'. This fellowship represented a pattern which had been evolving since the death of Linacre. Thomas Fryer, with an MD from Padua, was the only Englishman with a continental medical qualification.[8] Apart from Fryer and Huicke the ten most senior

4 Clark, *History*, I, pp.132–3; Annals, 25 June 1584, 27 April 1590.
5 Annals, 12 November 1585, 17 March 1599/1600.
6 *Statuta vetera*, in Clark, *History*, I, pp.385–7.
7 Annals, 7 December 1582, 14 September 1584, 23 October 1585.
8 The then President, John Symings, may have studied at Bologna.

members of the College were Oxford medical graduates.[9] They reflect the dominance of Oxford in English medical education before 1550. The four most junior Fellows of the College were medical graduates of Cambridge. Those in this second group were the first products of the mid-century wave of expansion experienced at the Cambridge medical school. The Fellows listed in 1572 were no doubt capable physicians, but they made little impact as scholars, and none had published or had contributed to a publication either in medicine or in any other subject.

The fellowship in 1589 had expanded to twenty-eight, and there were in addition two strangers. At the senior level the College was now evenly divided between Oxford and Cambridge medical graduates, with Fryer still the only one with a foreign medical qualification. The College as a whole was dominated by medical men whose education in arts had been undertaken at Cambridge. Of the eleven most junior Fellows, seven obtained their MD abroad (three in Basel, three in Leyden, one in Heidelberg). Thus a phase in which Cambridge recruits were dominant had given way to one in which continental medical education was becoming popular. This trend was not altogether welcome since it produced intellectual diversification among humanistic physicians which weakened the coherence of the College. The intellectual standing of the College was much higher than in 1572. William Gilbert and Thomas Mouffet were major scholars; many of the twenty more junior Fellows made minor contributions to the literature of medicine, natural history, mathematics and philology (see Plate 7). The College was within sight of the scholarly standards set by Linacre and Caius.

Repercussions of a more buoyant intellectual atmosphere within the College are to be detected in initiatives undertaken during the last two decades of the century. In 1585 it was proposed to produce a pharmacopoeia for the use of apothecaries throughout the country. Four years later the task of compiling the pharmacopoeia was divided between the Fellows. But there were difficulties in gathering in the material, and the project collapsed, before being revived nearly twenty years later.[10] The *Pharmacopoeia Londinensis* (1618) was hastily produced for the benefit of the newly-formed Society of Apothecaries. Probably related to the pharmacopoeia project was a decision of the College to establish a garden. Two different sites were considered, and John Gerard

9 Robert Huicke took his BA and MA at Oxford, transferring to Cambridge, perhaps briefly, for his MD.
10 Annals, 25 June 1585, 10 October 1589.

was appointed gardener. There is little sign that the garden was actually established.[11] The plan was inconsequentially revived in 1631.

The most significant innovation at the College was the establishment in 1581 of the Lumleian Lecture in surgery, the stipend for the lecture being derived from a joint gift of Lord Lumley and Richard Caldwell, one of the Fellows. The significance attached to this lecture is demonstrated by the large outlay countenanced by the College for a new anatomical theatre. This was the most important single investment by the College in the sixteenth century.[12] The first lecturer appointed, Richard Forster, an Oxford medical graduate, held the office until 1602. Forster is primarily remembered as a mathematician; he was singled out by Richard Harvey as one of 'our chief doctors in physic' favouring astrology. Little is known about Forster's lectures, other than from references in the Annals which suggest that they were poorly attended by Fellows, candidates, licentiates and surgeons. However highly favourable references to Forster by the surgeon Clowes imply that the lectures would have been useful.[13] Earlier holders of the office were completely eclipsed when William Harvey was appointed lecturer in 1615.

Surgeons were much more entrenched in London civic life than their brother physicians.[14] Their gilds were of long ancestry and the Barbers' gild had received its first royal charter in 1462. This charter dealt almost entirely with the regulation of surgery, and it confirmed that this organization was as much concerned with surgeons as with barbers.[15] In 1520 the Barbers amalgamated with the much smaller sister Fellowship of Surgeons to form the 'Mystery and Communality of Barbers and Surgeons of London'.[16] This company occupied a well-established place in the hierarchy of London companies, and apart from minor problems it enjoyed good relations with the civic authorities. Surgeons played an

---

[11] Annals, 12 July, 6 October 1587. The garden scheme may have originated with Gerard, who put forward similar plans to the Barber-Surgeons' Company and to the University of Cambridge: S. Young, *Annals of the Barber-Surgeons* (1890), pp.542–3. See Plate 10.

[12] Clark, *History*, I, pp.150–2; F. W. Steer, 'Lord Lumley's benefaction to the College of Physicians', *Medical History*, II (1958), 298–305, Frank, 'Institutional renaissance'.

[13] Richard Forster, *Ephemerides meteorologicae* (1575). Richard Harvey, *Astrological discourse upon the conjunction of Saturne and Jupiter* (1583), sig. Aii r. William Clowes, *Profitable and necessarie booke of observations* (1596), pp.73, 83, 114.

[14] For London surgeons, see F. J. Furnivall and P. Furnivall (eds.), *The Anatomie of the Bodie of Man by Thomas Vicary*, Early English Text Society, XXXIII (1888); Young, *Annals*; J. F. South, *Memorials of the Craft of Surgery in England*, ed. D'Arcy Power (1886).

[15] Young, *Annals*, pp.52–71. The Barbers' gild in 1499 was known as 'mistere Barbitonsorum et Sirgicorum': ibid., p.71.

[16] Young, *Annals*, pp.78–80, and appendix C.

important part in the hospitals, and in public health work at the time of epidemics. The fortunes of the large Barber-Surgeons' Company depended less on individual initiative than did the College of Physicians. During the sixteenth century the Company built on its strengths, resisted the subjugation of surgery to physic, and grew to a position where its leading members could challenge the authority of the College of Physicians.

The Barber-Surgeons adopted the traditional livery–yeomanry pattern of organization. Within the Company there was a strict separation of duties of barbers and surgeons. Their Company was not rich, but it was large, being governed by four Masters and a Court of Assistants of between twenty and thirty members drawn from the livery. This hierarchical structure was repeated in the yeomanry. It is difficult to assess the precise strength of the medical element within the Company. At the outset of episcopal licensing in 1514 72 surgical licences were issued in London, mostly to surgeons practising locally.[17] In 1537 the freemen of the Barbers' Company numbered 185. The company was at this time the largest in the city. It is reasonable to suppose that half the members were involved in surgery.[18] At a more impressionistic level a pessimistic observer estimated *c*.1560 that the number of London surgeons able to give service in times of war had slumped from 72 to 34.[19] In 1578 90 freemen and 10 'foreigns' contributed to the levy for raising soldiers.[20] Thus it is reasonable to assume that in the latter years of the century the expanding Company contained between 70 and 100 surgeons. There was no attempt to restrict the numbers entering the yeomanry, and there was no barrier to the admission of women. An important group attached to the Company were the 'foreign brothers', comprising members who had trained outside London. The foreign brothers included the Sea-Surgeons, a group whose registration was controlled by the Barber-Surgeons' Company (see Plate 11). One of the most important and difficult official duties of the Company was the supply of surgeons for military service. It was a constant cause of complaint both in the army and navy that press-

---

[17] Reg. Fitzjames 1506–1522, fol.52: R. R. James, 'The earliest list of surgeons to be licensed', *Janus*, XLI (1937), 255–60.

[18] P.R.O., Exchequer, Treasury of Receipt, Misc.Bk 93, fols.1–3; Young, *Annals*, pp.95–6. The membership comprised 26 Court of Assistants, 42 Livery, 117 Yeomanry.

[19] Thomas Gale, Interpolation in François Valleriola, 'The office of a chirurgion' [1562] in Gale, *Certain works of Galens* (1567), p.117.

[20] Young, *Annals*, p.106. Between 1603 and 1674 the Company entered an average of 48 freemen per annum: ibid., p.259.

gang methods of recruitment had resulted in military medicine's becoming dominated by surgeons the calibre of horse-leeches.[21] For a short time at the turn of the century the Barber-Surgeons attempted to control all inferior classes of practitioner. After a brief and unsuccessful experiment, coercion was abandoned in favour of the traditional practice of recruitment to the Company on a goodwill basis.

The Barber-Surgeons' Company embraced many classes of practitioner. The majority of its members where no doubt humble mechanics, but the Company also contained a group of articulate and effective surgeons who were not content to allow their practice to be limited in scope by deference to rules imposed by the College of Physicians. These surgeons exercised increasing influence in the Company in the latter decades of the century. They introduced stricter rules for entry, and more effective machinery for the education of freemen. In 1555 four examiners were appointed by the Company; this number was soon increased to seven. Examiners were drawn from within the Company, whereas previously to 1555 it had been customary to employ a physician as examiner.

Candidates applying for admission to the Barber-Surgeons' Company were required to have served the statutory period as apprentices and to satisfy the examiners that they were 'well exercised in the curing of infirmities belonging to surgery of the parts of man's body commonly called the anatomy'.[22] In 1557 a rule was introduced insisting on familiarity with Latin as a precondition for apprenticeship. The ecclesiastical authorities were increasingly pressed to avoid licensing surgeons not previously certified by the examiners.[23]

The regulations were complemented by increasingly well-codified arrangements for surgical demonstrations and anatomical lectures. The substantial body of information relating to these lectures suggests that the surgeons were more successful than the College of Physicians in securing the participation of their members in anatomical exercises. The original charter of the Barber-Surgeons' Company allowed them access to the bodies of four executed criminals each year. In 1556 more formal rules were introduced for the anatomies, allowing for a regular succession of two Masters and two Stewards of Anatomy. The Masters of Anatomy were important functionaries, who examined surgeons and

---

[21] J. J. Keevil, *Medicine and the Navy* (2 vols., Edinburgh/London, 1957–8), I, pp.139–44; C. G. Cruikshank, *Elizabeth's Army*, 2nd edn (Oxford, 1966), chapter 11.

[22] Young, *Annals*, pp.312, 316.

[23] Roberts, 'London apothecaries', pp.186–7.

held the keys to the library and instrument collection. In 1567 the improved facilities introduced for viewing the anatomies indicate that these exercises were regarded as an attraction for visitors to London, although the lectures were primarily intended for members of the Company. The records of the Company indicate that strict observance of attendance rules was expected. In anatomies, as with examinations, surgeons moved towards a position of greater independence from the College of Physicians.[24] In the years following the establishment of the Company, its lectures had been given by John Caius. In 1567 the Venetian Julio Borgarucci was appointed lecturer in anatomy for four or five years in order that 'the college of the physicians should not put him from us' because of Borgarucci's lack of official standing.[25] In 1566 Thomas Hall was awarded a bursary to enable him to study 'surgery annexing physic thereunto' at university, sufficient for him to lecture on the subject. Thereafter he was appointed examiner and dissector for ten years.[26] The lectures of John Banister on the *De re anatomica* of Realdo Colombo are commemorated in an illustration dating from 1581. Banister, one of the leading surgeons of the time, came under censure from the College of Physicians for illegal practice of medicine.[27]

English surgeons of the later sixteenth century were led by men of sound learning and assured skill. They produced useful translations of texts selected discriminatingly from recent medical literature. Through their work a wide range of continental medical authors became accessible to English readers.

A good impression of the sources valued by an experienced surgeon is gained from the schedule attached to the will of Robert Balthrop in 1591, bequeathing his medical works to three assistants. To one he gave two editions of Guidi's *Chirurgia*, one in Latin and one in French, Bartholomaeus *De proprietatibus rerum*, Cataneus *De morbo gallico*, Valescus *Practica*, and the works of Albucasis, Dioscorides, Cornelius Celsus, Johannes Mesue, Leonhard Fuchs, and a manuscript translation of Curtius into English. To the second he gave certain English writings: the Geminus edition of Vesalius (see Frontispiece), Vigo *Chirurgerye*, Turner *Herbal*, and manuscript translations of works by Guidi and

24   Young, *Annals*, pp.79, 102, 170, 180, 183, 187, 308–15, 361–78.
25   Young, *Annals*, p.314. Borgarucci's relations with the College are not clear. He was referred to as belonging to the College at the incorporation of his degree in 1567, and as a stranger of the College in a list of *c.*1572. According to the Annals of the College for 1560 he was restrained as a quack. He is not listed as a Fellow by Munk.
26   Young, *Annals*, pp.183–7.
27   Anatomical Tables of John Banister, Glasgow University Library, Hunterian MS. 364.

Fuchs. To the third he gave a bound edition of surgical works in Latin by Guy de Chauliac, Bruno and Lanfranc.

The most interesting bequest of Balthrop was to the Barber-Surgeons' Company, of his own manuscript text and translation of the important modern surgical works of Tagault and Paré. He declared: 'I have written into English for the love that I owe unto my brethren practising chirurgery and not understanding the Latin tongue and given them into the Hall for their daily use and reading both in Latin and English'.[28]

It is difficult to avoid the impression that the elite of the Barber-Surgeons' Company were, in the last decades of the century, making a more active and original contribution to medicine than their colleagues in the College of Physicians (see Plates 10 and 11). The earlier medical writers among the surgeons, Thomas Vicary, John Hall and Thomas Gale, prepared the way for William Clowes, George Baker, John Banister and John Read. The former group represented a more traditional view of surgery, using vernacular writings to improve the educational standing of surgeons, and to familiarize them with the basic tenets of Galenic medicine. They viewed the physician as their mentor and senior partner. The latter group employed the vernacular for more original and advanced handbooks. They sought to raise the status of surgeons; Galen was quoted to undermine the traditional division between physic and surgery. They were receptive to new ideas in medicine, and were quick to exploit the advantages of Paracelsian remedies. Their writings deliberately instigated a breach of the College monopoly of medical practice. It is therefore not surprising that Banister and Baker were singled out for censure by the College, or that in 1595 the College should issue a formal warning to the Barber-Surgeons' Company 'that they should refrain completely from the practice of medicine'.[29]

Apart from the College of Physicians and Barber-Surgeons' Company, the other main identifiable group in London medicine was the apothecaries.[30] London apothecaries were independently minded,

---

[28] Young, *Annals*, pp.530–2. Balthrop was Sergeant-Surgeon to Queen Elizabeth, and the friend of Clowes and Banister. Balthrop's master Nicholas Alcocke (d. 1550) left his apprentice his 'Guido in English', and gave to others editions of Lanfranc and John of Arderne: Young, *Annals*, p.527.

[29] *Annals*, 7 November 1595.

[30] C. R. B. Barrett, *History of the Society of Apothecaries* (London, 1905); C. Wall, H. C. Cameron and E. A. Underwood, *A History of the Worshipful Society of Apothecaries of London* (London, 1963), I.

wealthy, and numerous; many of their shops were to be found in Bucklersbury, near Cheapside. By the end of the century there were probably about 100 apothecaries practising in London, since 121 were listed shortly afterwards at the foundation of the Apothecaries' Society.[31] In the sixteenth century apothecaries were not separately organized. They formed an important element within the Grocers' Company, and there were no limitations on the sale of drugs by grocers. Indeed, members of other companies engaged in the retail trade were actively involved in the sale of products which were used medicinally such as oils, conserves, tobacco, cordials and distilled waters. In the later part of the century John Hester was the leading figure in a small faction of 'practitioners in the art of distillation' who specialized in the supply of chemically prepared medicines.[32] The chemists were openly critical of the polypharmaceutical practices of apothecaries. They regarded as worthless most of the products dispensed: 'your syrups be but sauces, your purgations for the most part poisons, and ... your confortatives, exhilaratives, and regeneratives, are by nature so fast fettered that they cannot move against their enemies'.[33]

Although possibly slower than surgeons to take advantage of chemical therapy, apothecaries were often keen gardeners, and botanists; figures like James Garrett and Hugh Morgan pioneered the importation of drugs or the cultivation of plants from the New World. This was still a small-scale operation in the sixteenth century; the value of imported drugs had not reached an annual value of £1,000 by 1600. Twenty years later this figure had reached £8,000.[34]

The gardeners Garret, Morgan and John Parkinson were among the substantial group of apothecaries prosecuted by the College of Physicians for the illegal practice of medicine.[35] Apothecaries were also found guilty of dispensing for the numerous unlicensed physicians. Edward Barlow was actively pursued by the College for illegally practising medicine; he was also dispensing for such eminent College physicians as William Gilbert and Richard Forster, for the Paracelsians

---

[31] Barrett, *Society of Apothecaries*, pp.xxi–xxii. In testimonies recorded in Guildhall MS. 8286 for the 1630s, estimates of between 140 and 185 apothecaries were made (fols.14, 21).

[32] For Hester, see below, p.326.

[33] T.W., *The copie of a letter sent by a learned physician to his friend* [1587], sig.B4v–5r.

[34] R. S. Roberts, 'The early history of the import of drugs into England', in F. N. L.Poynter (ed.), *The Evolution of Pharmacy in Britain* (London, 1965), pp.165–86.

[35] C. E. Raven, *English Naturalists from Neckam to Ray* (Cambridge, 1947), pp.136, 170, 172, 185, 192 (Garret); 115–17, 135, 192, 213, 242 (Morgan); chapter 15 (Parkinson). The most distinguished apothecary practising medicine at this time was Roger Gwyn, apothecary to St Bartholomew's and St Thomas's hospitals.

Peter Turner and Richard Taylior, and for the unlicensed practitioners Raphael Thorius and Johann Vulpe.[36] In 1585 the apothecaries sought to secure their position in medicine by petitioning the College of Physicians for a monopoly over compounding medicines and over the sale of substances used in the practice of medicine. This demand was impracticable then, as it was after 1618, when it was revived by the newly formed Society of Apothecaries. The petitioning of 1585 signifies that the apothecaries were beginning to tire of being in an inferior position to grocers in the Grocers' Company. Only hesitantly, and after complex manoeuvering, did they move towards separation, since they were aware that such a move would expose them to greater control by the College of Physicians, including the imposition of an official pharmacopoeia.[37]

At the fringe of official medicine were the midwives. The College of Physicians had general authority over physicians, surgeons and apothecaries. The latter two groups were also under the jurisdiction of city companies; surgeons were also under ecclesiastical control.[38] Midwives throughout England came only under a system of ecclesiastical jurisdiction.[39] Ecclesiastical licensing of midwives was not always rigorously enforced. Nevertheless midwifery licensing was a serious consideration, since the religious conformity and co-operation of the midwife was seen as one of the essential means towards securing a conformist baptism for the infant. As indicated by the oath sworn by midwives, strict exercise of midwifery was important for the prevention of abortion, the establishment of paternity, and for ensuring that birth took place in an atmosphere of sound religion and without regard for magical practices. The midwife was an established figure in the London parish. In 1589 the daughter of a foreign merchant was 'brought to bed in the house of Lieven Allette a Dutch midwife dwelling in the Dukes Place . . . where the said child was born'. In the same parish of St Botolph without Aldgate a midwife named Mrs Pullet was active in 1590; between 1610 and 1624 the burials of three midwives were reported, one being 'an ancient midwife, and a long dweller in our parish'.[40] It was

[36] Bodleian Library, MS. Ashmole 1487, 'Liber E. Barloui', fols.7–27.
[37] Roberts, 'London apothecaries', chapter 7; Barrett, *Society of Apothecaries*, chapter 1; and Wall, Cameron and Underwood, *History of the Apothecaries*, pp.8–22, 216–20.
[38] For a case of a surgeon's being excommunicated in 1595 in his parish for failing to obtain an ecclesiastical licence, see T. R. Forbes, *Chronicle from Aldgate* (New Haven, Conn., 1971), p.91. See Plate 8.
[39] T. R. Forbes, *The Midwife and the Witch* (New Haven, Conn., 1966); J. Donnison, *Midwives and Medical Men* (London, 1977), pp.1–20, 203–6.
[40] Forbes, *Chronicle from Aldgate*, pp.67–8, 194.

Plate 8. Ecclesiastical medical licence, 1566
A licence granted to Robert Hauust of Great Yarmouth for the practice of medicine and surgery, 8 June 1566, on the authority of the Bishop of Norwich. Reproduced by permission of the Norfolk Record Office (Aylsham Collection 76).

probably by no means unusual for three English and one foreign midwife to be active at any one time in a London parish.

Although hospitals and public health agencies in London were poorly developed in comparison with major cities on the continent, numerous individuals were employed in this work on a permanent or temporary basis. After the middle of the century, the rump of medical charities to weather the storm of the Reformation, such as the reorganized major hospitals of St Bartholomew and St Thomas, or minor establishments ranging from the military hospital of the Savoy and the lunatic hospital of St Mary of Bethlehem, down to the few surviving lazar houses, offered posts as renter clerks, hospitalers, butlers, matrons, sisters, surgeons, porters and beadles.[41] At St Bartholomew's women were

---

[41] Important hospitals like St Mary Roncevall and St Anthony's were among the numerous medical charities which collapsed in the mid-sixteenth century. See R. M. Clay, *The Medieval Hospitals of England* (London, 1909); W. J. Loftie, *Memorials of the Savoy* (1878); N. Moore, *The History of St Bartholomew's Hospital* (2 vols., London, 1918); F. G. Parsons, *The History of St Thomas's Hospital*, 1 (London, 1932).

employed to treat the numerous cases of skin diseases. Later in the century the main hospitals expanded their medical staff to include apothecaries and physicians. The civic authorities managing the hospitals adopted an independent attitude towards medical staff appointments. St. Bartholomew's employed William Clowes, the leading English writer on surgery, and convert to Paracelsianism. Its apothecary Roger Gwyn was pursued by the College of Physicians as an unlicensed practitioner. The Paracelsian sympathizer Peter Turner was employed as physician (1581–4). Upon his retirement the College of Physicians strongly urged the appointment of Henry Wotton, who, like Turner, was the son of a celebrated naturalist. The College claimed that 'in all other honourable cities and towns in all Europe, where the like hospitals are maintained, the physician is always provided out of the body of the Society and College of the Physicians of the same city'.[42] The governors responded to counterpetitioning from the Privy Council, and appointed Timothie Bright, who, like his friend Turner, was threatened with imprisonment by the College of Physicians for illegal medical practice in London.[43]

Civic authorities in London were slow to move beyond the medical assistance given on an occasional basis through poor relief, to evolve public health measures appropriate to the escalating burden of mass-illness occasioned by epidemics (see Plates 1 and 2). A hospital for contagious diseases was lucidly delineated in More's *Utopia* (1516), but a purpose-built civic pesthouse was established only after a long period of agitation, and it had barely reached the construction stage by the end of the century.[44] In the meantime victims of epidemics were housed, if at all, in temporarily appropriated buildings, lazar houses and prisons. In time of plague a ramshackle machinery administered by Constables and temporarily appointed Surveyors was brought into operation to enforce isolation and provide for rudimentary domiciliary care. The male and female officers included: surgeons; wardens or watchers; keepers, providers, purveyors or acaters; searchers, viewers, and nurses. These latter followers of dangerous occupations terminate the roll-call of official medicine. The best of the nurses were regarded as compassionate saviours of the sick; many were feared as 'night-crows' hastening the

[42] Letter from the College of Physicians to the governors of St Bartholomew's, 7 January 1584/5: Munk, *Roll*, I, pp.70–1.
[43] Moore, *History of St Bartholomew's Hospital*, pp.429–33. In 1591 Bright was dismissed for neglect of duties. In 1609 William Harvey secured this post.
[44] F. P. Wilson, *The Plague in Shakespeare's London* (Oxford, 1927), pp.74–84.

end of plague victims while scavenging among their possessions.[45]

As far as the vast majority of the population of London was concerned, regular contact with official medicine would have been limited to the lower echelons of the Barber-Surgeons' Company, to poorer apothecaries, and to midwives. Most of their medical assistance came from the internal resources of the family, from neighbours, priests, or finally from the local unlicensed male practitioners or wise women having no formal authorization to practise medicine from either ecclesiastical or civil bodies. This situation was not unlike that in the smaller town or village, except that London offered a greater variety of practitioners, and the greatest opportunities for honest innovators, or unscrupulous mountebanks. The extent of this unauthorized practice was a constant annoyance, particularly to the College of Physicians, which periodically met to consider means of curtailing the 'bold and ignorant multitude' of empirics practising in London.[46] Conscientious attempts by the College of Physicians, as an extra-municipal corporation, to restrict the activities of the Barber-Surgeons' Company or to stamp out other practitioners, ran contrary to the common-law tradition of free service and infringed the customs of the City of London. Hence unlicensed practitioners of medicine could generally rely on sympathy not only from their patients but also from the Privy Council and municipal authorities.

Unauthorized practitioners devoting sufficient of their time to medicine to be designated as 'professors' of surgery and physic, or as surgeons or apothecaries, outside the fellowship of the recognized medical bodies, constituted a major element in London medical practice. Just how important they were quantitatively is difficult to establish in view of the scattered evidence relating to this diverse fraternity. In making the following estimates for the last two decades of the century, we have endeavoured to utilize least estimates in cases where accurate data are not available. Subsequent correction would then be expected to indicate the larger rather than the smaller extent of unauthorized practice. It will be assumed that the number of practitioners detected in a twenty-year period represents the number practising at any one time during that period.

One impression of the scale of unauthorized practice may be gathered from the records of prosecutions contained in the Annals of the College

45 See Wilson, *Plague*, pp.64–9, for an excellent brief account of plague officials.
46 Letter from the College to William Fleetwood, Recorder of London, 3 February 1582, quoted from Annals of the College of Physicians.

of Physicians. Between 1550 and 1600 proceedings are recorded against 236 individuals. A small number were well-qualified physicians who had committed minor infringements of the complex statutes of the College; the great majority had been openly practising medicine with no intention of seeking a College licence. The list derived from the Annals is by no means a complete enumeration of those detected as being engaged in unauthorized practice. The records of the College are deficient or missing for most of the period 1564–80. Seventy-seven of the cases date from before 1581; 159 (including 36 surgeons and apothecaries, and 13 who ultimately became candidates or licentiates of the College) from the more fully reported period 1581 to 1600. Hence there were prosecuted 110 unauthorized practitioners outside the Barber-Surgeons' and Grocers' Companies, and who formed no attachment with the College. Many unauthorized practitioners escaped prosecution. Individuals like Robert Recorde, John Dee and Timothie Bright were too highly-qualified and well-connected to be subject to effective harassment. At a more humble level it is doubtful whether unauthorized practitioners were normally reported to the College. Bolder empirics were 'discovered' by the Fellows without difficulty; others might be reported by disgruntled patients seeking retribution.

It is likely that the practitioners prosecuted by the College were matched by an equal number also unrecognized by the College, and outside the fellowship of the Barber-Surgeons' or Grocers' Companies. The biographical index of medical practitioners in progress at the Wellcome Unit for the History of Medicine currently, for 1550–1600, lists just over 100 practitioners (the majority of whom were active after 1580) outside the recognized medical bodies, in addition to those prosecuted by the College of Physicians. Thus it is not unreasonable to suppose that the miscellaneous category of physicians, surgeons and apothecaries outside the three main medical organizations practising in London in the period 1581 to 1600, numbered 250.

A second estimate of the strength of unorganized practice may be based on Thomas Gale's calculation of 60 women practitioners, which relates to 1560. Gale may have exaggerated the extent of female practice; he probably included in his estimate midwives who dabbled in medicine. However the Gale figure might well not be an exaggeration for the later decades of the century. Between 1581 and 1600 the College of Physicians prosecuted 21 women practitioners, leaving 39 to be accounted for. Biographical records made this identification difficult, since women practitioners must often have been described as midwives, or keepers of women in childbed. The ratio of female to male practitioners prosecuted (excluding members of the Barber-Surgeons' and Grocers' Companies, and offenders who ultimately became candidates or licentiates of the College), is 21 : 78 for the 1581–1600 period. Application of this ratio to the Gale estimate of women practitioners suggests that there would have been 223 male practitioners who neither belonged to the two Companies nor were ultimately attached to the College. Thus the total for male and female practitioners on this estimate is 283.

A third very approximate estimate may be made on the basis of the records of St Botolph without Aldgate (for vicinity see Plate 5). These supply more information about occupation than is usual in parish records. Twelve practitioners were mentioned between 1595 and 1625, in addition to three midwives. None of the medical practitioners was licensed by the College of Physicians; four were possibly freemen of the Barber-Surgeons' Company. The remaining eight were more humble practitioners of physic and surgery.[47] It is not known to what degree the midwives practised medicine. If it is assumed there was at this time a minimum of eight unauthorized practitioners for a population which is unlikely to have exceeded 6,000, and if the ratio of unauthorized practitioners to population was constant throughout the metropolis, on the basis of a population of 200,000 there would have been 270 practitioners outside the ranks of the organized medical bodies.[48]

The above calculations are offered hesitantly and on a tentative basis. As such however the three independent methods have produced remarkably similar results. They substantiate the impression given by such contemporary witnesses as John Halle, Gale and Clowes, that men and women from a variety of backgrounds were flooding into civil and military medical practice. It might well be a minimal estimate to suppose that in the latter decades of the sixteenth century the body of practitioners outside the three major medical organizations stood at 250.

In the eyes of the College of Physicians all those practising medicine outside the College tended to be designated as 'ignorant' and 'dangerous'. Little is known about many of the outsiders, but it is clear from the available evidence that they represent a wide social spectrum.

---

[47] Forbes, *Chronicle from Aldgate*, pp.90–3.
[48] Forbes, *Chronicle from Aldgate*, p.81, provides a population estimate for 1631 derived from Graunt, whose total related to part of the parish. Parish returns for 1694 giving a population of 9,750, represented under-registration: P. E. Jones and A. V. Judges, 'London population in the late seventeenth century', *Economic History Review*, VI (1935/6), 45–63.

At one extreme their professional credentials were as good as those of the Fellows of the College. Such celebrated medical writers of the Tudor period as Sir Thomas Elyot, William Bullein, Robert Recorde and John Hester escaped the censure of the College. However the famous mathematician Thomas Hood, having acquired between 1578 and 1595 a BA, MA, medical licence, and MD from Cambridge, was summoned before the College on two occasions, and completely forbidden to practise medicine.[49]

Medical practice was one of the favoured vocations for immigrants, both male and female. Some practised predominantly within their own community, others operated more widely. Some of the immigrants prosecuted by the College were well qualified. When Gerard Gossen, an MD of Louvain, was prosecuted in 1570 he promised to leave the country. However he seems to have remained in England until his death in London in 1603, publishing an almanac in 1571. He was granted an archiepiscopal licence to practise medicine in 1582. Even Julius the 'quack' who was restrained in 1560, was probably Julio Borgarucci, an MD of Padua, and brother of Prosper Borgarucci, a celebrated medical humanist. As already mentioned, Borgarucci lectured on anatomy to the Barber-Surgeons' Company – to the annoyance of the College – and he practised in London until his death in about 1580. He was even included as a 'stranger' in one list of members of the College of Physicians.[50] Among the surgeons prosecuted by the College are to be found George Baker and John Banister, both prominent writers and translators, as well as leading members of their profession. Equal to these surgeons in educational standing among the prosecuted practitioners were such Puritan ministers as Richard Surphlet and Henry Holland.[51]

The great majority of practitioners possessed no licence and only a limited education. They relied on their natural gifts. Many were simple tradesmen. Critics were fond of reciting the catalogue of 'honest trades' deserted by intending medical practitioners. Some had been 'painters, some glaziers, some tailors, some weavers, some joiners, some cutlers, some cooks, some bakers, and some chandlers . . . it is too apparent to see how tinkers, toothdrawers, pedlars, ostlers, carters, porters, horse-gelders, horse-leeches, idiots, apple-squires, broomsmen, bawds,

[49] *Annals*, 17 October 1595, 25 February 1597.
[50] Clark, *History*, I, p.130.
[51] For Surphlet, see a forthcoming study by Mr M. A. L. Cooke of Oxford. Surphlet published two important translations, *A discourse of the preservation of eyesight* (1599), and *Maison rustique* (1600).

witches, conjurers, sooth-sayers and sow gelders, rogues, rat-catchers, renegades, and proctors of spittle-houses, with such other like rotten and stinking weeds ... in town and country, ... abuse both physic and chirurgery'.[52]

Many of the new recruits into medicine prospered, and London was the most attractive centre for their practice. Upon prosecution many faded from the scene; others (like Paul Buck, Simon Forman, John Not, Leonard Poe and Roger Powell), despite being energetically pursued by the College, found powerful protectors who successfully prevented their protégés from being excluded from medical practice. Stigmatized as dangerous empirics by physicians, they were regarded as resourceful practitioners by their noble patients.

A representative collection of practitioners is found in the parish of St Botolph without Aldgate. The most prestigious representative was Richard Foster (d. 1624), the barber-surgeon who had treated a parishioner suffering from syphilis in 1599. Nathaniel Thorey was described as a grocer, free of the Barber-Surgeons' Company. David Warde was pursued by the College of Physicians at various times between 1580 and 1590. Thomas Woodhouse was excommunicated in 1595 for practising surgery without a bishop's licence. David Muller, like one of the midwives, was an immigrant. The lower ranks were represented by Matthias Evans, 'professor of physic and other curious arts', Edward Askew, 'a poor man, professor of physic', and Margaret Mott, the only woman, wife of a silkweaver and 'a counterfeit physician, and surgeon ... and old quacksalver'. Matthias Eggere, a visiting ship surgeon, unexpectedly entered the records of the parish by dying as a result of a brawl with another stranger.[53]

Women played a substantial part in medicine in sixteenth-century London, as already implied. Besides occupying posts at hospitals, taking on public health duties during epidemics, and collecting the information for the bills of mortality, women were recognized as apothecaries and surgeons. Mrs Cook was appointed resident surgeon-apothecary at Christ's Hospital. She was reprimanded by the governors for practising medicine privately.[54]

The twenty-nine female practitioners prosecuted by the College of

---

[52] William Clowes, *A brief treatise of Morbus Gallicus* (1585), fol.8r.
[53] Forbes, *Chronicle from Aldgate*, pp.90–3.
[54] For Mrs Cook see F. N. L. Poynter, *Selected Writings of William Clowes* (London, 1948), pp.22–3.

Physicians between 1550 and 1600 occur evenly throughout the period. 'Itinerants and old women' were a cause of particular concern to the College.[55] Those prosecuted almost certainly represent only a fraction of the women practitioners. Gale described female practice in the following terms:

three score women, that occupieth the arte of physick and chirurgerye. These women, some of them be called wise women, or holy and good women, some of them be called witches, and useth to call upon certaine spirits, and some of them useth plain Bawderie, and telleth gentlewomen that cannot bear children how they may have children.[56]

Gale's caricature is revealing about the exploitation of magical practices by wise women, and about their concern with fertility and childbirth. Many specialized primarily in the medical problems of women and children.

It is likely that nurses as well as midwives were apt to trespass into medical practice. The parishes regularly employed women to nurse orphan children or to give lodgings to the sick poor. Nurses would be assigned additional duties during epidemics relating to the care of families subjected to isolation.[57] The monthly nurse, wet–nurse and children's nurse were a common part of the establishment of higher social classes. It was common for London babies to be sent out for nursing to villages like Brentford.[58] The practice of employing wet–nurses was, however, coming under increasing criticism. John Lyly, one of the earliest critics of this practice, declared that 'the infant will ever smell of the nurse's manners having tasted of her milk'.[59]

John Dee was typical in employing wet–nurses for his children. They were paid at the rate of six shillings per month, and their charges regularly involved the cost of candles and soap. His daughter Katherine was born on 7 June 1581. Shortly afterwards she was placed with nurse Maspely at Barnes, but returned to Mortlake on 4 August because of illness at the nurse's home. She was given suck by goodwife Benet before being taken by Jane Dee to nurse Garret at Petersham on 11 August. Nurse Garret cared for the child until 25 August 1582, when she was

---

[55] Letter from College of Physicians to William Fleetwood, Recorder of London, 28 January 1582: College Annals.

[56] Gale, Interpolation in Valleriola, in Gale, *Works of Galens*, p.102.

[57] Forbes, *Chronicle from Aldgate*, chapter 7.

[58] Thomas Middleton, *A chaste maid in Cheapside*, act II, scene ii, ll.15–16, 162–4, 176.

[59] John Lyly, *Euphues*, in *Works*, ed. R. Warwick Bond (3 vols., Oxford, 1902), I, p.265; C. Webster, *The Great Instauration: Science, Medicine and Reform 1626–1660* (London, 1975), p.104.

returned home to be weaned. On 22 August 1582 nurse Garret had taken in the next child of the Dees.[60]

Having delineated the strata which constituted medical practice in London, it is appropriate at this stage to collate the various estimates and to hazard a tentative assessment of the quantitative availability of medical care.

For the period 1580 to 1600, the medical profession in London was evolving towards the position where at any one time there would have been practising:

Physicians   : 50–*c*.30 Fellows; *c*.20 candidates, and licentiates, of College of Physicians.
Surgeons   : 100–Surgeons in Barber-Surgeons' Company, freemen and licentiates including those prosecuted by College of Physicians.
Apothecaries : 100–Apothecaries in Grocers' and other Companies, including those prosecuted by College.
Practitioners : 250–Comprising 110 practitioners outside the College, Barber-Surgeons' and Grocers' Companies prosecuted by the College; 140 miscellaneous, some with licences, mostly unlicensed. Not including midwives and nurses.

Total   500

Since the population of London was approximately 200,000 in 1600, there was at least one practitioner to every 400 individuals, not taking into account the numerous body of midwives, nurses and public health officers.[61]

By modern standards the medical profession in London was disorganized and disunited. There was no adequate institutional basis for the treatment of acute diseases, and no effective public health service. In all of these respects London compared unfavourably with Italian cities.[62] But London was not lacking in medical practitioners. The medical profession spawned varieties of practitioner accessible to all segments of the population, and their practice evolved flexibly to meet health needs as they arose. The work of these practitioners may seem woefully misguided, but there is every indication that they fulfilled their brief conscientiously, and, like their rural counterparts, fully maintained the

---

[60] J. O. Halliwell (ed.), *The Diary of Dr John Dee*, Camden Society, XIX (1847), pp.14–17.
[61] These estimates are consistent with those given for later dates by Roberts, 'The London apothecaries', pp.381–2.
[62] C. M. Cipolla, *Public Health and the Medical Profession in the Renaissance* (Cambridge, 1976).

confidence of the community in their effectiveness in satisfying the needs of the sick.

In view of the disorganized state of English medicine, and the failure to impose minimal professional standards even in London, it might be expected that there would be little incentive for practitioners to opt for prolonged and expensive medical education of the kind offered at the universities. It is a revealing reflection on the mentality of those seeking entry into the higher ranks of the medical profession that they increasingly sought to obtain qualifications of the kind required for admission to the College of Physicians, and that neither the College nor the universities experienced any detectable dilution in standards. Whether strictly necessary or not, the educated classes of medical practitioner amassed academic qualifications with the same avidity as their twentieth-century counterparts. The training of the sixteenth-century physician was often so involved and prolonged that by comparison moderns seem distinctly underqualified.

The profile of the academically educated physician which gradually emerged was that of a humanistically inclined scholar, familiar alike with classical tongues and the medical sciences. This physician had spent many years studying at English universities, and sometimes also a few years abroad at one or more of the continental medical schools. This course of education frequently involved seven years in preparation for an MA, and a further seven years or more accumulating medical qualifications. During this period the medical student often held a college fellowship, minor teaching posts in medicine or other subjects, and practised medicine. He might also have prepared himself for an alternative career in the church, civil service, or in some other faculty of the university. If the doctor sought to practise in London he might then become involved in a lengthy process of selection for a fellowship of the College of Physicians. By establishing this profile the physician could claim a dignified position in society, dress according to this rank, and establish his right to charge high fees, and to dominate all inferior groups within the medical profession.

Edward Wotton, the naturalist, followed the cosmopolitan pattern of medical education established by such humanistic pioneers as Thomas Linacre. After obtaining his BA and MA at Magdalen College, Oxford, Wotton transferred to Corpus Christi College, and in 1524 was granted permission to spend from three to five years in Italy perfecting his knowledge of Greek. He took an MD at Padua some ten years after commencing his medical studies, and he concluded them by incorporating at Oxford in 1526. William Harvey abbreviated this pattern at the end of the century. After graduating as BA from Caius College in 1597 and spending two further years as an arts student at Cambridge, Harvey began a brief term of study at Padua in 1600, taking his MD in 1602. There is no firm evidence that he incorporated his MD at Cambridge upon his return to England.

John James, physician to Leicester and Sidney, went through the full course of study at Cambridge, obtaining in turn a BA, MA, MB and MD. Having completed his English medical education James transferred to the new university of Leyden, where in 1578 he became its first medical student, and, in 1581, the second to receive a medical degree. By this stage he had been engaged for seventeen years in higher education. Robert Huicke, physician to Queen Elizabeth, obtained his BA and MA at Oxford, followed by MB and MD at Cambridge, the last being incorporated at Oxford in 1556.

The search for academic qualifications was not limited to court physicians. Thomas Twyne, a practitioner of Lewes, obtained his BA, MA and MB at Oxford, the last being incorporated at Cambridge. He then studied for several years at Cambridge before taking his MD there. Thomas Turswell, physician and steward to Whitgift, took his BA and MA at Cambridge, then a licence to practise surgery, followed by a licence to practise medicine, and finally an MD. He then took out both a licence to practise medicine and an MD at Oxford. He was arguably the most qualified physician in the land.

Universities provided the most prestigious accreditation for all ranks of practitioner. Not only did Oxford and Cambridge award medical degrees, but they also granted licences to all classes of practitioner, giving authority to practise surgery or medicine throughout the nation. It might be anticipated in view of the great authority of the leading continental medical schools, and the relative weakness of formal medical teaching in England, that Englishmen would prefer continental medical education, as they were to opt for the Edinburgh medical school in the eighteenth century. But, as already indicated, apart from foreign physicians settling in England, English physicians educated abroad remained a small, albeit influential, group. For reasons of taste, and perhaps expense, continental medical education remained the privilege of the few. In the course of the century only twelve scholars left Cambridge to study on the continent and then returned to incorporate their medical degrees. Thus William Gilbert was the more typical in completing his education at Cambridge, while William Harvey was exceptional in studying medicine at Padua. The majority undertaking academic peregrinations followed Linacre to Italy, usually visiting more than one Italian university, before graduating at Padua. William Turner visited major cities in the low countries, Germany and Switzerland, and Italy, probably taking his doctorate at Ferrara or Bologna. His son, Peter Turner, studied in Switzerland and Germany, taking his doctorate at Heidelberg in 1571. Peter Turner's friend, Thomas Mouffet, visited many towns in Italy and Germany, taking his doctorate at Basel in 1579. Basel, rather than Padua or Montpelier, was the most popular continental medical school for English medical students graduating in the later sixteenth century. Besides Mouffet, Richard Taylior, Thomas D'Oylie, Robert Jacob, James Cargyll and Matthew Lister graduated at Basel between 1570 and 1605. As their correspondence indicates, a small community of English medical students built up on the continent in the later sixteenth century. As in the case of the Protestants William and Peter Turner, or the Catholics Thomas and John Fryer, extreme religious convictions were often the occasion for long visits to the continent.

Continental medical education was almost obligatory for serious scholars of the generation of Linacre. Afterwards there was a gradual falling off in the habit of studying abroad. In 1572 only one, or possibly two, of the fourteen Fellows of the College of Physicians possessed continental medical degrees. The position changed sharply shortly afterwards. Of the nine Fellows recruited between 1585 and 1589, seven possessed foreign medical qualifications. Of these, three came from the new medical school at Leyden, which was ideally situated to become the main continental centre for English medical students in the next century. This trend caused alarm in the College of Physicians, for it was regarded as a potential threat to the English medical schools. Measures were taken by the College to deter students from studying medicine abroad; accusations were made about inferior standards elsewhere; but it proved impossible to stem the flow of students towards Leyden. However the continental medical schools posed no threat to Oxford and Cambridge in the sixteenth century. Linacre and Caius believed that only benefits could emerge from interchange of personnel.

In addition to granting degrees, the English universities cherished the right to grant surgical and medical licences, bestowing unrestricted rights of practice throughout the nation. The universities took their licensing and degree-granting functions equally seriously; in the sixteenth century degrees and licences were granted in approximately equal numbers; ninety-eight MDs, twenty-two MBs, and ninety-five licences were issued.[63] These licences became highly regarded: practitioners and civil authorities alike were tending to display an ever-increasing sensitivity about formal credentials. The licensing function was a cause of friction between the universities and the College of Physicians, especially when the latter body sought to become the sole medical licensing authority for London and its environs. It was then appreciated that every university medical licentiate was a potential source of threat to the jurisdiction of the College over medical practice in London. Although the College was apt to accuse the universities of abusing their licensing privileges by granting degrees and licences to illiterate empirics, there is very little evidence to support this accusation. On the whole, as the following survey demonstrates, licences were granted with care and discrimination.

Practitioners obtaining licences from the University of Cambridge fall into three approximately equal categories; first, those who were also granted medical degrees; secondly, those who graduated in arts at the university, but who proceeded to take a medical licence rather than a medical degree; thirdly, a miscellaneous category comprising those licentiates in medicine and surgery having a more remote association with the university than the previous group.

It was not uncommon throughout the century for medical students to take out a licence to practise medicine at some stage during their prolonged preparation for a medical degree. Thus medical students practised medicine, probably independently, well before graduation. It

---

[63]   The following survey of licences and degrees at Cambridge is based primarily on W. G. Searle (ed.), *Grace Book Γ, Containing the Records of the University of Cambridge for the Years 1501–1542* (Cambridge, 1908); J. Venn (ed.), *Grace Book Δ, Containing the Records of the University of Cambridge for the Years 1542–1589* (Cambridge, 1910); Cambridge University Library (CUL), 'CU Grace Book Liber E 1589–1620'; *Venn*; R. Richardson, 'A catalogue of all the graduates in the University of Cambridge from 1500–1735', CUL, Univ. Arch. Degr.14.

Evidence from the above works has been collated with that derived from other biographical sources (see note 1). On quantitative aspects the authors reach slightly different conclusions from previous authorities, including the only detailed studies, A. H. T. Robb-Smith, 'Medical education in Cambridge before 1600', in A. Rook (ed.), *Cambridge and its Contribution to Medicine* (London, 1971), pp.1–25; A. Chaplain, 'The history of medical education in the Universities of Oxford and Cambridge 1500–1850' (1920), typescript, London, Royal College of Physicians, MS. 663. See also: H. D. Rolleston, *The Cambridge Medical School* (Cambridge, 1932); P. Allen, 'Medical education in seventeenth-century England', *Journal of the History of Medicine,* 1 (1946), 115–43; V. Bullough, 'The mediaeval medical school at Cambridge', *Mediaeval Studies,* xxiv (1962), 162–8. Of less relevance are M. H. Curtis, *Oxford and Cambridge in Transition 1558–1642* (Oxford, 1959), chapter 6; W. J. Costello, *The Scholastic Curriculum at Early 17th Century Cambridge* (Cambridge, Mass., 1958); J. B. Mullinger, *The University of Cambridge* (3 vols., Cambridge, 1873–1911).

is also not unlikely that those without the licence practised medicine. Of the twelve sixteenth-century Cambridge medical graduates with MBs only, five possessed medical licences. Of the ninety-eight Cambridge MDs, twenty-one possessed medical licences, and one, Thomas Turswell, a surgical licence also. In 1572, one year after obtaining his BA, and at the age of 24, Turswell was granted a licence to practise surgery, on the basis of six years' study and practice of surgery. In 1578 and 1581 he was granted medical licences on the basis of studies since his MA in 1574. He was accorded an MD in 1583. In a more representative case, Lancelot Browne was granted a medical licence in 1570 on the basis of six years' study of medicine. Browne had taken his BA in 1563 and his MA in 1566. The university recognized in the cases of Turswell, Browne and others, that it was permissible to begin the study and practice of surgery or medicine before the completion of the liberal arts course. For the purpose of granting medical licences to medical students, medical studies were usually accepted as beginning after the BA and before the completion of the MA. Usually four or five years' experience was thought sufficient for granting licences to medical students.

The majority of medical students obtained neither licence nor MB before proceeding to the MD, which then constituted their sole and sufficient qualification for the practice of medicine throughout the nation, although the applicability of this or other university qualifications in the London area was constantly challenged by the College of Physicians.

Medical licences were the sole medical qualification of twenty-eight of the sixteenth-century arts graduates. This practice was uncommon before 1550, but continued at a fairly constant rate of about five per decade thereafter. It is difficult to generalize about the college associations of these licentiates, but the pattern is different from that pertaining in the case of licences granted to students who went on to take medical degrees. The largest group (six) came from Christ's College; but even there, at a rate of never more than one per decade over the century. None was granted both medical and surgical licences, and only three (Geoffrey Bell, John Parman and William Thomson), licences for surgery. The very first Cambridge licence had been the surgical licence granted in 1498 to Robert Yaxley, later one of the founders of the College of Physicians. Most arts graduates preferred to qualify for general medical practice. Almost all of the licentiates gave evidence of a length of study in medicine after completion of an arts education which was comparable to that of scholars who went on to take medical degrees.

The statutes seem to have recommended six years of study for medical licentiates.

In a few cases licences were granted after periods of three years or less. This category included George May, who took out a licence one year after obtaining his BA, but claimed seven years' study and practice of medicine. More typical was the famous William Butler, who was granted a licence after six years' study of medicine. In an extreme case, Thomas Barwick was granted a medical licence after twenty years' study of medicine after graduating in arts. Of these licentiates, five are recorded as being ordained, and a total of nine beneficed. For instance, Peter Aschton was granted a licence to practise medicine in 1533 on the basis of five years' study and practice in Paris and London. He was later ordained, and from 1537 held a variety of ecclesiastical places of benefit, while also being elected a Fellow of the College of Physicians.

The third and final category of licentiate comprised mainly outside practitioners having no Cambridge arts degree, who came to the university specifically for the purpose of obtaining licences. In the sixteenth century eighteen applicants were awarded medical licences, seventeen, surgical licences, and three were granted both surgical and medical licences. Most of the licences were awarded between 1540 and 1570, six being granted before 1540, and six after 1570. The growth of the practice may be associated with the rise in the reputation of the medical faculty, and the increase in pressure for certification within the profession, and from outside authorities; its decline is unlikely to represent a response to pressure from the College of Physicians. More probably it is to be explained by the emergence of the rival system of ecclesiastical licensing.

Although information about the academic and professional standing of this third category of licentiate is usually sparse, there is no indication that licences were given freely to empirics; indeed those outsiders who applied for medical and surgical licences seem on the whole to have been skilled and experienced, and often well educated. Indeed the medical licentiates in this last category were of very similar academic standing to those licentiates who had proceeded to the study of medicine after taking an arts degree at Cambridge. This of all the groups contained the largest section of foreigners. In some cases it is evident that these visitors had studied at Cambridge. The theologian John Venetus returned to Cambridge twelve years after obtaining his DD, in order to take out a medical licence in 1531. A close connection with Cambridge is also likely for Miles Blomefield who was granted a licence after seven years' study and practice, which included one dissection; or for Florentius Semar, described as a graduate in arts of Paris and a one-time student at Cambridge, who was granted a licence after ten years' 'diligent and enthusiastic' study of medicine. There is little difference in academic standing between Semar and the Hungarian Johann Vulpe, whose MD was negotiated by his patron the Duke of Sussex. It was attested that Vulpe had studied medicine for ten years, partly abroad, partly in Cambridge. Sussex arranged for the degree to be granted without the candidate's undertaking all of the statutory exercises.

The outsiders who were granted surgical licences tended to be of lesser academic standing than their brother medical licentiates. Nevertheless the surgeons were of good standing within their profession. Typically Thomas Surphlet and Leonard Duffield were granted licences after giving evidence of 'many years'' study and practice. Edward Overton had studied and practised for ten years, while Philip Barrough, author of *The Method of Physic* (1590), declared seven years' study of surgery when granted a surgical licence in 1559. In 1572 he was granted a licence to practise medicine. Geoffrey Bell, described as a one-time student of Cambridge, was granted a licence after ten years' study and practice of surgery.

For those taking medical degrees, the MD was the more popular option. Only seven individuals took both an MB and an MD, four of these cases occurring within the first decade. In the course of the century ninety-eight MDs were granted, compared with only twenty-two MBs. There are grounds for believing that the MB and the ML were regarded as equivalent to each other. The MB was often granted to foreigners, or, for a variety of technical reasons, to a handful of English scholars. Academic arrangements were sufficiently flexible for there to be no particular incentive to opt for the more junior qualification. Thus the practice of granting MBs, which had been common during the first decade of the century, virtually fell into abeyance after 1550. The sixteenth-century university statutes gave no particular incentive for incepting for the MB before proceeding to the MD, or for opting for an MB rather than an MD.

Grants of doctorates, indicated in Table 1, provide a convenient barometer of the scale of operation of the Cambridge medical school. The position was by no means uniform throughout the century. In the first four decades very few doctorates were awarded. Then between 1540 and 1560 there was a sharp acceleration, doctorates being awarded at an average rate of one per annum. In the next decade there was

Table 1. Medical degrees granted at Cambridge University in the sixteenth century

	1501–10	1511–20	1521–30	1531–40	1541–50	1551–60	1561–70	1571–80	1581–90	1591–1600	Total
(a) MDs											
Caius							2	2	2	2	8
Christ's								1		3	4
Clare				1					1	4	6
Corpus							1			1	2
Jesus					1	1				1	3
King's	1			2		2	2		5	2	14
King's Hall	1	1	1								3
Magdalen									1		1
Pembroke								1	2	1	4
Peterhouse						2	1	4	1	2	10
Queens'									2	1	3
St John's					1	1	4	2	1		9
Trinity				1		2	4	5	2	4	18
Unknown	2	1	1		4	1	2	1		1	13
Total	4	2	2	4	6	9	16	16	17	22	98
(b) MBs	6			3	5	2		5	1		22
Total MD + MB	10	2	2	7	11	11	16	21	18	22	120

another sharp rise. In the last four decades of the century, doctorates were awarded at an average rate of almost two per annum. There was a distinct concentration of medical students at certain colleges. Virtually half of the medical graduates in the period 1561–80 were drawn from St John's and Trinity Colleges. Thereafter the distribution became more even. Despite the activities of John Caius, his college does not appear to have emerged as a major centre of medical studies.

In estimating the strength of the student body involved at any one time in preparation for a medical degree, it is necessary to take into account the duration of medical education. Regulations about residence were defined, albeit briefly and slightly imprecisely, in the university statutes. Before 1570, it was assumed that an MD would be taken not less than five years after the MA, and after 1570, that an MD would be taken not less than five years from obtaining the MB, or not less than seven years after the MA. The slightly more detailed and specific character of the regulations in the 1570 statutes seems to have had very little effect on established practice. Both before and after 1570 medical studies tended to be preceded by the full term of arts studies. The term spent in preparation for a medical degree was frequently not as long as that prescribed in the statutes, but the spirit of the regulations was broadly preserved. For one third of the doctorates the length of medical studies cannot be assessed with accuracy. The remainder are divided evenly between those who studied medicine for between four and ten years, and those who studied medicine for eleven years or longer. Within these groups there is such wide variation that it is difficult and possibly misleading to isolate an average pattern of medical education. The statutory norm of seven years was taken sufficiently seriously for the College of Physicians in 1585 to introduce penalties for doctors who had spent less than seven years preparing for their medical degree.[64] In the majority of cases for which evidence is available, the impression is given that short-cuts were rarely sanctioned. There is no justification in statutes, grace books, or biographical records, for the commonly held myth that the 1570 statutes marked a radical change in procedures relating to medical degrees, permitting students to qualify more rapidly by entering directly into medical studies without first undergoing an arts education. The ambiguity in the 1570 statutes respecting requirements for entrance into MB studies was not exploited to produce any noticeable change in academic practice until well after the sixteenth century.

[64] Annals, 23 October 1585.

Thomas Lorkin, who became Regius Professor in 1564, obtained his BA in 1552, his MA in 1555, and the MD after the statutory five years in 1560. When William Gilbert incepted for an MD in 1569, five years after his MA, he was described as a student of medicine of eight years' standing. Of Gilbert's medical contemporaries at St John's, William Baronsdale spent five years, Richard Smith and John Coldwell six years, and William Lakyn, Thomas Randall and George Bonde thirteen years over their MD studies after graduating in arts. It was by no means uncommon at Cambridge in the sixteenth century for more than ten years to be spent in preparation for an MD. Twenty-four instances are recorded, and it is likely that many of the uncertain cases fall into this category. As examples of longer preparation, in 1545 the celebrated mathematician Robert Recorde was granted his MD after twelve years of medical study; in 1579 Timothie Bright was granted his MD after eleven years of medical study.

On the basis of the above information it is possible to speculate about the effective size of the Cambridge medical faculty. During the last four decades of the century, as already mentioned, two students per annum graduated in medicine as MB or MD. Our working estimate for the average length of study is seven years. Thus at any one time fourteen students would be preparing for a medical degree. This category would be matched by a group of perhaps equal size, comprising various elements: local practitioners, medical men in college fellowships or medical teaching positions, and especially students of other faculties and visiting scholars studying medicine privately, sometimes with the intention of taking out a medical licence. Even in the 1530s some dozen medical graduates were working in Cambridge. In the loosely structured teaching system of medicine in sixteenth-century Cambridge, all of these components would be relevant to determining the character of the medical faculty and the tone of the education of its students.

The official teachers of medicine were so few by the standards of continental medical schools, that medical education would have collapsed had it depended on their efforts alone. The unstructured nature of Cambridge medical teaching may have had certain disadvantages from the professional point of view, but it carried the compensation that medicine would have retained its broad cultural appeal. Thus members of other faculties were not inhibited from taking an active interest in medicine. Sir John Cheke, the leading humanist innovator and Regius Professor of Greek, examined medical candidates; the prominent mathematician Henry Briggs served as Linacre lecturer; the lay polymath Gabriel Harvey succeeded the medical man Lancelot Browne as medical fellow at Pembroke College; the theologian Joseph Mede provides us with invaluable evidence about the study of anatomy at Cambridge.[65] John Fletcher, MA, a fellow of Caius College, was much in demand as a mathematics teacher, astrologer and physician. At King's College William Burton lectured in astronomy and philosophy before being appointed Regius Professor of Physic in 1596.

At this time of religious turmoil, clerics prudently studied medicine as a safeguard. Such Puritan leaders as William Alley, William Turner and John Burgess turned to medical practice during times of persecution. Many other intending clerics like John Favour would have studied medicine to assist their work with the sick poor of their parishes. The academic records of many university-educated physicians, including such well-known names as Peter Baro of Boston and Gabriel Harvey of Saffron Walden, show no evidence of formal medical studies. Nevertheless in most cases it is likely that their preparation for a medical career began at university.

The practice of granting licences to scholars who ultimately entered the church was disapproved of by the College of Physicians. A substantial body of priest-physicians existed, who were beyond the control of the College, and who could compete effectively with specialist physicians. The College might complain about the granting of medical degrees and licences to priests, but this practice was almost impossible to restrain in view of the close connections between the clerical and medical professions. There were so many cases of transfer between the two professions, or of pursuit of both simultaneously, that priest-physicians constituted a dominant group in the medical profession. It was also unrealistic to expect priests to relinquish their duties towards the sick, even if these involved profit from better-off patients, while physicians continued to enjoy the fruits of ecclesiastical offices. Thomas Linacre himself owed his wealth to this practice, and other members of the College, including William Harvey's father-in-law, Lancelot Browne, were rewarded from ecclesiastical sources during

---

[65] Letter from Mede to Martin Stuteville, 15 March 1627/8, in J. Heywood and T. Wright (eds.), *Cambridge University Transactions during the Puritan Controversies* (2 vols., 1854), II, p.364, refers to the intention of John Collins (1572–1634), the new Regius Professor, to perform anatomies every year, suggesting previous neglect of this practice. It was noted that Mede was 'usually sent for when they had any anatomy in Caius College': John Worthington, Introduction to Mede's *Works* (1664), sig.a2v. In 1646 the senate drew attention to the neglect of anatomies by Regius Professor Francis Glisson: Heywood and Wright, *Cambridge University Transactions*, II, pp.471–2.

the century. An extreme case of versatility was Richard Argentine, a Cambridge medical graduate in 1541, who practised medicine and taught at the grammar school at Ipswich, as well as serving at various times as a Catholic priest and Puritan minister.

Although the Cambridge medical faculty was small by continental standards, and also the smallest faculty within the university, after 1540 its numerical and intellectual record was by no means insignificant. The upturn in the fortunes of the medical faculty coincides with the appointment in 1540 of the first Regius Professor of Physic. It is also relevant to note that the first direct evidence about the appointment of a Linacre lecturer dates from 1546. As demonstrated above, from 1560 onwards there were at any one time fourteen students preparing for medical degrees, and an equal number intending to take out licences, or involved in medical studies in some other capacity. From 1540 onwards there would have been in residence a sufficiently large number of medical graduates to fill academic posts, conduct examinations, and fulfil ceremonial functions. There was also a sufficiently stable body of medical students to sustain a lively interest in the acquisition of knowledge of the medical sciences. Thus in the second half of the century Cambridge emerged as a viable centre for medical studies, and the momentum created was preserved for the whole of the seventeenth century. Whereas, at the time of Linacre, serious medical students had no choice but to study abroad, William Gilbert was very much the rule in his generation in spending the whole period of his medical education at Cambridge. From the time of William Harvey the pendulum swung in favour of Padua and Leyden, but then continental medical education was becoming fashionable as much for its brevity and connection with continental travel as for its academic and professional quality.

John Blyth, the first Regius Professor of Physic (1540–54), was very much of the stamp of the older generation of humanist physicians. After initial education in arts at King's College he travelled widely on the continent, obtaining his MD at Ferrara in 1533. He married the sister of Sir John Cheke, the first Regius Professor of Greek. Of the other Regius Professors of Medicine in the sixteenth century only Henry Walker (1555–64) studied abroad, and he had only spent a short time at Angers where he was awarded his MD. The other incumbents John Hatcher (1554–5), his son-in-law Thomas Lorkin (1564–91) – and, amazingly, their successors until after 1850 – were educated almost exclusively at Cambridge.

The rise of the medical faculty at Cambridge is one manifestation of the general expansion of English education in the century before 1660. This 'educational revolution' was manifested in the growth of educational institutions of all types, and by the foundation of new colleges and schools. Student numbers at the universities rapidly increased; the greater numbers graduating in medicine correlate closely with this general increase, and with the rise in numbers at those colleges like Caius, for which accurate data are available.[66] This expansion does not seem to have taken place at the cost of academic standards. The universities cultivated the humanistic curriculum, and there is ample evidence of the emergence of a new spirit of criticism and enquiry during this renaissance, which benefited medicine and the natural sciences as well as other disciplines.

The transformation of studies at Cambridge was reflected in the statutes to only a limited degree. Academic developments were more a function of individual example and initiative than of institutional change. Hence improvements were sometimes spectacular, but they were often transitory. In medicine informal developments took place against a background of minor institutional change. The creation of the Regius chair in physic in 1540 provided the basis for continuous lecturing on important medical texts. Perhaps more significant changes occurred at the college level. St John's College under Nicholas Metcalfe, was singled out by Ascham as possessing 'such a company of fellows and scholars as can scarce be found now in some whole university'.[67] Lectures in arithmetic, geometry, perspective and cosmography were instituted, and in 1524 Metcalfe signed an agreement with Thomas Linacre establishing 'a free lecture of physic continually hereafter to be kept, read and maintained sufficiently and openly in the common schools of the said University of Cambridge'.[68] Although St John's College fell short of the utopian visions of its founders John Fisher and Metcalfe, it became a centre for the diffusion of interest in natural philosophy, mathematics and medicine. All of these subjects were taken up at St John's by laymen such as John Dee, John Gwyn, Richard Bostocke and Henry Briggs, or by physicians such as William Gilbert. In the 1560s Gilbert was mathematical examiner at St John's. He, and his contemporaries William Baronsdale and Thomas Randall, both of

---

[66] J. Venn, *Biographical History of Caius College* (4 vols., Cambridge, 1897–1912), III, p.392 and accompanying graph.

[67] Roger Ascham, *The scholemaster* (1570), ed. E. Arber (London, 1909), p.135.

[68] J. E. B. Mayor, *Early Statutes of the College of St John* (Cambridge, 1859), p.250. Agreement between Linacre and the Master and Fellows of St John's College, Cambridge, respecting the Linacre lectureship: Maddison *et al.*, *Linacre Studies*, pp.172–4.

whom served as Linacre lecturers, went on to become prominent Fellows of the College of Physicians.

Five colleges at Cambridge had provision for a fellowship in medicine. The most explicit arrangements were made by John Caius in his revision of the statutes of Gonville and Caius College in 1557. Caius set aside two fellowships in medicine, to be occupied by candidates possessing doctorates in medicine. These Fellows were obliged to conduct regular disputations with medical students of the college. In winter of each year the entire college was supposed to witness the dissection of a human body, an exercise which Caius defended as dignified and essential for the study of medicine. Finally medical students, along with lawyers and theologians, were encouraged to take leave to spend three years perfecting their knowledge in Padua, Bologna, Montpelier or Paris. Before his period abroad the student was expected to have studied Greek and the texts of Aristotle, Plato and Galen.[69]

The *Statuta antiqua*, the more humanistic university statutes of 1549, 1559 and 1570, and the various college statutes, furnish an incomplete impression of the character of the education received during the long periods spent in study by medical students at Cambridge. It is possible that before 1570 the Regius professor lectured regularly from a variety of compendia which had dominated the medical curriculum of the Middle Ages, and after 1550 more specifically from Hippocrates and Galen.[70] College lectures and exercises would have reflected this drift in fashion. Despite explicit stipulations by visitors and in the statutes from 1549 onwards, anatomies were not performed regularly, although a few students at the time of incepting for their degree, or applying for a licence, claimed to have witnessed an anatomy. On the other hand Thomas Mouffet doubted in 1584 whether a medical student would see one dissection in a decade.[71] It is probable that the most regularly performed academic exercises were those relating to degrees or licences. These were partly of a ceremonial nature and they seem to have been

---

[69] 'Statuta Collegii de Gonville et Caius', 1557: Venn, *Caius College*, III, pp.357, 359, 367, 377.

[70] J. Lamb, *Collection of Letters, Statutes and other Documents Illustrative of the University and Colleges of Cambridge* (1838); Rolleston, *Cambridge Medical School*, chapter 1.

[71] Lamb, *Collection of Statutes*, pp.127, 322–3. Thomas Mouffet, *De jure chemicorum medicamentorum* (Frankfurt, 1584), p.105. There is some dispute as to whether the first anatomy performed in England *c.*1531, and described by David Edwardes, took place at Oxford or Cambridge: A. Rook and M. Newbold, 'David Edwardes: his activities at Cambridge', *Medical History*, XIX (1975), 389–92. Despite the good intentions of Collins (see note 65 above), dissections were performed rarely. Rolleston, *Cambridge Medical School*, pp.47–55; A. Macalister, *The History of the Study of Anatomy in Cambridge* (Cambridge, 1891).

performed with care. Candidates for degrees were expected to take part in formal disputations, whereas licentiates were examined by two or more senior members of the faculty. Examinations were supervised not only by the Regius professors, but also by such resident physicians as Isaac Barrough of Trinity College. As we have seen, medical students regularly practised medicine, probably mainly away from Cambridge, and often under the guidance of an experienced physician. But at Cambridge the student would have no opportunity to work under supervision in a hospital or even to study medicinal plants in a botanical garden.[72] In the sixteenth century formal clinical training and teaching of medical botany were limited to continental universities. Statutory medical studies at Cambridge were literary and philosophical in character. In this system medical men were unlikely to become narrow specialists. Indeed, there was a conscious attempt to preserve the liberal spirit pioneered by Linacre, in which medical, mathematical and philological studies were pursued in harmony. It was as natural for William Gilbert to become an authority on cosmology and magnetism, as it was for Nicholas Carr, the Regius Professor of Greek, to practise and examine in medicine. Reference to the examples of William Burton, William Cuningham, Thomas Fale, John Fletcher, Oliver Grene, Thomas Hood and Robert Recorde shows that it was by no means uncommon for Cambridge-educated medical practitioners to earn a reputation as mathematicians.

It would be a mistake to regard medical studies at Cambridge as irrelevant to practice. The Regius professors and other medical lecturers possibly performed their official duties mechanically; they had very little reputation as original scholars, but, along with William Ward, each might be characterized as an 'excellent, judicious, and careful physician, a good housekeeper, and an honest and true-hearted man'.[73]

The libraries of medical men indicate eclectic tastes, and a concern with recent specialist medical literature. Typical of the smaller libraries was that valued at £49 belonging to Edward Raven, MA, a licentiate in medicine and fellow of St John's College. This contained major editions of the works of Aristotle, Hippocrates and Galen, a number of separate works by classical authors, particularly Galen, also medieval authors like

---

[72] The Botanic Garden at Oxford was instituted in 1621, the Radcliffe Infirmary, Oxford, in 1769 and Addenbrooke's Hospital, Cambridge, in 1766. In the period before 1800 none of these institutions was employed systematically in medical education along the lines pioneered at Padua in the sixteenth century.

[73] Rolleston, *Cambridge Medical School*, p.138.

Avicenna and Mundinus, more recent works by Mattioli, Monardus, Tagault and Montanus, and finally a few works on herbs, medical astrology, phlebotomy and urines. The main English work was Recorde's *Urinal of Physic*.[74] A smaller library of John Seward, 'scholar and surgeon' of Clare Hall, contained about forty books. The small number of more important works specifically listed included a volume of works by Galen, Mundinus *Anatomia*, Fuchs *De natura stirpium*, and Vigo *Opera in chirurgia*.[75] The larger medical libraries derived from such physicians as Thomas Twyne, Sir William Paddy and Robert Welles (now deposited in Corpus Christi College, Oxford, St John's College, Oxford, and Caius College, Cambridge, respectively), contain substantial and wide-ranging collections of the medical writers of the Renaissance.

The works of Galen provided a general structure for medical education, but it would not be correct to conclude that the medical outlook of practitioners trained at Cambridge can be characterized as narrowly Galenic. Their debt to ancient medicine was not limited to Galen; they continued to rely upon writings which dominated the medieval medical curriculum and which contained many Arabic influences; they were receptive to the ideas of the more original humanistic commentators; their practice was often deeply affected by astrology, alchemy and natural magic. The Cambridge humanists Cheke and Sir Thomas Smith had followed astrology; Roger Ascham's medical practitioner brother Anthony Ascham composed almanacs. Towards the end of the century, such well-known Cambridge figures as Isaac Barrough, John Fletcher, the Harveys and Thomas Twyne were ardent exponents of astrological practice. The practical and indeed popular tone of Cambridge medicine is suggested by Lancelot Browne's recommendation to Gabriel Harvey of Brunschwig's *Homish Apothecary* (1561) and other similar works, as outstandingly reliable guides to medical practice; or by the Regius professor William Ward's translation of the *Secrets of Alexis of Piedmont* (1558–62) and *Book of the famous doctor and expert astrologer Arcandam* (1578); or indeed by Timothie Bright's two short books *Hygieina* (1582) and *Therapeutica* (1583), based on lectures which he had delivered as a medical student at Cambridge.

The eclectic nature of Cambridge medical culture is well indicated by Lancelot Browne's recommendations about medical studies. He advised

---

74 CUL, Vice-Chancellor's Court, Inventories, box 2, 1547–1561.
75 CUL, Vice-Chancellor's Court, Inventories, box 2, 1547–1561.

not only the standard ancient and medieval medical authorities, but also that Hermes Trismegistus, Pliny and Celsus should be studied alongside the innovators Colombo and Cardano; Brunschwig's practical *Homish Apothecary* was to be followed by Mattioli, Petrus Hispanus, and antidotaries. Of the modern authorities Browne recommended Wecker, Fernel, Bruel, Heurne and Fioravanti, authors who were strongly influenced by the natural magical and alchemical tradition.[76] Eighty years later Sir Thomas Browne was relaying similar but suitably updated information to a medical student at Christ's College. He advised that '*materia medicamentorum*, surgery and chemistry, may be your diversions and recreations; physic is your business'. Power's library catalogue and case books indicate that Browne's advice was faithfully followed by the provincial medical practitioner.[77]

Regardless of their proportionate numerical strength, university-educated medical practitioners came in the course of the sixteenth century to dominate medical practice at the level of the social elite. By 1600 they constituted an important element in the emergent medical profession. Although not as systematically trained or as rigidly organized as their counterparts in Italy, the English graduate practitioners had many of the qualities of the humanistically educated physician held up as a model by Linacre and Caius. If classical standards were inadequate completely to determine the routines of medical practice, they were sufficient to provide a code of common cultural experience, serving to cement relations among physicians, and to unite them with the class of educated patrons which constituted their clientele.

Medical practitioners educated at the universities could choose a career in London or in the provinces. The largest identifiable group practised in London; but these were not a majority. One third of the ninety-eight Cambridge doctors became Fellows of the College of Physicians. A second identifiable group of twenty-four remained in Cambridge, occupying college fellowships, public or college teaching positions (sometimes for a short period), or merely practising medicine locally. Eight practitioners had careers involving association with both Cambridge and with the College of Physicians. Thus more than half of Cambridge medical graduates, and a larger proportion of the licentiates and unlicensed practitioners from the university, settled in the provinces. Perhaps as many as 250 graduate and licentiate practitioners

[76] G. C. Moore-Smith, *Gabriel Harvey's Marginalia* (Stratford-upon-Avon, 1913), p.132.
[77] Letter from Sir Thomas Browne to Henry Power [1646], in Browne, *Works*, ed. G. Keynes (4 vols., London, 1964), IV, pp.255–6.

Plate 9.   Norwich in 1558
    The first printed map of an English provincial town; produced by the
    physician William Cuningham, probably engraved by John Betts, and
    included in Cuningham's *Cosmographical Glass* (1559). Reproduced by
    permission of the Curators of the Bodleian Library.

emerged from Cambridge during the century to practise in the
provinces.[78] This is a creditable total, but closer examination of the
situation in the provinces is necessary in order to assess the claim of
Raach that graduate physicians were a dominant element in provincial
medical practice.[79]

The provincial side of medical practice can be conveniently examined
on a sample basis with reference to East Anglia. This prosperous and

[78] This 250 comprises 63 MDs (or MD + MB), 15 MBs, 72 non-medical graduate licentiates, and
    100 Cambridge-educated scholars with no formal medical credentials. This last figure is
    approximate and subject to later correction.
[79] J. H. Raach, *A Directory of English Country Physicians 1603–1643* (London, 1962), p.14.

populous area might be expected to exhibit a higher density of graduate practitioners in view of its close associations with and proximity to Cambridge. The local records for East Anglia and the diocese of Norwich are moderately good, but in view of the scattered and fragmentary nature of evidence relating to medical practitioners, the following pilot survey is presented as a tentative approach.

Norwich, in 1500, had a long-established character as a centre of trade and population second only to London. As a dominant inland port, in conjunction with the subsidiary coastal town of Great Yarmouth, it served as a focus of long-distance trade as well as a market for a rich and varied hinterland. Land and sea routes to London were well defined. Its substantial manufacturing industry was beginning to diversify after a lengthy dependence upon the textile trades. The surrounding county, to which neighbouring Suffolk was subordinate, remained among the most densely populated and prosperous in England. This population was still not concentrated in towns, although the percentage of inhabitants of Norfolk living in Norwich doubled between 1524 and 1670. As an old town, Norwich showed a capacity for self-renewal which ensured its status until the end of the eighteenth century. Although the town suffered in the sixteenth century from declines in trade, the effects of the Reformation, and drastic fluctuations in population brought about by plague and immigration, this period cannot be defined comparatively as one of great change. There is some agreement that in this century Norwich became increasingly a centre for consumption and for professional and social life. This development was heralded by the Duke of Norfolk's setting up his town house in Norwich in 1540.[80]

In its essential physical characteristics too, Norwich remained stable, the wideflung boundaries of river and city wall enclosing large areas of field and garden as well as parishes crowded with buildings. William Cuningham's perspective view of 1558, possibly the earliest such view of any English town, shows the major features of castle and cathedral but gives little indication of the poorer, more ephemeral classes of housing.[81]

For the purposes of this study the most striking feature of Norwich life

---

[80] On towns in the sixteenth century, see P. Clark and P. Slack (eds.), *Crisis and Order in English Towns 1500–1700* (London, 1972). On Norwich see also J. Campbell, 'Norwich', *The Atlas of Historic Towns*, ed. M. D. Lobel, ii (London, 1975); W. Hudson and J. C. Tingey (eds.), *The Records of the City of Norwich* (2 vols., Norwich and London, 1906); J. H. C. Patten, 'The urban structure of East Anglia in the sixteenth and seventeenth centuries' (unpublished University of Cambridge Ph.D. dissertation, 1972).

[81] See Plate 9.

is the over-riding influence of the municipal corporation. Sixteenth-century Norwich was ruled by an independent and durable oligarchical structure in which craft and trade organizations had constant reference to the mayor and aldermen. Aldermen were elected for life, whereas it was extremely rare, until towards the end of the century, for gild officials to hold office for extended periods. One major phenomenon of the period, the influx of perhaps as many as 4,000 Dutch and Walloon Protestant refugees after 1565, was to some extent a matter of national concern, but the elaborate plans evolved in the third quarter of the century to deal with the problem of the local and itinerant poor seem to have been an entirely municipal construction and were regarded as providing an example for the rest of England to follow. The 'Mayor's Book of the Poor' provides the bulk of the evidence relating to medical practice in Norwich, together with the proceedings of the municipal courts.[82] Both sources supply examples of the contract system of employment subsisting between the practitioner and the patient, or (more commonly), the patient's friends and sponsors. The only isolable professional or medical institution, the Company of Barber-Surgeons, may have kept its own records but its elections and judgments derived their validity from their appearance in the records of the municipality.

It is convenient to deal with the types of practitioner in turn, although the artificiality of this will soon become apparent.[83] Of the three main groups the physicians, or those who practised physic, were perhaps the most heterogeneous. At the one extreme were those 'practitioners of physic' who were given licences to erect stages and sell medicines. It might be argued that these persons could be excluded; but the spectrum

---

[82] The Mayor's Book of the Poor exists in two versions (bk I: 1571–9; bk II: 1571–80) in the Norfolk and Norwich Record Office. The Norwich Library also holds J. M. Dixon's transcriptions of parts of the Books and of other records relating to the poor: 'Poor relief in Norwich', 1926 (typescript). See also J. F. Pound (ed.), *The Norwich Census of the Poor 1570*, Norfolk Record Society, XL (1971); J. M. Dixon, 'Poor relief in Norwich during the reign of Queen Elizabeth' (University of Leeds M.A. dissertation, 1927); E. M. Leonard, *The Early History of English Poor Relief* (Cambridge, 1900).

[83] Information on Norwich practitioners has been obtained from the following sources unless otherwise stated, together with general reference works already cited: Hudson and Tingey, *Records of Norwich*. W. L. Sachse (ed.), *Minutes of the Norwich Court of Mayoralty 1630–1631*, Norfolk Record Society, XV (1942); *1632–1635*, Norfolk Record Society, XXXVI (1967). P. Millican (ed.), *The Register of the Freemen of Norwich 1548–1713* (Norwich, 1934). W. M. Rising and P. Millican (eds.), *An Index of Indentures of Norwich Apprentices... Henry VII–George II*, Norfolk Record Society, XXIX (1959). B. Cozens-Hardy and E. A. Kent, *The Mayors of Norwich 1403–1835* (Norwich, 1938). W. J. C. Moens, *The Walloons and their Church at Norwich: Their History and Registers 1565–1832*, Huguenot Society Publications, I (1887–8). J. F. Williams (ed.), *Diocese of Norwich. Bishop Redman's Visitation, 1597*, Norfolk Record Society, XVIII (1946). E. H. Carter, *The Norwich Subscription Books... 1637–1800* (London, 1937). M. A.

is continuous, providing as examples Edmund Hewes 'of the Cathedral', accused in 1597 by the ecclesiastical authorities of practising physic without a licence; Adrian Colman, widow of the practitioner of physic Nicholas Colman, who, being experienced in the art and having 'not any other thing to relieve her' was licensed by Howard and Knollys at the court of Whitehall, 1596, to 'minister the best skill and cunning to women, children and such other persons as are not able to go to physicians in all and every place and places whatsoever in the county of Norfolk'; James Mayes, licensed in 1581 by the Archbishop of Canterbury to practise surgery and 'medicine as far as necessary for surgery' in Norwich and the counties of Suffolk and Norfolk; Richard Fisher, surgeon of Norwich, excommunicated in 1597 for practising physic without a licence; Augustin Steward, 'gentleman', licensed by the Bishop of Norwich to practise medicine in 1595, one of his referees being Richard Sherman, MD of Cambridge; Matthew Rycke, 'doctor medicus', who came to Norwich with his family from Flanders in 1567; and finally the larger group of practitioners known to have been educated in the English or continental universities. Of these John Caius (MD Padua 1541), a native of Norwich who may have practised in Norwich as well as Cambridge, Shrewsbury and London, or Tobias Whitaker (1600–66), MD Leyden, who began practice in Norwich and later became physician to Charles II, cannot be regarded as typical. C. Williams, writing in 1897, could find only one Norwich physician of the period who was given that designation: Martin Corembeck. Later investigation shows that practitioners of physic were perhaps as numerous as apothecaries, but the academically qualified physician

Farrow, *Consistory Court of Norwich Wills 1550–1603*, The Index Library, LXXIII (1950). M. A. Farrow and T. F. Barton, *Index of Wills Proved in the Consistory Court of Norwich... 1604–1686*, Norfolk Record Society, XXVIII (1958). [M. Knights], 'Physicians and barber-surgeons in Norwich', in J. L'Estrange (ed.), *Eastern Counties Collectanea* (1873), pp.247–54; 'More about surgeons and physicians', ibid., pp.270–1. C. Williams, *The Barber-Surgeons of Norwich*, 2nd edn (Norwich, etc., 1897). Idem, *The Masters, Wardens and Assistants of the Guild of Barber-Surgeons of Norwich from the Year 1439–1723* (Norwich, 1900). M. Beverley, *Some Norfolk Medical Worthies* (Norwich, 1890). T. A. Walker, *A Biographical Register of Peterhouse Men* (2 vols., Cambridge, 1927–30). In the Norfolk and Norwich Record Office: T. F. Barton, 'Norwich diocesan archives. Probate inventories 1553–1603'; idem, 'Consistory Court inventories: index of occupations' (bound typescripts). [M. A. Farrow], 'Norwich archdeaconry wills 1604–1660' (bound typescript). 'Dean and chapter of Norwich registers of wills and administrations 1461–1559' (typed index). Bishop's Administrative Records: Registers of Licences... 1582–7, SUN 2. Mayor's Book of the Poor, I and II, City Records, Case 20, Shelf c, Rep. 140 and 141. Alysham 156, Names of householders and others in Norwich for [1589]. *Correspondence of lady Katherine Paston 1603–1627*, ed. R. Hughey, Norfolk Record Society, XIV (1941). R. R. James, 'Licences to practise medicine and surgery issued by the Archbishops of Canterbury, 1580–1775', *Janus*, XLI (1936), 97–106.

whom later periods have singled out is difficult to find. Medical doctorates were rare; medical licences, often with a training in arts, were much more common. Between 1501 and 1600 only Caius, Robert Harridance (MD Cambridge, d. 1513), William Cuningham. (MB Cambridge 1557, MD Heidelberg *c.*1559), Martin Corembeck (MD Bologna, d. 1579), and perhaps James Bylney ('doctor of medicine', fl.1560), Henry Bagot (Bologna, ?MD Cambridge, d. *c.*1525), 'Mr Dr Bowne' (fl. 1562), and William Rant (1564–1627) possessed MDs; George Walker (1533–97), MD Cambridge and Fellow of the College of Physicians, may have practised in Norwich. Of these nine, several were more representative in that they combined medicine with another business or profession. Harridance was 'Mercerii et Civis Norwici'; Bagot was rector at Markshall. Only Caius and Cuningham are known to have published. From the academic remainder may be selected Paul Gould, who was born in Norwich, graduated MA from Caius College, Cambridge, in 1576, was a student of medicine there without taking a degree, and later lived in Norwich as a practitioner of medicine and schoolmaster. An appropriate counter-weight to the humanist Caius is perhaps William Blomfild (*c.*1509–*c.*1574), who knew modern languages as well as Latin, Greek and Hebrew, called himself 'philosopher and bachelor of physic', was a radical Puritan appointed by Parkhurst to St Simon and St Jude, Norwich, from which church he was expelled by his congregation, and a skilled alchemist and distiller who was tried in 1547 for conjuring. His younger contemporary Cuningham (b. *c.*1531), who was also learned and had in addition full academic credentials, was eminent in London, where he practised after leaving Norwich, as an astrologer and physician. Cuningham lectured publicly at Surgeon's Hall in 1563, and was a friend of the surgeon Thomas Gale.

It is plain that the paucity of academically qualified physicians in Norwich cannot be regarded as a measure of practice. Further broadening the definition of the practitioners of physic is their inclusion in the 1550s in the Gild or Company of Barbers or Barber-Surgeons. The chief evidence for this is an isolated petition of the 'Company of Physicians and Barber-Surgeons within the City of Norwich' of 1561, which proposed various measures to preserve the exercise of 'these mysteries' exclusively to members of the Company and their indentured apprentices.[84] From 1550 the Company is called that of the Barber-

---

[84] The petition is reprinted by M. Knights (1873) and C. Williams (1897) from the Assembly Books of the Norwich corporation, where also appear annually the names of the newly elected officers of the Company.

Surgeons and Physicians, and there is no reason why the names of its officers should not be those of practitioners of physic as much as surgeons. Physicians, unlike surgeons, do not appear at all in the list of freemen for the city, although 'surgeon' itself appears only once before 1540.

Several examples can be given of practitioners of physic who held office in the Company. Robert Britiffe, who obtained a Cambridge medical licence in 1560 and called himself 'physician of Norwich' in his will (proved 1575), was a warden of the Company in 1561 and its headman or master from 1568 to 1574. Similar to Britiffe was Walter Haugh (senior), who in addition was commissioned *c.*1560 by the College of Physicians in London to pursue Norfolk empirics. An ambiguous case is that of Dr James Bylney, who with 'Mr Dr Bowne' was taken before the mayor in 1562 by the wardens of the 'occupation of Barbers and Surgeons' for refusing to pay dues to the Company. Bylney at first repudiated the authority of the Company and also of the mayor, but it is not at all clear that he and Bowne did so because they felt the Company did not represent the interests of physicians. Both men eventually agreed to pay their dues and Bylney reappears as headman of the Company two years later. At about the same period the Barber-Surgeons' Company in London shifted from prosecuting members who practised physic, to tacitly accepting that the two pursuits were indissolubly linked.

The place of physicians and other practitioners in the simplified gild structure of Ipswich, as mentioned below, is more typical of the provincial centres than their separation into distinct companies, which occurred in Norwich as a function of the size and importance of the town. Norwich in 1630 had twenty-two craft or trade companies requiring the election of officials, and although the Barber-Surgeons had a separate existence, so did both the Mercers and the Grocers. The company including the surgeons was then called indifferently the Barbers, or the Barbers and Surgeons. Gild organization varied more with locality than any other factor, and in all towns the companies were shifting and conglomerate in character. With respect to physicians in Norwich, their failure to reappear in corporate records under a specific designation cannot be regarded as indicating that physic was little practised in the city.

The surgeons or barber-surgeons constitute the largest group of practitioners in Norwich and their activity provided the staple of medical practice. Any estimate of their number is of course subject to the reservation already mentioned, since their service to their Company is the only fact known in the case of more than forty names. Of the total of about seventy names found for the century, nearly fifty held office at some time in the Company, so that this total must represent only a proportion even of the full complement of barbers, surgeons, barber-surgeons, physicians and possible members of other crafts who belonged to the Company, setting aside apprentices and journeymen. The Company underwent some changes of definition and structure during the century. Two 'Magistri Barbitonsorum' are recorded almost continuously each year from 1511 to 1549. In 1550 the Company began to call itself 'Barber-Surgeons and Physicians', and in 1554 the number of assistants or wardens was raised to two, an arrangement which persisted into the seventeenth century. A set of six ordinances was adopted in 1561 on an annual basis but left unrevised until 1684, when thirty-three were found necessary, and a further increase in the number of assistants. It is most unlikely that gild practices remained static over the intervening period.[85]

As a gild to which surgeons were admitted from an early period the Company dates to before 1300. A constitution of 1388 gives an entirely religious cast to the organization but takes for granted the inclusion of women. A more comprehensive picture is perhaps given by a longer return for Lincoln of the same date, which includes provisions for office-bearing, apprenticeship and the support of sick members. The religious element is represented by restrictions on property holding and on the purposes of meetings.[86] As in the sixteenth century, the gild had no independent powers of giving leave to practise. The change of title in 1550 echoes the displacement in lists of freemen, of 'barber' by 'barber-surgeon' and 'surgeon'. In general the changes in title and constitution of the sixteenth century seem to have imitated events in London.

After a preamble complaining of the intrusion into physic and surgery of other tradesmen (in this case shoemakers, hatmakers, dornixweavers, smiths and worsted weavers), and of 'sundry women', the ordinances of 1561 also follow an established pattern. They are few in number, excluding a number of provisions included in the revised ordinary of the Barbers and Surgeons of York of 1592 which might come under the

---

85 The ordinances of 1684 specified a quorum for assemblies of the headman, four assistants, and six other barbers or barber-surgeons, being freemen. The earlier set of six ordinances may have been additional to a larger set common to all the Norwich companies. See C. Williams, 'The ordinances of the Gild of Barber-Surgeons of Norwich', *The Antiquary*, XXXVI (1900), 274–8, 293–7.

86 The constitutions of 1388 are reprinted in Young, *Annals*, p.21.

heading of standing orders as to dress, attendance, election procedure and entertainment.[87] There is a stronger statement in the Norwich than in the York statutes of the principle that no sanctions applied to those undertaking cures or care without payment: 'Provided always that if any person or persons will do or minister any thing of neighbourhood and God's sake and of pity and of charity taking by no means anything for the same then it shall be lawful for every of them so to do'. The Norwich ordinances further differ from those of York both in providing for consultation in the case of dangerous cures, a limitation often placed on licences by the London College of Physicians, and in making no explicit provision for barbering. The Norwich practitioners also provided for compulsory attendance at a lecture in their art held every three weeks, in the manner of the London Company in 1529. York laid down more elaborate procedures for dissections as well as lectures in 1614. No lectures were mentioned in the York rules of 1592, but the tone of such ordinances is less that of innovation than of the ratification of or making compulsory already existing practice. A possible exception to this is the attempt of the York practitioners to inhibit their patients as well as their rivals by fining every freeman or woman who consulted a stranger or unlicensed practitioner without first consulting a member of the Company. In Norwich as well as London and York, the superintendence of the Company by the corporation is emphasized by the division of the profits from fines between the two bodies.

It was very unusual before 1570 for the same man to hold office in the Norwich Company for more than two consecutive years. Normally a man was a warden one year and headman the next, reappearing in either office five or often ten years later. This pattern is broken in Norwich by the tenure of the headship 1554–9 by John Porter, and a series of lengthy tenures became established in the late 1560s by such men as Robert Britiffe, William Pickering and James Fisher or Fisherman. This is typical of changes observed elsewhere in town government at the end of the sixteenth century.[88] Britiffe has already been mentioned. Fisher was Porter's apprentice, receiving his freedom *c.*1562. Porter, a friend or colleague of William Bullein, appears as a prominent member of the Company from 1540. In 1549 he received wages from the corporation as

---

[87] See previous note. For the York ordinances see Furnivall and Furnivall, *Anatomie*, appendix xv. On the companies and medical practice of York, see D. M. Palliser, 'The trade gilds of Tudor York', in Clark and Slack (eds.), *Crisis and Order*, pp.86–116; G. A. Auden, 'The Gild of Barber-Surgeons of the city of York', *Proceedings of the Royal Society of Medicine*, xxi (1928), 1400–6; M. Barnet, 'The Barber-Surgeons of York', *Medical History*, xii (1968), 19–30.

[88] See Clark and Slack, 'Introduction' to *Crisis and Order*, pp.21–2.

surgeon and barber to the poor in one of the city hospitals. There are very few other records of barbering as opposed to barber-surgery. As we shall see, a contract with the city such as Porter's was not an indication of low status on the part of the practitioner.

Instances of the regulation of practice show that while the judgment of expertise was left to the officers of the Company, the process of arrest and punishment was dependent upon the municipal courts. Allen Sendall was presented to the Mayor's Court in 1559 by John Porter as practising surgery without learning or knowledge. It was ordered that he be examined, and admitted if found fit. If not, he would be 'sequestered' and told to cease practising. More drastic measures had been taken with George Hill, an apothecary imprisoned around 1539 for practising surgery when he was neither expert nor admitted according to the law. Evidence of the ill-effects of his practice was presented to the Convocation of Aldermen, who gave him a few days to leave the city. Nonetheless, they envisaged the possibility of his being lawfully admitted to practice. The case of John Cross in 1584 involved an 'Inquisition of Surgeons' but shows that much regulation of practice is better seen as a legal investigation of claims against contracts. Cross was alleged to have undertaken the cure of the badly hurt hand of Christian, wife of John Preston, having said from the first that her hand 'was not to be recovered'. Cross's 'artificial ministrations' were investigated for the court by four surgeons including James Fisher. John Grove, surgeon, who was accused in 1608 of 'using things not fit administered' was ordered by the court to be examined by Dr Rant, physician, and John Cropp the younger, physician-surgeon, in the presence of John Mingay and George Birch, aldermen who were also both apothecaries.

The Norwich Company in 1561 asked that its governors should have 'full power and authority during the time of their office to oversee, search, punish and correct all such defaults and inconveniences as shall be found amongst the said Company using the mysteries abovesaid as well of freemen as foreigners, aliens and strangers within the said city, and the suburbs'. It is probable that, as in the case of outsiders in general, action was taken only against those who showed signs of 'dwelling' in the town. The barber-surgeons of York allowed an intruder to practise for five days without search or fines. Such itinerants must have included those practitioners already mentioned who were licensed by the city to erect stages. In 1620 in Norwich Peter Verbruge was licensed to cut corns for ten days, and a note taken of his lodging. With respect to itinerants practising particular specialities, who might be expected to do a limited business and then move on, such tolerance is perhaps less surprising. It seems likely, however, that an outsider who was prepared to pay for the privilege might be able to stay and practise or open a shop in the town for a period of years before further demands, for example that he take out his freedom, were made of him. He would of course always be liable to search and examination. In the later Norwich ordinances of 1684 a barber or barber-surgeon did not have to be a freeman if he were retained by the year by an inhabitant of Norwich or Norfolk, and confined his practice to the house of his employer and 'to such work as shall be for the proper use of the family wherein he shall be so retained'.

It must already be clear that, although ratification and temporary licensing were in the hands of the corporation, and admission the prerogative of the Company under the corporation, a late-sixteenth-century practitioner might be licensed by any one or more of a number of different authorities. A Norwich practitioner might hold a licence in medicine or surgery or both from the University of Cambridge, the Bishop of Norwich, the Archbishop of Canterbury or a variety of agencies in London, including the Bishop of London and the Privy Council. The Bishop of Norwich's licence usually had as its area the city of Norwich and its liberties, and parts of the counties of Norfolk and Suffolk. The applicant's plea was commonly supported by testimonies, often from medical men (whose denominations did not necessarily bear any relation to the part of practice given in the licence), or by 'the credible report of divers worshipful and honest men', or by proof of successful cases already conducted by the applicant.

The strong connections between Norwich and the capital were evident in licensing. The licence granted to the cleric Robert Cripps in 1590 by the Archbishop of Canterbury gave him access to Ely, Norwich and London. In a procedure analogous to the custom of allowing widows to carry on their husbands' businesses, Nicholas Colman's licence from the archbishop was in effect transferred to his widow Adrian by the Privy Council, giving her access to the county of Norfolk. Local and national spheres of influence were combined in the affidavit given in 1565 to Valerian Danske, a surgeon, by Martin Corembeck, doctor of medicine, and presented to the authorities in Norwich. Corembeck, who was physician to the Duke of Norfolk, bore witness to Danske's experience and skill and to his having lost his proof of admission to the Company of Surgeons in London. Corembeck himself, another associate of William Bullein, was fined by the College of

Physicians in 1553 for practising illegally in London. He became a Fellow of the College after incorporating his Bologna degree at Oxford, but then left London for Norwich. Like Walter Haugh rather earlier, he was used by the London College as an agent in the punishment of local empirics. Norwich empirics came before the College of Physicians in London; attempts by the College to repress unlicensed practice in the eastern counties were embarrassingly undermined by one of its Fellows, George Walker, who prospered by illicitly selling licences to such practitioners. Through Corembeck's agency Walker was accused in 1570 'de examinatione et admissione medicorum Norwici et Norfolciâ' and the following year 'repetundarum et pecuniae extortae ab indoctis quibusdam empiricis, quibus medicinam factitandi facultatem concessit'.[89]

The licensed had no monopoly of skill or virtue. The Redman visitation of 1597 excommunicated Robert Hempinstall, 'glover, empiric and astrologer', but also cast suspicion on, among others, the Cropps, father and son, strangers who were by then well established as surgeons in the town. The elder Cropp was then licensed and had been officially described in 1593 as 'a surgeon of great knowledge and experience'. Being unlicensed could hardly have been equivalent to being unskilled while licences themselves were granted on the basis of previous skill and experience.

There is no clear evidence from Norwich as to the order of superiority of licences from different sources, or the Company's procedures with respect to licences granted by ecclesiastical and other agencies outside the town. The searches conducted by the ecclesiastical visitors into medical licences late in the century seem to have been the most strict of any. During the Redman visitation Richard Fisher was found to be unlicensed, and pleaded in reply that he was 'prentice to a surgeon by his indenture'. However this related rather to the parts of practice, since Fisher was accused of practising physic, not surgery. In York in 1598 William Padmore was complained of by the Company for practising surgery while not a freeman. The corporation court refused to accept Padmore's excuse that he was 'licensed to practise by my Lord's grace under his seal', and eventually forced him to take out his freedom at a cost of £6 13s 4d. The factor of revenues to the authorities is more apparent in this case than in those such as Fisher's.

---

[89] This extract from the College Annals is reprinted by Munk, *Roll*, 1, 55n. The College's brief attempts to control provincial empirics also extended to Chester.

A special case among the surgeons was the bonesetter. In York, the ordinance of 1614 imposing fines upon freemen who used unlicensed practitioners made a special exception of bonesetters. The presence of a highly successful bonesetter in Norwich has been interpreted as evidence of a dearth of surgeons even in the largest cities, but this is obviously a false assumption. Richard Durrant (d. 1602) may have been the first in a series of generations of Norwich bonesetters extending at least to 1669. A later representative began as a weaver's apprentice but subsequently reverted to the family vocation. Richard Durrant died prosperous and apparently well established in private practice, though he may, like Adrian Johnson who was made freeman as 'surgeon and mercer' in 1543, have made his money in other ways. Durrant held office in the Barber-Surgeons' Company, being headman 1593–6, but he did not feel it necessary to call himself other than 'bonesetter' in his will. Having 'taken pains' with the dislocations of two poor patients in 1571–2, and otherwise earned a reputation for skill, Durrant accepted the next year an annual salary from the corporation to live in the city and attend to the 'relief of those who break bones and are poor and unable to pay for their healing'. He was succeeded after his death in this post by Mr Reve, probably the Phineas Reve noted as bonesetting without a licence by the Redman visitors in 1597. That the corporation continued to require the services of such a specialist is shown by its employing a later Richard Durrant, bonesetter, in 1669.

Although publicized by Norwich as a model for other urban centres, there was nothing essentially new about the measures taken with respect to the poor in the 1570s and 1580s.[90] This effort of organization involved a high degree of surveillance and institutionalization, and an enforced distinction between the infirm and those who could be put on work. Much of the relief supplied to the ill or infirm was in the form of money, fuel or clothing which would put them into a better condition to survive the illness and perhaps allow them to be nursed. The corporation was also interested in preventing costly diseases brought on by idleness, indigence, cold or surfeit, and paid minor officials, the 'proctors', to take into their houses and out of circulation the diseased, including the 'leprous'. To a considerable extent the organization set up in the 1570s was aimed at rationalizing and reducing the costs of earlier, more pragmatic attempts to deal with vagabondage, infirmity and

[90] The Norwich census of the poor of 1570 gave a total of 2,359 persons, that is, perhaps 14 per cent of the population.

mendicancy, and sudden outbreaks of epidemic disease. Before the regular institution of Courts of Guardians and workhouses, the individual or his friends had normally to apply for permission to make a special collection, or, a collection was made in church by local clergy with the licence of the bishop and the recommendation of the Mayor's Court.[91] Such a 'licence to collect' was issued in 1593 to Thomas Jenkinson, reduced to penury by an accident to his leg.

The new poor scheme does not seem to have involved practitioners in any novel way, nor was a particular class of practitioner called upon. Many of the better-known surgeons of the town were parties to contracts with the corporation for the cure of poor persons. As we have seen in the cases of John Porter in 1543 and Richard Durrant in 1573, the corporation sometimes retained the services of a practitioner, but the regular practice was for it to act in the place of the friends or relatives of the patient who normally agreed on a contract, often with conditions, with a practitioner for the cure of a particular disability. William Lever or Fever, a surgeon employed on several occasions by the corporation, was in 1586 paid 30s for healing the legs of three women in one of the hospitals. He had 10s at once, 10s when he cured one woman, and the last 10s when he had cured all three. Most patients were of course treated outside institutions, and the practitioner was commonly expected, as part of the contract, to 'keep' or house the patient until the cure was effected. Leonard Wright, a warden of the Barber-Surgeons in the 1590s, who undertook in 1614 to cure a person called Singlewood of a 'thistely', was to be paid conditionally like Fever and promised also to keep Singlewood until he was well. The period of keeping in one York case was two years. If the patient was wealthy, he either retained his own practitioner or required the latter to take up residence for the duration of the cure. There were many ways in which the contracts between practitioner and patient or patient's proxy might prove unsatisfactory, and much evidence of sixteenth-century practice is to be obtained from court proceedings. The case of John Cross has already been mentioned. In a Norwich case of 1602, the defendant claimed, unsuccessfully, that he had not sent for the surgeon who attended a person bitten by his dog and was not therefore liable to pay the surgeon's fee of £3.

The conditions for which the poor of Norwich were treated were chiefly strikingly apparent, being on exposed parts; those affecting the

---

[91]   See C. Williams, *The Treatment of the Sick in Norwich during the Seventeenth Century* (Norwich, 1903).

mobility of the patient; or those likely to affect others. Sores, sore faces, sore legs, sore hands, broken bones and scald head were the most common. Mouth canker, 'small pock', 'pocks', dropsy, bloody flux, swelled knee, and the 'French disease' are also mentioned. The Paston family and connections called in Norwich practitioners to treat them for agues (for which Katherine Paston also had her own palliative), a lame arm, swelled face, cough and consumption. The practitioners used by the corporation in the 1570s and 1580s were both numerous and varied. Many of them were women, who sometimes took an ancillary role but, as we shall see, were more often given sole responsibility for the patient. The names of men included John Cobbe, apothecary; Richard Durrant, bonesetter; William Fever, surgeon; Edward Fisher; James Fisher; Richard Fisher, surgeon; Stephen Horne, surgeon; Mr More, surgeon; Mr William, surgeon; Robert Wretham, barber-surgeon; Leonard Wright, barber-surgeon; and a 'Dutch man'. Durrant, James Fisher, Horne, Wretham and Wright held office in the Barber-Surgeons' Company, before or after their services to the city.

Accounts giving the cost of the care of the poor provide much of the early evidence about the long-established practice of 'cutting for the stone' in Norwich and surrounding districts.[92] The earliest record of stone so far discovered for this area is a deposition of 1566. An Agreement was reached after much haggling between John Sympson of King's Lynn, and a stranger surgeon Hans or John Hesse of Norwich, such that Hesse would travel to King's Lynn to cut Sympson's son 'for a certain disease he then had called the stone', but without guaranteeing the child's life. For this Hesse was prepared to ask £10, with board and lodging for himself and two others 'while the child should be in healing'. Nearly thirty years later, it was deposed before the Mayor's Court that a stone had been removed by John Hobart, surgeon and officeholder in the Barber-Surgeons' Company, without cutting. In 1618 Miles Mayhew, a warden of the Company in 1616, was paid by the corporation 30s down and 30s for the cure, in a case of stone in a child. The corporation and the parishes paid for the treatment for stone of several other poor children by Mayhew between 1616 and 1618. Women were employed to keep the children in the meantime. Usually the alderman of the ward in

---

[92] See W. Rye, *Depositions taken before the Mayor and Aldermen of Norwich 1549–1567*, Norfolk and Norwich Archaeological Society (Norwich, 1905); Williams, *Treatment of the Sick*; idem, 'Extracts from the court rolls of the City of Norwich relating chiefly to instances of stone in the bladder', *Lancet*, 1896 (ii), pp.1181–2; A. Batty Shaw, 'The Norwich school of lithotomy', *Medical History*, xiv (1970), 221–59.

which the poor patient lived was given overall responsibility for him. This kind of arrangement continued long after 1673, when the alderman of Colegate ward took charge of David Brand's child, who had sores. A surgeon was to view the sores and to consult with Sir Thomas Browne the physician as to their nature and cure.

Norwich suffered major outbreaks of plague in 1579–80, 1584–5 and 1589–92. These epidemics may have caused in sum 9,000 deaths.[93] The city appears on these occasions to have made temporary arrangements, including special levies, of the usual kind. With respect to medical personnel, more is known of the city's proceedings in the 1660s, when the town clerk was sent to London by flying coach to negotiate with physicians and surgeons 'as to their coming to Norwich to visit and prescribe for the infected poor'. In addition to the usual expenses the corporation paid for accommodation and compensated those concerned for not going abroad or treating others in the city.[94]

Apothecaries, although undoubtedly active as practitioners, are seldom mentioned by name in records of the treatment of the poor. In the accounts of institutions like the Bridewell, a brief entry only is made of the cost of medicines for the sick patient. Money allocated 'for the comfort' of a poor patient was no doubt partly laid out in medicines and palliatives. A specific mention occurs in the Mayor's Book of the Poor in 1571, where John Cobbe is recorded as receiving payment for medicines for Mother Stowe. The medicines for Mother Stowe's sore face were probably administered by Mother Waterman, to whom the case was entrusted, although another person (probably a parish official) was recompensed for 'looking to' Mother Stowe. About as many apothecaries can be found in Norwich as practitioners of physic, and they were clearly integrated in an orderly and respectable way into the municipal structure. However their status among the companies seems unclear. It has been claimed that they were admitted into the Barber-Surgeons' Company, in which case this gild, by including exclusively all three parts of practice, pre-dates the otherwise unique medical gild in Glasgow, which did so in 1599.[95] There is however no sign of an apothecary among the Norwich gild's officebearers, and it seems more likely that the apothecaries' allegiance should have been determined by

93 Campbell, 'Norwich', pp.17–18. It is estimated that the population by 1602 was again 15,000. Another epidemic of plague in 1603–4 caused perhaps 3,400 deaths. For plague in Norwich see P. Slack, *The Impact of Plague in Tudor and Stuart England* (forthcoming).
94 Hudson and Tingey, *Records of Norwich*, II, pp.cxxvi–viii.
95 See T. D. Whittet, 'The apothecary in provincial gilds', *Medical History*, VIII (1964), 245–73.

their traditional affinity with grocers and mercers. Mercer, merchant, spicer and especially grocer were terms interchangeable with apothecary in the sixteenth century. George Walden of Norwich, grocer, who died in 1593, had two apprentices, John Wagstaffe and the well-known John Mingay, who were both apothecaries. Richard Bayley, son of a grocer, died as a grocer in 1596, but took out his freedom in 1587 as an apothecary. His son Henry was made free as a grocer. In York, a town smaller than but comparable with Norwich, the apothecaries belonged to the Society of Merchant Adventurers, and thus to the mercantile rather than to the less-well-documented handicraft sector of the gild structure.[96] In lesser centres apothecaries might be found with a great variety of trades under a single mercantile umbrella which could be given the name of Grocers, Merchants or Mercers. Some atypical associations could occur according to local circumstances. In Andover in 1625 the apothecaries belonged to a combined retail-craft gild called the Company of Leathermen, while the surgeons joined the barbers and the grocers in the more mercantile Haberdashers' Company. In other centres as well as Norwich, the comparative dearth of information on apothecaries is no measure of the strength of their position in the town. An extreme case is that of Cambridge, where it is abundantly clear that apothecaries were numerous, wealthy, and of high social standing. Apothecaries' families were also strongly inter-connected. The son of Thomas Carter (fl. 1589), apothecary of Norwich, was also an apothecary; Thomas's apprentice George Baron was an apothecary whose son was mayor of Norwich in 1649. The John Mingay (1556–1625) already mentioned was a well-known apothecary and member of a prominent local family which produced others in the same trade. What an apothecary might achieve is well represented by George Birch, grocer and apothecary, who was sheriff in 1604 and mayor in 1621. In his will (1632), Birch called himself simply 'alderman'. A nephew was mayor in 1627. One son was a goldsmith, another, John, an apothecary. Four apprentices of the elder Birch took out their freedoms between 1595 and 1614. In 1632, following the death of George Birch, the Mayor's Court ordered that John should 'perform the place of ministering physic and surgery to the poor in the Hospital' at an annual fee of £4, as his father had done before him. That George Birch had achieved status as a practitioner is clear from a reference by Katherine Paston to his treatment of members of her household at Palgrave,

[96] See Palliser, 'Trade gilds of Tudor York'.

suffering variously from agues, cold, and swelled face. Birch stayed at the house some days and 'did us much comfort. He went home in my coach.'

Women practitioners were important enough to be treated separately here as a sector of Norwich practice. As already noted the early constitution of the Norwich Barbers' Company implied in its references to 'brothers and sisters' some equality of women with men. In the sixteenth century women could take out freedoms, run businesses and indenture apprentices, but it is not clear that they could do this in their own right, rather than in that of a deceased husband. The London Barber-Surgeons' draft rules of 1529 bracket together for payment of certain dues 'every widow keeping an open shop', and 'every man out of the clothing'.[97] The Norwich ordinances of 1561 complain in familiar style of the intrusion of 'women giving over the good and profitable arts that they have been brought up with from their youths hitherto even for lucre's sake and idleness of life being unskillful and utterly ignorant of . . . those things that they do minister', but this adverse attitude need not have affected other women practitioners. In any case the women who had abandoned more fitting but less lucrative pursuits for medicine must have done fairly well, since the complaints of 1561 regarded their activities as discouraging the fully trained, and inhibiting the training of male apprentices.

The Mayor's Book of the Poor gives the names of a number of women of seemingly similar status, but there was probably a spectrum of female practitioners as there was of male. The Norwich census of the poor of 1570 includes Elizabeth Brother, a spinster of 40 'that helped women'. The only midwife who went by that name so far located in Norwich was a stranger, the widow of Henry van Brabant, 'obstetrix', who came from Flanders with her children in 1567. Adrian Colman of Norwich, like the surgeon Isabel Warwike of York, was a licensed practitioner but there were, at least nominally, restrictions on her practice, whereas the seven women who were employed by the corporation from time to time in 1571–4 apparently undertook whatever was required. There is no indication that they were employed only after other practitioners had failed. Of the seven, Widow or Mother Waterman is a substantial example of an independent practitioner. As well as healing the sore face of Mother Stowe she managed the cases of 'Anne Morkerke a young maid', Widow Williams

---

97 See Furnivall and Furnivall, *Anatomie*, appendix xiv.

who had the pocks, Grimes and Grimes's wife in Bridewell in 1574, and Margaret Cooper of Berestreet, who was suffering from scald head. In the last case Mrs Waterman was paid for healing and 'the warrant to keep it whole for woman's life'. Another practitioner, Mother Colle, seems to have specialized in broken limbs. In three further cases the woman may have become involved by virtue of her husband's position. Mrs Bradley, who was paid for healing a poor girl of dropsy, was the wife of the proctor of St Bennet's Gate. Proctors were minor municipal officials akin to caretakers or stewards, who could also be responsible for collecting alms for occupants of a spitalhouse or for others debarred from begging for themselves. We have already seen that they took in members of the sick poor. Mrs Bradley, however, did not merely 'minister to' but healed her patient. The husband of Mrs Fyddell who healed the scald head of a poor boy, may have been in employment at the Bridewell as an official. Alice Glavin (d. 1591), who was given responsibility for several cases, including one of the pocks, was, like Adrian Colman, the wife of a surgeon (John, d. 1573). Her son may also have practised surgery.

The last group to be considered is the strangers. As a major city Norwich attracted a number of these, including John de Marbrier, a French surgeon naturalized in 1541, before the massive influxes of Dutch and Walloons after 1560. Since the strangers constituted a third of the population later in the century it is to be expected that they cared for their own sick, as they did for their own poor. It does not affect this assumption that most sixteenth-century religious refugees were of the artisan class. Some names (van Brabant, midwife; Matthew Rycke, medicus) have already been mentioned. The position of a foreign practitioner who wished to practise among other than his own people must have been more problematic. The restrictions placed upon strangers were explicit and detailed according to whether the trades they pursued threatened local interests. The 'Book of Orders' for the Norwich strangers of 1571 greatly limited their retail outlets but, apart from the textile trades, mentioned specifically only tailors, butchers, cobblers and shoemakers. Characteristically the corporation itself showed no inhibitions about employing 'a Dutch man' to heal the swelled knee of a poor patient in 1571–2, or a 'Dutch surgeon' for cutting two poor men's children at the same period, but the constitutions of gilds regularly placed restrictions on the activities of foreigners. The ordinances of the Norwich Barber-Surgeons and Physicians of 1561, composed before the major immigrations, do not complain of the intrusion of aliens and merely include them among those over whom the officers of the Company were to have jurisdiction. The Walloon surgeon John de Buss was banished the city in 1599 for debt, but this was hardly special treatment: one of his debtors was a Walloon silkweaver. The same could be said of Peter de No, charged in 1597 for practising surgery without a licence. Abraham Hacker, physician of Norwich in 1622, his contemporary Peter Hiborne, surgeon, John Cropp the younger, and Martin Corembeck may all be examples of successful practitioners who were born of stranger parents in the land of adoption. Although commonly given their parents' nationality, these English-born foreigners would not necessarily suffer any form of exclusion from trade and professional institutions.

Highly illustrative are the careers of the John Cropps, father and son, both surgeons or surgeon-physicians.[98] The elder came to Norwich from Flanders in 1567, as a surgeon; his son John was born in 1572, presumably in Norwich. He acquired in 1577 letters testimonial, or the equivalent of a licence to practise, from the Bishop of Norwich. These he used thirteen years later to obtain an admission to surgery from the Bishop of London, evidently as part of an attempt to establish himself in the capital, where the family had relatives and where his younger son Joseph settled as a merchant. This enterprise seems to have been abortive, since the Redman visitors in 1597 noted that both father and son were practising surgery in Norwich, possibly without licences. The elder Cropp died around 1598 and the younger redeemed his unlicensed state by obtaining the Archbishop of Canterbury's licence to practise both medicine and surgery in 1602. In 1605, at the age of 33, the younger Cropp was described as 'practitioner in physic, licentiate of the City of Norwich'. Two years later he became in the same year a freeman, and a warden of the Norwich Barber-Surgeons' Company. This might imply that the first was formally necessary for the second, though not for any form of participation and advancement other than that of officeholding in the Company, since Cropp was already of sufficient standing to become headman immediately after acting as warden 1607–8. As in other cases already mentioned, Cropp's commitment to the Company indicates its catholicity. He was described as 'physician' in 1615, at a time when he was holding office in the Company. Around 1625 some account of his practice is given by Katherine Paston: 'I am very glad to

98 On the Cropps see also [P. O. Bramble], 'Walloons in Norwich', *Proceedings of the Huguenot Society of London*, XVI (1937–41), 277.

see he [Tom Hartston, a neighbour's son] has so much strength in his arm, for I did fear he had been stark lame of it . . . on Monday Mr Crope I think will take it in hand, first by physic and after by applying strengthy things to it'.

This account of Norwich may be concluded by making an estimate of the number of practitioners per head of population. On the basis only of known names, a total of 73 persons can be said to have practised some form of medicine in the city between 1570 and 1590. Counting each one only once, which as already indicated enforces arbitrary distinctions, the total can be divided into 37 surgeons or barber-surgeons, 12 apothecaries, 10 women practitioners, 6 practitioners of physic, 5

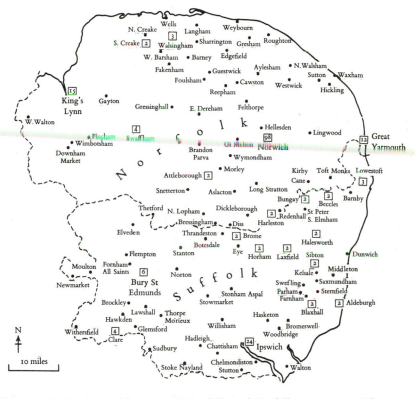

Fig. 1.   Medical practitioners on Norfolk and Suffolk 1550–1600. The map indicates settlements at which medical practitioners have been located at any time during the period 1550–1600. Where more than one practitioner has been located, the total number for the settlement is indicated in the box near the name of the settlement.

academically trained physicians, and 3 miscellaneous. Remembering that many of its members may, like Cropp, have been physicians or have practised physic, the first group is confirmed as that performing the bulk of practice in the city. The total of 73 must be regarded as a minimum. The population of Norwich in 1575, after the arrival of many of the strangers but before the major outbreaks of plague, is estimated as 17,000. This is probably nearer to the maximum than the minimum figure. It therefore appears that there was at least one practitioner for every 220 to 250 persons living in Norwich at this period.

The combined population of Norfolk and Suffolk by 1600 had probably reached 250,000.[99] Apart from Norwich the major centres of population were Yarmouth, Ispwich, King's Lynn and Bury St Edmunds (Fig. 1). The remainder of the population was distributed variously in substantial settlements, smaller villages, and sparsely inhabited fenland. East Anglia was a rich, agricultural, fishing, trading and industrial area.

The organization of poor relief and medical practice followed the pattern already described for Norwich, every settlement developing in addition idiosyncratic elements. The whole region came under the ecclesiastical system of medical licensing inaugurated in 1512 and designed to give a unified basis for the accreditation of all practitioners apart from medical graduates and licentiates of Oxford and Cambridge. This mechanism was extremely slow to come into operation, and even then it tended to function sporadically, with each diocese developing its own characteristic pattern of licensing.[100] Generally most licences were given for surgery, and a much smaller number for medicine, or medicine and surgery.[101] By contrast with other areas, the relatively small number of licences recorded for the diocese of Norwich includes a higher proportion granted for both physic and surgery (see Plate 8). It is doubtful whether these distinctions had much practical significance; like their London brethren, East Anglian practitioners would have adopted a flexible definition of their professional duties.

In the Norwich diocese medical licensing began in earnest in 1583, and the Redman visitation of 1597 was one of the first serious attempts in

---

99 Patten, 'The Urban Structure of E. Anglia', p.21.
100 For surveys of provincial medical practice, see Roberts, 'The personnel and practice of medicine... Part I. The provinces'; R. M. S. McConaghey, 'The history of rural medical practice', in Poynter (ed.), *Evolution of Medical Practice*, pp.117–43; Raach, *Directory of English Country Physicians* (note 79 above). See also scattered information in *Devon and Cornwall Notes and Queries*, 2nd ser., XIII (1925), 142–51, 237–46, 333–44; XIV (1926), 45–56, 138–53, 234–48, 329–40.
101 Roberts, 'Personnel and practice', p.369.

England to ensure that all practitioners were licensed.[102] The first evidence for the systematic licensing of midwives comes from the 1630s. By contrast there is no evidence in the adjacent diocese of Ely that either practitioners or midwives were under pressure to take out ecclesiastical licences until the visitation conducted by Bishop Wren in 1638.

Norwich licences were generally given for the whole diocese, occasionally for an archdeaconry only. Some practitioners in East Anglia possessed licences given by the Archbishop of Canterbury – usually covering a number of dioceses – and others were in possession of licences issued by the University of Cambridge. The ecclesiastical and university licensing systems were grafted onto an already established gild system operating in the towns; as in London, the relationship between the two is altogether obscure. The more inclusive gild pattern was exhibited in King's Lynn where medical practitioners of all kinds affiliated with the Merchants' Gild. By contrast a reorganization undertaken in Ipswich in 1551, which ordered all crafts and trades into only four gilds, placed physicians and apothecaries with the mercers, surgeons with the drapers, and barbers with the tailors.

Collation of evidence from various sources suggests that, with respect to East Anglia at least, previous assessments have tended to underestimate the numbers practising medicine, as well as giving a misleading impression about the relative strength of different groups. Our continuing census of East Anglian medical practitioners currently indicates that at least 250 practitioners, excluding midwives, were operating in Norfolk and Suffolk in the second half of the sixteenth century. Despite fragmentary and defective evidence, 170 practitioners working elsewhere than Norwich have been located.

The diversity and richness of medical practice in the small towns of England is well illustrated by closer examination of Ipswich and King's Lynn. We have recorded the presence of twenty-four practitioners in Ipswich and fifteen in King's Lynn in the second half of the century, most being active after 1580.[103] At Ipswich, seven practitioners were of MD status. However they were not such a dominant element as this proportion suggests. Besides practising medicine during his stay in Ipswich Richard Argentine also taught at the local grammar school, held ecclesiastical appointments, and established a reputation as a scholar and

---

[102] Carter's valuable statistical study, *The Norwich Subscription Books*, overlooks Norwich medical licences issued before 1637. For other sources on licensing see note 83 above.

[103] Taking the maximum combined population of King's Lynn and Ipswich as 12,000, on present estimates of the number of medical practitioners there would have been one practitioner to every 400 persons.

religious controversialist. The two friends Timothie Bright and Thomas Mouffet spent a short time in Ipswich after qualifying, before settling in London. One of the few medical graduates to base his practice on Ipswich was Eleazar Duncan, whose experience of local medical practice is the likely source of a strenuous attack on empirics which he published in 1606.[104]

There is an enormous educational gulf between the small elite of humanistically trained medical graduates, and the other medical practitioners operating in Ipswich, whose expertise would have been gained by apprenticeship or by casual means. At least four of these practitioners were strangers. Discounting the two apothecaries, the remaining thirteen, whether or not known as 'surgeons', would have engaged in general practice. No fewer than seven of these practitioners were in 1597 suspected of practising without a licence. This irregularity was consistent with the disconcerting level of religious disobedience and unlicensed teaching reported of the town by the 1597 visitation.[105] To the annoyance of critics like Duncan, 'empirics' were not prevented by the action of civic authorities from playing a key role in public health and poor-law relief work.[106] Thus a shadowy figure like Peter emerges with the reward of 13s 4d for healing a leg; Hercules Quick, a poor man, who had himself been in receipt of poor relief, was employed in medical relief work during a plague epidemic. At the time of the plague in 1585 Ipswich appointed an official town physician charged with 'visiting certain infected poor people' and ministering 'sundry drinks and medicines to them at the charge of the town'.[107]

The first town physician, a Mr Lufkyn, was granted a 10s bonus by grateful citizens after a brief term of service. It is possible that Lufkyn was Thomas Lufkin, formerly a fuller, and later an unlicensed practitioner, whose activities in Maidstone in 1558 were censured by John Halle. Lufkyn was succeeded as town physician by Cornelius Hubright who was paid a substantial salary of £30 per annum.[108] Through the apothecary William Loy, another alien, Hubright supplied the poor with 'meat, drink and poticary diet'.[109] At the time of the 1597 ecclesiastical visitation Hubright, together with three other surgeons

---

[104] For Ipswich, see J. Webb (ed.), *Poor Relief in Elizabethan Ipswich*, Suffolk Record Society, IX (1966); Nathaniel Bacon, *The Annalls of Ipswche*, ed. W. H. Richardson (Ipswich, 1884). Eleazar Duncan, *The copy of a letter written by E. D. to a gentleman* (1606).

[105] *Redman Visitation*, pp.156–9.

[106] Webb, *Poor Relief*, pp.110–14, 118–19.

[107] Ibid., p.115.

[108] Ibid., pp.115, 118.

[109] Ibid., pp.110, 114, 118. For Loy, see Bacon, *Annals*, p.320.

employed in poor relief, was accused of practising without a licence.[110]

Apart from recognized surgeons, work of a medical nature was undertaken in Ipswich by such individuals as midwives, nurses, women who were employed to foster orphan babies, and by soothsayers. In 1582 a case was reported in which a sailor, worried about the illness of his daughter, obtained satisfactory guidance from a cunning man after a local physician had refused to comment about witchcraft as a cause of the condition. In 1597 Thomas Pemerton was accused of practising as a soothsayer.[111]

The spectrum of medical practice in King's Lynn closely resembled that in Ipswich. Of the fifteen practitioners known to be associated with King's Lynn, three were of MD status, but none of these medical graduates had more than a limited association with the town. At least four of the fifteen practitioners were strangers. One is identified as an apothecary. Five became freemen of the Merchants' Company.[112] The major responsibility for medical care fell to practitioners of humble status. Of this group the best qualified were figures such as John Bale and Thomas Surphlet. The former had obtained a medical licence at Cambridge in 1568 on the basis of ten years' study and practice. Surphlet obtained a surgical licence at Cambridge in 1559. Thereafter he became a freeman of the Merchants' Company, his admission being conditional on his giving his services free to the poor and needy upon request of the mayor. Surphlet was a well-known oculist, whose work was noticed by Richard Banister, a fellow-specialist of the next generation: 'He lived till he was four score years of age, lived most in Norfolk, and died at Lynn, and in good estate. He lay two or three years at a barber's house at Lynn, to whom he taught some skill, who now professeth it with weak understanding and given to drink. I cannot commend this Mr Surphlet for any extraordinary skill, though of long experience'.[113]

---

[110] *Redman Visitation*, pp.156–9. The poor-relief surgeons accused were Cornelius Hubright, Robert Gooding, Robert Kenington, and Elias Kempe: Webb, *Poor Relief*, pp.49, 70.

[111] W. W., *A true and just recorde . . . of all the witches taken at S. Oses (1582)*, sig. E1. *Redman Visitation*, p.157.

[112] *Calendar of the Freemen of Lynn 1292–1836* (Norwich, 1913); H. Ingelby (ed.), *Red Register of King's Lynn* (2 vols., King's Lynn, n.d.); L. G. Matthews, 'Apothecaries and the spicers of King's Lynn Norfolk', *Pharmaceutical Historian*, II, no.3 (1971).

[113] British Library, Sloane MS. 3801, fol.3, quoted by R. R. James, *Studies in the History of Ophthalmology Prior to the Year 1800* (Cambridge, 1933), p.54. Banister himself practised in East Anglia; he noted: 'many poor people wanted help, as well as rich, were not able to travel so far to me for help; both in respect of the weakness of their bodies, and the disability of their estates' (fols.8v–9r). See A. Scorsby, 'Richard Banister and the beginnings of English ophthalmology', in E. A. Underwood (ed.), *Science, Medicine and History. Essays in honour of Charles Singer* (2 vols., London, 1953), II, pp.42–55.

At the visitation of 1597, six practitioners in King's Lynn were accused of being without licences. Two produced credentials which satisfied the authorities. Those convicted included Robert Green, a freeman of the Merchants' Company and former apprentice of Surphlet; another was described as a hat-dresser by trade.[114]

Although evidence concerning rural medical practice even in East Anglia is distressingly fragmentary, information about certain districts is sufficient for us to gain an impression of the extent to which medical practitioners were active in the countryside. In the Saxmundham area of Suffolk we have so far recorded nineteen practitioners between 1550 and 1600 including two early medical writers, William Bullein and Philip Moore. The former spent a brief time as rector of Blaxhall, before becoming a medical writer and practitioner in London. Philip Moore of Halesworth, Bullein's 'well-beloved friend', remained in Suffolk, where he wrote minor medical and astrological works. Neither Bullein nor Moore seems to have possessed medical qualifications, but each firmly identified with the learned physician. Their writings popularized herbal medicine, while vehemently criticizing empirics. A similar figure was Thomas Short of Farnham, who probably commenced practice after taking his MA at Cambridge in 1592. It was not until 1607 that he obtained a medical licence from the university. At a lower level no fewer than four local practitioners – at Middleton, Sibton, Sternfield and Swefling – were granted licences to practise surgery in 1584 and 1585.

Nicholas Fiske (1575–1653) spent his early years in the Framlingham and Laxfield area. He was 'educated in country schools' and 'at home both astrology and physic' which he then practised in Suffolk, Colchester and London.[115] He was acknowledged as contributing greatly to the revival of English astrological medicine. James Mayes of Laxfield was described as 'medicus' in legal documents between 1578 and 1600, but there is no evidence that he possessed a licence. At the 1597 visitation five individuals in the Saxmundham area were accused of practising without a licence; one was able to satisfy the authorities that he had been granted a licence in 1584; another was excommunicated; and a third, a curate at Dunwich, was censured for practising medicine and neglecting his clerical duties.[116] The extent of unlicensed practice was certainly greater than that recorded in the visitation. Bullein and Moore fulminated against empirics, while recognizing the hold which

114   *Redman Visitation*, p.68.
115   Bodleian Library, Ashmole MS. 421, fols.192v–193.
116   *Redman Visitation*, pp.128–30.

these 'impostors' maintained on the affections of the population. Bullein attacked Mrs Line and Mrs Didge, 'witches' at Kelsale and Parham who cured by prayer and spells, as 'more hurtful in this realm than either quarten, pox or pestilence'. Nevertheless Bullein recognized that, in counties like Suffolk where there were few physicians, old empirics like John Preston were 'greatly sought unto', and charged fees as little as one penny. Bullein admitted that 'Custom hath commenced him amongst the common people to be their doctor. I was this man's patient a great time, but yet I never heard him talk of Hippocrates and Galen, he troubles not his house with any of their books'.[117]

Enjoying a similar following later in the century was Margaret Neale of Aldeburgh. The 1597 visitation reported that 'she taketh upon her to cure diseases by prayer, and therefore hath recourse of people to her far and nigh'. She confessed 'that she useth a prayer to God and then the paternoster, the creed and another prayer, and before this she useth to wash'. Margaret Neale was ordered to do penance in the church, bearing a placard inscribed 'for witchcraft and enchantment' in capital letters, and carrying a white wand.[118]

The Walsingham district of Norfolk displays similar characteristics to Saxmundham. Twelve practitioners are currently recorded for this area between 1550 and 1600. William Boyton, an MD of Cambridge and described in his will as a doctor in physic, lived in this vicinity for at least thirty years, but he might not have practised medicine. This applies also to George Walker, MD, Fellow of the College of Physicians, who may have lived at Langham in his later years. It will be recalled that Walker in 1570 earned notoriety for illegally licensing empirics of Norwich and Norfolk.[119] Two local clerics, the rectors of North Creake and Sharrington, both with Cambridge arts degrees and medical licences, probably practised in their neighbourhood. Christopher Beane, who was of Gresham and for a short time student at Cambridge, obtained a licence to practise surgery from the Archbishop of Canterbury. At the other end of the scale, six individuals were accused of practising without a licence in 1597. Two men proved to have licences. At South Creake Bridget Dike and Giles Michell claimed that they practised bonesetting rather than surgery without a licence. However this was also an offence. At Wells a woman was censured for practising surgery without a

[117] William Bullein, *Bulwarke of defence againste all sicknes* (1564), pp.56v–57r.
[118] *Redman Visitation*, p.134. Nearby to Aldeburgh, at Walton, Mary Cole was accused of curing sores and ulcers by 'blessing': *Redman Visitation*, p.145.
[119] Munk, *Roll*, pp.55–6, 66.

licence, and at Barney Elizabeth Clerke admitted 'she hath been heretofore noted for a witch and dealeth in physic not licensed'. At the turn of the century Walsingham was visited by the oculist Richard Banister, who performed there the operation of couching for cataract.[120]

Following up hints contained in earlier local studies, J. H. Raach compiled a directory to demonstrate that university-educated practitioners were much more widely distributed in the provinces than was generally appreciated. Raach concluded that a great number of well-qualified practitioners were residing in villages and hamlets, hence providing the population with 'well-trained doctors by their standards'.[121] The present provisional study of East Anglia suggests a greater total population of medical practitioners and a radically different composition of the spectrum of 'well-trained doctors'. Even the impressive total of 814 country doctors listed by Raach must represent only a small fraction of the total of medical practitioners outside London. In the present study, for a similar time span, in an earlier period in which evidence is sparse, and the population size less, we have already located more than 250 practitioners for only two counties (see Fig. 1). It might be suggested that some of these individuals should be eliminated on the basis of their being quacks or charlatans. But, for reasons given at the outset of this essay, it is impossible to arrive at satisfactory criteria for narrowing the definition of medical practice. It is much more realistic to accept that the entire body of individuals identified as healers by the community should be regarded as eligible for inclusion in a study of medical practitioners.

This extension of the conception of medical practitioner is particularly important for a balanced assessment of rural medical practice. It is evident that Raach's university-educated practitioners were themselves an extremely heterogeneous group, and that they represent only a small fraction of those dispensing medical care in rural communities. If there was a medical graduate living locally it is quite possible that he was not engaged in medical practice, or, that he restricted his services to a narrow social group. Even towns like Ipswich or King's Lynn supported only a single practising medical graduate for most of the time. Thus Peter Baro (MA 1585), son of the Lady Margaret Professor of Divinity of the same name, established a medical practice at

---

[120] *Redman Visitation*, pp.52–62; Richard Banister, *A treatise of the one hundred and thirteene diseases of the eyes* (1622), sig.c4r–v.

[121] Raach, *Directory*, p.14.

Boston, Lincs.; and his son Samuel Baro (MD 1628) practised at King's Lynn. Graduates practising medicine were more likely to be the local clergymen, some of whom had taken out medical licences at university. The 1597 visitation exposed the great diversity of educational attainment, formal qualifications, and sense of vocation among the clergy of East Anglia. We find that the curate at Thetford suspected of being unordained, and accused of teaching children and of practising medicine, had actually been granted a medical and surgical licence by the Bishop of Norwich. The curate at Aslacton neglecting his clerical duties and practising medicine, was in possession of an MA, but neither a medical licence nor holy orders.

The majority of practitioners, whether English or foreign, in provincial towns and villages were not educated at a university. Some were formally apprenticed, and associated with gilds; many recognized the value of taking out a bishop's or university licence. It is doubtful whether even freemen, or licentiates, represent a majority of those dispensing medical care. In most cases knowledge was acquired by casual means, and it is likely that medicine was not the only source of income for many practitioners. It is noticeable that in smaller as well as larger towns strangers were active in medical practice, and that women played an important although sometimes ancillary role. In the countryside there were fewer strangers, and women were more dominant. Cecily Baldrye was granted a surgical licence by the Bishop of Norwich in 1568. More commonly women practised without a licence. Twelve women outside Norwich were prosecuted during the 1597 visitation. This number suggests that women were playing a substantial part in bonesetting, surgery and medical practice, as well as following the traditional vocations of midwifery and nursing.

Within the local community much of the available medical assistance was delivered cheaply. It was by no means uncommon for a local gentleman, clergyman, or their wives, to dispense medicine gratis, or for small reward. This service was matched by surgeons, midwives, or cunning men and women, employing their skill as practitioners either to court celebrity or for fees amounting to a few pence. Advice from outsiders or itinerant practitioners would be used in difficult cases, or for special complaints, such as stone or cateract. By exploiting simple medicines, and by deploying prayer and magical rituals, the community was able to furnish from its internal resources the appropriate level of medical assistance. What was lacking in therapeutic effectiveness was amply made up in psychological support. Away from the influence of the few doctrinaire modernists attempting to follow Galen, there would have been a remarkable consistency of outlook on matters relating to disease and health between the educated and uneducated classes. They shared simple herbal lore, and maintained, albeit at different levels of sophistication, a predominantly magical medical outlook.

Health care was finely integrated into the traditions and customs of rural communities. Established mechanisms of care came under pressure in the later sixteenth century in cases where ecclesiastical authorities were inclined to exercise their licensing function severely, or to impose sanctions against magical practices. It is a complex matter to determine why useful and seemingly popular members of the community should increasingly be exposed to official disapprobation. The forces against the traditional healer were various; they included the humanist physicians and their lay sympathizers favouring rationalistic medicine and the rational division of labour within the medical profession, and ecclesiastical authorities aspiring to a more rigid supervision of the ministry, teachers and medical practitioners, in the course of attempts to improve parish discipline. Healers risked being suspected of indulging in illegal and sinful magical practices, and hence they were liable to prosecution for either perpetuating Catholicism, or for fostering the innovations of radical Protestantism. Thus it is not surprising to find that the move to enforce medical licensing coincides with the rising concern about witchcraft. Magical medicine and witchcraft were stigmatized as related evils. Sophisticated neo-Platonists like John Dee and traditional healers alike risked designation as 'witches' or 'conjurers', and hence were likely to become victims of popular resentment, or to be placed under legal prohibitions. Women healers in particular were vulnerable to accusations of witchcraft. Others in East Anglia who came under suspicion for conjuring included the Puritan minister and alchemist, William Blomfild, the churchwarden and medical practitioner Miles Blomefield, the astrological medical practitioners Gabriel and John Harvey, and Nicholas Fiske. The last, who practised in Suffolk and London, reported that astrology had been in his youth 'strangely kept under', discussed only in secret, and 'aspersed by men malicious and unlearned'.[122]

Despite cultural, professional and legal pressure against traditional healers, unlicensed practitioners and exponents of magical medicine, it is

[122] John Heydon, *An astrological discourse* (1650), 'To the Reader', by Fiske. For further discussion of the above issues see Thomas, *Religion and the Decline of Magic*; A. MacFarlane, *Witchcraft in Tudor and Stuart England: A Regional and Comparative Study* (London, 1970).

doubtful whether any noticeable erosion of the influence and standing of these groups occurred in the sixteenth century, either in rural communities, towns like Norwich, or in the capital itself. Indeed any success achieved by the licensing mechanisms of the College of Physicians or the church was more than compensated for by the growth in the general popularity of magic, astrology and alchemy. The tripartite division of labour within the medical profession as favoured by humanist physicians was largely a utopian dream. Medical practice in London and the provinces was dominated by general practitioners, some licensed, most unlicensed, some urban practitioners within gilds, and many more rural practitioners who had no formal organization. Each community, whether metropolis or rural parish, generated its characteristic constellation of male and female medical practitioners, whose talents could be employed whenever there was need to seek medical assistance outside the family circle. Evidence accumulated in the course of the present study for London, Norwich and East Anglia has consistently pointed to there being one medical practitioner at least for every 400 members of the population. It was probably not unusual for the ratio to reach 1 : 200. When it is appreciated that the influence of these practitioners was reinforced by midwives, nurses, and laymen of all social classes exercising their skills in the art of physic, it is evident that early modern western society called for a high level of medical assistance from outside the limits of the family. This complexity and high intensity of medical care links early western culture with present-day traditional societies. It may well be the case that the high level of intensity of medical care was generated by the limited efficacy of therapeutic procedures. Thus a system of compensations operates which permits society to absorb the effects of ill-health regardless of its level of medical knowledge. In the sixteenth century this system was largely independent of the services of medical graduates, notwithstanding the emergence of a university-educated elite at the head of the nascent medical profession. This group attained significant proportions, but it was not sufficiently cohesive or influential to undermine the authority of other sections of the medical community. Humanistic physicians were welcomed as adding to the diversity of medical practice, but they were not allowed to sever the strong bonds which united the community with its traditional healers.

7

Mirrors of health and treasures of poor men: the uses of the vernacular medical literature of Tudor England

PAUL SLACK

It was the 'compassion that I have of the poor people' which moved the author of the most popular medical work of the sixteenth century to put pen to paper, so that 'every man, woman and child' might 'be their own physician in time of need'. So wrote Thomas Moulton, whose *Mirror or Glass of Health* went through at least seventeen editions between 1530 and 1580.[1] Other writers followed what seemed to be a sure recipe for success. Claims to popular utility became as commonplace in the prefaces of the English medical works of the Tudor period as appeals to the 'general reader' on the dustjackets of academic books today.

Like their modern equivalents, however, these were pious hopes or calculated advertisements rather than statements of fact. Such works can scarcely have reached the illiterate poor, and the extent of their diffusion even among the literate may well be questioned. Neither can they be taken without qualification as reflections of 'popular' attitudes towards disease, still less of popular treatment of it.[2] They were one small and specialized part of a medical world in which there were several alternative sources of knowledge and advice, from the educated practitioners to the more numerous 'cunning' men and women who represented a well-worn and well-known tradition of magical and folk medicine.[3] Nevertheless, the literature existed, found a market and grew in volume, and it is important to ask what, in an already well-peopled medical universe, its function was. How great was the contribution of the printed book to medical attitudes and medical care, and how much can it tell us about them?

---

[1] Thomas Moulton, *This is the myrour or glasse of helthe* [before 1531], chapter 1.
[2] There is a useful general account of these works in H. S. Bennett, *English Books and Readers 1475–1557*, 2nd edn (Cambridge, 1970), pp.97–109, and idem, *English Books and Readers 1558–1603* (Cambridge, 1965), pp.179–89.
[3] On popular and magical medicine, see K. Thomas, *Religion and the Decline of Magic* (London, 1971), especially chapters 7 and 8.

I

The answers to these questions depend upon some initial assessment of the quantity and quality of the literature itself. We need to determine its volume and its subject-matter. This is no easy task since the works involved were so various. The vernacular literature of the sixteenth century is readily identified and already pre-packaged for us (if the occasional Latin work is excluded) in the *Short-Title Catalogue*;[4] but the term 'medical' does not have such a sharp definition. As one would expect in a society in which the care of the sick was not yet a specialized professional activity, and in which astrologers and priests practised medicine, there were several works which straddled the borders between medicine and other subjects. Compiling a list of 'medical' books for the early modern period is therefore an even more subjective and arbitrary exercise than most bibliographical classifications. For the purposes of calculating the figures which follow, 'medical literature' has been taken to cover all books and pamphlets deliberately and largely devoted to the description, analysis or treatment of human health and disease. Herbals and works on anatomy have been included but not books on the care of animals.[5] Books of 'secrets' almost wholly concerned with disease have been counted, but not a more general encyclopaedia like that of Bartholomaeus Anglicus,[6] or works on astrology which may refer to medical matters among others.[7] More questionably, perhaps, almanacs and most religious tracts on epidemics and other diseases have been excluded from the figures, although they will necessarily be referred to at a later point in the discussion. Of the religious tracts, only those few works which included some relatively technical enquiry into the natural remedies for or protections against disease have been counted.[8]

Using this definition, it has been possible to identify 153 medical titles published before 1605. The first was the *Little Book*, a plague tract attributed to Canutus, published about 1486;[9] one of the last was

---

4   *STC* A; *STC* B, vol. II.
5   An example of the latter is anon., *Remedies for diseases in horses* (1576, and later edns).
6   Bartholomaeus Anglicus, *De proprietatibus rerum*. transl. John Trevisa (1495).
7   E.g., Claude Dariot, *A breefe introduction to the astrologicall judgement of the starres* (1583), though the 1598 edition, which has the addition of a treatise on 'mathematical physic', has been included.
8   E.g., Henoch Clapham, *An epistle discoursing upon the pestilence* (1603) and idem, *H. Clapham, his demaundes and answeres touching the pestilence* (1604) have been included.
9   [Canutus], *Here begynneth a litil boke the whiche traytied and rehersed many gode thinges necessarie for the pestilence* [c.1486].

another work concerned with plague, Francis Herring's *A Modest Defence*, published in 1604.[10] Between them came a variety of books covering many other aspects of health and disease. The number of recorded titles tells us little in itself, however. In one sense it is a minimal estimate, for it comprises only works listed in the *Short-Title Catalogue*, that is works which are known to survive.[11] Several others must have been lost, especially no doubt the smaller more popular tracts which were probably never bound. In another sense it may be too large a figure. Quite apart from the amount of borrowing by one author from another, some titles are in fact only slightly different versions of earlier books.[12] Duplicates of this kind have been excluded where possible, but it is likely that not all have been spotted. In any case the number of titles is less indicative of the quantity of medical literature available than the number of editions. Several of the 153 titles were reprinted again and again. If we count all known editions (but not variants) as well as originals, there were 392 editions of medical works between 1486 and 1604 inclusive.

In order to calculate at all reliably the total book-stock implied by this number, we should need to know the size of each edition, a subject on which we have no accurate information. In the early part of the sixteenth century editions may well have been quite small, but a not unrealistic estimate of the average for the whole period might be 1,000 copies.[13] That would give a total of nearly 400,000 copies printed between 1486 and 1604. The number of volumes in use at any one time was, of course, much smaller. Even at the end of the sixteenth century, when the number of publications was increasing, it cannot have been very large. If we allow each book a life of around thirty years – probably a generous estimate – there may have been some 166,000 medical books still in use in 1604, one for every twenty people or so, had they been equally distributed. Despite some contemporary fears that the market was being flooded, these are quite modest figures. Medical works represent only a small proportion of English publishing, probably some 3 per cent of the

10 Francis Herring, *A modest defence of the caveat given to the wearers of amulets* (1604).
11 The figures in this and the following paragraphs have been calculated from *STC* A, revised as far as possible with reference to *STC* B, vol. II, and to the information on the revision of letters A to H available in the Bodleian Library, Oxford. *STC* B adds few new titles (two works on baths by John Jones are examples: *STC* B 14724a.3, 14724a.7), but many editions not known to the original compilers of the work.
12 Conrad Gesner, *The newe jewell of health* (1576) and idem, *The practise of the new and old phisicke* (1599), both translated by Thomas Hill and George Baker, are examples.
13 Bennett, *English Books and Readers 1475–1557*, p.228; *English Books and Readers 1558–1603*, p.298; L. Febvre and H.-J. Martin, *The Coming of the Book*, English edn (London, 1976), p.262.

total output of books.[14] We can scarcely attribute any major social or medical impact to a volume of literature of this size. Having said that, however, rather less than half a million books is not a negligible number. If medical books did not force themselves on the attention of the literate by their numbers, they probably existed in sufficient quantity by the end of the period to be accessible to most of the readers who positively wanted them.

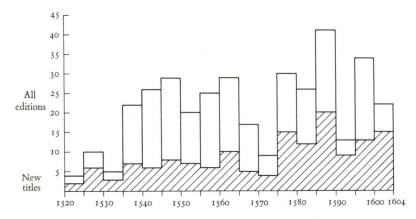

Fig. 1.   The publication of vernacular medical literature 1520–1604, showing number of titles and editions for each five-year period. Source: see note 15.

The output of these books was unevenly spread over time. Fig. 1 shows both the total number of editions and the number of new titles printed in each quinquennium after 1520 (before that date the number of publications was very small).[15] The gradual growth in the volume of medical publishing is evident, from an average of one or two editions a year to an average of four or five. So too is the heavy dependence during the middle decades of the century on reprints rather than new texts. This reinforced the second- or third-hand quality of medical writing, which was already well established by authors borrowing from foreign texts or fifteenth-century collections. Only after 1575 did the number of new

14   Bennett, *English Books and Readers 1475–1557*, p.20; *English Books and Readers 1558–1603*, p.269. John Jones thought there were so many medical books 'that books may seem rather to want readers than readers books': *A diall for all agues* (1566), sig. A viiir.
15   Fig. 1 is based on information in *STC* B, vol. 11, and on the information so far available on vol. 1 in the Bodleian Library. The dates of several works published between 1520 and 1570 are only approximate, being the suggestions of the revisers of *STC*. They are often significantly different from those of *STC* A. Where the revisers suggest no date (saying, for example, 'before 1546'), the edition has not been included in the figure.

works slightly exceed the number of reissues, and even then there was no period like the 1650s when the number of new publications rose dramatically.[16]

Output was, however, more prolific in some years than in others, and there were clusters of productive years, some of which are masked by the quinquennial divisions in Fig. 1. Two such were in 1539–41 and 1546–8, when the genre of medical works intended for laymen, pioneered by Moulton, Sir Thomas Elyot, Andrew Boorde and Thomas Paynel, achieved instant success and gave rise to several new editions.[17] Another prolific period occurred between 1560 and 1562, partly owing to reprints of Elyot and Moulton after a hiatus in Mary's reign, partly perhaps because of the epidemic fevers of the later 1550s which must have boosted sales and editions of relevant works.[18] Later in the century epidemics of plague certainly inspired authors to seize the main chance. Outbreaks of the disease across the country, together with the government's interest in encouraging public health measures against it, may have helped to produce a cluster of publications between 1578 and 1580, for example;[19] and it was literature on plague which pushed up the total number of new publications to a record height in 1603.[20]

The very high productivity of the years 1585–7, on the other hand, was much more varied in its make-up and cannot be attributed to any single cause. Rather it illustrates the range of 'medical' literature with which we are dealing. It included Bostocke's defence of Paracelsian medical theory,[21] and treatises by an Oxford professor, on eye diseases and medicinal springs in Warwickshire.[22] There was a translation of a foreign work on surgery, as well as an edition of a book on the French

---

[16] See C. Webster, *The Great Instauration: Science, Medicine and Reform 1626–1660* (London, 1975), p.489. My total for 1600–4 is slightly larger than Dr Webster's, no doubt because of our different definitions of 'medical' literature.

[17] Moulton, *Mirror* [edns in 1540?, 1541?, 1545?, 1548?]; Sir Thomas Elyot, *The castel of helth* [first edn, *c*.1536; probably six further editions before 1549]; Andrew Boorde, *Here foloweth a compendyous regyment or a dyetary of helth* (3 edns, 1542–7); idem, *The breviary of healthe* (1547); *Regimen sanitatis Salerni*, trans. Thomas Paynel (first edn, 1528; another, 1541).

[18] E.g., William Bullein, *Bulleins bulwarke of defence againste all sicknes* (1562), and the reprints [John XXI], *The treasury of healthe* [*c*.1560], and Jehan Goeurot, *The regiment of life* (1560).

[19] E.g., Pierre Drouet, *A new counsell against the pestilence* (1578); Thomas Brasbridge, *The poore mans jewell, that is to say, a treatise of the pestilence* (4 edns, 1578–80).

[20] E.g., Thomas Thayre, *A treatise of the pestilence* (1603); Thomas Lodge, *A treatise of the plague* (1603); James Balmford, *A short dialogue concerning the plagues infection* (1603); S. H., *A new treatise of the pestilence* (1603); Francis Herring, *Certaine rules, directions or advertisements for this time of pestilentiall contagion* (1603).

[21] R. B[ostocke], *The difference betwene the auncient phisicke . . . and the latter phisicke* (1585).

[22] Walter Bayley, *A briefe treatise touching the preservation of the eiesight* (1586); idem, *A briefe discours of certain bathes or medicinall waters in the counties of Warwicke* (1587).

pox by the English surgeon, William Clowes.[23] There were three small tracts trumpeting the virtues of particular medicines,[24] a treatise on melancholy,[25] a handbook of medical receipts intended for household use,[26] and – inevitably – reprints of Elyot's *Castle of Health* and of Boorde's *Breviary of Health*. And there were other works besides.

It is time, therefore, that we tried to define the content of this varied literature. Perhaps its most striking feature, apart from the large number of reprints, is the number of translations of foreign works. Exactly one third of the titles, fifty-one, were explicitly translations. Some of them were versions of prestigious authorities, of Galen or modern writers such as Gesner.[27] Of wider appeal, however, were books billed as revelations of the 'secrets' of some foreign sage, such as Fioravanti, or Alexis of Piedmont whose collection of remedies appeared in four parts and several editions between 1558 and 1614.[28] In addition there were works which, while claiming to be by English authors, were borrowed from continental sources. Thomas Lodge's *Treatise of the Plague* (1603), which historians have sometimes supposed to refer to English conditions, has been shown to be such a case,[29] and detailed comparison of texts would no doubt reveal others.[30] For English medical literature was very often derivative in the sixteenth century. Translations, and works ostensibly by English authors, covered much the same variety of themes, and they must be grouped together when considering the literature's subject-matter.

---

[23] Hans Jacob Wecker, *A compendious chyrurgerie*, trans. John Banister (1585); William Clowes, *A briefe and necessarie treatise touching the cure of the disease called Morbus Gallicus* (1585).

[24] Anon., *A briefe and short discourse of the vertue of balsame* (1585); anon., *A discourse of the medicine called mithridatium* (1585); Andreas Bertholdus, *The wonderfull and strange effect of a new terra sigillata found in Germania* (1587).

[25] Timothie Bright, *A treatise of melancholie, containing the causes thereof* (1586).

[26] John Partridge, *The treasurie of commodious conceits, and hidden secrets, and may be called, the huswives closet, of healthfull provision* (1586 edn). Cf. the same author's *The widowes treasure, plentifully furnished with secretes in phisicke* (1585).

[27] *Certaine workes of Galens called methodus medendi*, trans. Thomas Gale (1567); Gesner, *New Jewel of Health*, and idem, *The treasure of Euonymus: conteyninge the wonderfull hid secretes of nature*, trans. P. Morwyng (1559). On Gesner, see A. G. Debus, *The English Paracelsians* (London, 1965), pp.52–7 passim.

[28] Leonardo Fioravanti, *A compendium of the rationall secretes*, trans. John Hester (1582); [Alessio], *The secretes of Alexis of Piemont containing remedies against diseases*, trans. William Warde (1558 onwards). On the latter, see J. Ferguson, 'The secrets of Alexis. A sixteenth-century collection of medical and technical receipts', *Proceedings of the Royal Society of Medicine*, XXIV (1930–1), 225–46.

[29] E. Cuvelier, '"A treatise of the plague" de Thomas Lodge (1603)', *Etudes Anglaises*, XXI (1968), 395–403.

[30] Compare, for example, T.C., *A godly and learned sermon, upon the 91. Psalme* (1603), with Andreas Osiander, *How and whither a christen man ought to flye the horrible plage of the pestilence*, trans. Miles Coverdale (1537).

Accordingly, Table 1 divides the totals of 153 titles and 392 editions into eight distinct categories.[31] Although determined by the content of the books themselves, these are not rigid thematic groups. They represent an attempt to impose strict subject divisions on works which often ranged across several themes. Hence the vagueness of some of their

Table 1. *The subject-matter of English vernacular medical literature 1486–1604*

Category	Titles		Editions		Editions in octavo or smaller format	
	No.	Per cent	No.	Per cent	No.	Per cent
1. Anatomy and surgery	23	15.0	39	9.9	7	3.5
2. Reflections on theory and practice	17	11.1	26	6.6	12	6.0
3. Herbals	10	6.5	27	6.9	13	6.5
4. Plague tracts	23	15.0	42	10.7	15	7.5
5. Other specific diseases	16	10.5	27	6.9	16	8.0
6. Single or specialized remedies	13	8.5	19	4.8	9	4.5
7. Explanatory textbooks and regimens	33	21.6	115	29.3	64	32.0
8. Collections of remedies	18	11.8	97	24.7	64	32.0
Totals	153	100.0	392	(99.8)	200	100.0

Source: STC (see note 11).

headings. There were inevitable difficulties in pigeon-holing several publications, and nice distinctions have had to be drawn. The categories 'Anatomy and surgery' (1) and 'Herbals' (3) are self-explanatory and their contents readily recognizable. Works on these subjects were relatively well defined and specialized in their subject-matter in the sixteenth century.[32] Our other groups are more artificial. 'Reflections on

---

[31] Some 13 per cent of the works (20 titles) have not been seen by the present author in any edition; and their themes have had to be judged from their titles or from secondary literature. This may have introduced some slight inaccuracy in the table.

[32] See F. N. L. Poynter (ed.), *Selected Writings of William Clowes 1544–1604* (London, 1948), pp.13–17; A. Arber, *Herbals. Their Origin and Evolution . . . 1470–1670*, 2nd edn (Cambridge, 1938). See Plate 10.

Plate 10. Title-page of Gerard's *Herbal*
The London surgeon John Gerard's *The Herbal or General History of Plants* (1597) was the most elaborate herbal, and arguably the most ambitious vernacular medical work produced in England in the sixteenth century. The title-page was engraved by William Rogers, who also produced the title-page of Mouffet's *Theatrum insectorum* (see Plate 7). Reproduced by courtesy of the Wellcome Trustees.

theory and practice' (2) comprises works, some of them controversial, on medical practice in general. It includes, for example, Timothie Bright's *A Treatise wherein is declared the Sufficiency of English Medicines* (1580), R. Bostocke's *Difference between the Ancient Physic... and the Latter Physic* (1585), and other books criticizing or defending the medical profession and its current treatments. It is perhaps the loosest of our eight categories, determined largely by exclusion from the others. Works solely concerned with 'Plague' (4) are numerous enough to justify a group of their own.[33] Several further publications have long sections concerned with this disease, but if they consider other matters besides they have been allocated to groups (7) or (8). 'Other specific diseases' (5) takes in books concentrating on such complaints as syphilis, the sweating sickness, pleurisy, melancholy and diseases of the eye.[34] 'Single or specialized remedies' (6) is a similarly mixed bag. It includes works on English medicinal springs and spas, as well as on such ancient remedies as mithridatium; but all are publications on a single theme.[35]

The works in categories (7) and (8) range over a wider field, and the line between these two groups was the most difficult of all to draw. Each of them contains books giving advice on how to combat a great variety of diseases, and claiming to be popular handbooks for the use of the layman. A distinction can be made, however, between those which simply list remedies for named complaints, and those which attempt also to explain the origins and symptoms of disease or to show how health can be preserved; between simple practical manuals on the one hand, and more discursive works of literature on the other. Examples of the latter, from the category 'Textbooks and regimens' (7), are Elyot's *Castle of Health* and Thomas Cogan's *Haven of Health* (1584); and of the former, from 'Collections of remedies' (8), Moulton's *Mirror or Glass of Health* and T.C., *An Hospital for the Diseased* (1578).[36] Some works bridged the gap between the two, like Thomas Phaer's edition of Jehan Goeurot's *The Regimen of Life* [1543?]. This has been classed here as a regimen since the French original was based on the *Regimen sanitatis Salerni*, but the English version is largely devoted to the provision of

---

33 For examples, see the works mentioned in note 20 above.
34 E.g., Clowes, *A Brief and Necessary Treatise Touching ... Morbus Gallicus*; Phillippus Hermanius, *An excellent treatise teaching howe to cure the French-pockes*, trans. John Hester (1590); John Caius, *A boke, or counseill against the disease commonly called the sweate, or sweatyng sicknesse* (1552); William Bullein, *A comfortable regiment against pleurisi* (1562); Bright, *A Treatise of Melancholy*; André Du Laurens, *A discourse of the preservation of the sight* (1599).
35 See the works cited in notes 22 and 24.
36 Other examples of these two categories will be referred to later in this essay.

specified remedies for specific complaints. There are, however, evident differences of style and purpose between the works at the two extremes.

Which were the most popular of these categories? The first column in Table 1 shows that the largest in terms of titles are textbooks and regimens (7), books on anatomy and surgery (1), and plague tracts (4). If we look at the number of editions in each category, however, a different picture emerges. Textbooks and regimens retain their prominence, even increasing their share of the total output; but they are joined now by the simple collections of remedies (8) whose few titles went into many editions, five each on average. All the others except herbals (3) lose ground by comparison. Between them, textbooks and regimens and collections of remedies supplied half the medical books published during the period.

Much of this unequal distribution of editions is readily explained. Works on single or specialized remedies (6) were clearly advertisements, of short life. Most of the reflections on theory and practice (2) were tracts for the times of little continuing importance, as were some of the works on specific diseases (5). Plague tracts (4), though still the third-largest category, were published during or shortly after epidemics and not reprinted until the next outbreak. They also concerned a subject, the most intractable of all diseases, on which no single author could hope to make himself the obvious authority. On the other hand, collections of remedies, like herbals and to some degree regimens, belonged to an established 'genre' in which little variety but much reprinting might be called for.

The difference between the distribution of new titles and that of all editions was also in part a function of chronological changes in the pattern of publishing. The older the book, the more opportunity there was for it to be reprinted before our closing date of 1604. It is significant therefore that works in some of the more specialized areas appeared in large quantity only after 1575. Before then the literature was more heavily dominated by collections of remedies and by textbooks and regimens: 39 per cent of pre-1575 titles were in categories (7) and (8), compared with 29 per cent in the later period. The literature was much more varied in content at the end of the sixteenth century than it had been thirty or forty years before.

The need for new editions might depend also on the physical durability of the work in question. Large bound volumes lasted longer than small pamphlets of twenty or thirty pages and were reprinted less often. The format of a book has its own story to tell, however, since it reflects the author's and publisher's view of the purpose and audience for it. The larger the volume, the less likely it was to be put to everyday household use, the more likely to be designed for the study or library. Table 1 shows that the distribution of books of smaller format – octavo, duodecimo and sexto-decimo – was even more unequal than that of editions. Very few works on anatomy and surgery were printed in less than quarto size. Even octavo plague tracts were few in number, though they were much shorter than the surgical folios and quartos and can rarely have been bound. More than half the textbooks and regimens were in small format, however, and nearly three quarters of the collections of remedies. These were clearly the most popular categories of medical work. The particular hold which the collections exercised on such 'mass' market for medical literature as existed in Tudor England is indicated by the fact that they comprised only an eighth of titles, but a quarter of all editions and nearly a third of works of 'pocket' size.

The limited information available about the price of books is consistent with the evidence of popularity given by editions and format. Prices depended in part on whether or not a work was bound, and they also varied between different works in each category. On average, however, publications in categories (7) and (8) were much the cheapest. Whereas the surgical works of Vigo cost 4s, and Dodoens's herbal 6s (Gerard's herbal cost as much as 48s), textbooks and regimens could be got for as little as 1s (*Regimen sanitatis Salerni*, 1575) or 6d (Elyot's *Castle*), and collections of remedies for 6d (T.C., *An Hospital for the Diseased*, 1578) or 2d and 3d (Moulton's *Mirror*). These copies of Moulton were as cheap as any publication on the market in the later sixteenth century.[37]

Consequently it is not surprising that regimens, textbooks and collections of remedies dominated the list of medical best-sellers between 1485 and 1604. Table 2 shows the thirteen titles which achieved more than six editions before 1604. No less than eleven of these works are in categories (7) and (8). Three of them are rather more specialized than the others and should be mentioned first. *The Seeing of Urines* was a popular version of larger works which, 'considering that it is expedient for every man to know the operation and qualities of his body', expounded the techniques by which disease could be identified by

[37] Information on prices from H. R. Plomer, 'Some Elizabethan book sales', *The Library*, 3rd ser., VII (1916), 328; F. R. Johnson, 'Notes on English retail book-prices 1550–1640', ibid., 5th ser., V (1950), 83–112.

Table 2. *Medical best-sellers 1486–1604*

Category (see Table 1)	Work	No. and date of editions
8	T. Moulton, *This is the myrour or glasse of helthe*	17 (pre-1531–1580)
7	T. Elyot, *The castel of helth*	16 (1536–9 to 1595)
8	Anon., *Here begynneth a newe boke of medecynes intytulyd or callyd the treasure of pore men*	15 (1526?–1575)
7	Anon., *Here begynneth the seynge of uryns*	13 (1525–1575?)
3	Anon., *Here begynneth a newe mater: the which is called an herball*	11 (1525–1560)
7	E. Roesslin, *The byrth of mankynde*, trans. Richard Jonas	10 (1540–1604)
7	J. Goeurot, *The regiment of life*, trans. Thomas Phaer	9 (1543?–1596)
8	T. C., *An hospitall for the diseased*	8 (1578–1598)
4	[Canutus], *Here begynneth a litil boke the whiche traytied and rehersed many gode thinges necessarie for the pestilence*	7 (c. 1486–1536)
7	*Regimen sanitatis Salerni*, trans. Thomas Paynel	7 (1528–1597)
8	Anon., *The antidotharius, in the whiche thou mayst lerne how thou shalt make playsters, salves, etc.*	7 (1535?–1556?)
8	[John XXI], *The treasury of healthe*	7 (1550?–1585)
8	J. Partridge, *The treasurie of commodious conceits, and hidden secrets*	7 (1573–1600)

Source: STC (see note 11).

simple inspection of the urine.[38] Roesslin's *Birth of Mankind* was the standard work, translated by Richard Jonas from the Latin, on childbirth. *The Antidotharius* covered the making of ointments and plasters. All were relatively narrow in scope, but all referred to several different diseases and complaints and can thus be counted with more general textbooks and collections.

[38] Anon., *The judycyall of uryns* [1527?], title page. Cf. anon., *Hereafter foloweth the judgement of all urynes* [1555?]

The two exceptions noted from Table 2 were further removed in character from the other best-selling titles. The first is the herbal, published by Banckes and once attributed to Cary, which, like similar works, was based on medieval manuscripts listing various plants and their medicinal uses. It was swept from the market after 1560 by the more extensive volumes of Turner, Dodoens and finally Gerard.[39] The plague tract attributed to a fifteenth-century Swedish bishop, Canutus,[40] was similarly descended from manuscript tractates of the later Middle Ages, and it was overtaken by an even larger volume of literature on plague in the second half of the sixteenth century. Essays on the precautions to be adopted to prevent infection and on treatments for the disease were appended to other works, like Moulton's *Mirror* and Goeurot's *Regimen*. There were also several separate publications, one of the first a tract translated by Thomas Paynel,[41] and one of the most popular, Thomas Brasbridge's *The Poor Man's Jewel, that is to say a Treatise of the Pestilence* (1578). Although they continued to be written from a traditionally Galenic standpoint, stressing the miasmic origins of epidemic infections, these later works introduced into the literature both variety and a new note of controversy, with disputes about the nature of contagion and about the virtues of various treatments.[42] The variety of the literature on plague was further increased at the end of the period by a succession of devotional works, prescribing prayers and meditations as defences against the disease.[43] Although Canutus alone occurs in Table 2, therefore, his work is a reminder of the very large number of publications, twenty-three 'medical' titles and thirteen 'religious' works, devoted to this single disease between 1486 and 1604.

The character of textbooks and regimens, and of collections of remedies, the main titles in Table 2, changed much less in the course of the period. Of the textbooks and regimens, Elyot's *Castle* was reprinted

[39] Anon., *Here begynnyth a newe mater: the which is called an herball* (publ. R. Banckes, 1525); Bennett, *English Books and Readers 1475–1557*, pp.98–9; William Turner, *A new herball* (1551); Rembert Dodoens, *A nieuwe herball or historie of plantes* (1578); John Gerard, *The herball or generall historie of plantes* (1597). If works similar to Banckes's, e.g. anon., *A newe herball of Macer* [1535], are counted as editions of the same work, there were in fact nineteen, not eleven, editions before 1561. See Plate 10.

[40] For an edition of this tract, see *A litil boke*, ed. G. Vine, John Rylands Library Facsimiles, no.3 (Manchester, 1910).

[41] *A moche profitable treatise against the pestilence* (1534).

[42] See, for example, Clapham, *An Epistle*; Herring, *A Modest Defence*; Peter Turner, *The opinion of... concerning amulets or plague cakes* (1603); Balmford, *A Short Dialogue*.

[43] Examples are, Anthony Anderson, *An approved medicine against the plague* (1593); William Cupper, *Certaine sermons concerning Gods late visitation* (1592); Henry Holland, *Spirituall preservatives against the pestilence* (1593); John Sanford, *Gods arrowe of the pestilence* (1604).

throughout the century, and so too was the work on which it was partly based, the *Regimen sanitatis Salerni*. It was not until 1607 that Sir John Harington's verse translation of the latter[44] partially replaced Paynel's version; and works like Boorde's *Dietary* (1542), Bullein's *Government of Health* (1558) and Cogan's *Haven of Health* (1584), though popular, did not dethrone the *Castle*. Some of them indeed gave the game away by copying Elyot *verbatim*.[45] Sir Thomas Elyot could have claimed therefore to be both the originator and chief representative of this genre of publication, the main characteristic of which was the provision of simple rules for a healthy diet and course of life. As he made clear in his book, Elyot had earlier models whose work he adapted. Salernitan writings on these themes, like the 'Isagoge' of Johannitius, had been widely available before the invention of printing, and the *Regimen* itself was accessible in Latin even before Paynel's translation.[46] There was also Erasmus's version of Plutarch, *De tuenda sanitate* (1513), which had a similar subject-matter.[47] But it was Elyot who built on Galenic, Salernitan and humanist foundations a didactic and beguiling essay incorporating humoral theory, dietary advice and a few practical remedies, a work, as the author said, combining moral philosophy with physic.[48] Elyot established a model which was influential for at least a century, and which produced echoes even in medical textbooks concerned more narrowly with 'physic'.

The collections of remedies, which occupy even more space in Table 2, had no single influential hand behind them, and were hence very different in quality. Where the regimens discussed humoral theory, explained the origins of disease and advised on how to maintain health, the collections simply listed illnesses, sometimes in alphabetical order, more often according to the part of the body affected, and added one or more remedies. They had direct roots in the vernacular literature of the Middle Ages. Moulton's *Mirror* and *The Treasure of Poor Men* prescribed remedies, most of them purgative or soothing concoctions of herbs, in as

---

44 *The Englishmans docter. Or, the Schoole of Salerne*, trans. John Harington (1607).

45 For an example compare Henry Wingfield, *A compendious or shorte treatise, conteynynge preceptes necessary to the preservacion of healthe* [1551 ?], sig. A v v, with Elyot, *Castel of Helthe* [1541], ed. S. A. Tannenbaum, Scholars' Facsimiles (New York, 1937), fol. 43r; and see S. E. Lehmberg, *Sir Thomas Elyot, Tudor Humanist* (Austin, Texas, 1960), p.147.

46 For brief accounts of early Salernitan writings, see C. H. Talbot, *Medicine in Medieval England* (London, 1967), chapter 3, and H. E. Sigerist, *Landmarks in the History of Hygiene* (Oxford, 1956), chapter 2.

47 Translated into English as, *The gouernaunce of good helthe, by the moste excellent phylosopher Plutarche, the most eloquent Erasmus beynge interpretoure* [1549 ?].

48 Elyot, *Castel*, ed. Tannenbaum, fol.65 [*recte* 67]; see also Lehmberg, *Sir Thomas Elyot*, pp.132–47.

direct a way as the manuscript collections of receipts of the fifteenth century.[49] There were close similarities between the remedies in manuscript and printed works, and there was a minimum of explanation in both.[50] Although one reader of *The Treasure* felt moved to scribble against a prescription a note of the humoral theory behind it,[51] few can have expected such information in a book of this kind. One or two collections, like Humphrey Lloyd's translation of *The Treasury of Health* attributed to Pope John XXI, contained rather more comment on symptoms than others, but their origin and purpose was the same. Unlike the regimens, they were handbooks apparently intended for everyday use.

As Table 2 suggests, there were some changes in this literature in the later sixteenth century. There was no reprint of *The Treasure of Poor Men* after 1575, of Moulton after 1580, or of *The Treasury of Health* after 1585. In their place came works which incorporated more up-to-date information without changing the established format. A very few chemical remedies and practices such as distillation made their appearance.[52] There were new drugs like guaiacum to be mentioned.[53] John Partridge's *Treasury of Commodious Conceits* also appealed because it had recipes for quinces, marmalades and perfumes alongside medicines. But the basic formula in Partridge, in T.C.'s *An Hospital for the Diseased*, in *A Book of Sovereign Approved Medicines and Remedies* (1577), and in A.T.'s *A Rich Store-house or Treasury for the Diseased* (1596) was the same as before. Old remedies by far outnumbered new, and the lists of complaints had changed scarcely at all.

The largest sectors of medical publishing in the sixteenth century were thus the most conservative in quality. The many works on plague

[49] For examples of the latter, see *The 'Liber de diversis medicinis'*, ed. M. S. Ogden, Early English Text Society, original ser., CCVII (London, 1938); *A Leechbook or Collection of Medical Recipes of the Fifteenth Century*, ed. W. R. Dawson (London, 1934).

[50] Compare the remedies for headaches in *Liber de diversis medicinis*, p.1; *Leechbook*, p.19; Moulton, *Mirror*, cap. vii; anon., *Here begynneth a newe boke of medecynes intytulyd or callyd the treasure of pore men* (1540 edn), fol. xv; for fevers in *Leechbook*, pp. 129–31 and *The Treasure of Poor Men*, fol. xxxv v; and for flux in *Leechbook*, p. 47, and Moulton, *Mirror*, cap. lxx.

[51] *The Treasure of Poor Men* (1540), Bodleian Library, Oxford, Crynes 873, fol. xxviii r.

[52] See the simple account of distilling in Partridge, *Treasury of Commodious Conceits* (1591 edn), sigs C4v–C5; and cf. C. C. Mambretti, 'William Bullein and the "lively fashions" in Tudor medical literature', *Clio Medica*, IX (1974), 290–1. For other new remedies and medicines see R. Multhauf, 'Medical chemistry and the Paracelsians', *Bulletin of the History of Medicine*, XXVIII (1954), 101–26; O. Temkin, 'Therapeutic trends and the treatment of syphilis before 1700', ibid., XXIX (1955), 309–16.

[53] The growth in imports of foreign drugs is criticized in William Harrison, *The Description of England*, ed. G. Edelen (Ithaca, N.Y., 1968), pp.266–8; and described in R. S. Roberts, 'The early history of the import of drugs into Britain', in F. N. L. Poynter (ed.), *The Evolution of Pharmacy in Britain* (London, 1965), pp.168–70.

may have increased in variety and scope at the very end of the sixteenth century, but they were never in such great demand as the textbooks and regimens based on Elyot's model and the collections of remedies which had roots even further back in time. The most popular medical works covered familiar ground and were no doubt successful for that reason. For one must assume that, in this as in other areas of publishing, authors were well attuned to the requirements of their readers. Having considered the quantity and content of the literature, we must examine the authors and the audience who between them determined both.

II

The authors were a miscellaneous group, not all of whom deserved the title.[54] We have noted the extent to which publications drew on the past and on each other. As the similarity of their titles suggests, they were scarcely original works, and it is significant that the most hackneyed of them, the collections of remedies, often had anonymous authors. Few of their compilers can be identified and it is scarcely profitable to make the attempt. The 'T.C.' who according to its title page 'gathered' the remedies in *An Hospital for the Diseased*, for example, has sometimes been identified as the Puritan divine, Thomas Cartwright. Even if he was, he was the author of no more than the Preface describing God's gift of medicines; and he may equally well have been Thomas Cooper, who before becoming a bishop had studied medicine at Oxford.[55] His exact identity is of little more than bibliographical importance. The question does, however, illustrate one important feature of the literature with which we are concerned: the small role which the medical establishment played in it. Only a third of the textbooks, regimens and collections of remedies with identifiable authors came from the pens of established physicians; and the latter can have provided few of the several authors who are unidentified.

This is not to say that the medical elite as a whole disdained to write vernacular works. Dr John Caius's apologia to his English work on the sweating sickness suggests some initial reluctance to adopt the habit.[56] There may equally be some significance in the fact that Christopher Langton, who had published two general works on physic, was expelled

---

54 In what follows, information on authors is taken from *DNB* unless otherwise stated.
55 *Cartwrightiana*, ed. A. Peel and L. H. Carlson (London, 1951), pp.9, 14–15.
56 Caius, *A Book or Counsel*, in *Works*, ed. E. S. Roberts (Cambridge, 1912), pp.4–8.

from the College of Physicians in 1558 for his arrogant and immoral behaviour: his publishing record may have been one symptom of a personality ill suited to the conservative confines of the College.[57] By the end of the century, however, established physicians were publishing works in English, though normally on rather specialized subjects. Francis Herring, and Peter Turner, physician at St Bartholomew's Hospital, wrote on plague; Walter Bayley, Regius Professor of Physic at Oxford, produced works on eye diseases and medicinal waters; Edward Jorden published a book on hysteria.[58] Works on surgery were also the province of the specialists: Thomas Gale, William Clowes, John Banister and Peter Lowe were all surgeons with military or naval experience on which they drew in their works.[59]

Yet the majority of the more popular medical works of the period, the textbooks, collections of remedies and even the plague tracts, were not written by professional medical men in the modern sense. Their authors made their living in other ways. They were lawyers and civil servants, clergymen, or, by the end of the century, professional writers, most of whom would have regarded themselves as socially and intellectually superior to mechanic surgeons. Many of them had studied medicine at one or other of the universities; a few went abroad to further their medical education; and some of the clergy certainly practised physic. As their other activities show, however, they belonged to an age in which divisions between the learned professions were not yet clearly drawn, and in which humanist teachings positively encouraged the blurring of such distinctions.

Sir Thomas Elyot is the most eminent example of a lawyer, civil servant, diplomat and humanist who wrote on subjects outside medicine. A somewhat similar figure at the end of the century was William Vaughan, author of *Natural and Artificial Directions for Health* (1600), who was also a lawyer, colonial pioneer, poet and writer of

---

57 Christopher Langton, *An introduction into phisycke* [1545?]; idem, *A very brefe treatise, ordrely declaring the principal partes of phisick* (1547); Sir George Clark, *A History of the Royal College of Physicians of London* (2 vols., Oxford, 1964–6), I, pp.108–9.

58 Herring, *Certain Rules*, idem, *A Modest Defence*; Turner, *The Opinion of... Amulets*; Bayley, *A Brief Treatise of Eyesight*, idem, *A Brief Discourse of Baths*; L. G. H. Horton-Smith, *Dr Walter Baily (or Bayley) c.1529–1592* (St Albans, 1952), pp.30–1; Edward Jorden, *A briefe discourse of a disease called the suffocation of the mother* (1603); Clark, *History of the Royal College*, I, p.165.

59 See *STC* for their works, and, on some of their lives: Poynter (ed.), *Selected Writings of William Clowes*, pp.17–18; T. Finlayson, *Account of the Life and Works of Maister Peter Lowe* (Glasgow, 1889). The quality of some surgical writings is discussed in P. H. Kocher, 'Paracelsan medicine in England (c.1570–1600)', *Journal of the History of Medicine*, II (1947), 466–80; S. V. Larkey and O. Temkin, 'John Banister and the pulmonary circulation', in *Essays in Biology in Honor of Herbert M. Evans by His Friends* (Berkeley, Calif., 1943), pp.287–92.

devotional tracts. Two more professional authors were John Partridge, who produced poems and translations as well as *The Treasury of Commodious Conceits*, and Thomas Lodge, who turned to the study of medicine and wrote on plague only after a successful literary career in other fields had been disrupted by suspicions of his Roman Catholicism.[60] The translators, who were of first importance in determining the character of the literature in the first half of the century, were similarly involved in non-medical projects. Humphrey Lloyd, who was responsible for *The Treasury of Health*, was an M.P. and author of antiquarian works. Thomas Paynel was an almost full-time translator of Latin works in the years after 1528, a plague treatise and the *Regimen sanitatis Salerni* being only two of his renditions.[61] Thomas Phaer, a lawyer and Doctor of Medicine, published legal handbooks and a translation of Virgil besides the 'Book of children' which he added to his edition of Goeurot's *Regimen*.

The clergy's contribution to the literature was particularly large. The study of medicine had flourished among members of religious orders in the Middle Ages, and it is not surprising to find among the most successful authors of the early sixteenth century, Thomas Moulton, a Dominican, Andrew Boorde, once a Carthusian,[62] and Paynel, once an Austin friar. Schoolmasters like Thomas Brasbridge of Banbury and Thomas Cogan of Manchester also practised and wrote about medicine. Cogan, who was also a Fellow of Oriel College, Oxford, directed his work particularly to students.[63] William Turner, a convinced Protestant and Dean of Wells, used his periods of religious exile on the continent to develop his contacts with foreign medical scholars, and published herbals and a book on medicinal springs as well as *A New Book of Spiritual Physic* (Emden, 1555).[64] Thomas Newton of Cheshire, rector of Little Ilford, was another clergyman who wrote on other subjects

---

[60] On Elyot, see Lehmberg, *Sir Thomas Elyot*, and J. M. Major, *Sir Thomas Elyot and Renaissance Humanism* (Lincoln, Nebraska, 1964); and on Lodge, W. D. Rae, *Thomas Lodge* (New York, 1967), p.101, and E. A. Tenney, *Thomas Lodge* (New York, 1935), pp.160–77.

[61] Bennett, *English Books and Readers 1475–1557*, pp.153, 165; J. K. McConica, *English Humanists and Reformation Politics* (Oxford, 1965), pp.138–9.

[62] On Boorde, see the introduction to *The Fyrst Boke of the Introduction of Knowledge made by Andrew Borde...*, ed. F. J. Furnivall, Early English Text Society, extra ser., x (1870).

[63] Brasbridge, *The Poor Man's Jewel*; Thomas Cogan, *The haven of health* (5 edns, 1584–1605); Clark, *History of the Royal College*, I, p.167. John Stockwood, translator of two works on plague, was also a schoolmaster (*DNB*). Other works partially directed towards students were Philip Moore, *The hope of health* (1564), see sig. Ai; Gulielmus Gratarolus, *A direction for the health of magistrates and studentes*, trans. Thomas Newton (1574).

[64] Arber, *Herbals*, pp.120–3.

besides medicine.[65] If William Bullein found it easy to move from a career as a country parson to the study of medicine, Timothie Bright, writer on melancholy, could make the opposite transition from St Bartholomew's Hospital to a country rectory.[66]

The authors of the medical literature were thus men of diverse accomplishments and interests, not professional scientists working within the conventions of an established discipline. This did much to determine the range of their output, and it also explains the blurred boundaries between 'medical' and other types of publication in the sixteenth century. There was, for example, considerable overlap with religious literature. Although physicians like Caius disclaimed any intention to trespass on the territory of 'divines',[67] and devotional tracts on sickness showed by their titles that their authors were aware of the same distinction, there was in practice a marked identity of interest. There were at least twenty-seven devotional works for the sick, prescribing prayers and meditations as aids to health, published before 1605. The most popular was Thomas Becon's *The Sick Man's Salve*, which ran to twenty editions between 1560 and 1604. There were also books of 'ghostly medicines', 'godly gardens' of herbs, and 'pomanders of prayer'.[68] The authors of these normally confined their attention to spiritual remedies for disease, but the shared vocabulary demonstrates the basic similarity between their concerns and those of medical writers, and the two sets of publications cannot always be distinguished. This was especially the case with tracts describing the actions to be taken during epidemics of plague. Pamphlets by the London preachers James Balmford and Henoch Clapham on the plague of 1603, for example, contained a good deal of medical as well as theological argument.[69]

The medical literature was equally close to the world of astrology and particularly to the world of the almanac. Andrew Boorde, author of the *Breviary* and *Dietary*, was also the first English author of almanacs. John

[65] Thomas Newton, *Approoved medicines and cordiall receiptes* (1591); idem, *The old mans dietarie* (1586).

[66] W. S. Mitchell, 'William Bullein, Elizabethan physician and author', *Medical History*, III (1959), 188–200; Mambretti, 'William Bullein and the "lively fashions"', p.285; G. Keynes, *Dr Timothie Bright 1550–1615. A Survey of his Life with a Bibliography of his Writings* (London, 1962), pp.1–20.

[67] Caius, *A Book or Counsel*, in *Works*, p.36; there is a full account of this theme in the literature in P. H. Kocher, *Science and Religion in Elizabethan England* (San Marino, Calif., 1953), especially pp.265–79.

[68] E.g., Paul Bushe, *Certayne gostly medycynes to be used to eschew the plage of pestilence* (n.d.); anon., *A godly garden out of the which most comfortable herbs may be gathered* (1574); Thomas Becon, *The pomander of prayer* (1558); William Perkins, *A salve for a sicke man* (Cambridge, 1595).

[69] Balmford, *A Short Dialogue*; Clapham, *An Epistle*, and idem, *Demands and Answers*.

Securis, a Salisbury practitioner, published almanacs as well as a criticism of current medical practice.[70] Although not included in our quantitative survey of the literature, almanacs themselves contained, along with other matter, much medical information: advice on bloodletting, indications of the days favourable or unfavourable for medical treatment, and prognostications of the sicknesses most likely to prevail at particular seasons of the year. They were also much more popular publications than any so far considered. More than 600 almanacs were published before 1600, far exceeding in number all the literature classed as medical here.[71] If religious works on the one hand and almanacs on the other show the loose boundaries to 'medical' literature, they also point by way of contrast to its limited quantity and hence to its relatively small audience.

The composition of that audience is much less easy to assess than its probable size. The limited evidence available suggests, however, that the readers of medical works, though larger in numbers, were probably not very different in character from their authors. Works of anatomy and surgery were obviously aimed at and perhaps reached a group of specialized practitioners. Vicary, for example, wrote for new members of the surgeons' gild; and like other surgeons he added recommended remedies to his work in recognition of the fact that – however much the College of Physicians might wish otherwise – physic and surgery were in practice not often distinguished.[72] More remarkably, however, apparently 'popular' medical works were also intended in part for practitioners. One or two, like Boorde's *Breviary*, gave the names of herbs and medicines in Latin, while A.T.'s *A Rich Store-house*, although ostensibly designed for 'the poorer sort of people ... that are not of ability to go to the physician', included a section of 'divers and sundry good instructions and rules for all such as are the true practisers of

70   Thomas, *Religion and the Decline of Magic*, p.294; John Securis, *A detection and querimonie of the daily enormities and abuses committed in physick* (1566). Securis was following the example of the French astrologer Nostradamus, whose works, including *An excellent tretise, shewing suche perillous, and contagious infirmities, as shall insue. 1559. and 1560* (1559), had recently been translated.

71   Bennett, *English Books and Readers 1558–1603*, pp.204–5; E. F. Bosanquet, *English Printed Almanacks and Prognostications: A Bibliographical History to the Year 1600* (London, 1917), provides an extensive list. Two examples containing the sort of medical information mentioned are the almanacs and prognostications for 1589 by John Dade, 'gentleman, practitioner in physic', and John Harvey, 'M.A. and practitioner in physic'.

72   Thomas Vicary, *The Englishemans treasure* (1596 edn), sig. Bi; Joannes de Vigo, *The whole worke* (1586), fols. 363 *et seq.*; Thomas Gale, *Certaine workes of chirurgerie* (1586), 'Instit. of a surgeon', sig. Aii v.

physic and surgery'.[73] It is possible that one of the purposes of the literature was the instruction of less well-educated popular practitioners, of men like the shoemaker in Elizabethan Chelmsford who also acted as a surgeon,[74] or of clergymen practising medicine far from the learned worlds of the universities and London.

The defensive tone adopted by the prefaces to medical books scarcely suggests so respectable a purpose, but it need not be taken at face value. If writers seem to have felt the need to justify opening the secrets of the 'noble science' of physic to the multitude,[75] a large part of this was a calculated appeal for readers. There is little evidence that physicians as a whole disapproved of these works, and more that it was empirics and astrologers who wished to keep their practices confidential.[76] Most of the medical works reinforced the establishment view of physic as a complex art demanding learning and judgment, and attacked the amateur tamperings of untrained and illiterate practitioners. As the translator of one work remarked, vernacular books might serve to increase respect for physicians and to instruct their less prestigious colleagues such as apothecaries.[77]

Yet it would be difficult to argue that printed literature of this kind was as important an instrument for the instruction of medical practitioners as its authors hoped. It probably helped to keep them familiar with the vocabulary of their trade, with the language of the humours and the nomenclature of diseases, but it seems not to have materially affected their treatments. Doctors' casebooks suggest that the remedies prescribed by them were in general much simpler than those in the printed collections. They might include plague waters of the kind authors recommended, but simple purges were the great standby. Doctors were also as likely to borrow remedies from other physicians, from well-known cunning women, and especially from their more

---

[73] A.T., *A rich store-house or treasury for the diseased* (1596), sigs. A2v, B1–C4; cf. anon., *The antidotharius, in the whiche thou mayst lerne how thow shalt make playsters, salves, etc.* [1535?], sig. Biii r.

[74] Essex Record Office, Q/SR 41/31, 10 July 1572.

[75] Examples in Bennett, *English Books and Readers 1558–1603*, pp.180–1.

[76] Compare the attitude of the Elizabethan astrologer, Forman: A. L. Rowse, *Simon Forman: Sex and Society in Shakespeare's Age* (London, 1974), p.89. Archbishop Cranmer, however, thought that physicians as well as alchemists deliberately used 'strange languages' to 'hide their sciences from the knowledge of others': *Writings and Disputations of Thomas Cranmer*, Parker Society (Cambridge, 1844), pp.310–11.

[77] Joseph Du Chesne, *The practise of chymicall and hermeticall physicke*, trans. Thomas Tymme (1605), 'To Reader'. Cf. William Bullein, *A newe booke entituled the governement of healthe* (1558), fols. vi–vii; William Clever, *The flower of phisicke* (1590), 'To the Reader'; Bullein, *Bulwark*, 'Book of the use of sick men', fol. lii v; Jones, *Dial for All Agues*, sig. Ciii v.

eminent patients, as from printed works.[78] Though they possessed books and must occasionally have used them, they were clearly working in a society in which personal recommendation and oral communication were more important than the printed word.

If medical practitioners were one part of the audience for medical literature, who were the rest? They clearly were not the 'poorer sort', the 'ignorant' and the wholly 'unlearned' referred to in authors' prefaces.[79] Neither is it likely that they included many of the 'middle sort', the increasingly literate tradesmen and yeomen of the later sixteenth century. Only almanacs were available in large enough quantity to reach the lowest ranks of the literate, and even they contained medical advice which demanded a knowledge of dates and times, and assumed a choice of diet and exercise (tennis, for example) which must have been foreign to many of their readers. Some almanacs explicitly referred to a narrower audience when they included medical rules 'worthy the observation amongst all practitioners'.[80] The less voluminous literature considered here necessarily had a smaller readership, and it was probably a more select one. The content of the textbooks and regimens certainly presupposed a choice of activities which can have had little meaning outside the leisured elite, and although the simpler collections of remedies ought to have had wider appeal, it is difficult to show that they reached a wider audience before the end of the sixteenth century.

Hard evidence of possession or purchase, the real test of readership, is scanty. Regimens and collections of remedies are not mentioned in the library catalogues and probate inventories of the period, but this may simply be because these sources tended to concentrate on more valuable and less ephemeral books.[81] There ought to be more evidence of them in

---

[78] F. N. L. Poynter and W. J. Bishop (eds.), *A Seventeenth-Century Doctor and his Patients: John Symcotts, 1592?–1662*, Bedfordshire Historical Record Society, xxxi (Streatley, 1951), pp.xix–xxi, 97; W. R. Le Fanu, 'A North-Riding doctor in 1609', *Medical History*, v (1961), 179. Compare the similar practices recorded in British Library, MS. Sloane 1529 (commonplace book of an Essex practitioner 1644–5), e.g. fol. 239r; MS. Egerton 2065, Case Book of John Hall 1622–36; Bodleian Library, Oxford, MS. Rawlinson A.369, Case Book of an Oxford doctor 1589–1614.

[79] A.T., *A Rich Store-house*, title page; Bullein, *Bulwark*, 'Epistle dedicatory'; Boorde, *Breviary*, bk ii, fol. 1v.

[80] Gabriel Frende, *A new almanacke and prognostication for the yeere ... MDLXXXIX* (1589), sigs. Cvv, Aii v.

[81] S. Jayne, *Library Catalogues of the English Renaissance* (Berkeley, Calif., 1956), p. 54; P. Clark, 'The ownership of books in England, 1560–1640: the example of some Kentish townsfolk', in L. Stone (ed.), *Schooling and Society* (Baltimore, 1976), p.103. Only herbals commonly occur in booklists: e.g. *The Lumley Library: the Catalogue of 1609*, ed. S. Jayne and F. R. Johnson (London, 1956), p.273; John Caius, *The Annals of Gonville and Caius College*, ed. J. Venn,

the few surviving lists of booksellers' stock, but there is none before the reign of Elizabeth, which suggests that their circulation may well have been very narrow indeed in the early sixteenth century, perhaps even confined to London. In 1585, however, a Shrewsbury bookseller was selling some of the more reputable, that is less anonymous, items in the vernacular literature. He experienced some demand for the works of Bullein, Gesner, Fioravanti and Recorde, as well as for Beza's tract on plague, although we should note that he needed more copies of Becon's *Sick Man's Salve* and of the latest almanacs than of any of these.[82] His customers are not recorded. They may have been local clergy and doctors; but one piece of evidence from the same year suggests that they probably also included country gentlemen. In 1585 a Huntingdonshire gentleman, Edward Wingfield, ordered from his London bookseller an interesting range of medical works, all of them from our categories (7) and (8): they were Bullein's *Bulwark*, Boorde's *Dietary* and *Breviary*, Barrough's *Method of Physic*, and, at the cheaper end of the market, Thomas Newton's *Approved Medicines* and T.C.'s *Hospital for the Diseased*, each of which cost him 6d.[83]

This reference to the *Hospital* is not the only evidence for the appeal of collections of remedies, as well as of the more sophisticated textbooks and regimens, to an upper-class audience. The collections were the source of many of the prescriptions copied into the commonplace books kept by the gentry, by scholars, and by the richer inhabitants of towns in the later sixteenth and early seventeenth centuries. There are examples of such borrowings in the books begun shortly after 1610 by a northern gentry family and by a Norwich citizen,[84] and the annotations in them,

Cambridge Antiquarian Society Publications, xl (1904), p.213. But the celebrated collector of ballads, Captain Cox of Coventry, had a copy of Boorde's *Breviary* in 1575: *Robert Laneham's Letter*, ed. F. J. Furnivall, New Shakspere Society, vi, pt 14 (1890), p. xiii.

[82] A. Rodger, 'Roger Ward's Shrewsbury stock: an inventory of 1585', *The Library*, 5th ser., xiii (1958), 250–61 passim. There is no sign of the earliest publications in F. Madan (ed.), 'Day-book of John Dorne 1520', in *Collectanea I*, Oxford Historical Society (Oxford, 1885), pp.71–178; or in D. M. Palliser and D. G. Selwyn, 'The stock of a York stationer, 1538', *The Library*, 5th ser., xxvii (1972), 207–19.

[83] Plomer, 'Some Elizabethan book sales', p.328. Herbals were even more clearly destined for gentry and professional men: for examples of purchase and use, see *Trevelyan Papers*, pt ii, ed. J. P. Collier, Camden Society, old ser., lxxxiv (1863), p.98; M. M. Knappen (ed.), *Two Puritan Diaries* (Chicago, 1933), pp.103–4.

[84] *Arcana Fairfaxiana Manuscripta. A Manuscript Volume of Apothecaries' Lore and Housewifery nearly Three Centuries Old, Used, and partly Written by the Fairfax Family*, intro. by G. Weddell (Newcastle-on-Tyne, 1890), pp.xlii–xliii, 10 and passim; Bodleian Library, Oxford, MS. Tanner 397, fol. 4 *et seq.* (from rear). Other examples are in Bodleian Library, Oxford, MS. Tanner 169, fols. 78 *et seq.*; MS. Rawlinson C.506, fols. 122v–123.

like the manuscript additions to some of the printed volumes,[85] show that the remedies were occasionally used.

The elite nature of a large part of the readership suggests conclusions about the circumstances in which the medical literature might be drawn upon. One was no doubt the consultation between the gentleman or woman and the doctor. The prefaces to the regimens and textbooks often insist on their usefulness in patient–physician relationships. Elyot, for example, saw his task as the provision of background knowledge so that the patient might 'instruct his physician whereunto he may adopt his counsel and remedies'.[86] The upper classes found some basic acquaintance with medical theory essential if they were to judge the expertise of the doctor, to shop around between different practitioners, and to engage in a relatively equal exchange of information with a medical man who was their employee rather than their master.[87] Collections of remedies on the other hand were helpful tools for the literate in the absence of the physician. They were perhaps used especially by women and they were employed initially, as Partridge noted, by the housewife 'amongst her own family'.[88] Their influence might extend further than this, however. They could assist women in the social elite in giving advice to others. The preface to an early edition of Goeurot's *Regimen* referred to one such lady who 'according to her custom' advised the 'poor' who came to her; and several other works claimed to be of use, not so much to the sick themselves, as to those who visited or cared for them, their 'friends' and 'neighbours'.[89] The vernacular literature thus contributed something to the exchange of information between doctor and patient and perhaps between neighbour and neighbour. Far from challenging, let alone overturning, the oral culture of a 'face-to-face' society, printed medical books simply gave a few people more to talk about.

[85] E.g., the Bodleian Library copy (Douce P. 90) of [John XXI], *The Treasury of Health* [1550?], sigs. Qii–Qiv; and the Wellcome Historical Medical Library, London, copy of Moulton, *Mirror* (1546), in which plague remedies are underlined.

[86] Elyot, *Castel*, ed. Tannenbaum, p.v; cf. [John XXI], *The Treasury of Health*, sig. Aiiir.

[87] For examples of doctor–patient relationships, see F. N. L. Poynter, 'Patients and their ills in Vicary's time', *Annals of the Royal College of Surgeons*, LVI (1975), 145–9, and the letters in *Letters and Papers, Foreign and Domestic, of the Reign of Henry VIII*, ed. J. S. Brewer and others (38 vols., 1862–1932), XIII, pt I, nos.431, 538, 1491; *The Official Papers of Sir Nathaniel Bacon of Stiffkey*, ed. H. W. Saunders, Camden Society, 3rd ser., XXVI (London, 1915), pp.221–2.

[88] Partridge, *Treasury of Commodious Conceits*, title page.

[89] Goeurot, *Regimen* [1543?: *STC* B 11966.5], prologue; anon., *The key to unknowne knowledge* (1599), 'Judgment of urines', sig. Aii; Bullein, *Bulwark*, 'Dialogue', fol. 6r; Nicholas Gyer, *The English phlebotomy* (1592), sig. A6. The correspondence of the early seventeenth century contains many examples of ladies giving medical advice to their friends and relations: e.g. *The Oxinden Letters 1607–42*, ed. D. Gardiner (London, 1933), pp.179, 191–2.

The evidence for the readership of medical books, though slight and inconclusive, points therefore in the direction of the social elite: members of the professions, gentlemen, no doubt some merchants, and their wives. The collections of remedies were cheap enough and available in sufficient quantity to be rather more accessible. They may have reached apothecaries and others at the lower levels of medical practice. They may have been bought also by a few yeomen and tradesmen, especially perhaps in London, of whose purchases no trace remains; but we cannot be sure that this occurred and it is perhaps unlikely to have happened before the very end of our period, or outside the capital. It would hence be impossible to argue that the literature had any major social effects. That does not mean that it has no historical utility, however. Much of it, the collections of remedies in particular, can be thought of as analogous to modern cookery-books. They were bought both by professionals and by laymen, but not heavily used by either in their everyday activities. They may have been bought by people who could not afford the recipes they contained, as well as by those rich enough to experiment. The ordinary practice of the craft with which they dealt cannot be deduced from them. But they formed part of the background knowledge to the craft, they reflected some of its techniques and assumptions as well as its ambitions, and they helped to some degree to form attitudes towards it. Thus the textbooks and regimens and collections of remedies helped to mould or to confirm the attitudes of the social establishment towards disease and health, and these subjects are of interest in themselves.

Moreover, in one important respect the analogy with cookery-books does not hold. The collections of remedies and many of the regimens made no attempt to change attitudes or practices; they did not try to introduce new fashions or to innovate. They were conventional and conservative, reinforcing rather than conflicting with other sources of medical knowledge, and they may thus tell us something about the medical problems of a wider section of the population than that which read them. A brief examination of the content of the more 'popular' medical works might be expected to reveal some of the common assumptions and anxieties surrounding sickness in sixteenth-century England.

III

Medical knowledge and traditional medical practices in other societies have been seen to have a dual role. First, they provide mechanisms for action, instruments which, while not necessarily totally effective in combating disease, are more often than not thought to be so. Secondly, they provide explanations for disease which, by reassuring the sick that their pains are part of the natural order of things, help to reduce distress and uncertainty.[90] Although sixteenth-century England was in many ways different from the societies on which these observations have been based,[91] its medical literature can be approached from a similar standpoint. For illness is always a social as well as biological phenomenon. It produces strains and anxieties which need treatment as much, if not more than, the disease itself, and the doctor's role has never been simply that of an administrator of an effective physical cure. Similarly, when Andrew Boorde wrote his *Breviary* 'for simple and unlearned men that they may have some knowledge to ease themselves in their diseases and infirmities', it is likely that he meant 'ease' to imply more than physical comfort.[92]

Other authors made it plain that they wrote to calm the fears raised by illness in a society much more at the mercy of infections, deficiency diseases, accidents and functional disorders than our own. One writer described the 'strange and unknown diseases that swarm among us, and more in number than can be found remedy for', while Elyot drew up a long list of 'grievous diseases' for which physicians had few remedies. T.C. also knew the concerns of his audience. 'Art thou diseased in thy head?', he asked. 'Art thou pained with an ache? Art thou tormented with a fever?... Doth thy youth wear away?... Dost thou feel thyself infected with the poison of the plague and pestilence? Then delay no time, but with a small price buy a gem worth gold.'[93] The ways in which these tracts tried to reassure their readers can illustrate the demands made on medical care of all kinds in the sixteenth century.

Some of the questions to which medical authors provided answers were of immediate practical concern to the sick or those close to them. Several described symptoms so that a man might tell, for example, whether he had the plague or some other less terrible disease.[94] Most of

90 See for example U. Maclean, 'Some aspects of sickness behaviour among the Yoruba', in J. B. Loudon (ed.), *Social Anthropology and Medicine*, ASA Monographs, no.13 (London, 1976), pp.288–90.
91 It had, for example, a much more diverse intellectual heritage from different historical traditions: see Thomas, *Religion and the Decline of Magic*, p.627.
92 Boorde, *Breviary*, bk ii, fol. 1v.
93 *The Secrets of Alexis of Piemont* (1558), sig. +ivr ; Elyot, *Castel*, ed. Tannenbaum, fol. 79r; T.C., *An hospitall for the diseased* (1579), sig. Aii.
94 Nostradamus, *An Excellent Treatise*, sig. Aviiiv; *The Judicial of Urines*, title page; Partridge, *Treasury*, sigs. F5–F6; A.T., *A Rich Store-house*, fol. 64v.

the collections tackled the still more crucial problem of how to know whether a sick man would live or die.[95] Some of the complaints described were also of general social importance. Since disease was defined as dysfunction, the inability of the body or any part of it to perform 'that office and action that nature hath ordained it to do',[96] it covered vital subjects such as infertility, as well as others like lovesickness and masturbation, which might not now be defined as illness at all.[97]

The vast majority of the complaints discussed were much more ordinary, however. If we can presume that the collections gave readers what they required, they wanted remedies for common physical pains and common infectious diseases. Toothache and corns, smallpox and dropsy were frequent entries, as were disorders connected with menstruation and pregnancy, the remedies for which sometimes strayed onto the forbidden territory of abortion.[98] The complaints which filled the most space in two collections are shown in Table 3. They are the

Table 3. *Common complaints in two collections and the number of remedies given for them*

Agues and fevers	46	Sore eyes, webs in eyes	22
Stone (in bladder) and 'collic'	41	Headache and megrim	17
Coughs and phlegm	38	Bruises	17
Burns and scalds	33	Pain in reins (kidneys)	15
Aches and sciatica	31	Boils	15
Plague	30	Spots, pimples, skin diseases	12
Urinary complaints ('cannot piss', etc.)	29	Flux and bloody flux (dysentery)	11
Bleeding (inc. nose-bleed)	27	Canker in mouth	11
Pain in back	24	Jaundice (black and yellow)	11

Sources: T.C., *An Hospital for the Diseased* (1579 edn); A.T., *A Rich Store-house or Treasury for the Diseased* (1596).

95 Anon., *The boke of knowledge: whether a sycke person beynge in peryll shall lyue or dye* (1535). One commonly cited means of prognostication was to add the patient's urine to a woman's milk and to see whether they mixed or not; if the former, he would live: ibid., sig. Aiiir; *Liber de diversis medicinis*, p.58; *Arcana Fairfaxiana*, p.45. Cf. *The Treasure of Poor Men*, fol. xvv.

96 Moore, *Hope of Health* (1564), fol. 45v. See also Bartholomaeus Anglicus, *On the Properties of Things*, trans. John Trevisa (2 vols., Oxford, 1975), I, p.342. The problems involved in defining health and sickness are discussed on Loudon (ed.), *Social Anthropology and Medicine*, pp.xix, 506–7.

97 [John XXI], *The Treasury of Health*, sigs. Ovir, Oiiij; Partridge, *Treasury*, sigs. D2, D6v; Vicary, *Englishman's Treasure*, p.87; Boorde, *Breviary*, fols. lxxiiv, cxir, cxixr.

98 E.g., [John XXI], *The Treasury of Health*, sig. Oviv–Ovii. Cf. Boorde, *Breviary*, fols. lxxxxv, ixr.

entries for which the most remedies were listed, and not necessarily those most frequently encountered by readers, although it is unlikely that the two were unrelated. Plague may not often have killed members of the social elite, for example, but it certainly threatened them and they felt the need for protection against it. Many adults must have come across all of these afflictions in the course of a life-time.[99] No detailed picture of the health of sixteenth-century Englishmen can be drawn from descriptions such as these. Apart from plague, they are all symptoms rather than diseases, and several of them are conditions which may be manifestations of more than one disorder.[100] Dietary deficiencies and poor hygiene may well have been at the root of many of the bladder, eye and skin complaints,[101] but agues and fevers might include anything from typhus and typhoid to malaria and influenza. Simply listed as they are, however, they paint a picture of the infections, disorders, accidents and straightforward aches and pains with which Tudor Englishmen had to cope.

Whether the remedies prescribed in the collections were of any instrumental help is a question which would merit pharmacological investigation. The very profusion of the medicines suggested for each complaint perhaps indicates that they were not.[102] In any event, most of the conditions were either self-limiting, or liable to recur only after periods of remission which might be attributed to some remedy. The simplest and broadest recommendations were often sensible ones. Fresh milk and clean rain-water were prescribed against dysentery by Nostradamus, for example.[103] But the collections depended for their existence on their more complicated recommendations. Throughout the sixteenth as in the fifteenth century, theriac ('treacle') and

---

99 The seventeenth-century diarist, Ralph Josselin, for example, was continually pestered by colds, aches and pains and threatened by plague and fevers around him: *The Diary of Ralph Josselin 1616–1683*, ed. A. Macfarlane, British Academy, Records of Social and Economic History, new ser., III (London, 1976), passim.

100 Similar classifications of complaints in other societies are discussed in J.-P. Peter, 'Malades et maladies à la fin du XVIIIe siècle', *Annales: Economies, Sociétés, Civilisations*, XXII (1967), 711–51; F. Lebrun, *Les hommes et la mort en Anjou au 17e et 18e siècles* (Paris, 1971), pp.277–8; D. M. Spencer, *Disease, Religion and Society in the Fiji Islands*, Monographs of the American Ethnological Society, no.2 (Seattle, 1941), pp.80–1.

101 J. C. Drummond and A. Wilbraham, *The Englishman's Food. A History of Five Centuries of English Diet*, 2nd edn (London, 1957), pp.82, 83, 133. The several remedies for 'loose teeth' may suggest scorbutic conditions, which some observers thought common in England: see *Harrison's Description of England in Shakspere's Youth*, ed. F. J. Furnivall, New Shakspere Society (1877–1908), I, p.lxv.

102 E. H. Ackerknecht, *Medicine and Ethnology: Selected Essays* (Baltimore, 1971), p.128, suggests a different view of the efficacy of much traditional medical folklore.

103 Nostradamus, *An Excellent Treatise*, sig. B4v.

mithridatium were the great panaceas. Since they had scores of ingredients there could be dispute about their proper constituents, but theriac roasted in an onion was said to be an infallible remedy for plague, and it was a point in mithridatium's favour that when Oliver Cromwell took it to protect himself from plague he found that it also cured his pimples.[104] There were many herbal preparations, usually based on a simple basic ingredient. Bitter herbs, for example, especially rue or 'herb of grace', were thought to drive out most poisons and hence infections. There was heavy reliance also on counter-irritants and purges to draw out either the disease itself, regarded as a foreign body, or the surplus, corrupt humours which were its manifestation.[105]

When explanations for these remedies were given, they were usually based on humoral theory, hot and moist herbs being used to counteract cold and dry diseases and so on. Yet many remedies had their origins in other traditions, often magical ones. Notions of contagious magic and action at a distance, colour symbolism and the doctrine of sympathies between different parts of creation, lay behind several recommendations. A new German medicine was effective because it had the virtue of the sun and of gold. Against measles 'any cloth dyed purple hath virtue of attraction'. Part of a stag's heart, hung in a silk bag around the neck, would draw poison from the body. 'A red stone found in a swallow, carried about the patient and tied in a cloth of linen and put under the left arm' was supposed to 'heal frantic and lunatic persons'. The rump of a live cock applied to a plague botch would attract the infection.[106] Precious stones on the one hand and human waste products on the other also had medicinal power. A sapphire held in the hand would be effective against the sweating sickness. 'One drop of the

[104] G. Watson, *Theriac and Mithridatium. A Study in Therapeutics* (London, 1966), passim; Partridge, *Treasury*, sigs. F2v–F3r; Vicary, *Englishman's Treasure*, p.87; Poynter and Bishop, *A Seventeenth-Century Doctor . . . Symcotts*, pp.xxiii, 76 (Cromwell). For doubts on the virtues of some theriac concoctions, see Goeurot, *Regimen* [1543?], 'Treatise of the pestilence', fol. xx; Cogan, *Haven of Health* (1584), p.277; Timothie Bright, *A treatise wherein is declared the sufficiencie of English medicines* (1580), p.14.

[105] W. S. C. Copeman, *Doctors and Disease in Tudor Times* (London, 1961), pp.143–9. Cf. Bullein, *The Government of Health* (1558), fols. xiiv, lxir, and for parallel uses of bitter herbs elsewhere, V. W. Turner, *Lunda Medicine and the Treatment of Disease*, Rhodes-Livingstone Museum, Occasional Papers no.15 (Lusaka, 1963), p.54; Loudon (ed.), *Social Anthropology and Medicine*, pp.80, 299, 455.

[106] Bertholdus, *A New Terra Sigillata*, p.14; [John XXI], *The Treasury of Health*, sigs. Tvr, Dvr; Leonhard Fuchs, *A most worthie practise of L. Fuchsius* [1562?], sig. Avir; Goeurot, *Regimen*, 'Treatise of the pestilence', fol. xxxvii. Cf. T.C., *An Hospital for the Diseased*, pp.2–3; and for parallels, see O. G. Simmons, 'Popular and modern medicine in Mestizo communities of coastal Peru and Chile', in D. Apple (ed.), *Sociological Studies of Health and Sickness* (New York, 1960), p.77.

patient's own urine' would 'mightily heal the wateriness of the eyes'.[107]
The rationale behind such remedies was never articulated. They
represented, it has been remarked, 'the debris of many different systems
of thought', and it would be difficult to trace their genealogies.[108]
Obviously magical cures were also rather less common in the collections
of the sixteenth century than in the manuscript leechbooks of the
fifteenth. One reader of T.C.'s compilation, for example, found it
necessary to add in the margin his own cure for nose-bleed: 'Write in a
paper *confirmatum est*, and put it up your nostril'.[109] If the cruder sorts of
charm were disappearing, however, a strong magical element remained
in many sixteenth-century medical recipes.

The collections of remedies thus repeated, and to an extent
legitimized, some of the cures advocated by popular medical
practitioners. In doing so, they reflected something of the pluralist
medical system of Tudor England, the appeal of which lay less in any
understanding of its diverse intellectual origins than in respect for
tradition and the habits engendered by repetition. The sources given for
remedies also lent authority to them: these included not only writers
from Hippocrates to Paracelsus but also figures nearer home such as
Henry VII, Henry VIII or Archbishop Parker, whose virtues added
power to the remedies they advocated. T.C. appealed to a similar
authority, and also showed a nice appreciation of differential life-
expectations, when he described 'a restorative which divers noblemen
have used, and it hath prolonged their life'.[110] The rituals involved in
preparing and administering these medical recipes must have been a
further source of reassurance, whether or not they were effective.
Remedies should be taken nine times to produce results, or buried in the
ground for twelve days before use, or prepared from herbs picked only

[107] Boorde, *Breviary*, fol. cxxvii; [John XXI], *The Treasury of Health*, sig. Eivv. Cf. Herring,
Certain Rules (1625 edn), sig. C2; Gesner, *New Jewel of Health*, fol. 244v.
[108] Thomas, *Religion and the Decline of Magic*, p.185. Part of the descent of some such cures has been
painstakingly traced in the notes to the *Liber de diversis medicinis*, ed. M. S. Ogden, and many of
them occur in Anglo-Saxon compilations: W. Bonser, *The Medical Background of Anglo-Saxon
England* (London, 1963), chapters 12, 24.
[109] T.C., *An Hospital for the Diseased*, in Bodleian Library, Oxford (G. Pamph. 2156(1)), p.18. The
reader of another collection, however, thought one of its remedies 'witchery': [John XXI], *The
Treasury of Health*, in Bodleian Library (Douce, P.90), sig. Gvv. See Thomas, *Religion and the
Decline of Magic*, pp.179–81 for the popular use of such charms, and *Liber de diversis medicinis*,
p.63, for a fifteenth-century example in a collection.
[110] T.C., *An Hospital for the Diseased*, pp.3, 52, 65, 73; Partridge, *Treasury*, sig. D6r. See also anon.,
A booke of soveraigne approved medicines and remedies (1577), sig. Bviii; Lodge, *Treatise of the
Plague*, sig. Elv.

at certain seasons.[111] The complex astrological rules about favourable times for medical treatment, criticized though they were by some authors, provided an apparently profitable and satisfyingly active role for those looking after the sick.[112]

These satisfactions depended, however, on the prescribed formulae being followed to the letter, which they perhaps rarely were. A more immediate reassurance provided by the literature lay simply in its naming of diseases. Diagnosis is usually more acceptable than uncertainty, since the identification of a condition distances it to some degree from the sufferer, shows that his experience is not unique, and raises the possibility of treatment.[113] There is, for example, much of the appeal of Dr Spock in the assertion by Phaer and other writers that smallpox and measles were very common children's diseases, as well as in Phaer's conclusion that 'the best and most sure help in this case is not to meddle with any kind of medicines but to let nature work her operation'.[114] The need for a diagnosis scarcely applied to the ordinary aches and pains in Table 3. It did apply, however, to many epidemic infections and especially to the apparently 'new' diseases of the sixteenth century. A.T.'s *Rich Store-house* was written, as its title page proclaimed, because of 'divers and sundry diseases which have been long hidden, and not come to light before this time'.

Syphilis was the most alarming new disease and it produced a sequence of works throughout the century.[115] Fevers of various kinds from the sweating sickness onwards raised similar anxieties. Shortly after the influenza of the later 1550s, John Jones wrote his *Dial for All Agues* because of the fevers which were 'so often frequent in these our days, and . . . so hard to be understanded, discerned or judged; and also therewith so perilous and moreover so neglected'.[116] In this case the difficulties of identification were compounded by the similar symptoms

---

[111] T.C., *An Hospital for the Diseased*, p.73; Gesner, *New Jewel of Health*, fol. 223. See Bayley, *A Brief Discourse of Baths*, pp.20–1, for the superstition that medicinal baths should not be used in leap years.

[112] See the rules in *Key to Unknown Knowledge*, 'Judicial rules of physic'; Dariot, *A Brief Introduction* with *A breife treatise of mathematicall phisicke* (1598). For critical views, see Thomas, *Religion and the Decline of Magic*, p.354.

[113] See U. Maclean, *Magical Medicine: A Nigerian Case-Study* (London, 1971), p.21.

[114] Thomas Phaer, *The Boke of Chyldren* (reprint, Edinburgh and London, 1955), pp.56–7, originally published as part of Goeurot's *Regimen*; Hieronymus von Brunschwig, *A most excellent homish apothecarye* (Collen [Cologne?], 1561), fol. 41v.

[115] See for example, Ulrich von Hutten, *De morbo gallico*, trans. Thomas Paynel (1533), preface; Clowes, *A Short and Profitable Treatise Touching . . . Morbus Gallicus*, sigs. Bi–Bii.

[116] Jones, *Dial for All Agues*, sig. Aivv.

exhibited by different infectious diseases, and by the consequent lack of any clear conception of disease entities. It was commonplace to remark for example that once an epidemic of bubonic plague occurred, all other diseases 'will shortly after be turned into it', and even the sweating sickness was thought 'one of the kinds of the plague or pestilence'.[117] As a result authors resorted to complex subdivisions of 'pestilential fevers' to give an impression of precision: Jones's *Dial* contained a table of twenty-four 'simple agues' classified according to humoral theory.

The tracts on fevers and syphilis show that the naming of diseases and the prescription of remedies were not enough for more inquisitive and more educated readers. They required explanations. Only if disease was given a cause as well as a name and a cure could it be accounted for satisfactorily.[118] It was the function of the textbooks and regimens to meet this demand, and they did so in terms which reflected the contemporary assumptions that all human activities were related to one another, and that natural and supernatural forces were interconnected. They made illness less disturbing by setting it in the context of familiar assumptions.

On the natural plane disease was the result of disorder and excess of any kind. According to Galenic theory any breach in the precarious balance of the humours within an individual could produce 'putrefaction' and 'corruption' and thus disease, and the balance could be broken as much by psychological as by physical excesses. Disease sprang, according to Phaer, from 'the abuse of things not natural, that is to wit of meat and drink, of sleep and watching, of labour and ease, of fullness and emptiness, of the passions of the mind, and of the immoderate use of lechery, for the excess of all these things be almost the chief occasion of all such diseases as do reign among us nowadays'.[119] Physiological disturbances could have psychological causes therefore, and the proper frame of mind was as important as the proper diet in preserving health. Those who had the French pox, according to Partridge, should not be troubled with anything 'to bring them out of patience, for that corrupteth the blood'. In the case of plague, the very idea of the disease was dangerous and those threatened should avoid thinking of the

---

[117] Brasbridge, *The Poor Man's Jewel* (1592 edn), sig. Civr; Boorde, *Breviary*, fol. cxxvii.

[118] In the legal case in which Edward Jorden claimed that hysteria was a consequence of natural disease not of witchcraft, the judge asked him first what he 'called' the disease, and then what its 'natural cause' and 'natural remedy' were: I. Hunter and R. A. Macalpine, *Three Hundred Years of Psychiatry* (London, 1963), pp.74–5.

[119] Goeurot, *Regimen*, 'Treatise of the pestilence', fol. xi.

subject.[120] Psychological symptoms might equally have physiological causes. The prime example here was hysteria, which was thought to arise from movements of the womb. Jorden's celebrated tract on the subject was the most sophisticated account of its causes, but earlier writers had also treated it as a physical disease.[121]

All these were the natural origins of disease. They were, however, only secondary causes, since God was the first cause of all human afflictions. Although Jorden's work was concerned to refute claims that hysteria was a consequence of demonic possession, and the medical writers made little reference to popular beliefs that sickness might arise from witchcraft and black magic, divine intervention played an important part in their explanatory system. God normally worked through secondary causes, and in the case of minor and common illnesses he was a distant influence. His role here was implicit, and seldom mentioned, although it might be cited to account for the failure of prescribed medicines.[122] References to divine intervention were much more common, however, in explanations of the great epidemic diseases, which struck whole societies and against which there was little protection. Poisonous vapours in the air came from disorders in the macrocosm of the universe, which were the signs of God's displeasure. The influence of the stars brought corruption on men, said Bullein, and so 'all Christian men must pray to God to be their defence, for they be God's instruments to punish the earth'. Cogan thought the gaol fever at the Oxford Assizes in 1577 was 'sent only by the will of God as a scourge for sin'. Ulrich von Hutten might criticize those who thought the French pox wholly divine, as if 'nature hath no power to bring in new diseases, which in all other things maketh great changes', but Clowes and other authors did not doubt the reality of God's hand in it and his power to alter the disease at will.[123] Above all it was plague which elicited from all authors an acknowledgment of God's handiwork and

---

[120] Partridge, *Treasury*, sig. E6v; Brasbridge, *The Poor Man's Jewel,* sig. Bi. See R. and E. Blum, *Health and Healing in Rural Greece* (Stanford, Calif., 1965), pp.122, 134, for modern parallels.

[121] Jorden, *A Brief Discourse of the Mother*; Boorde, *Breviary*, fol. lxxxxivr; Goeurot, *Regimen* (1560 edn), sigs. Jiv–Jii; [John XXI], *The Treasury of Health*, sig. Pii. See also I. Veith, *Hysteria. The History of a Disease* (Chicago, 1965).

[122] Fioravanti, *A Compendium of the Rational Secrets* (1582), bk I, p.24. In Peter Levens's *A right profitable booke for all disseases. Called the pathway to health* (1582), 'by god's grace' was added at the end of many remedies. Similar theories of multiple causation of disease are described in S. F. Nadel, *Nupe Religion* (London, 1954), p.153; E. E. Evans-Pritchard, *Witchcraft, Oracles and Magic among the Azande* (Oxford, 1937), p.510.

[123] Bullein, *The Government of Health*, fol. xliir; Cogan, *Haven of Health,* p.281; von Hutten, *De morbo gallico*, fol. 2r; Clowes, *A Short and Profitable Treatise Touching . . . Morbus Gallicus*, sigs. Aivv, Biijr.

the admission that all remedies depended for their efficacy on his assistance.[124]

From the multiple interpretations of disease which they provided, writers drew conclusions about the roles to be adopted when sickness occurred. Just as the regimens laid down a 'convenient form or discipline of living' to conserve health, so some textbooks also showed 'how a man shall behave himself that is . . . diseased'.[125] Since sickness was God's will and perturbations of mind were dangerous, those ill should be calm under their afflictions, even welcome them as a means of spiritual and physical purification, and use both natural and spiritual remedies.[126] The relatives, friends and neighbours of the sick should visit them, help to comfort them and supervise their diet. In cases of hysteria, for example, Jorden recommended 'good instruction and persuasions' to remove fears, apparently to be given by 'the friends and assistants unto the patient'.[127] It was not only the specialist 'medical' literature and devotional tracts which gave advice and commented on behaviour in this way. An interesting new development by the end of the sixteenth century was the appearance of works describing fictional events during epidemics, which besides providing entertainment, had a similar function. The earliest example was Bullein's *A Dialogue Against the Fever Pestilence* (1564), which satirized the activities of doctors, lawyers, and others who surrounded the sick, and drew pointed morals about their real obligations.[128]

As Bullein's *Dialogue* shows, it was during major epidemics that questions of how to act arose in their most contentious form. Infectious diseases brought the desire for self-preservation and the duty to visit the sick into conflict. They also necessitated provisions for public health which interfered directly with personal freedom. Many authors touched on these issues. They discussed the circumstances in which men could flee from infected places and when their obligations were such that they

---

[124] E.g., Jones, *Dial for All Agues*, sig. Givr; Caspar Hueber, *A riche storehouse or treasurie, for the sicke* (1578), fol. 45v. Brasbridge, *The Poor Man's Jewel*, is an example of a plague tract combining 'medical' and 'religious' approaches in equal quantities.

[125] Wingfield, *A Compendious or Short Treatise*, sig. Aviiir; von Brunschwig, *A Most Excellent Homish Apothecary*, fol. 44r.

[126] See Brasbridge, *The Poor Man's Jewel*, sigs. B2–C4; Boorde, *Breviary*, fol. ivv, in addition to the exclusively devotional literature cited in note 43.

[127] Jorden, *A Brief Discourse of the Mother*, fols. 23v, 25v. Cf. Boorde, 'A dyetary of helth' in *The Fyrst Boke of the Introduction of Knowledge*, ed. Furnivall, pp.301–2; Caius, *A Book or Counsel*, in *Works*, p.30; anon., *A myrrour or glasse for them that be syke* [1536?], sig. Biv.

[128] William Bullein, *A Dialogue against the Fever Pestilence*, ed. M. W. and A. H. Bullen, Early English Text Society, extra ser., LII (1888); Mambretti, 'William Bullein and the "lively fashions"', p.289. *The Plague Pamphlets of Thomas Dekker*, ed. F. P. Wilson (Oxford, 1925) gives later examples of similar, but slightly less didactic, works.

should stay behind. They stressed the necessity for those infected with plague to isolate themselves.[129] They advised magistrates, 'the second surgeons appointed by God', on their duties, not only during epidemics but at other times. The exclusion of vagrants from towns and the punishment of sexual immorality were among the precautions necessary to preserve the body politic from infectious disease.[130]

In prescribing behaviour the medical literature did more than advise on means to preserve or restore health. It also reinforced social norms which were commonly accepted, though not always practised, in sixteenth-century England. This function is obvious and explicit in the advice to magistrates; but it can also be seen as a central element in the interpretations of disease advanced by the textbooks. If sickness was the consequence of disorder and sinful excess, existing moral imperatives could logically be emphasized by medical writers. Thus it was common to remark that gluttony not only brought famine to the poor, but also ruined the health of those indulging in it. Accordingly Elyot found medical justification for sumptuary legislation 'although perchance bodily health was not the chief occasion thereof'.[131] Dr Caius's observations on the incidence of the sweating sickness reflected the same attitude: those who caught it 'with peril or death, were either men of wealth, ease and welfare, or of the poorer sort such as were idle persons, good ale drinkers, and tavern haunters. For these by the great welfare of the one sort, and large drinking of the other, heaped up in their bodies much evil matter by their ease and idleness'.[132] In a similar way commentators on plague did not hesitate to draw the obvious conclusion from the fact that the disease spread most rapidly in taverns, at plays and bear-baitings.[133] It is not only Boorde's simple preservative against gaol fever – man should 'so live and . . . do, that he deserve not to be brought into no prison' – which illustrates that interpretations of disease could act as a means of social control.[134]

---

[129] Osiander, *How and Whither a Christian Man Ought to Fly the Plague*; A.T., *A Rich Store-house*, fol. 65v; Brasbridge, *The Poor Man's Jewel*, sig. Cviv; Cogan, *Haven of Health*, p.266; Fuchs, *A Most Worthy Practice*, sig. Aviii.

[130] Clowes, *A Short and Profitable Treatise*, sig. Aivv; Walter Cary, *A briefe treatise called Caries farewell to physicke* (1587 edn), pp.48–9; Lodge, *A Treatise of the Plague*, chapter 8.

[131] Elyot, *Castel*, ed. Tannenbaum, fol. 43r. The 'strong ethical' element in the Galenic system is well described by J. C. Bürgel, 'Secular and religious features of medieval Arabic medicine', in C. Leslie (ed.), *Asian Medical Systems: A Comparative Study* (Berkeley, Calif., 1976), pp.47–8.

[132] Caius, *A Book or Counsel*, in *Works*, p.19. Cf. Clever, *The Flower of Physic* (1590), 'To the Reader', p.11.

[133] E.g., Brasbridge, *The Poor Man's Jewel*, sig. Biiiv.

[134] Boorde, *Breviary*, fol. xxxi.

It would be easy to exaggerate the function of medical ideas as a mechanism of social control and the role of medical literature as a vehicle for it. There were many more effective means for those in authority to proclaim moral standards; and the association of illness with wrong-doing was not invariable or automatic. Disease was not thought inevitably to follow a breach of some accepted rule of behaviour. Sixteenth-century Englishmen needed no telling that chance or fortune as well as an ordered providence played a part in their affairs. Nevertheless, as a common source of stress and anxiety, disease is particularly suited to use as a sanction, however fallible, against activities which are disapproved of for non-medical reasons.[135] The literature shows how contemporary explanations tried to channel anxieties and to turn them to some normative purpose. One cannot dismiss the weight of comment to the effect that disease was a product of actions which perverted 'the order that nature hath appointed',[136] or the medical vocabulary which, by its stress on 'corruption', 'disorder' and 'unnatural' activities, made for associations which were more than metaphorical between different aspects of life. The medical literature articulated a system of thought in which 'health' had wide social and moral implications.

IV

Much more could be written than there is space for here about the common concerns and attitudes revealed in the medical books of Tudor England. The examples which have been given are perhaps sufficient to show the eclectic system of medical thought which the published works embodied, and the sort of functions which such a system could serve. Its variety was its great strength. It was able, for example, to incorporate new diseases like syphilis and new remedies like those of the chemical physicians, without too radical a readjustment. It was not, however, quite the harmonious whole which may have been suggested by previous paragraphs. It contained confusions and inconsistencies within it which could, when specified, lead to conflict. Different writers could draw different conclusions about the virtues of arsenic amulets, or the efficacy of astrological rules in medical treatment, or even about the

---

[135] Cf. A. Macfarlane, *The Family Life of Ralph Josselin* (Cambridge, 1970), pp.173–6; Spencer, *Disease, Religion and Society in the Fiji Islands*, pp.33, 71.
[136] Goeurot, *Regimen* [1543?], 'Treatise of the pestilence', fol. xviir.

details of the humoral system itself.[137] There could be conflict between different interpretations of the extent to which God interfered with the working of secondary causes, and between the dictates of public and private health.[138] But such disputes never threatened the whole structure, and most of them raged most fiercely in the seventeenth century, not in the sixteenth. Until 1600 the assumptions and attitudes expressed in works like those of Elyot, Moulton and Canutus held together.

It is in their reflection of common assumptions and attitudes that the main value of the textbooks and collections of remedies considered here lies. Exactly how 'common' the views they represented were, is a question which cannot be answered precisely. We have concluded from the volume of the literature and from its audience that it was not a major factor in the provision of medical knowledge and treatment, but of ancillary help to a relatively small elite of practitioners and laymen. It lay at the opposite end of the spectrum from the practices of cunning women and the diseases of the poor. Yet it was not entirely cut off from that other more popular world. There were not two distinct medical cultures. The need for diagnosis, rituals and meaningful explanations which the literature tried to meet was felt as much by the illiterate who sought out the local cunning woman as by the ladies who employed physicians. The illnesses in Table 3 were as much those of the poor as the rich, and if the collections of remedies embodied less overt magic than the techniques of genuinely popular medicine, they were not wholly devoid of it. The vernacular medical literature is of wider interest than its limited circle of readers might suggest. The 'Treasures of Poor Men' may not have reached the poor, but they do provide a 'Mirror' reflecting some of the medical problems and attitudes in Tudor England.

---

[137] Some doubts about the precise interpretation of humoral theory are expressed in Clever, *Flower of Physic*, pp.46–9, 54.

[138] See the works cited in notes 8 and 129. I hope to discuss these controversies at length on a later occasion.

8

Astrological medicine

ALLAN CHAPMAN

That the stars and planets were somehow capable of influencing terrestrial affairs, and occasioning major changes in the human condition, was an established part of the mental equipment of Tudor England. The study of celestial analogies provided valuable explanations for a wide variety of phenomena, and it was probably in medicine that astrology reached its most extensive development. Yet it is not altogether easy to disentangle the specifically medical, from the other departments of the art. Whilst it is true that forecasting the outcome of a commercial venture or the location of stolen goods had little apparent medical content, a cursory acquaintance with the sources is enough to show that medical astrology went far wider in its scope than the sickroom consultation of an ephemeris. Astrological medicine for the sick, indeed, was often the forlorn hope of the art, and the wise man expected it to function primarily as a system of preventative and explanatory physic. The stars were thought to exercise a profound influence on the weather, the harvest, the humours, and the tranquillity of the soul, and a proper appreciation of medical astrology required an understanding of the adjacent branches.

Astrology, medical and otherwise, depended on the doctrine of free will. The heavens gave a man his general character and inclination, but they could not compel him against the wise exercise of preventative conduct. Similarly, the infliction of disease was not necessarily inescapable, and good health, like good fortune, was best achieved by the judicious avoidance of obstacles. Without this element of freedom, the whole of astrology would have become hopelessly fatalistic, and could never have developed therapeutic aspirations. The preventative medical horoscope aimed to instruct a man how to act, so that free will could ally with nature in the preservation of health. The astrological Doctor Arcandam was only repeating a tenet of the profession, when he emphasized that 'the said stars do not enforce and constrain thee to any thing'.[1]

I

The basic precepts of Renaissance astrology corresponded with those laid down in the classical period, in Ptolemy's *Tetrabiblos*.[2] Some refinements had been added by the Arabs, which included, according to one authority, the association of the humours of classical physiology with specific planets.[3] Once a link was postulated between celestial configurations and specific bodily functions, it became possible to prognosticate the course of a disease mathematically.

Astrological lore was an integral dimension of medieval English medicine, and by the fifteenth century astrological medicine was accessible to the vernacular readership. However, the Tudor astrologers largely bypassed this tradition, tending rather to derive their ideas from the flood of continental astrological writings of the Renaissance. It is doubtful whether Bosanquet is correct in asserting that the Henrician 'Sorcery Act' of 1541 had an inhibiting influence on the development of Tudor astrological medicine. The time-lag in this area was no greater than in other areas of science in which English authors took their cue from the continent.[4]

The revised *Short-Title Catalogue of Books Printed in England* lists, for

1 'Arcandam', *The most excellent, profitable and pleasant book, of the famous doctor and expert astrologian Arcandam or Aleandrin, to finde the fatal destiny* (1592), sig. B2r.

2 *Ptolemy's Tetrabiblos. Or Quadripartite*, trans. J. M. Ashmand (London, 1917), pp.152–71. On the place of astrology in the sixteenth and seventeenth centuries, see L. Thorndike, *A History of Magic and Experimental Science* (8 vols., New York, 1923–58), v, chapter 10; vi, chapter 33; and K. Thomas, *Religion and the Decline of Magic* (London, 1971), pp.283–389. For further bibliography, see C. Camden, 'Astrology in Shakespeare's day', *Isis*, xix (1933), 26–73; idem, 'Elizabethan astrological medicine', *Annals of Medical History*, ii (1930), 217–26.

3 B. G. Lyons, *Voices of Melancholy* (London, 1971), p.4.

4 H. S. Bennett, 'Science and information in English writings of the fifteenth century', *Modern Language Review*, xxxix (1944), 1–8. For background, see Thorndike, *History of Magic and Experimental Science*, iv, chapters 44, 47 and 55; K. Sudhoff, *Iatromathematiker vornehmlich im 15. und 16. Jahrhundert* (Breslau, 1902); V. Fossel, *Studien zur Geschichte der Medizin* (Stuttgart, 1909), pp.1–23; W. Osler, *Incunabula Medica*, Bibliographical Society Illustrated Monographs, no. 19 (Oxford, 1923); E. F. Bosanquet, *English Printed Almanacks and Prognostications. A Bibliographical History to the Year 1600* (London, 1917), especially p.5; idem, 'English printed almanacks and prognostications. A bibliographical history to the year 1600. Corrigenda and addenda', *The Library*, 4th ser., viii (1928), 456–77; idem, 'English seventeenth-century almanacks', ibid., 4th ser., x (1930), 361–97; idem, 'Notes on further addenda to English printed almanacks and prognostications to 1600', ibid., 4th ser., xviii (1938), 39–66; D. Singer, 'Survey of medical manuscripts in the British Isles dating from before the sixteenth century', *Proceedings of the Royal Society of Medicine*, xiii (1919), sect. 'History of medicine', 96–107. See also D. C. Allen, *The Star-Crossed Renaissance* (Durham, N. Carolina, 1941), especially p.101; S. V. Larkey, 'Astrology and politics in the first years of Elizabeth's reign', *Bulletin of the Institute of the History of Medicine*, iii (1935), 171–86. For a typical example of a fifteenth-century vernacular work on astrological medicine, see Oxford, Bodleian Library, Rawlinson MS. D.1220.

between 1498 and 1560, thirty-five separate almanac-makers, some of whom published consistently over several years. As well as these attributable works, there have survived another thirty almanacs of the same period, the authors of which are not known.[5] Of the thirty-five known almanac-makers, eight wrote under probably English names.[6] Eighteen writers have names suggesting an origin in Germany or the Low Countries, and two, including Nostradamus (Michel de Nostredame), seem to have been French. One, William Parron, was Italian. The remaining six writers have names of uncertain origin; these are 'Erra Pater', M. Walter, John Ryckes, Johannes Mussemius, William Red and 'J.A.'.[7]

How many of the almanacs were original products, and how many were derivative or baselessly attributed to some famous scholar, is hard to establish. The almanac attributed to 'Otto Brunfelsius', dated 1536, is simply a case of exploitation of the name of one of Europe's most prolific and effective popularizers of humanistic medicine. The German had never visited England and had been dead two years at the time of publication of the almanac.[8] Although it is impossible to ascertain what percentage of almanacs has survived, the distribution of names and dates tends to confirm Allen's conclusions about the degree of reliance on the continental tradition. It was not until 1537 that an almanac was composed by an Englishman (Andrew Boorde). There were perhaps three English authors publishing in the 1540s, and five in the 1550s. This, however, represents more a natural growth of the genre, than a sudden release following the repeal of the Sorcery Act under Edward VI. A native English mathematical school did not emerge until the publications of Digges, Ascham and Recorde in the 1550s. Recorde was the first major writer on mathematics in English.[9]

[5] *STC* B. I am indebted to Mr Paul Morgan of the Bodleian Library for allowing me to see the sheets of vol. I of this work.

[6] See Bosanquet, 'Almanacks and prognostications ... Corrigenda and addenda'.

[7] The names of the almanac makers are as follows. English: Henry Low, Thomas Hill, Lewes Vaughan, Anthony Ascham, Andrew Boorde, William Cuningham, Leonard Digges the elder, and John Field or Feild. French: Michael Nostradamus,? Henry Rogeford. Germany or Low Countries: James Sauvage, Achilles Gasser, James Gesner, Alphonse Laet, Gaspar Laet (elder), Gasper Laet (younger), Adrian Velthoven, Arnoldus Bogaert, Simon Huring (Heuringius), Mathias Brotbeihel, Otto Brunfelsius, Valentine Butzlin, Antonius de Montulmo (Motulind), Cornelius Scute, George Seyfridt ('of Sulzfeld'), Jaspar (Kaspar) Vopell, Joachim Hubrigh and John Thibault. Italian: William Parron (of Piacenza).

[8] In 1531 Otto Brunfels printed Georg Tannstetter's *Artificium de applicatione astrologiae ad medicinam ... canones aliquot & quaedam alia ...* (Strassburg, 1531). On one occasion, Tannstetter's own name was 'stolen' to give authority to a prediction: Allen, *Star-Crossed Renaissance*, p.249.

[9] Thomas, *Religion and the Decline of Magic*, p.347; Allen, *Star-Crossed Renaissance*, p.102. A. M. McLean, *Humanism and the Rise of Science in Tudor England* (London, 1972), chapter 6.

Although it was not until the last few decades that sixteenth-century English almanac production reached its zenith, astrological beliefs had always been endemic in Elizabethan society.[10] The mathematician and physician Robert Recorde considered all terrestrial events to be presaged in heaven; Robert Burton ascribed his melancholy temperament to Saturn; while the number of astrological allusions in Shakespeare is enormous.[11] As early as 1560, moreover, these beliefs were sufficiently well established to warrant a full-dress refutation by William Fulke.

The hold of astrological interpretation upon the minds of the educated classes accounts for the success of practitioners like Simon Forman. The medical and psychological advice sought from Forman by the well connected illustrates a general addiction to astrology so deeply rooted that it could withstand innumerable failures. From the career of Forman, it is clear that astrology was used to ease a range of mental states. The use of astrology to divine the fates of absent friends and enemies might also be seen as a form of psychological therapy. William Lilly was to develop a successful practice of this kind during the Civil War.[12]

The character of sixteenth-century astrology was pinpointed by Christopher Heydon, when he argued that the influence of celestial configurations upon the human frame was analogous to that of a lodestone upon iron. The heavens made their first imprint upon the child in the womb, and had an especially strong influence from the time of birth onwards, when the child first began a separate existence. However, as already noted, what the stars gave to the child were its overall constitution and dominant inclinations, rather than a detailed, irreversible fate. A wise man made sure he was always aware of these influences, and organized his conduct accordingly.[13]

Astrological practice took several forms, each having a specialized function. Robert Fludd stated of the 'four parts or kinds of astrology' that 'the first is conversant about the mutation of the air, and foretelling of tempests, diseases, famine, or plenty'; the second foretold the

---

[10] Entries in *STC* indicate the enormous increase in almanac production in the period 1560–1600. The almanac achieved its widest currency *c.*1650.

[11] [Robert Recorde], *The castle of knowledge* (1556), preface; Robert Burton, *The Anatomy of Melancholy*, ed. A. R. Shilleto (3 vols., London, 1904), I, p.14; Camden, 'Astrology in Shakespeare's day'.

[12] A. L. Rowse, *The Case Books of Simon Forman* (New York, 1974), chapter 7. Lilly's surviving casebooks are in the Ashmole Collection, Bodleian Library, Oxford. There has been no full investigation of the source material on Lilly. See D. Parker, *Familiar to All: William Lilly and Astrology in the Seventeenth Century* (London, 1975), especially p.125; C. H. Josten (ed.), *Elias Ashmole: His Autobiographical and Historical Notes* (5 vols., Oxford, 1966).

[13] Christopher Heydon, *Defence of judiciall astrologie* (Cambridge, 1603), p.164.

'alterations of states, as also wars, or a pacific dispo[si]tion in the minds of men'; the third 'entreateth of the election of times, and of nativities', and the last was directed towards the 'fabricating of characters, seals and images'. As was acknowledged by Fludd, himself a physician and astrologer, each of these branches could have medical implications. Traditionally however, astrology consisted of two broad departments of practice. One, judicial astrology, attempted to predict specific future events, especially with respect to 'nativities'. In addition, there was the much wider use of the art to explain human temperaments, behaviour, and the general pattern that future events might take, if the exercise of human free will did not avert them. This was the department of the art condoned by Calvin as 'natural astrology'. Whilst himself an advocate of judicial astrology, Richard Harvey also affirmed the more commonly held belief that 'diverse alterations in the four elements do proceed from stars, and not only temperaments of men's bodies, but also dispositions of their minds are greatly governed by those shining lights of heaven'. Even the 'natural' theory of temperaments was far from infallible, however, for as Howard scornfully pointed out, it was common to find 'melancholy students under Jupiter; jestes [jesters] under Saturn; and constant friends under the moon, which giveth a proud check to the bas[e] conjectures of astrology'.[14]

A considerable degree of scepticism towards astrology is encountered in the literature of the period, although it is chiefly of a qualified kind. Critics were inspired by a variety of motives, but their attacks were usually directed against specific details, or concepts of practice, rather than against the validity of the art as a whole. The most frequently heard complaint on technical grounds asserted the inadequacy of current knowledge in the construction of horoscopes. Unless the exact minute of birth was known, the disposition of the heavens and the nature of their influence upon the individual could never be correctly ascertained. John Chamber, one of the most trenchant of the late Elizabethan critics, clearly defined, in the manner of Renaissance criticism, the inadequacies inherent in the commonly proposed expedient in which an observer sitting by the mother signalled the moment of birth (itself indefinable, according to Chamber and his predecessors) to the astrologer waiting under the open sky outside. As valid was the argument which stressed

[14] Robert Fludd, *Doctor Fludds answer unto M. Foster or, the squeesing of Parson Fosters sponge* (1631), pp.13[5]–6; Jean Calvin, *An admonicion against astrology judiciall*, trans. G. G[ylby] [c.1560], fol. Bir; Richard Harvey, *An astrological discourse upon the great and notable conjunction of the two superiour planets, Saturne & Jupiter ... 1583* (1583), sig. Aiiir (quoting Melanchthon); Henry Howard, *A defensative against the poyson of supposed prophesies* (1583), fol.56r.

the impossibility of knowing the time of conception, which, some asserted, was of greater importance than that of nativity. The diverse fates and temperaments of twins – especially Siamese twins – were cited against the astrologers, as well as the imprecision involved in the practice of computing a medical horoscope from the time at which the patient took to his bed.[15]

Not surprisingly, most of this criticism was directed against judicial, rather than natural, astrology. In its medical aspect the former was mainly concerned with techniques of prognosis, though it is clear that the basis of these techniques was astronomical, rather than physiological. This observation holds good for most other formulations in astrological medicine where the techniques involved did not begin with the disposition of the patient, but represented instead the imposition of natural celestial patterns, such as the seasons or the phases of the moon, upon a given set of symptoms. The astrological distinction between acute and chronic diseases provides a characteristic example: an acute disease was governed by the moon and so could last for only twenty-seven days, whereas, if the illness persisted, its governance shifted to the sun and it was regarded as chronic.[16]

The severest criticisms of judicial astrology arose from its ostensible tendency to deny free will by predicting categorically, rather than explaining overall tendencies. To divine the future was somehow to pre-empt the authority of the Almighty, and it was for this that it was condemned by men who were quite in accord with other departments of astrology. Calvin's attack on judicial astrology repeated and strengthened several of the arguments against astrological divination. As already noted, Calvin was willing to recognize 'natural astrology', which included most of the medical branches of the art, as a legitimate part of liberal learning.[17] Certainly by the end of the Elizabethan period, the arguments for and against judicial astrology had become quite familiar, and received their best public statement in the Chamber versus Heydon controversy after 1601.[18]

---

[15] John Chamber, *A treatise against judicial astrologie* (1601), chapters 4 and 6, and especially pp.49ff. See the childbirth scene in Plate 3.

[16] The best statement of these rules is in Nicholas Culpeper, *Semeiotica uranica or an astrological judgment of diseases from the decumbiture of the sick* (1651), pp.22–39.

[17] Calvin, *Admonicion*, sig. [Avi]r.

[18] This controversy began with Chamber's *Treatise* (1601), and elicited Heydon's *Defence* (1603) and later George Carleton, *The madnesse of astrologers. Or an examination of Sir Christopher Heydons booke* (1624), John Melton's *Astrologaster, or the figure-caster* (1620), and other works. Heydon's *Defence* came to be regarded as the intellectual bulwark of the art by seventeenth-century astrologers: see the MSS of William Lilly, Jeremy Shakerly and others, Oxford, Bodleian Library, Ashmole Collection.

Specific incidents or failures were also instrumental in the stimulation of critical literature. In the wake of the dreaded conjunction of Jupiter and Saturn in 1583, Richard Harvey predicted that 'many infirmities and diseases, shall generally reign, both amongst men, women, and children, proceeding of unnatural moistness, and distemperate heat'. The latter conditions would be occasioned by the presence of cold Saturn in the watery sign Pisces, and Jupiter in the fiery sign of Aries. When nothing unusual occurred, Thomas Heth launched an attack against the astrologers for terrifying simple folk with their predictions. Though it was not Heth's intention to deny the possibility of celestial influence, he argued that current knowledge of this influence was so imperfect as to make it impossible to arrive at any useful conclusions. In the same spirit as Heth's squib, William Perkins published his *Four Great Liars*, in which he compared the predictions of four well-known almanac-makers, 'B', 'T', 'D' and 'F' (probably Buckminster, Twyne, Dade and Frende), in order to highlight their mutual disagreements. Like Heth, Perkins had no doubt about the existence and significance of celestial influences but considered them to be too diverse to permit exact prognostication. He likened the influence of the stars and planets to that of the contents of a pot including an unspecified number of herbs: the brew would produce some reaction in the taker, but it would be impossible to establish which herb had been effective.[19]

All the critics of astrology so far mentioned shared, whatever the grounds of their criticism, a belief in the correlation between celestial phenomena and human affairs. Complete sceptics were very rare, and staunch critics like Stubbes and Brasbridge acknowledged that astrology possessed a genuine, if impious, core. One of the closest approximations to a thoroughgoing sceptic was William Fulke, but even he accepted a necessary connection between celestial and terrestrial phenomena, and he attempted to provide alternative natural explanations for this in his *Goodly Gallery*. He claimed, for example, that comets caused pestilence and war not because they were in any way intrinsically portentous, but because their inherent dryness parched the land and overheated men's brains, thus disposing them to war. Comets were especially dangerous to princes since, 'living more delicately than other men, [they] are more

---

[19] Harvey, *Astrological Discourse*, p.74. Thomas Heth, *A manifest and apparent confutation of an astrological discourse, lately published to the discomfort (without cause) of the weake and simple sort* (1583). W[illiam] P[erkins], *Foure great lyers, striving who shall win the silver whetstone* [1585], sigs. [C6]v–[C7]r. See H. G. Dick, 'The authorship of *Foure Great Lyers* (1585)', *The Library*, XIX (1939), 311–14. *Four Great Liars* was modelled upon Nicholas Allen, *The astronomers game, or a game for thre[e] whetstones, played by two maisters of the arte and a doctor* [1569].

subject to infection, therefore die sooner than other men'. Fulke attacked the whole scheme of astrological interpretation, and in *Antiprognosticon* challenged astrologers to show the evidence on which they ascribed malicious characters to Saturnians and wholesomeness to Jovians. Because he denied the real existence of the zodiac signs and houses, Fulke was naturally contemptuous of the practice of consulting the signs before performing surgery. Furthermore, he considered the uselessness of this practice to be so obvious to sincere men that he virtually accused all astrological doctors of falsehood, asserting 'that the most part of astrologians are by profession physicians, which if they be indeed as they profess, and have learning according to their degree... they know assuredly, that the causes of sickness and health hang nothing upon moving of the celestial bodies'.[20] Condemnation apart, this statement emphasizes the close connection between astrology and medical practice, and the extent to which competent physicians – with 'learning according to their degree' – had recourse to the art. Though not a physician himself, Fulke was an able scholar, and his use of the word 'physician' seems to have indicated the academically qualified practitioner.

Fulke's critique of astrology was motivated by philosophical and theological factors. In the case of Thomas Vicars, a childhood incident involving a totally spurious prediction started him on the road to scepticism, and later inclined him to consider all astrologers to be 'doting liars'. Vicars's opinions were stated in his preface to George Carleton's posthumous *Madness of Astrologers*, a work which Carleton had intended as a counter to Heydon's *Defence*, around 1604, but which remained unpublished for some twenty years. Carleton himself denied that any form of astrology could belong to 'natural learning', and in this respect, forced a distinction which went beyond that made by Calvin. Carleton ascribed diseases to natural causes within the human body, and denied that they had any necessary connection with the stars. 'It is true', he emphasized, 'that a physician may judge of a man's health or sickness, but not by astrology, but by the disposition of his body'. Carleton's primary reference in cases of disease was therefore the reverse of that of

---

[20]   Philip Stubbes, *The anatomie of abuses* (1583); Thomas Brasbridge, *The poore mans jewell, that is to say, a treatise of the pestilence* (1578), chapters 2 and 7; sections on physic and judicial astrology in Henry Cornelius Agrippa, *Of the vanitie and uncertaintie of artes and sciences*, trans. J. San[ford] (1569), fols. 44, 140; William Fulke, *A goodly gallery ... to beholde the naturall causes of all kind of meteors* (1571), fol. 16r; idem, *Antiprognosticon that is to saye, an invective agaynst the vayne and unprofitable predictions of the astrologians* (1560), sigs. Biiir[sic], [Dvii]v. 'Astrological types' were already established by the time of Ptolemy: see *Tetrabiblos*, pp.149–52.

the astrological doctor. Between these varied attitudes to astrology lay a middle way which is perhaps best exemplified in the views of Francis Bacon. The moderate position accepted the broader concepts of planetary influence, but rejected detailed prescriptions relating to exact birth times and hororary government. That the heavens could influence the 'tender humours' seemed to pass without question, but this influence operated across the population and was not localized to specific individuals or brief periods of time. Because of the generalized nature of the influence, its medical uses would have been limited by a lack of exact data upon which to base conclusions. Bacon concluded that 'celestial bodies have other influences besides heat and light ... But these lie hid in the profound parts of natural philosophy'.[21]

Most of what can be gleaned respecting astrological medicine is to be found in astrological, rather than specifically medical books. This indicates not that writers of physic books were opposed to astrology, but rather that they recognized a certain specialism of purpose. Dr Walter Bayley's *Preservation of Eyesight* (1586), for instance, rehearses common and herbal eye treatments without recourse to astrology. That many such writers were not opposed to astrological physic is demonstrated by their having written on the subject elsewhere. The astrological content of Andrew Boorde's *Breviary of Health* (1557) and *Regiment ... of Montpelier* (1549–56) is minimal, both books being concerned with basic hygiene and diet, whereas in his *Principles of Astronomy*, Boorde speaks as an astrological doctor, for 'astronomy doth elucidate physic'. William Bullein's books on the rules of health generally exclude astrological allusion from their interpretation of disease, although when dealing with bloodletting and purging, Bullein included a picture of the zodiac man and referred his readers to an almanac.[22]

Of particular interest are those works which offer non-astrological discussion of conditions generally ascribed to celestial causes. Melancholy was the classic astrological disease, and whilst attributed to

---

[21] Carleton, *Madness of Astrologers*, preface (by Thomas Vicars), and chapter 1, pp.1–11; 74–5. Francis Bacon, *Of the advancement and proficience of learning*, trans. Gilbert Watts (Oxford, 1640), bk III, chapter 4, p.95.

[22] Walter Bayley et al., *Two treatises concerning the preservation of eye-sight* (Oxford, 1616). Andrew Boorde, *The pryncyples of astronomye* [c.1542], preface. William Bullein, *A newe booke entituled the governement of healthe* (1558), fols. xxiii r, xxxii r [sic]. Idem, *Bulleins bulwarke of defence against all sicknesse, soarenesse and woundes* (1579) is similarly devoid of astrological interpretation. John Securis, one of the best-known astrological medical writers of the early Elizabethan period, discussed astrology only briefly in his *A detection and querimonie of the daily enormities and abuses committed in physick* (1566).

Saturn both by common consent and reputable medical opinion,[23] it was discussed quite differently in two of the best-known Elizabethan treatises on melancholy. Timothie Bright, a formally qualified physician, explained the disease in terms of malnourishment of the humours. Although acknowledging that the latter were subject to seasonal variations, he suggested purely physical treatments. Similarly, Thomas Wright implied in the preface to his *Passions of the Mind* that the chief governor of the mind's condition was the degree of external, climatic heat, rather than any malignant planetary influence. Andrew Boorde, in his non-astrological capacity, offered a purely humoral explanation for melancholy; Sir Thomas Elyot stated explicitly that the disease originated in the dregs of the blood. None of these writers denied the potential influence of the planets on the humours, but their willingness to pass silently over this factor indicates a reluctance to acknowledge Saturn to be the root cause of melancholy.

Richard Jonas's *Birth of Mankind*, although dealing with an apparently ideal subject for astrological interpretation, remained singularly aloof from formulations of this kind, restricting itself to empirical observations and practice.[24] Closely allied to popular medicine as astrology had become by 1580, it was still possible to see the art as an appendix to or gloss upon the corpus of classical medicine. Hippocratic and Galenic medicine could be practised without recourse to astrology, but an astrological practitioner tended to conceive his subject in terms of the premises of humoral physiology. This connection was accentuated by a reliance upon spurious classical writings having an astrological bias, and numerous humanistic medical textbooks of astrological medicine.

Perhaps the best measure of the position occupied by astrological physic is the contemporary proliferation of almanacs, many of which were replete with medical information. By the beginning of the Elizabethan period the annual almanac booklet had become a commonplace. Almanacs were cheap, selling for a few pence each. They contained a miscellany of information, and were probably the only pieces of secular literature to be encountered by most of the population. Their supplementary ingredients could vary greatly, some giving dates

---

[23] Burton, *Anatomy of Melancholy*, I, 14; Augier Ferrier, *A learned astronomical discourse, of the judgement of nativities*, trans. Thomas Kelway (1593), fol. 21r.

[24] Timothie Bright, *A treatise of melancholy* (1586), pp.1–3; Th[omas] W[right], *The passions of the minde* (1601), preface; Andrew Boorde, *The breviary of healthe* (1557), fol. lxxviii; Thomas Elyot, *The castel of helth* (1541), fol. 9v. Even when dealing with seasonal diseases, Elyot avoided astrological metaphor: fols. 84v–85v. Richard Jonas, *The byrth of mankynde, newly translated* (1540). Jonas's work derived from Eucharius Roesslin, *De partu hominis* (Frankfurt, 1532).

of fairs, distances between towns, and similar information, but their astrological content was always extremely conservative. In addition to the calendar, most almanacs contained a zodiac man, the rules for bleeding and purging, and simple medical astrology. A 'prognostication' for the coming year was often included. These features underwent little change between 1550 and 1660. While it is probably true that most Elizabethans already had some belief in the overall concepts of astrological medicine, the almanacs must have been significant in popularizing and codifying these beliefs.[25]

Between a half and a third of the almanac writers listed by Bosanquet claimed for themselves some sort of medical qualification, and, in another recently compiled checklist of pre-1640 almanacs, twenty out of sixty-four authors are found to have made similar claims.[26] How far such designations as 'Practitioner of Physic and Chirurgery' indicated the possession of a licence or formal degree is debatable, although in the case of the 'Doctor in Physic' claimed in Michael Nostradamus's medical prognostication of 1559, it seems certain that the author was medically qualified. Other popular titles included 'Master of Arts' – probably indicative of a genuine degree – 'Chirurgion', 'Priest', and the ubiquitous 'Gent.'. Predictably, those claiming a higher professional qualification also spoke disparagingly of the lower orders of practitioner, as when John Securis, 'Master of Art and Physic', and a practitioner in Salisbury, advised his readers to consult first a 'good and learned' physician before trusting to 'the unlearned chirurgion' in cases requiring phlebotomy. However, the possession of a 'medical qualification' was, in the context of the sixteenth century, no certain guide to the competence of its possessor. Although sent for to consult with foreign physicians and astrologers concerning the Queen's health, 'Dr' John Dee held no formal medical qualifications, while the almanac writer Dr Low probably did. Andrew Boorde, who practised at court in the 1530s, is not recorded as having taken out a degree, although he is said to have undergone a period of study.[27] The notorious Simon Forman started life as a grocer's apprentice and school-teacher. He became a successful astrological practitioner who was singled out for

---

[25] Bosanquet, *Almanacks and Prognostications* (1917).

[26] See the checklist, seen by the present author in typescript, and later incorporated into *STC* B, vol.I. The lists of almanac writers given by Bosanquet also include professional designations, genuine and assumed.

[27] Michael Nostradamus, *An excellent tretise, shewing suche perillous, and contagious infirmities, as shall insue 1559 and 1560* (1559). John Securis, *An almanacke, and prognostication, made for the yeere... M.D.LXXIX* (1579), sig. Aiii. *DNB*, art. 'Dee, John'; ibid., art. 'Boorde, Andrew'. For Low, 'doctor in physic', see Allen, *Star-Crossed Renaissance*, pp.104 and passim.

persecution by the College of Physicians. The College maintained its attack until about 1601 ; in 1604 Forman was granted a licence to practise by the University of Cambridge.[28] It is hardly possible to estimate the true qualifications of most of the persons mentioned in this study though it can be stated with fair certainty that Anthony Ascham, Timothie Bright, John Harvey, John Securis, Walter Bayley and William Cuningham possessed either a licence or a formal medical degree.[29]

II

The foundations of medical astrology rested upon the supposed interaction between the celestial influences and humoral physiology. Its working concepts, however, seem to have been formulated more from an astronomical, than from a medical viewpoint, and the patient was seen as exhibiting less a set of physical symptoms than a collection of numerical possibilities. To most astrological doctors disease originated in a humoral imbalance, the root cause of which was a star. The celestial influence itself might have been a manifestation of God's displeasure with human conduct, but it was left to man's free will to decide what precautionary measures to take. Epidemics, of the type frequently heralded by comets or eclipses, were usually sent as general scourges to punish the collective sins of a city or nation, although the wise astrologer was able to read the portents in advance. Preventative measures could take the form of charms, rituals, drugs or, most efficacious of all, a return to prayer and godly living. The mechanics of this system harmonized with a retributive theory of illness in which the afflicted organ was not the seat, but rather the relayer of a discomfort that began in the greater heaven. In this respect, astrological medicine fitted neatly into a world-view that interpreted all phenomena in terms of moral agency. Alternatively disease could be considered as caused by organic malfunction, so that diagnosis and therapy were aimed at repairing a specific physical defect, without the need for interpreting the heavens. Fulke and Carleton seem to have adopted this latter approach, in their assertion of the primacy of the patient in physic, although their denial of celestial influence would not have precluded divine retribution, for God, unlike the stars, was omnipotent.

The correlations drawn between specific regions of the heavens and

---

[28] Rowse, *Case Books of Forman*, pp.294, 297–8, 300, 301 and passim.
[29] Information obtained from the biographical index of sixteenth-century medical practitioners compiled by Charles Webster and Margaret Pelling.

the parts of the body, which were the basis of the medical horoscope, seem to have been quite arbitrary, and more in accordance with the astronomical cardinal points than with the incidence of disease. Aries, the first sign from the vernal equinox, was allotted the head, while Pisces, the last sign, was given governance of the feet, and the intermediary signs the intermediary limbs. No sources for the justification of these arrangements survive in contemporary literature, and they seem to have been accepted as a form of immemorial knowledge by all but a few critics. One of the latter was William Perkins, who stressed that 'the government of the signs in the body is not taken from experience in nature, but feigned long ago by some drowsy pate, and now because it hath a cloak of antiquity, it is allowed'. He went on to remark that it was absurd to give Aries, a hot sign, control over the cool brain, rather than over the heart and vital blood, but did not question why Aries should have been considered a hot sign in the first place.[30] The principles of planetary government also went unexplained, although it is easier to imagine a qualitative relationship for the planets than for the constellations. It seems obvious that to the sun should be ascribed hot, powerful qualities; to the changing lunar phases, mutable diseases; and to Saturn, a dim planet requiring twenty-nine years to creep around its orbit, slothful melancholy. This was doubtless the logic behind, for instance, the purging of phlegm – a cold moist humour – when the hot dry sun was favourably aspected.[31] In all its operations the medical horoscope depended upon qualitative connections between the surface appearances of phenomena, and was most frequently used in prognosis. Although the general explanatory tenets of the art could be considered as parts of natural astrology, the construction of detailed horoscopes for particular cases of specific diseases brought it into contact with the judicial branches.

At the beginning of his consultation it was traditional for the astrological doctor to establish the precise time at which the patient had been first smitten with sickness, for this time of 'decumbiture' supplied the basis of a horoscope. However it was this practice of computing a disease from the hour at which the patient had taken to his bed, which attracted the most severe criticism. John Chamber argued that if the hour of decumbiture was all important, the patient could improve his chances of recovery by refusing to take to his bed until the most favourable hour by the ephemeris, and thus 'play bo peep with death'.

[30] Perkins, *Four Great Liars*, sig. D4r. See also Fulke, *Antiprognosticon*, sig. [Bi]v.
[31] Boorde, *Principles of Astronomy*, chapter 11.

Chamber also enquired, what would be the fate of each of two persons who took to their beds at the same time, one with a trivial disease, the other with a grave affliction? By the 1650s it was considered best to interpret the hour of decumbiture as that time at which the patient felt manifest discomfort, for a weak man would be likely to take to his bed before a strong one, given the same disease.[32] Richard Saunders preferred to judge a case from the time at which the physician examined the patient; in 1583 Richard Harvey recommended the rule of Hermes Trismegistus as given in his *Iatromathematica*: 'it profiteth much to observe that hour in which a disease beginneth to breed'.[33] Yet no matter how the doctrine of decumbiture was interpreted, it remained an astronomical rather than a physiological point of reckoning, in which the time was of greater importance than the symptoms.

For ease of computation, the time of decumbiture, together with the other astronomical details, was entered on a horoscope plan, devised as three interlocking squares, the twelve corners of which corresponded to the celestial houses. To calculate the horoscope of a disease the astrological doctor followed a procedure similar to that used in computing a nativity, with the hour of decumbiture corresponding to the 'birth' time of the disease. Just as the zodiac itself was broken into twelve signs, so there were twelve corresponding 'houses' which were regarded as immovable in relation to a terrestrial observer, and through which the zodiac signs moved once in every twenty-four hours. The first step in computing a horoscope was to establish which sign had occupied the 'Ascendant' house on the eastern horizon at the hour of decumbiture, and what planets it had contained. In this way the astrologer determined the 'Lord of the Ascendant' and the other principal powers of the horoscope.

The basic influences of the horoscope were decided from the situations of the planets, but these were moderated by the special qualities of the signs which they currently occupied. It was therefore essential to notice how the respective planets were 'aspected' one with another, especially if the ascendant sign was the one that had governance over the organ in question, for example Taurus in throat ailments. Planetary aspects were expressed in angles from the ascendant sign, the number of possible aspects being five, of varying degrees of amity or malignancy. When two or more planets were aspected within the same sign they were said to be in 'conjunction', and such a configuration was

---

[32] Chamber, *Treatise against Judicial Astrology*, p.33. Culpeper, *Semeiotica uranica*, p.28.
[33] Harvey, *Astrological Discourse*, p.75.

held to be one of great strength. In cases where planets faced each other across the zodiac, at 180 degrees, that is at 'opposition', or at 90 degrees, that is, in 'quartile', the influences were towards discord and enmity. The 60 degree and 120 degree positions, known as 'sextile' and 'trine' respectively, were regarded as friendly. Mars and Saturn were especially dangerous in the quartile aspects, unless the force of these naturally malignant planets was moderated by that of good planets in better positions.[34]

It was also essential to take careful note of the place of the moon for, being a fickle, mutable planet, it could be the author of sudden as well as cyclical changes. The moon governed all acute diseases, and was indispensable when purging or performing surgery. Phlebotomy, the most widely practised treatment of the day, was strictly governed by the moon. Luna, indeed, was one of the most commonly consulted of all bodies in astrological medicine, and Richard Harvey was expressing the general view in stressing that 'it behoveth the physician to know the moon'.[35]

The elemental qualities of the signs currently occupied by the moon and planets had also to be ascertained, for in addition to their own characters the signs had affinities with earth, air, fire and water, and the elements acted in sympathy with their corresponding humours. Thus Aries, a fire sign, was associated with hot, choleric diseases. Boorde advised his readers not to shave when the moon occupied this sign, for the operation would leave small pores in the face, through which noxious vapours might gain access. Conversely Pisces, being a watery sign, caused coughs and rottenness.[36]

Once the basic astronomical details had been obtained from the ephemeris, the horoscope could be 'progressed', and a prognosis arrived at. This last operation involved a knowledge of the doctrine of crises, and the computation of critical days. The first crisis came upon the day when the patient fell sick, and was reckoned from either the hour of decumbiture or the first hour of illness. Several accounts exist of methods to be used in determining the critical days. John Dade went so

---

[34] One of the most comprehensive treatises on the properties of the celestial configurations was Richard Saunders, *The astrological judgment and practice of physick. Deduced from the position of the heavens at the decumbiture of the sick person* (1677); see especially pp.2–4.

[35] William Bourne, *An almanacke and prognostication for three yeares that is to saye ... 1571 and 1572 & 1573* (n.d.), section headed 'A rule for letting of bloude'; also Securis, *Almanac and Prognostication for MDLXXIX,* section headed 'Certaine observations concernyng phisicke', sigs. Aii v–Aiii r. Harvey, *Astrological Discourse,* p.5.

[36] Saunders, *Astrological Judgment,* pp.13–19. The qualities of the planets and signs were commonplace in astrological medical books and almanacs. See also Boorde, *Principles,* chapter 6.

far as to lay down rules for persons falling sick on specific days of each month. Precisely how subsequent crises would fall depended upon whether the disease was considered to be acute or chronic. With an acute disease the next critical time would come when the moon moved to quartile, at 90 degrees, seven days after decumbiture, although the fourteenth, twenty-first, and twenty-eighth days would also be significant if the disease persisted.[37] More favourable turns could be expected when the moon moved to sextile and trine. The same rules applied in chronic diseases, but as their governance fell to the sun, the periods in question were of longer duration.

An imaginary horoscope might be constructed as follows. A patient falls ill with inflammation of the lungs when the moon is waning in Cancer, Saturn being in opposition, and Jupiter approaching trine. The moon is cold, moist, and situated in the house governing the lungs. Saturn, cold and dry, is placed in a bad aspect and greatly aggravates the condition by contributing a dry, hacking cough. The chief hope lies with Jupiter which, in addition to being a generally beneficent planet, has special powers over the lungs, and is moving to the favourable trine aspect. Much will also depend upon the moon. If the patient can hold his ground until the new moon, when everything begins to 'grow' again, his chances will be much strengthened, and Luna's moistness will help to mitigate the hard cough. A powerful, hot planet like the sun could also be beneficial if well placed, for Sol's heat would drive out the cold humours. Medication should take the form of warming applications, and, possibly, bleeding on the right days, to release the heavy Saturnine humours.[38]

However, it was necessary to consider factors other than those of a purely hororary nature in forming an opinion upon a person's health. The patient's age of life, the day of the week on which he had been born, and the day of the week on which he had been taken ill, were all considered important. Several writers dealt with the 'ages' as a means both of classifying human dispositions and of predicting possible fates. Traditionally, these ages were seven in number, each being ruled by its particular planet in a progression upwards through the spheres, from the changeable moon-likeness of infancy, to the Saturnine decrepitude of old

[37] John Dade, *An almanacke and prognostication, in which you may beholde the state of this yeere of our lorde god MDLXXXIX* [?1589]: see the 'Prognostication'. Saunders, *Astrological Judgment*, pp.23–4; Saunders himself was critical of these older rules.

[38] Culpeper, *Semeiotica uranica*, p.39. Culpeper constructs an imaginary horoscope for a man falling sick in Paris on a certain day, pp.40ff.

age.[39] Some writers used fewer ages. Arcandam employed only five, comprising three main designations, and two degrees of old age, terminating in 'extreme feebleness'. Godfridus used a simpler symbolism, in which he divided a lifetime into twelve ages of six years each. Similar to the theory of ages was the supposed connection between the day of the week on which a person was born, and his condition, temperament and health. This could be used to elucidate human types, and also to 'weigh' the respective planets governing a patient's horoscope. Like the ruling planet of that day, a child born on a Sunday was said to be 'great and shining' while the Saturnine Saturday child 'shall seldom be profitable, but if the course of the moon bring it thereto'.[40]

Each season of the year had its cycle of particular diseases, which was usually included amongst the prognosticatory pages of almanacs, and could be reckoned into an individual horoscope. For the first half of 1568, for example, John Securis predicted that as a consequence of an eclipse of the sun the previous year, there would be reigning 'wild, strong, and inconstant diseases ... ulcerations and botches ... and, chiefly toward the East parts ... corrupt blood ... migraines, leprosies, lunatic diseases' and others besides. The 'second revolution' of the year would be remarkable for 'cold and corrupt humours as, rheums ... gouts, colics, palsies ... dropsies, phthisis, black jaundice ... gravel and stone', and a variety of other afflictions. Alexander Mounslowe's revelations following the 1579 eclipse were hardly more encouraging. Indeed, there seem to have been few years when some terrible portent was not expected, and from an astronomical point of view, it would have been an unusual twelvemonth that did not contain at least one eclipse of either sun or moon, a conjunction or opposition of malefic planets or a conspicuous shower of meteors. In the light of so much doom-warning, it is hardly surprising that hypochondria and melancholy were so common; although one assumes that in the face of so much real disease, the terrors of the almanac must have taken second place in the imaginations of its readers.[41]

[35] For a thorough treatment of the doctrine of the 'seven ages' and their astrological characteristics, see [Thomas Milles], *The treasurie of auncient and moderne times ... translated out of ... Pedro Mexio. And M. Francesco Sansovino ... As also, of ... Anthonie Du Verdier ... Loys Guyon ... Claudius Gruget*, I (1613), pp.336–9.

[40] Arcandam, *The Most Excellent, Profitable and Pleasant Book*; 'Godfridus', *The knowledge of things unknown: shewing the effects of the planets, and other astronomical constellations* (1649), pp.64–7, 4.

[41] John Securis, *A new almanacke and prognostication for the yere of our saviour Christ MDLXVIII* [1567]: see the 'Prognostication', sigs. [Aviii], B[i]. Alexander Mounslowe, An almanacke and prognostication, made for ... MDLXXXI (n.d.). See Lyons, *Voices of Melancholy*, pp.1–6.

One of the demands placed upon medical astrologers concerned the prediction of life expectancy. The brevity of life was a cause of some concern; Thomas Paynel noted in 1541 that, while Old Testament characters had often lived many centuries, and even Galen 'that famous doctor [had lived] a hundred and forty years, but nowadays, alas, if a man may approach to forty or sixty years, men repute him happy and fortunate'. Physiognomy and chiromancy could also be used, in conjunction with the horoscope, to predict life expectancy and define character details. These arts detected the imprints of the planets on the face and hands respectively. Thomas Hill's *Contemplation of Mankind* (1571) demonstrated the link between facial lines, the planets, and the ages of life. On the forehead, for example, there were three principal lines, governed by Mercury, Jupiter and Saturn respectively, and corresponding to youth, maturity and old age. When three lines ran close together across the forehead it indicated that the subject would live until he was seventy; if four lines, eighty. Similar rules were drawn up for the hands. Hill laid no claim to originality in his book, and constantly referred to the 'physiognomer' from whom he had learned his business. This was probably Bartholomaeus Cocles, whose treatise on physiognomy of 1554 seems to have been a prototype for Hill's, both in content and illustrations. Physiognomy and chiromancy were, like the other divinatory arts, highly conservative, and probably received their most comprehensive treatment in Cornelius Agrippa's *Occult Philosophy*.[42]

The end of all these arts was to understand the nature of man and his afflictions, but to put understanding into practical effect required resort to therapy.

III

Therapy was aimed at bringing about a change in a patient's condition, thwarting the malefic influences that caused disease, and facilitating the action of more beneficent forces. This could involve a variety of techniques, some of which were overtly magical, although it was usual to combine astrological treatment with some form of physical medication. The latter could be humoral in its intentions, like bloodletting, or it could depend on some sympathetic or quasi-magical reaction which was designed not to affect the diseased organ itself but to

---

[42] Thomas Paynel, *Regimen sanitatis Salerni* (1541), sig. Aiir; Thomas Hill, *The contemplation of mankinde, contayning a singuler discourse after the art of phisiognomie* ([London?], 1571), fols. 39v–44v, 'The judgment of certain lines seen in the forehead'; and preface. Bartholomaeus Cocles, *Physiognomiae et chiromantiae compendium* (Strassburg, 1554). See also Henry Cornelius Agrippa, *De occulta philosophia libri tres* (Antwerp, 1531).

thwart the celestial influences at source. Physical medication could take
the form of herbal or chemical drugs, or it could consist of a charm, in
which the physical substance formed the neutral vehicle for a magical
therapeutic agent.

Characteristic of the last approach were the 'cures' being described by
John Blagrave as late as 1671, in which he recommended the treatment
of plague-sores by the application of 'a dried toad macerated in vinegar'.
To cure an atrophied limb, the practitioner was advised to bore a hole
into a tree, and bind the wood turnings onto the afflicted part. After
twenty-four hours the sufferer's hair cuttings, nail parings and scrapings
of the skin from the defective limb, were to be placed in the hole in the
tree, and stopped with a peg of the same wood. To guarantee the success
of this charm, with its symbolism of growth and sympathetic action, it
had to be performed under a waxing moon, with Saturn in a weak
position.[43]

Lunar symbolism was crucial to all astrological therapy. Lunatics
were considered as being at their most agitated around the time of new
moon. Thomas Vicary affirmed the notion that the brain 'followeth
upwards' in the cranium at the waxing moon, whilst at the onset of the
wane 'the brain descendeth downwards, and vanisheth in substance of
virtue'. Medicinal herbs had also to be collected under an auspicious
moon, and cat's eyes were believed to vary in size according to the
prevailing phase. So powerful was the lunar influence thought to be, that
John Maplet spoke of a plant called Selenotropion, the growth of which
followed the moon as that of Heliotrope followed the sun.

Dr Richard Mead was in no way an astrologer, and instead attempted
to explain causes in terms of Newtonian physics. He was nonetheless, at
this later date, to confirm many of the lunar phenomena on which
astrological doctors had based their conclusions. Mead was especially
impressed with the influence of the moon on times of death, as well as of
the existence of seventh-day, fourteenth-day and twenty-first-day crises
in fever cases.[44]

The form of therapy in which astrological considerations were of
paramount importance was bloodletting. Because the moon was
thought to control the amount of blood in the veins, astrology
inevitably became the handmaiden of phlebotomy, and even physicians
who generally refrained from astrological discussion made an exception

---

[43] Joseph Blagrave, *Blagraves astrological practice of physick* (1671), pp.158–9.
[44] Thomas Vicary, *The anatomie of the bodie of man*, ed. F.J. Furnivall and P. Furnivall (1888), p.33.
John Maplet, *The diall of destiny* (1581), fol. 15v. Richard Mead, *A treatise concerning the influence of the sun and moon upon human bodies, and the diseases thereby produced* (1704; 1748).

when dealing with this topic. The few astrological references in Bullein's *Government of Health* (1558) and Boorde's *Breviary of Health* relate mainly to phlebotomy, though Paynel paid no attention to astrological connections when dealing with phlebotomy in his edition of *Regimen sanitatis Salerni*. The rules for bleeding formed an indispensable part of most almanacs, usually following the wood-cut of the zodiac man, and were, like most other parts of astrological physic, deeply conservative. The most important of these rules was that prohibiting bleeding at a time when the sun, moon or Lord of the Ascendant occupied the sign controlling the disease in question. Thus it was inadvisable, for instance, to bleed a patient for a disorder of the spleen when the moon was in Cancer, although most almanacs stressed that exceptions could be made in extreme or critical cases. Along with most of the other astrological rules, William Fulke ridiculed those of bloodletting, asking the grounds on which they had been formulated. This was valid criticism, for there seemed, as Fulke argued, to be no more reason in delaying phlebotomy seven days in cases of pleurisy, than there was in postponing treatment in suspected cases of poisoning.[45] According to orthodox practice, however, it was permitted to bleed on prohibited days in extreme cases, such as the 'pestilence, the frenzy, the pleurisy, the squinancy, for a continual burning ague, a continual or great headache, proceeding of choler, or hot and superfluous blood'.[46]

In ordinary cases phlebotomy was most likely to be successful when the sextile and trine aspects were favourably occupied, and especially when the moon was conjoined with Jupiter. But certain signs were always 'unmeet' for bloodletting when occupied by the moon, namely, Taurus, Gemini, Leo, Virgo, Capricorn, and the cusps of Libra and Scorpio. Bloodletting was also forbidden on the unlucky 'Canicular' or Dog Days, when the star Sirius was believed to rule. The Dog Days began with the helical rising of Sirius, and were said to bring with them fearful heat and disturbance. Godfridus stated that they fell between the fifteenth Kalendar of August and the Nones of September, although in fact the astronomical rising could fall in different seasons for any given cycle of years. It was recommended that not only bloodletting but all manner of physic and even copulation should be suspended during

---

45 Bullein, *Government of Health*, fol. xxiiir; Boorde, *The Breviary of Health*, fol. iiiir. Paynel, *Regimen sanitatis Salerni*, confines itself to manipulative clinical advice. Fulke, *Antiprognosticon*, sigs. B[i]v–Biir.

46 Securis, *Almanac and Prognostication for MDLXXIX*, sig. Aiiir. This advice is given by many writers, with little variation: see also Harvey, *Astrological Discourse*, p.81; John Dade, *A triple almanacke for the yeere of our Lorde God 1591* (1591), see the 'Prognostication', sig. Aiiir.

these dangerous days, when the star occasioned debility, pestilence and death. Venomous reptiles, and even flying snakes, were also said then to abound. The only preservative came from keeping up a great fire, day and night, though whether this measure was intended to produce a sympathetic reaction in the already over-heated blood, or to frighten away the flying snakes, is not made explicit.[47]

An elaborate ritual preceded the operation of phlebotomy, in addition to that required by the astronomical conditions described above. 'Let blood at no time, without great cause', stressed Leonard Digges, 'for it bringeth weakness and many infirmities. If ye do, see it be after good digestion, and fasting, in a fair temperate day. Beware before of all manner [of] exercise, bathings, watchings, and carnal copulation'. After reckoning all these factors it was also necessary to be sure that the patient would be bled under the correct sign for his temperament or 'complexion': for example, Aries for the phlegmatic, Libra for the melancholic, and Cancer for the choleric.[48] A further relevant factor was the age of the patient. Just as the 'ages of life' of man were governed by their respective planets, so there was an equivalent correlation between the age of the patient, and the 'age' or phase of the moon under which he was to be bled. It was considered best not to bleed children at all, but youths were in general bled during the moon's first quarter, middle-aged men as it approached the full, and the elderly and the old during the waning phases. Again, there is nothing in the literature to suggest that these correlations met any purely medical criteria, and they seem rather to have represented the imposition onto approximate periods of human life of four easily demarcated stages of an astronomical event. Versions of these rules were widespread in contemporary publications and may be found in detail in the works of Bourne, Harvey and Dade.[49]

---

[47] Boorde, *Principles*, chapter 11; Godfridus, *Knowledge of Things Unknown*, pp.20–4. In the 'Everlasting Prognostication' attributed to 'Leopoldus Austriacus and others', the Dog Days were said to begin around 7 July: Thomas Hill, *The profitable arte of gardening, now the thirde time set forth* (1574), appendix, p.53. A concise account of the Dog Days, astronomical, astrological and medical, is to be found in Milles, *The Treasury of Ancient and Modern Times*, pp.71–4.

[48] Leonard Digges, *A prognostication of right good effect*, Old Ashmolean Reprints no. 111 (1555; Oxford, 1926), p.44.

[49] Thomas Paynel advised that a patient under 17 years should not be bled at all, and stated that Galen recommended 14 years as the minimum age: *Regimen sanitatis Salerni*, fols. 103v–104r. Bourne, *An Almanac... 1571–1573*; Harvey, *Astrological Discourse*, p.80. In his *Almanac... 1591*, 'Prognostication', sig. Aiii v, John Dade gave the rule in verse, to aid the memory:

The moon in age, the ancient sort,
Their veynes may open best:
The younger sort tyll Moone be newe,
Must let their veynes have rest.

Blood was drawn from different veins for different diseases, such as from the temple in cases of headache; Culpeper provides a detailed list. Once again, the rules of treatment are astronomical rather than physiological: diseases that came under Aries were treated by bleeding from the head, and the diseases of Pisces, from the feet. Moreover, blood was drawn from different sides of the body according to the season. Bourne stated that in springtime the patient should be bled from the right side, and at harvest from the left. Godfridus affirmed, 'Whosoever on the seventh day of March is let blood in the right arm, and in the eleventh day of April in the left arm, he shall not lose the sight of his eyes'.[50] It was hoped, no doubt, to combine in this treatment the salutary qualities of the number seven, with the influence of two signs usually favourable to phlebotomy.

In sum, bloodletting was considered to be the 'universal evacuation of fullness of humours or plethory', and as acting like a safety valve, for 'plethory is the increase of humours above equality in the veins'. When properly applied, this release of disturbed humours could bring relief from a veritable infinity of diseases, for bloodletting 'cheereth the sad, appeaseth the angry; and keeps lovers from madness'.[51]

Because it would involve the spilling of blood, it was also necessary to ordain the time for an ordinary surgical operation astrologically. The connection between surgery and astrology was mentioned specifically by John Securis, whose rules for the timing of an operation were approximately the same as for phlebotomy. However, it seems that in practice these rules were observed less rigorously than the texts suggest, for William Perkins emphasized that it was well known among medical men that patients could be bled and physicked under the most dangerous signs, without the least discomfort. As is so often the case, theory and practice were clearly not in strict accordance. Nonetheless, with this proliferation of rules governing a single aspect of medical astrology, it is hardly surprising that the skills of a 'doctor of physic or astronomer' were necessary, but, as 'John Indagine' complained, not one practitioner in a hundred fully understood them.[52]

---

[50]   Nicholas Culpeper *et al., Two treatises: the first of bloodletting, and the diseases to be cured thereby. The second of cupping and scarifying*, 3rd edn (1672), pp.13ff; Bourne, *An Almanac . . . 1571–1573*, sig. [Bviii]v; Godfridus, *Knowledge of Things Unknown*, p.49.

[51]   Culpeper *et al., Two Treatises*, pp.1–2, 12; see also Harvey, *Astrological Discourse*, p.83.

[52]   Securis, *Almanac . . . for . . . MDLXVIII*, sig. aiiiv; Perkins, *Four Great Liars*, sig. D4; Boorde, *Principles*, chapter 11; also Jean de Hayn (ab Indagine), *Briefe introductions, both natural, pleasant and delectable unto the art of chiromancy*, trans. Fabian Withers (1575), sig.Jiiii. De Hayn considered astrology to be of such importance that physicians who were not learned in it were unfit to practise.

Though not as frequently discussed as phlebotomy, purging was another common recourse of Elizabethan physicians, and was usually performed according to astrological canons. Cold, moist signs were especially favourable, with the moon, it was stated by William Bourne, in Cancer, Scorpio, Pisces or Gemini. The signs under which purging was to be avoided were approximately the same as those at which bleeding was considered to be hazardous, and neither operation was without risk in excessively hot weather. Bullein recommended spring-time as the best season for taking a purge and, though he avoided astrological discussion, he stated that 'the apt days and signs are commonly known in the English almanacs'.[53] This remark itself is illuminating, for it indicates that as early as 1558 almanacs were already commonplace, and contained formalized medical rules.

Most of the drugs used in sixteenth-century medicine were herbal in origin, but there is little to suggest the practice of systematic astrological botany in England during the period in question. Several continental treatises on the subject were in existence by 1580, but these do not seem to have had any significant influence in England.[54] Nevertheless the herbals published in England from Turner (1568) to Gerard (1597) contained a great deal of astrological lore. The astrological virtues of medicinal herbs were believed to derive from the sympathies that subsisted between species of plants and the stars. During the sixteenth century, this doctrine drew strength from the alchemical tradition.[55] It usually worked in combination with the doctrines of signatures, which stated that each plant bore the physical impress either of the celestial influence which dominated it, or of the organ connected with the disease it was fitted to cure. Many of the plants illustrated in della Porta's widely read *Phytognomonica* (1588) were classified according to such principles. A crescent-shaped leaf, for example, was an indication of governance by the moon. Less well-known treatises by such authors as Winckler, Carrichter and Thurneisser also dealt systematically with the celestial virtues of herbs.[56]

---

53 Bullein, *Government of Health*, fol. xxxii r[sic].
54 For discussion of late-sixteenth-century astrological botany, see A. Arber, *Herbals, Their Origin and Evolution . . . 1470–1670*, 2nd edn (Cambridge, 1953), chapter 8.
55 W. Pagel, *Paracelsus, An Introduction to Philosophical Medicine in the Era of the Renaissance* (Basel, 1958), pp. 148–9; Thorndike, *History of Magic and Experimental Science*, v, chapter 10, and vi, chapter 33.
56 Giambattista della Porta, *Phytognomonica* (Naples, 1588), bk viii, see plate, p. 317. Bartholomaeus Carrichter, *Kreutterbuch* (Strassburg, 1575); Leonhardt Thurneisser zum Thurn, *Historia sive descriptio plantarum* (Berlin, 1578); both of these works are discussed by Arber, *Herbals*.

What did exist in Elizabethan England were a variety of astrological rules concerned with the collection of herbs, but these do not appear to have constituted a 'system' as such. The universal currency of such rules is indicated by references such as that of the Oxford philosopher and physician John Case, to the necessity of collecting herbs under their correct sign if they were not to lose their power.[57] Another work to touch upon the astrological affinities of herbs was the *Book of Secrets* of Albertus Magnus, a short tract printed in 1560. This was hardly a systematic study, and the thirty or so of its pages that dealt with herbs seem to have been directed towards a popular readership, which indicates the existence of a symbolism which was prevalent and familiar. In the first section four of the sixteen herbs described were allocated astrological affinities, and these were of a general character. 'Vervyn' or verbena, for example, gathered with the sun in Aries and mixed with 'pyonie' [peony] seeds, was said to be a preservative against the falling sickness. But when introducing the second section, the author stressed that the full efficacy of the drugs depended upon astrological considerations. Seven herbs were then described, each governed by its appropriate planet. The sun controlled a herb named 'Alchone', which was effective in cases of 'passions, and grief of the heart'; Venus controlled 'verven', which was of 'great strength in venereal pastimes', and so on.[58]

The widely diffused astrological lore about plants was ultimately synthesized into Nicholas Culpeper's celebrated *English Physician*.[59] Culpeper was at pains to stress the inherent rationality of the system, for his own experience had taught him that diseases varied with the sky, and his system of therapy depended upon the application of herbs possessing distinct astrological qualities. Although they were criticized by many physicians, Culpeper's doctrines were developed by various other writers after his death, and in particular by Joseph Blagrave, who wrote both a 'Supplement' to Culpeper's work and a new treatise on astrological physic. The rudimentary ascriptions of plants to diseases and planets set out by Albertus Magnus were here presented in greater detail. Thus, by 1675, the relationship between 'planetary' influences and drugs, which had been mentioned in passing a century earlier, had

57 John Case, *Lapis philosophicus* (Oxford, 1599), pp.182–3. Robert Fludd spoke of collecting herbs under the correct sign: see *Dr Fludd's Answer to M. Foster*, pp.136ff.
58 *The boke of secretes of Albertus Magnus, of the vertues of herbes, stones and certayne beastes* (n.pl., 1560), sigs. B[i]v, Biiiir, [Bvii].
59 Nicholas Culpeper, *The English physitian* (1652). For bibliography, see F. N. L. Poynter, 'Nicholas Culpeper and his books', *Journal of the History of Medicine*, XVII (1962), 152–67.

undergone considerable elaboration. In *Gerard's Herbal*, wormwood had been a hot drug, useful in the treatment of agues, but without specific astrological connotations. In Culpeper, however, it is accredited with a 'martial' quality, and said to be found growing near equally 'martial' forges and ironworks. Blagrave asserted that Culpeper had 'ridiculously romanced' about this drug; he himself placed the plant in a general 'martial' category, and stated that it should never be applied to the eyes but 'was said to provoke urine, help surfeits, and ease pains in the stomach', as well as reducing swelling and hardness of the spleen.[60] It would seem that in spite of the inherent conservatism of astrology as a whole, astrological botany at least was subject to change and development in the seventeenth century.

Many of the astrological aphorisms that surrounded plants in Elizabethan England were as much agricultural as medical in their intentions, like the rule advising farmers to sow seed when the waxing moon stood in a favourable sign and when Saturn was at trine. Although he devoted a whole section of his *Good Points of Husbandry* (1557) to the cultivation of medicinal herbs, Thomas Tusser made no allusion to astrology and dealt with herbs purely as simples. Similarly, Thomas Hill's 'Certain Husbandly Conjectures' discussed the connections between weather, plants, animals and health, but more in the manner of country-lore than systematic astrology. Hippocrates was cited to show how persistent north winds in summer brought rain, and hence hoarseness, coughs, consumptions and imposthumes. Other rules combined empirical weather lore with the astrological designation of lucky days, to ascertain the likelihood of sudden epidemics.[61] The simple aphorisms about the moon, plants, animals, weather and disease contained in writings on husbandry were probably a genuine reflection of English popular beliefs, rather than being dependent for their notions upon the more systematic astrological works then being published on the continent.

IV

The formal aspects of astrological belief are easily described. It is

---

[60] Nicholas Culpeper, *The English physitian enlarged* (1653), sig. [B8]v, p.375; Joseph Blagrave, *Blagrave's supplement or enlargement, to Mr. Nich. Culpeppers English physitian* (1674), especially p.233; see also idem, *Blagrave's Astrological Practice*. John Gerard, *The herball or generall historie of plantes* (1597), pp.936ff.

[61] See for example Boorde, *Principles*, chapter 13; Bourne, *An Almanac... 1571–1573*. Thomas Tusser, ... *His Good Points of Husbandry*, ed. D. Hartley (London, 1931), pp.151–6, 164; Hill, *Profitable Art of Gardening*, appendix, pp.45ff.

difficult, however, to establish the degree of confidence of the Elizabethan public in astrological physic. Was it as effective in the presence of the real crisis of disease as in the realm of academic discussion? It goes without saying that the failings of astrology must have become apparent, even to the most ardent devotee. But it was no more fallible than Galenic medicine. Indeed, in daily life astrological physic was rarely practised in isolation. By 1600 it had come to incorporate so much of the explanatory apparatus of classical medicine – especially the use of humours, elements, and their various affinities – that any thoroughgoing scepticism about the astrological system was likely to shake confidence in orthodox medicine. Though astrological medicines had developed as a gloss upon the classical corpus, the mutual borrowings of assumptions between the two systems had made it an indispensable gloss, which could not be removed without considerable embarrassment.

The degree of respect felt for astrology in the seventeenth century, fluctuated partly in accordance with the varying degrees of favour enjoyed by all the divinatory arts, and partly with the level of social tension. After a relative lull in the early Stuart period, interest in the astrological arts took a dramatic upward turn during the civil war and interregnum. The volume of astrological publications was then at its greatest, and certain reformers even advocated the inclusion of astrological teaching into the revised academic curriculum.[62] By the time of the Restoration, a comprehensive vernacular astrological corpus was available. All branches of this once obscure art had become available to English readers. In the post-Restoration treatises of Saunders and Blagrave, one sees both the ultimate systematization and the swan-song of astrological physic in England. By the end of the seventeenth century the explication of human afflictions in terms of celestial influences had ceased to be a serious part of medicine.

[62]   C. Webster, *The Great Instauration: Science, Medicine and Reform 1626–1660* (London, 1975), p.129.

9

Alchemical and Paracelsian medicine

CHARLES WEBSTER

The third kinde of *Magicke* containeth the whole philosophie of nature; not the brablings of the Aristotelians, but that which bringeth to light the inmost vertues, and draweth them out of natures hidden bosome to humane use, according to the Chymists, Albertus, Arnoldus de Villanova, Raymond, Bacon, and many others who understood the power of nature, and how to apply things that worke to things that suffer.

(Ralegh, *History of the World*, 1614, I, xi, 2)

The consolidation of the authority of Galen in the sixteenth century occasioned by the labours of such humanistic physicians as Linacre and Caius has tended to obscure the continuing relevance of alternative traditions in the practice of medicine at that period. The works of Galen, his editors, commentators, and disciples, flooded from the presses of Europe, and they came to dominate the teaching of medical faculties. The tenets of Galen were made to serve as a test of accreditation by colleges of physicians. But this system of knowledge was not the sole factor determining the character of medical practice. Galenic medicine was diluted, corrupted, even opposed by many other strands deriving from Arabic and Western sources during the Middle Ages. An important constituent part of this eclectic system was provided by alchemy.

It is tempting to believe that the rise of humanism, which was associated with the development of more critical, rational, and scientific standards in medicine, would have led to disenchantment with alchemy, and the relegation of alchemical medicine to the eccentric fringes of medical practice. But, as will be demonstrated below, the strength and importance of alchemical medicine has not been sufficiently appreciated. Alchemy not only failed to atrophy; it underwent, in a context of a rise of neo-Platonism, both revival and metamorphosis. To intellectuals like Sir Walter Ralegh, alchemical medicine was seen as a separate system of magical knowledge which challenged the values of Galenism and scholasticism, and had a superior ancient ancestry, a continuous history, and finally, full efflorescence in the medical philosophy of Paracelsus. Alchemical medicine and the Paracelsianism which it incubated, came to exercise a deep influence on medical practitioners and their public by the end of the sixteenth century.

Roger Bacon was the major authority cited by Englishmen as sanctioning the quest for eradication of disease and the prolongation of life by alchemical means. Bacon was venerated by subsequent generations of adepts and he was central to Ashmole's contention that 'no nation hath written more, or better' on alchemical subjects. However, Ashmole also believed that English alchemists had been too little honoured in their own country and that they had been reduced to 'covertly administering their medicine to a few sick, and healing them'.[1] The later medieval alchemical verse of Lydgate, Ripley, and Norton, is indicative of the seriousness with which practical aspects of the art were regarded. Norton commented that his older contemporary, Gilbert Kymer, had fallen short of Ramon Lull in his understanding of graduations, but conceded that 'in physic he had a noble mind' and had advanced knowledge of medicines.[2] Kymer, the only contemporary authority mentioned by Norton, was a leading figure in English medicine, and had been the architect of an abortive scheme for the establishment of a formally constituted society of physicians and surgeons practising in London.[3] Kymer also appears as one of a dozen signatories of a petition addressed to Henry VI, applying for a licence to practise alchemy. This petition gives valuable insight into the medical preoccupations of fifteenth-century alchemists, and testifies to the continuing relevance of Bacon's dreams about the perfectibility of human nature. The petition noted:

that in former times wise and famous philosophers in their writings and books, under figures and coverings, have left on record and taught that from wine, from precious stones, from oils, from vegetables, from animals, from metals, and from ordinary minerals, many glorious and notable medicines can be

---

[1] L. Thorndike, *A History of Magic and Experimental Science*, II (New York, 1923), pp.616–91. For useful background information on this general subject see C. Hill, *Intellectual Origins of the English Revolution* (Oxford, 1965); K. Thomas, *Religion and the Decline of Magic* (London, 1971). I am grateful to Walter Pagel, whose works are cited below, for general encouragement and specific comments on this essay. Elias Ashmole, *Theatrum chemicum britannicum* (1652), sig. A2r–v.

[2] *Theatrum chemicum britannicum*, p.57.

[3] A. B. Emden, *A Biographical Register of the University of Oxford to AD 1500* (2 vols., Oxford, 1958), II, pp.1068–9. G. H. Talbot and E. A. Hammond, *The Medical Practitioners in Medieval England* (London, 1965), pp.60–3.

made; and chiefly that a most precious medicine which some philosophers have called the Mother and Empress of Medicines, others have named it the Priceless Glory, but others have called it the Quintessence, others the Philosophers' Stone and Elixir of Life; of which potion the efficacy is so certain and wonderful, that by it all infirmities whatsoever are easily curable, human life is prolonged to its natural limit, and man wonderfully preserved in health and manly strength of body and mind, in vigour of limbs, clearness of memory, and keenness of intellect to the same degree; moreover, all kinds of wounds, which may be healed are healed without difficulty, and in addition it is the best and surest remedy against all kinds of poison.[4]

The above petition, and the licences which were granted subsequently, indicate both the importance of medicine in achieving official sanction for practical alchemy, and the unity of metallurgical and medical aspects of alchemy. Practitioners tended to be equally concerned with the production of medicinal oils by the method of circulation, and the purification of metals by the operation of 'medicines' in their furnaces.

In the first part of the sixteenth century, attention was temporarily shifted away from indigenous alchemical poetry by an increasing tide of hermetic and chemical literature produced on the continent.[5] Almost none of these works was at a sufficiently popular level to merit translation, although it is noteworthy that one of the outstanding practical handbooks, Brunschwig's *De destillandi*, was translated as early as 1527. Impetus to practical alchemy was supplied by the measures taken under Elizabeth I to diversify the economy. A high priority was given to the importation of 'foreign chemists and mineral masters' who were awarded grants for the exploitation of native mineral resources, not only salts, iron, copper, tin and lead, but also silver and gold. These projects were at least in part designed to provide an apprenticeship for dealing with the mineral resources of the New World. Immigrant technicians were active in stimulating interest in chemistry and chemical technology, areas which for the first time were absorbing substantial capital and manpower resources.

The two main groups of undertakers were respectively incorporated in 1568 into the Society of Mineral and Battery Works, and the Commonalty for the Mines Royal. Both companies were successful in exploiting economically profitable sources of base metals; they were even technically competent enough to locate and refine small amounts

4 T. Rymer (ed.), *Foedera* (20 vols., 1704–35), XI, pp.379–80. R. Steele, 'Alchemy in England', *The Antiquary*, XXIV (1891), 99–105; D. Geoghegan, 'A licence of Henry VI to practise alchemy', *Ambix*, VI (1957), 10–17.
5 L. Thorndike, 'Alchemy during the first half of the sixteenth century', *Ambix*, II (1938), 26–37.

of silver and gold.[6] These pioneer chemical undertakings were primarily concerned with prospecting, mining, and refining, but occasionally their sights were set on more complex operations. For instance, one partnership of merchants purchased a German recipe for the culture of saltpetre in artificial beds, which after feeding with a variety of cheap materials, would generate nitrous earth. This relatively simple manufacturing process offered independence from imported saltpetre, and hence greater security for the nation's gunpowder supplies. Nitre beds were never established on more than a limited scale in England, although on the continent they became the standard source for saltpetre supplies.[7]

An even more ambitious project involving earths and salt solutions was announced in 1571, when Sir Thomas Smith, Robert Dudley, William Cecil and Sir Humphrey Gilbert obtained a patent for the 'Society of the new art, discovered after long search by Smith, for making copper out of iron, and quicksilver out of antimony and lead'. Four years later it was reported that after 'long search in books of divers arts, divers trials... and manifold expense of his time and money', Smith, together with his assistant, William Medley, had perfected their technique. Under this scheme it was hoped to replace imported copper by copper 'transmuted' from native iron.[8] Medley was relying on the principle that iron could be used to secure the precipitation of copper from solutions of copper salts. As critics having a sounder understanding of the technical problems involved predicted, this project turned out to be an expensive failure.[9] By contrast, Sir Thomas Chaloner the younger, building on technical experience gained in Italy, succeeded in locating and exploiting deposits of alum at Guisborough in Yorkshire. Chaloner's friend, Sir Hugh Plat, was also successful in the investigation of the properties as agricultural fertilizers of the 'hidden treasures of minerals and their salts'.[10]

Projects requiring expertise in chemistry varied greatly in outcome,

---

6   *Calendar of Patent Rolls, Elizabeth*, IV, pp.211–12, 274–5. M. B. Donald, *Elizabethan Copper. The History of the Company of Mines Royal 1568–1605* (London, 1955); idem, *Elizabethan Monopolies: The History of the Company of Mineral and Battery Works from 1565 to 1604* (Edinburgh and London, 1961). See J. W. Gough, *The Rise of the Entrepreneur* (London, 1969), chapters 4–7, for a general survey.

7   *Cal. Pat. Rolls Eliz.*, II, pp.98, 104. A. R. Williams, 'The production of saltpetre in the Middle Ages', *Ambix*, XXII (1975), 125–33. Gough, *Rise of the Entrepreneur*, pp.204–7.

8   *Cal. Pat. Rolls Eliz.*, V, pp.483–5; VI, pp.509–10.

9   M. Dewar, *Sir Thomas Smith: A Tudor Intellectual in Office* (London, 1964), pp.149–55.

10 John Camden, *Britannia*, ed. E. Howe (1695), p.753. Gough, *Rise of the Entrepreneur*, pp.183–5. Sir Hugh Plat, *The jewell house of art and nature* (1594); quotation from p.58.

but whatever their degree of economic success, adventures in mining and refining, salt working, dyeing, brewing, and distilling, indicate the closing of the gap in expertise between English and continental practitioners. Technicians rarely limited themselves to one sphere of activity, and the heightened expectations relative to metallurgy tended to carry over into iatrochemistry. As in traditional alchemy, the two branches of the subject were inseparably linked by technique and practice. Thus one of the early immigrant technicians, Burchard Kranich, after mining for precious metals in Cornwall, established himself as a successful physician in London, where he was satirized as 'Dr Tocrub' in Bullein's *Dialogue Against the Fever Pestilence.* Kranich resumed his metallurgical activities in 1577 when, along with the Venetian alchemist and apothecary Giovanni Baptista Agnello, and the poet Sir Edward Dyer, he was consulted by the treasurer of the Mint on the quality of the gold ore brought back to England by Frobisher.[11]

Foreign iatrochemists were versatile, and not averse to advertising their skills. The letters of denization of Valentine Raseworme of Smalcalde described him as 'medicus, spagiricus, chirurgus, lithotomus, et ophthalmista'.[12] Figures such as Kranich, Raseworme, Agnello, or their contemporaries Elisaeus Bomelius and Cornelius de Alneto, were merely the most prominent and controversial representatives of a whole community of immigrant iatrochemists, astrologers, and natural magicians practising in the capital. Cornelius Drebbel, inventor of a perpetual motion, expert on dyeing, saltpetre and explosives, as well as chemical therapist, continued this tradition into the reign of James I. As medical practitioners the chemists attracted a wide following, influential patronage, and a reputation which endured despite opposition from medical authorities, or vilification in popular literature and in medical works by such writers as the surgeon William Clowes, or the physician John Jones. However this reaction against the more exotic members of the chemical fraternity should not be mistaken for total opposition to iatrochemistry. Clowes became a leading proponent of chemical therapy, while Jones was, like Paracelsus himself and Edward Jorden a few decades later, a student of the chemistry of mineral waters. Jones was also the author of a widely circulated manuscript alchemical work.

At the centre of the web of alchemical practice was John Dee (1527–1608). Dee represented the esoteric and practical aspirations of

---

[11] M. B. Donald, 'Burchard Kranick (*c.*1515–1578), miner and Queen's physician', *Annals of Science*, VI (1948–50), 308–22; *Cal. State Papers Dom. 1547–80*, pp.570, 571.
[12] *Cal. Pat. Rolls Eliz.*, VI, p.261, 25 Feb. 1574.

alchemy in their most sophisticated form. On the one hand Dee wrestled with the symbolic language of alchemy to secure insight into the pathway to spiritual harmony. On the other, he outlined projects which would maximize the economic potentialities of mathematical and experimental science. His work therefore encapsulated the religious and imperialistic ambitions of his generation.[13] Dee was recognized as a man of prodigious talent. His scientific library and laboratory at Mortlake were among the finest in Europe. He offered his services to rescue antiquities, or to discover hidden treasure and mineral deposits. He was consulted by the court on medical matters, and his circle of acquaintance included the leading English navigators of the time. Over the years his alchemical associates included Sir Philip Sidney, Sir Edward Dyer, Sir Thomas Chaloner, John Gwynn, Adrian Gilbert, William Blomfild, Thomas Twyne, John Chomley, and Robert Garland. Gabriel Harvey regarded him as the supreme exponent of the 'mystical and supermetaphysical philosophy'.[14]

Thomas Mouffet recorded that the young Sidney, not content with ordinary knowledge, pressed towards an understanding of innermost causes in nature by means of knowledge of chemistry, 'that astral science by which nature could be emulated' (eoque nomine chemiam, astralem illam naturaeque aemulam scientiam). In this study God was the ultimate guide, Dee the teacher, and Dyer a companion (Deo duce, Dio praeceptore, Diero socio).[15]

Sidney maintained the closest ties with his sister Mary, wife of Henry Herbert, Earl of Pembroke.[16] Wilton under Mary Herbert became an important intellectual centre – being variously described as a 'college' or 'university'. Alchemy and medicine were of central concern to this academy. Of Mary, Aubrey recorded that her 'genius lay as much towards chemistry, as poetry'. Her chief protégé was Thomas Mouffet, the famous naturalist, who will be discussed below as the major English exponent of Paracelsian medicine. Mary's household also contained Adrian Gilbert, half-brother of Ralegh and brother of Sir Humphrey Gilbert, described by Aubrey as 'a great chemist' who 'did many admirable cures with his chemical medicines'. At a lower level was one

---

[13] For recent introductions to the literature on Dee, see P. J. French, *John Dee: The World of an Elizabethan Magus* (London, 1972); A. G. Debus (ed.), *John Dee 'The Mathematicall Preface'* (New York, 1975).

[14] E. J. L. Scott (ed.), *Letter-book of Gabriel Harvey*, Camden Society, new ser., XXXIII (1884), p.71.

[15] V. B. Heltzel and H. H. Hudson, *Nobilis or A View of the Life and Death of a Sidney . . . by Thomas Moffet* (San Marino, Calif., 1940), p.13.

[16] John Jones dedicated to Henry Herbert his *Bathes of bathes ayde* (1572).

Boston, son of a Salisbury brewer, 'who was a great chemist: and did great cures by his art', but who eventually lost his entire fortune in the search for the philosophers' stone.[17]

At the turn of the century Roger Cooke, one of Dee's assistants, became employed as distiller to Henry Percy, ninth Earl of Northumberland, and Sir Walter Ralegh, during their imprisonment in the Tower of London. Ralegh had long been acquainted with Dee and the chemists Gilbert and Hester. His chemical notebooks date back to 1592. He persuaded the Lieutenant of the Tower to allow him to convert a hen-house into a still house, where he studied the chemistry of metals and prepared his celebrated cordials and other medicinal preparations. Among his scientific collaborators at the Tower was Peter Turner, one of Mouffet's closest associates.[18]

The above evidence illustrates the degree to which alchemy, in both its practical and esoteric forms, was an entrenched interest within court circles. The Queen employed Dee and Kranich as consultants, and was curious about Cornelius de Alneto and others who claimed knowledge of the art of transmutation.[19] Politicians such as Cecil, Dudley, Walsingham and Smith were avidly concerned with investment in chemical enterprises. Gabriel Harvey, mirroring Dee, offered his services to Sir Robert Cecil, claiming skill 'in the true Chymique without imposture (which I learned of Sir Thomas Smith not to condemn) and other effectual practicable knowledge'.[20] Within the ranks of the gentry, such figures as Sir Hugh Plat and Sir Thomas Chaloner sought to turn expertise in alchemy to practical advantage. They collected alchemical manuscripts, and engaged in philosophical speculation, but were also active in the medical and economic fields. Plat was the most resourceful patentee of his generation, while Chaloner, besides his interests in alum, was an associate of Drebbel, as well as

[17] John Aubrey, *Natural History of Wiltshire*, ed. J. Britton (1847), p.90; idem, *Brief Lives*, ed. A. Clark (2 vols., Oxford, 1898), II, pp.310–13. J. Buxton, *Sir Philip Sidney and the English Renaissance* (London, 1966), pp.173–204.

[18] Hill, *Intellectual Origins*, p.146; P. Lefranc, *Sir Walter Raleigh Ecrivain* (Paris, 1968), pp.436–40, 678–82; J. W. Shirley, 'The scientific experiments of Sir Walter Ralegh, the wizard Earl, and the three magi in the Tower, 1603–1617', *Ambix*, IV (1949–51), 52–66. For an alchemical notebook of Percy, see below, note 33.

[19] For Alneto (Lannoy), see *Cal. State Papers Dom. 1547–1580*, pp.249, 256, 273, 275–7, 289, 292; *Addenda 1566–79*, p.10. For other alchemists see *CSPD 1547–80*, pp.543, 570, 571 (G. B. Agnello); p.77 (John Dethicke); p.269 (John Bulkeley); p.403 (Johann Peterson); *CSPD 1580–1625*, *Addenda*, p.274 (Scory); *CSPD 1591–4*, pp.376, 422, 435, 488 (J. and R. Peterson). Both Alneto and Agnello published minor alchemical works: Agnello, *Expositione sopra un libro intitolato Apocalypsis spiritus secreti* (1566), trans. as 'J. B. Lambye', *Revelation of the Secret Spirit* (1623); for Alneto see below, note 35.

[20] G. C. Moore Smith, *Gabriel Harvey's Marginalia* (Stratford upon Avon, 1913), pp.72–4.

author of a work extolling the medicinal virtues of saltpetre, and adviser to Prince Henry on a project to separate silver from lead ore.[21]

Within the church, devotees of alchemy ranged from Edward Cradock, Lady Margaret Professor at Oxford, and John Thornborough, Bishop of Worcester, to the humble priest William Blomfild. Thornborough was the author of one of the most obscure alchemical works of the Jacobean period, while Blomfild's *Blossoms* was widely disseminated, even before its inclusion in Ashmole's *Theatrum chemicum*. Other alchemical poems included in Ashmole's volume which were indicative of the revival of alchemy in the mid-sixteenth century were Thomas Charnock's 'Breviary of Natural Philosophy', and shorter poems by Edward Kelly, John Dee and Thomas Robinson.[22] Not included by Ashmole was the 'Key of Alchemie' by Samuel Norton, a descendant of the author of the celebrated *Ordinal*. Another of Blomfild's major writings, 'Quintessence, or Regiment of Life' passed into the collection of rare manuscripts of his kinsman Miles Blomefield, who practised obscurely as a physician or 'cunning man' at Chelmsford.[23] In the nearby town of Saffron Walden lived Gabriel Harvey, another student of alchemy, who retired into Essex to practise medicine after his failure to obtain academic preferment at Cambridge.

The degree to which alchemy captured the interest of the Elizabethan intellectual would hardly be suspected from the handful of alchemical works published in the vernacular. The only important alchemical works published in English before 1600 were George Ripley's *Compound of Alchemy* (1591), edited by Ralph Rabbards, 'studious and expert in alchemical arts', and *The Mirror of Alchemy* (1597; translator unknown), which was a representative collection of medieval writings containing *Speculum alchemiae*, the Smaragdine Table, the commentary of Hortulanus on the Table, the Book of Secrets of Alchemy attributed to King Calid, and the 'Excellent discourse of the admirable force and efficacy of Art and Nature'.[24] This collection reflects the growing

[21] *A short discourse of the most rare vertue of nitre* (1584); *Biographia Britannia*, 2nd edn, ed. A. Kippis (1778–93), III, pp.419–22. For Plat, see C. F. Mullett, 'Hugh Plat: Elizabethan virtuoso', *University of Missouri Studies*, XXI (1947), 93–118.

[22] For Charnock (1526–1581), who described himself as 'student in the science of astronomy, physic and natural philosophy', see F. Sherwood Taylor, 'Thomas Charnock', *Ambix*, II (1946), 148–76.

[23] R. M. Schuler, 'William Blomfild Elizabethan alchemist', *Ambix*, XXII (1973), 75–87; I. Gray, 'Footnote to an alchemist', *Cambridge Review*, 30 Nov. 1946, pp.172–4; D. C. Baker and J. L. Murphy, 'The books of Myles Blomfylde', *The Library*, XXXI (1976), 377–85.

[24] The contents of the *Mirror* are very similar to those of the *Alchemia* issued by Johannes Petreus at Nuremberg in 1541, and of other, later alchemical collections. *Alchemia* contained the first published edition of *Speculum alchemiae*. *Epistolae de secretis operibus* was first published in 1542.

interest in Roger Bacon. The *Speculum* was an attributive work, while the *Epistolae de secretis operibus artis et naturae* became one of the most widely known of Bacon's works. A further medical work by Bacon, *De retardatione accidentium senectutis*, had already appeared in part in English in 1540. The full Latin text was published in Oxford in 1590, edited by John Williams the future Principal of Jesus College, Oxford.[25] In this latter work Bacon made constant reference to the *Secreta secretorum*, which he regarded without reservation as one of Aristotle's major writings. Bacon, along with many other medieval scholars, had produced a commentary on the *Secreta secretorum*. English editions of this wide-ranging courtesy book which touched briefly on alchemy, and much more extensively on medicine and hygiene, were issued in 1527 and 1570.[26]

The extent of a general diffusion of interest in alchemy and magic is indicated by the exploitation of the dramatic potentialities of these subjects in popular literature, ranging from Marlowe's *Dr Faustus* (*c.*1588), Greene's *Friar Bacon and Friar Bungay* (1589) and Lyly's *Gallathea* (1592), to Jonson's *Alchemist* (1610). Marlowe's *Faustus* brilliantly captured the spirit of writers such as Agrippa von Nettesheim. Platonists of the late sixteenth century paved the way for the deployment of alchemical imagery in the work of the metaphysical poets.[27] While some authors, like Lyly, displayed little real knowledge of alchemy, relying on easily accessible sources, or topical allusions, Gabriel Harvey, Donne, and Jonson, whether writing in a satirical vein or not, drew upon extensive reading of alchemical and hermetic sources.

English language publications were of little importance in diffusing alchemical lore, compared with works imported from the continent, manuscript collections, or even oral tradition within the many groups of adepts. By the turn of the century a large corpus of Latin alchemical literature had been built up; these editions found their way in large numbers into English libraries. Although vernacular writings were of less significance, it is interesting to note that Sir Christopher Hatton's extensive collection of Italian books contained *Il regimento della peste*

[25] Arnold of Villanova, *Defence of age and recovery of youth* (1540); *Libellus de retardandis senectutis accidentibus* (Oxford, 1590), see F. Madan, *Oxford Books* (3 vols., Oxford, 1895–1931), I, p.29. For Williams see A. Wood, *Athenae Oxonienses*, ed. Bliss (4 vols., Oxford, 1813–20), II, p.132.

[26] T. P. Harrison Jr, 'The Folger Secret of Secrets', in J. G. McManaway *et al.* (eds.), *Joseph Quincy Adams Memorial Studies* (Washington, 1948), pp.601–20. *Secreta secretorum* was much better known in the previous century, when it was widely copied in translations by many different hands.

[27] L. V. Sadler, 'Alchemy and Greene's *Friar Bacon and Friar Bungay*', *Ambix*, XXII (1975), 111–24. For further literature see below, note 55.

(1571), *Della fisica* (1582) and *Tesoro della vita humana* (1582), all by Fioravanti.[28] The libraries of John Dee, Thomas Twyne and Robert Burton, to which further reference will be made below, are illustrative of private collections rich in works on alchemy, astrology and natural magic.

The educated classes would have had little difficulty in obtaining access to collections of medieval alchemical writings such as the *Alchemia* (1541) of Johannes Petreus, or the *Verae alchemiae* (1561) of Guilielmus Gratarolus; to pioneering works on distillation and chemical technology by Biringuccio, Brunschwig, Ulstad, or Agricola; or to books of secrets and natural magic from medieval sources, or by Levinus Lemnius, Antoine Mizauld, J. J. Wecker and G. B. della Porta. Such works were widely available in private collections or institutional libraries.

Of greater importance than might be expected was the circulation of alchemical works in manuscript form. Sixteenth-century alchemical manuscripts have survived in surprisingly large numbers. For instance there have been traced twenty-four copies of Ripley's *Compound of Alchemy*, thirty-one of Norton's *Ordinal of Alchemy*, and sixteen of Blomfild's *Blossoms*. The great majority of these were produced in the sixteenth century. Latin works, such as the alchemical writings of Geber, Roger Bacon, or the *Liber de consideratione quintae essentiae* of Johannes of Ruprescissa survive to a similar extent.[29] The works of Ripley and Norton were copied in the later part of the century by such diverse individuals as Dee, Simon Forman, and Richard Walton, in London, and Francis Thynne (Lancaster Herald) at Longleat.

John Dee and Simon Forman represented the two ends of the social spectrum of London *magi*. Both built up large collections of alchemical manuscripts.[30] In one of the large number of manuscripts which he

---

[28] W. D. Hassall, *A Catalogue of the Library of Sir Edward Coke*, Yale Law Library Publication, no. 12 (New Haven, 1950), nos. 814, 815, 1113. This library absorbed many books from the library of Hatton. Other representative items of alchemical relevance include: H. Brunschwig, *De destillandi*; G. Gratarolus, *Alchemiae*; J. Lacinius, *Prestiosa margarita*; M. A. del Rio, *Disquisitiones magicae*; G. B. della Porta, *Magia naturalis*; V. Biringuccio, *Pyrotechnia*; and C. Agrippa, *De incertitudine et vanitate scientiarum*.

[29] D. W. Singer, *Catalogue of Latin and Vernacular Alchemical Manuscripts in Great Britain and Ireland dating before the XVI Century* (Brussels, 1928–31); R. H. Robbins, 'Alchemical texts in Middle English verse: corrigenda and addenda', *Ambix*, XIII (1965), 62–73; J. Reidy (ed.), *Thomas Norton: Ordinal of Alchemy*, Early English Text Society (London, 1975), Introduction; Schuler, 'William Blomfild'.

[30] The catalogue of the manuscripts of John Dee compiled in 1583 is contained in J. O. Halliwell, *The Private Diary of Dr John Dee*, Camden Society, XIX (1842), pp.65–89. The bulk of Forman's collections is contained in the Ashmole Manuscripts, Bodleian Library. For details see W. H. Black, *Catalogue of the Manuscripts ... bequeathed by E. Ashmole* (Oxford, 1845).

assiduously copied, Forman described himself as 'practiser in physic, chirurgery and astronomy, and searcher of the secrets of nature for the ph'ers stone'.[31] Many surviving alchemical manuscripts are probably the nuclei of small collections, which were annotated and expanded according to the tastes of the owner. Between 1560 and 1565 the London haberdasher Richard Walton compiled a volume which consisted mainly of works by Ripley, Norton and Lull, as well as miscellaneous notes about Walton's family, and a scattering of medical recipes.[32] Similar collections were in the possession of the aristocrat Henry Percy, and of two families of minor Suffolk gentry at different times in the later sixteenth century.[33]

The tendency of even modest integral collections of papers to contain Latin and English alchemical writings in verse from the medieval period, extracts from Renaissance and even contemporary works, as well as miscellaneous practical notes based on direct experience or the advice of informants, indicates the vitality of the alchemical tradition in the later sixteenth century. For instance Robert Garland, who described himself as 'practitioner in the art of spagerick', compiled a collection which comprised mainly English translations of medieval Latin works, some of them copied from transcriptions made by his friend Thomas Robson, as well as alchemical notes derived from Walton and Ralegh, recipes for chemical medicines containing antimony and mercury, and instructions by Garland himself for preparing a quintessence.[34]

Robson compiled a collection which, besides medieval works, contained recent and unpublished English alchemical writings by William Blomfild and John Jones, a translation made in 1575 of an important work on antimony by Suchten, a translation of Alneto on the Divine Elixir, and extracts from Thomas Lupton's *Book of a Thousand Sundry Things* (1597).[35] The manuscript of the London apothecary, Edward Barlow, for 1588–9 contains details of prescriptions dispensed for leading London physicians, a variety of medieval alchemical texts, a translation of Paracelsus, and a catalogue of Barlow's books, indicating

---

[31] Oxford, Bodleian Library, MS. Ashmole 1490, fol. 36b.
[32] Bodleian, MS. Ashmole 1479.
[33] Philadelphia University, E. F. Smith Library, MS. E. F. Smith 4 (Eng.). Edinburgh University Library, MS. Laing III 164.
[34] Bodleian, MS. Ashmole 1686, I. Aubrey, *Brief Lives*, II, p.203, credits Robson with the introduction into England of the art of making Venetian glass.
[35] Bodleian, MS. Ashmole 1418. Alexander Suchten, *Liber unus de secreto antimonii* (1570). Cornelius Alnetanus, 'Epistola de conficiendo divino elixire sive lapide philosophico' (1565), dedicated to Elizabeth; first published in *Secreta secretorum Raymundi Lulli et hermetis philosophorum in libros tres divisa* (1592).

his familiarity with recent alchemical and pharmacological publications.[36] Collections having a bias towards later sixteenth-century materials were drawn together by Sir Hugh Plat and Sir Thomas Chaloner, both of whose activities as chemists bore fruit in published works.[37] Gabriel Harvey possessed a small collection containing the work attributed to Solomon entitled the 'Key to Knowledge', 'This book of Doctor Caius' containing extracts from Agrippa, as well as miscellaneous conjurations; 'An excellent book of the art of magic' in the hand of Forman; and a collection of 'Visions' seen by Harvey and his skryer John Davis – possibly the navigator, who was also an associate of Dee.[38]

Surviving alchemical collections from the later sixteenth century tended to be constructed according to a typical pattern. They would contain extracts (or more rarely complete texts) from medieval English alchemical verse, texts or translations of medieval Latin alchemical works, excerpts from Renaissance authors, magical and astrological notes, and practical information about chemical and medicinal preparations. Alchemical 'secrets', like medical 'cures', were eagerly sought for, and carefully entered into their manuscripts by grateful recipients. Knowledge which was only rarely reflected in the vernacular literature of chemistry or medicine was rapidly propagated throughout a wide circle of alchemical practitioners, by oral transmission or correspondence. Consequently alchemical manuscripts provide ample information about the real or supposed sources of cures – Ralegh's cordial being perhaps the most celebrated example – as well as notes about informants indicating the extent of the following attracted by alchemy and especially alchemical medicine. Expensive secrets such as *aurum potabile* were the ultimate nostrum for the rich patient, and cheap secrets were the last resort of the poor. The knowledge that a medicine had undergone chemical preparation by the adept himself reinforced the purchaser's faith in the virtues of such a remedy. The phials of quintessences produced by the chemist gave by their appearance and qualities every promise of efficacy and potency.

Respect for alchemical medicine was diffused through all ranks of society. Not all 'secrets' were chemically prepared, but by the end of the

[36] Bodleian, MS. Ashmole 1487.

[37] For the Chaloner collection, see London, British Library, MS. Sloane 1198; and for Plat, MS. Sloane 2203. Plat's manuscript contains, besides miscellaneous chemical and cosmetical recipes, an abstract of Norton, extracts from Porta's *Magia naturalis*, and notes about Duchesne.

[38] British Library, MS. Add. 36, 674, fols. 5–63. The Caius manuscript passed to Harvey from Thomas Legg, who succeeded Caius as Master of Gonville and Caius College.

century distilled cordials and quintessences were predominant. It was a remarkable token of faith in alchemical medicine that Sir Walter Ralegh was allowed to dispense cordials for the dying Prince Henry during the former's imprisonment in the Tower of London. At about the same time a violent dispute arose over the increasing popularity of *aurum potabile*. The College of Physicians of London, with its traditional Galenic loyalties, was the body which stood to lose most by the efflorescence of alchemical medicine, and its Fellows mounted an attack on Francis Anthony and his *aurum potabile*. But they could neither quench the tradition nor afford not to take advantage of its benefits. Behind the scenes the Fellows of the College were scrambling to secure information about chemical cures and secrets. Significantly, in 1601 the statutes of the College were revised to remove the prohibition on Fellows engaging in the practice of alchemy, or the use of quintessences in treatment. Among the Fellows, Thomas Mouffet had paid £150 for the book of secrets of his friend Thomas Penny. William Harvey charged the dying Sir William Smith a large fee for treating him with a highly secret remedy. Prominent members of the College like Sir William Paddy collected alchemical books and manuscripts; and it was reported that William Gilbert 'addicted himself to chemistry, attaining to great exactness therein'.[39] Robert Fludd and Theodore de Mayerne confirmed the conversion of the Collegiate physicians to alchemical medicine.

Outside the College alchemical medicine was endemic. Its devotees extended from the monarchs of England and Scotland, through court circles, the aristocracy, gentry, scholars, churchmen and religious nonconformists, to lawyers like John Gwynn or Richard Bostocke, surgeons, apothecaries, and distillers. In its elementary form chemical medicine guaranteed the reputation of the poor practitioner among the poorest classes. Bullein's characterization of empirics of 1564 was already emphasizing their dependence on a small range of chemical medicines of a kind which was later regarded as the stock-in-trade of the Paracelsians: 'Small is their knowledge, much less is their speed. Yet lack they no brimstone, quicksilver, or litharge'.[40]

[39] C. J. Sisson, 'The magic of Prospero', *Shakespeare Survey*, XI (1958), 170–7; idem, 'Shakespeare's Helena and Dr William Harvey', in M. St Clare Byrne (ed.), *Essays and Studies* (London, 1960), pp.1–20. Lefranc, *Sir Walter Ralegh Ecrivain*, pp.678–82. For Gilbert, see Thomas Fuller, *Worthies of England* (2 vols., 1811), I, p.352. Oxford, St John's College, MS. 172, contains Paddy's copy of Johannes de Rupescissa's *Liber de consideratione quintae essentiae*. Paddy was a friend of the Rosicrucian alchemists Robert Fludd and Michael Maier. Paddy's friend, the royal physician Sir Matthew Lister, married the alchemist Mary, widow of the Earl of Pembroke. For the College and alchemy, see Sir G. Clark, *A History of the Royal College of Physicians of London*, I (Oxford, 1964), pp.97, 384.

[40] William Bullein, *Bulwark* (1564), sig. A6v.

The above evidence illustrates the pervasiveness of interest in alchemy in England in the later part of the sixteenth century. If there was a slight lag in the alchemical movement in the earlier part of the century, this was more than compensated for by the enthusiasm of adepts during the reign of Elizabeth. The impetus given to alchemy at this time created a momentum which continued without interruption until the end of the seventeenth century. The ridicule heaped upon impostors and the gullible fringes of this movement by satirists should not disguise the seriousness with which alchemical writings were studied, and their manipulative practices cultivated. As with astrology criticism affected the art only in its more naive and unsophisticated form.

The esoteric aspect of alchemy blended well with currents of religious thought which were gaining ground during the Reformation, and with the neo-Platonic philosophy which was beginning to attract the intelligentsia. The rather ramshackle edifice of hermetic and alchemical writings was stimulating, even exhilarating, to generations breaking away from the highly organized didactic regimen of scholasticism. It is not accidental that alchemy was taken up by those searching for new modes of philosophical expression, such as the Ramist Gabriel Harvey, and radical reformers within the church like William Blomfild.

Intellectually alchemy played an important unifying role. Its various branches drew upon many different intellectual skills. Its devotees included linguists, astrologers and mathematicians, as well as natural philosophers. It also entailed collaboration between the scholar and the technician. In the medical context alchemy was important in generating a concept of disease and therapy, based on such principles as sympathy and antipathy, or the macrocosm/microcosm analogy, which was the sophisticated counterpart of that which prevailed in the lower ranks of society. This confluence of ideas might have provided the basis for the protective attitude of the influential layman towards unqualified medical practitioners.

In the sixteenth century the complex world of alchemical symbolism was not regarded as an antiquated and primitive encumbrance, but rather as a key to ancient and fundamental truths which would only be revealed to those whose life was sanctified, and whose seriousness of purpose was guaranteed by dedication to manual and intellectual labour. This exercise demanded a range of intellectual skills which offered considerable opportunities for intellectual gratification. The medical relevance of alchemy lies not simply in its practical concern with chemical therapy, but also in its aim to create a total and harmonious relationship between man and the universe. This theosophic element was important in securing the serious commitment of the practitioner, and in introducing a convincing ritual context for the treatment of disease. But success in the practical field was obviously relevant to the generation of confidence in the esoteric aspect of alchemy. Indeed the manipulative branch of alchemy proved to be so fruitful that its gold-making dimension could be allowed to fall into the background. By the end of the sixteenth century techniques and apparatus were sufficiently refined for practitioners to embark on analysis of the chemical properties of natural products with every expectation that they would recover a variety of useful and valuable substances. Like Sir Hugh Plat they saw the world as a 'jewel house of nature' which, if subjected to chemical analysis, would yield a variety of potent medicines and reveal the secrets of vegetation. Hence man and his plants could be moulded towards perfection, so reversing the effects of the Fall, and vindicating Roger Bacon's claim that man's lifespan could be greatly extended.[41]

Although Francis Bacon was deeply suspicious of some of the pretensions of the alchemists, he was forced to concede that 'out of respect for that art' he was 'unwilling to include it among the unproductive philosophies, since, in fact, it has produced not a few useful inventions for the benefit of mankind'.[42] As confidence in their technical skills increased, many of the alchemists adopted the same attitude as Bacon to their art. Thus Plat announced that he was resolved to align himself with those authors who 'seek out the practical and operative part of nature', and he intended to leave to one side questions of theory which had been debated eagerly in every age. Plat (again like Bacon) admired authors like della Porta, who took delight in seeing 'a rarity spring out of their own labours', and who could 'provoke nature to play and show some of her pleasing varieties, when she hath met with a stirring workman'.[43]

This point of view was reiterated in a medical context by Sir Thomas Smith, who used his embassy to France in 1572 to improve his knowledge of practical chemistry, and to familiarize himself with recent publications: 'there can by that art be made and brought to pass most strange, wondrous, and incredible things both [*sic*] I have had experience myself and have read much more'. Some of the most immediate benefits of alchemy were accruing to medicine. 'For my

[41] Plat, *Jewel House of Art and Nature*. See Plate 4.
[42] Francis Bacon, *Cogitata et visa* (1607), in *Works*, ed. J. Spedding, R. L. Ellis and D. D. Heath (14 vols., 1857–74), III, pp.605–6.
[43] Sir Hugh Plat, *The Garden of Eden* (1608), quoted from 1675 edn, sig. A5r–A6v.

health I have found more help in it than all the physic hitherto in my life essayed'. Smith employed two servants as operators at his still house, communicating to them instructions regarding technical procedures for the production of quintessences and magisteria, and concerning the location and cultivation of plants such as eyebright, celandine and angelica, which were thought to yield useful medicines.[44]

The vigorous tradition of English alchemy promoted chemical therapy, and created an intellectual atmosphere which was ideal for the incubation of Paracelsianism. This receptivity to Paracelsianism is not surprising in view of the debt of Paracelsus to late medieval alchemy, and the close relationship which he and his adherents maintained with other currents in the alchemical movement. It would be arbitrary and misleading to regard Paracelsus and his followers as a sharply defined group of modernists who were distinctly polarized from a decaying alchemical tradition. Paracelsus was nevertheless important for his synthesis of alchemical and neo-Platonic elements into a consistent medical philosophy, which presented a viable alternative to the increasingly entrenched system of the Galenic humanists.[45] The formulations of Paracelsus had the disadvantages of imperfect systematization, and discordance with ideas which had been absorbed into the traditional framework of education. On the other hand Paracelsus expressed his medical and philosophical views in language which had a wide appeal among diverse groups searching for social values and modes of philosophizing which were in harmony with the Reformation. Paracelsian medicine emerged as the natural complement to the world view of Florentine Platonists, or the spiritual reformers. Paracelsianism was also in keeping with the new spirit of cultural assertiveness of the nations of northern Europe. Paracelsians dismissed Galenism as a relic of the decaying pagan, or Romanish Mediterranean culture. Theirs was the medicine of the reformed Christianity of the Germanic cultures. Paracelsus wrote in the vernacular, in a form accessible to a broad social spectrum, and in terms which could be connected with their values and needs. It is therefore not surprising that his writings should have had a particular appeal in England, and that the

[44] Letters from Smith to Richard Eden, 9 March 1572, from Smith to Robert Parsons, 17 May 1572, quoted from Dewar, *Sir Thomas Smith*, pp.140, 142–3. It is interesting to note that Smith found recently published writings of Lull 'worth their weight in pure gold'.

[45] The most important of the many recent studies on Paracelsus is Walter Pagel, *Paracelsus* (Basel, 1958). For the outlook of Oswald Croll, a leading Paracelsian popularizer, see O. Hannaway, *The Chemists and the Word* (Baltimore, 1975).

proponents of alchemical medicine should increasingly have become identified as 'Paracelsians' by friends and foes alike.

The assault which Paracelsus mounted on Galenic medicine escalated into a dramatic confrontation in the second part of the sixteenth century. Latin editions of his writings flooded from the presses, and at the turn of the century authoritative collected editions were issued in both Latin and German. From the ranks of adherents of alchemical medicine there emerged an effective group of commentators and popularizers. Paracelsians like Theodor Zwinger at Basel, and Johann Hartmann at Marburg, held important university posts; Joseph Duchesne in France and Petrus Severinus in Denmark were royal physicians; alchemical physicians dominated the courts of Rudolph II and the Czars.[46] Even cautious humanists like Conrad Gesner and Felix Platter became advocates of chemical therapy, and they became moderately sympathetic towards Paracelsus. Strongly developed Paracelsian movements emerged in most countries in northern Europe, which the representatives of official medicine were unable to suppress.[47]

Was the position similar in England? It is manifest that Paracelsus became a dominant influence in English medicine after 1640.[48] But detailed studies by Kocher and Debus of the earlier vernacular medical literature have suggested that the impact of Paracelsus was very much less marked before the Puritan Revolution. There is some evidence for the negative position. There were no translations of genuine works by Paracelsus before 1640, and only a handful of translations of spurious writings, or works by Paracelsian authors. Only two original works in English by English authors of a Paracelsian nature were issued; neither came from the pen of a medical man, and neither was devoted exclusively to an exposition of Paracelsian medicine. The Paracelsian works which were available in English tended to be little more than collections of recipes, without any detailed exposition of the natural philosophy or medical theories of Paracelsus.[49]

---

[46] See especially R.J.W. Evans, *Rudolf II and his World* (Oxford, 1973). See also: H.R. Trevor-Roper, 'The Sieur de la Riviere, Paracelsian physician of Henry IV', in A. G. Debus (ed.), *Science, Medicine and Society ... Essays to honor Walter Pagel* (2 vols., New York, 1972), II, pp.227–50; N. A. Figurovski, 'The alchemist and physician Arthur Dee', *Ambix*, XIII (1961), 35–51; N. Evans, 'Dr Timothy Willis and his mission to Russia', *Oxford Slavonic Papers*, II (1969), 39–61.

[47] The only detailed national study is Sten Lindroth, *Paracelsismen i Sverige Till 1600 – Talets Mit* (Uppsala, 1943). See also W. Hubicki, 'Paracelsists in Poland', in Debus (ed.), *Science, Medicine and Society*, I, pp.167–75.

[48] See C. Webster, *The Great Instauration: Science, Medicine and Reform 1626–1660* (London, 1975), pp.273–88.

[49] P. H. Kocher, 'Paracelsian medicine in England: (ca.1570–1600)', *Journal of the History of Medicine*, II (1947), 451–80; A. G. Debus, *The English Paracelsians* (London, 1965).

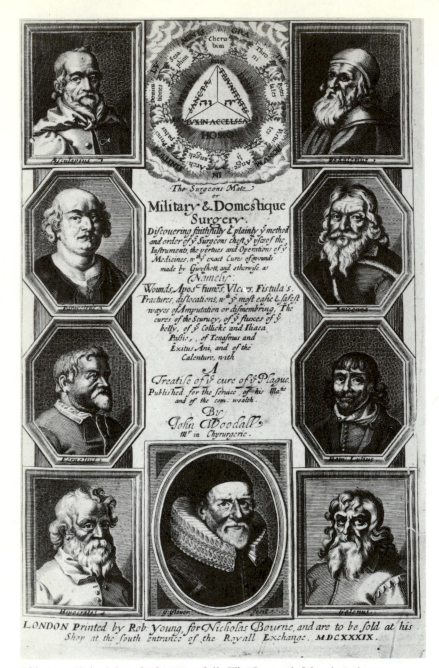

Plate 11. Title-page of John Woodall, *The Surgeon's Mate* (1639)

The 1639 edition of the surgeon John Woodall's popular handbook was for the first time furnished with an elaborate engraved title-page, making use of symbolism perhaps derived from Croll's *Basilica chymica* (1609), and including portraits of Paracelsus and the alchemist Lull, in addition to more orthodox medical authorities. Reproduced by courtesy of the Wellcome Trustees.

Perhaps the most important manifestation of the influence of Paracelsus was the increasing inclusion of Paracelsian remedies in the handbooks composed by leading English surgeons such as Banister, Clowes and Woodall (see Plate 11). Both Kocher and Debus believe that the acceptance of the useful part of Paracelsian medicine was delayed by distrust of the associated alchemical cosmology and occultism, which was distasteful to the increasingly pragmatically-minded Elizabethans. Dee and Fludd are portrayed as isolated mystics who were driven by unpopularity at home to publish their work abroad. Hence the emergence of iatrochemistry in England is thought to be correlated with the discarding of 'mystical alchemy'.[50] It is suggested that in the 'Elizabethan compromise' worked out by reputable surgeons and physicians, chemical remedies of accredited usefulness were absorbed into practice, while extraneous elements were rejected. This compromise must have contained a very small Paracelsian ingredient, since it is freely admitted that the chemical remedies were derived from a variety of sources; few of them can be proved to have had an exclusively Paracelsian ancestry.[51] Thus it might be tempting to conclude from the work of Kocher and Debus that Paracelsian medicine exercised only a limited appeal in England before the Puritan Revolution.

However, as indicated by Appendix II to the present chapter, accumulated findings about Paracelsian influences upon the vernacular medical literature suggest a by-no-means insubstantial impact, especially during the last twenty-five years of the sixteenth century. Not only was Paracelsus widely mentioned, but his ideas were also publicized in some of the most important medical works, and by leading medical authorities. Evidence from a variety of sources confirms that the trend evident in the vernacular literature is symptomatic of a wider receptivity to Paracelsian ideas. The vernacular medical literature gives only an incomplete impression of the development of interest in Paracelsian medicine, just as a census of published alchemical treatises in the vernacular would undervalue the contemporary interest in alchemy. Exigencies of the book trade required translators to concentrate on more practical Paracelsian works, which were seen as useful supplements to the more traditional books of recipes for which there was already an insatiable public demand. Thus Paracelsus himself, and even effective

[50] P. H. Kocher, *Science and Religion in Elizabethan England* (San Marino, Calif., 1953), pp.71, 91. Debus, *The English Paracelsians*, pp.49, 80–1, 86–7, 101–5, 127. Idem, Introduction to his edition of Ashmole, *Theatrum chemicum britannicum*, Johnson Reprint Corporation, Sources of Science, no. 37 (New York, 1967), pp.xxiv–xxv.

[51] Debus, *The English Paracelsians*, pp.49–85.

exponents of Paracelsian medical theory like Severinus, were excluded in favour of spurious writings and tracts by eclectic authors like Fioravanti, whose works were largely collections of chemical remedies. Stationers and translators would have appreciated that the educated reader interested in the natural philosophy of Paracelsus would have easy access to the Latin editions which were readily available from the presses of Europe. Hence published vernacular translations give as little insight into the degree of interest in the medical philosophy of Paracelsus as they would into the level of understanding of Aristotle, Plato, or the works of humanistic medical writers.

There is every indication that the works of Paracelsus were collected, studied and appreciated by English readers in the later sixteenth century. Works by Paracelsus occur commonly in private library catalogues of the period, and ultimately many of these sixteenth-century editions of Paracelsus found their way into libraries at Oxford and Cambridge.[52] Among the college libraries at each of the two universities are distributed copies of about twenty smaller collections of works, and a lesser number of the major collected editions. *Chirurgia magna* is found in three libraries at Cambridge and five at Oxford; *Fasciculus Paracelsicae medicinae veteris* also in three at Cambridge and five at Oxford; *Archidoxorum libri decem* in three at Cambridge and four at Oxford. Peterhouse was bequeathed a copy of *Chirurgia magna* by its Master, Andrew Perne, in 1589. This college in the next century was to receive, from Algernon Peyton, the only copy of the 1589/91 Huser German edition of Paracelsus to be found in the universities. The 1603/5 Latin folio collected works is more widely distributed; copies deposited before 1640 are located at Magdalen College, Oxford and Trinity College, Cambridge. The 1657 Latin collected works was donated to Caius College by Thomas Rudd. Typical of the small collections of Paracelsus are the five works bequeathed by Sir William Paddy to St

---

[52] For information contained in the following paragraphs about college libraries, the author is grateful for assistance given by the librarians and library assistants of the colleges mentioned, to Mr Paul Morgan of the Bodleian Library, Oxford, and to Mr J. F. Fuggles of the British Library, whose unpublished Oxford B. Phil. dissertation (1976) on the library of St John's College, Oxford, contains a valuable account of Sir William Paddy and his library. For works of Paracelsus in Aberdeen University Library, mainly derived from Duncan Liddle (d. 1613), see W. P. D. Wightman, *Science and the Renaissance*, II (Edinburgh, 1962), pp.28–39. I am indebted to Walter Pagel for this reference. See also S. Gibson and F. R. D. Needham, 'Two lists of Burton's books', *Cambridge Bibliographical Society, Proceedings and Papers*, I (1925), 222–46; R. F. Ovenell, 'Brian Twynne's library', *Oxford Bibliographical Society Journal*, new ser., IV (1950), 3–42. Most of Twyne's scientific and medical books were collected by his father, Thomas Twyne, a friend of John Dee. H. M. Adams, *Catalogue of Books Printed on the Continent of Europe 1501–1600 in Cambridge Libraries* (2 vols., Cambridge, 1967).

John's College, Oxford (*Chirurgia magna, Chirurgia vulnerum, Expositio vera harum imaginum olim Nurenbergae repertarum, Fasciculus Paracelsicae medicinae veteris* and *Pyrophila vexatiorum lib. V*), or the copies of *De gradibus, de compositionibus,* and *De meteoris, de matrice* derived from Thomas Twyne, or *Fasciculus medicinae veteris* from Richard Samwaies at Corpus Christi College, Oxford.

Even more widely distributed in college libraries are the writings of the followers of Paracelsus. Some of these works were little more than collections of recipes, but the majority were concerned with the exposition of the Paracelsian medical philosophy. Dorn, Severinus, Mouffet, Duchesne, Ruland elder and younger, and Croll, are particularly strongly represented in college libraries. Finally, the libraries also contain numerous writings by other authors relevant to the formation of the iatrochemical tradition (for example, Agrippa, Biringuccio, Brunschwig, della Porta) but who would not be classified as Paracelsians.

Works by Paracelsus and his followers were common in private libraries, such as those of Brian Twyne, Paddy and Burton, which were assimilated into college and university libraries, or those of Dee, Ralegh, Knyvett and the ninth Earl of Northumberland, which were dispersed or remained in private hands.[53] Notwithstanding Kocher's assertion that John Dee was not interested in Paracelsus, a catalogue of his library dated 1583 shows that he possessed a remarkable, and virtually complete collection of the writings of Paracelsus and his followers. Special prominence was given to 'Paracelsici' in this catalogue. Not only was every major writing, and almost every minor work, present, but many of them had been collected in more than one edition. One of the notable aspects of Dee's collection is the preponderance of German editions. The impression is given that Dee collected Paracelsian works with almost

[53] G.R. Batho, 'The library of the "Wizard Earl", Henry Percy ninth Earl of Northumberland, 1564–1632', *The Library*, 5th ser., xv (1960), 246–56; see p.254. Professor Batho has kindly supplied detailed information respecting Paracelsian works in Percy's library. The Earl possessed a particularly important collection of original writings and Paracelsian editions by Gerard Dorn. For Ralegh's Library Catalogue, 1608, see Lefranc, *Sir Walter Ralegh Ecrivain*, pp.439–40. Library Catalogue of Sir Thomas Knyvett (d. 1622), Cambridge University Library, MS. Ff. 2.30, fols. 5r–68r. This library comprises mainly books collected in the late sixteenth century by Edmund Knyvett. The *Chirurgia magna* (1573 Latin edn) of Paracelsus is listed in the reconstruction of Donne's library by G. Keynes: *A Bibliography of Dr John Donne*, 4th edn (Oxford, 1973) p.273. Even the small number of books possessed by the surgeon Richard Surphlet included *Centum quindecim curationes experimentaque* (1582) by G. B. Penot, the Paracelsian work which was translated into English by Hester in 1583. The author is indebted to Mr M. A. L. Cooke for information from his transcription of the will of Surphlet dated 1 March 1603/4.

obsessive zeal. A list of the editions of Paracelsus owned by Dee arranged in chronological order is included as Appendix I to the present chapter.[54]

In the case of such figures as Sir Hugh Plat, Francis Bacon, John Donne and Ben Jonson, where complete library catalogues have not survived, extensive acquaintance with the Paracelsian literature can be inferred from their published writings. These authors may have adopted a reserved attitude towards alchemy and Paracelsianism, but the literature of these subjects was too influential to be ignored. Bacon, Donne and Jonson clearly wrote for an audience which could be assumed to have a ready familiarity with the tenets of Paracelsianism. The satirical references of Jonson, the imagery of Donne, or the theories of matter of Bacon would have been placed in a Paracelsian context by an educated public which had gradually assimilated Paracelsian ideas into the framework of neo-Platonic philosophy that was becoming the common cultural standard during the final years of the sixteenth century.[55] At the time of Bacon's earliest writings, Paracelsus was still to be regarded as a major influence among the 'moderns'. According to Bacon, this was partly due to the effectiveness of Severinus and others in rendering Paracelsus's philosophy into an 'eloquent harmony'.[56] In 1598 John Donne was commenting favourably on Paracelsus in a verse letter addressed to Bacon's friend Sir Henry Wotton. Thereafter Donne's poems were deeply imbued with Paracelsian imagery, and in 1611 Paracelsus was accorded a major role in *Ignatius His Conclave*.[57] Already by 1594 Thomas Nashe, while exempting scholars like Dee from criticism, had identified the swarms of chemical therapists as 'metal-brewing Paracelsians, having not past one or two probatums for all diseases'. On the other hand Nashe's enemy Gabriel Harvey was

---

[54]   I am grateful to Julian Roberts, Keeper of Printed Books of the Bodleian Library, Oxford, for allowing me to consult his photocopies of the Dee library catalogue, and the card index of the edition of this catalogue which he is currently preparing for publication.

[55]   G. Rees, 'Francis Bacon's semi-Paracelsian cosmology', *Ambix*, XXII (1975), 81–101, 161–73. H. J. C. Grierson, *The Poems of John Donne* (2 vols., Oxford, 1912), I, pp.180–2. D. C. Allen, 'John Donne's knowledge of Renaissance medicine', *Journal of English and Germanic Philology*, XLII (1943), 322–42. E. H. Duncan, 'Donne's alchemical figures', *English Literary History*, XI (1942), 257–85. W. A. Murray, 'Donne and Paracelsus: an essay in interpretation', *Review of English Studies*, XXV (1949), 115–23. E. Crawshaw, 'Hermetic elements in Donne's poetic vision', in A. J. Smith (ed.), *John Donne: Essays in Celebration* (London, 1972), pp.324–48. E. H. Duncan, 'Jonson's *Alchemist* and the literature of alchemy', *Publications of the Modern Language Association of America*, LXI (1946), 699–710. P. Simpson, 'The Castle of the Rosi Cross: Ben Jonson and Theophilus Schweighardt', *Modern Language Review*, XLI (1946), 206–7. C. G. Thayer, *Ben Jonson* (Norman, Okl., 1963).

[56]   Bacon, *De augmentis*, in *Works*, I, p.564; B. Farrington, *The Philosophy of Francis Bacon...from 1603 to 1609* (Liverpool, 1964), pp.52, 57, 65–7, 71.

[57]   T. S. Healy (ed.), *John Donne: Ignatius his Conclave* (Oxford, 1969), pp.19–23.

welcoming Paracelsus as 'vir sagacissimus naturae, artisque secretarius', the founder of a school of Paracelsian medicine which had proved to be fertile in 'experimentis, et arcanis, tam chymico, quam pharmaceutico artificio praeparatis'.[58] Shakespeare realized that medical practitioners were polarized into camps supporting either Galen or Paracelsus. His comments on this situation imply that Galenists tended to pronounce difficult diseases incurable whereas Paracelsians were 'philosophical persons' who 'make modern and familiar, things supernatural and causeless. Hence it is that we make trifles of terrors.'[59]

Because of the ready availability of Latin editions of Paracelsus and his followers, it is difficult to outline the exact chronology of the rise of Paracelsianism in the later decades of the sixteenth century. As the library of John Dee indicates, during the 1560s Latin editions of Paracelsian works became increasingly easy to obtain. There was therefore little necessity for the circulation of his writings in manuscript form, or for translations except at the most popular level. Nevertheless the habit of devotees of copying key passages of Paracelsus into their manuscript notes provides useful confirmation as to the spread of serious interest in Paracelsus.

It can be assumed that Paracelsus was virtually unknown in England in 1560, but that his ideas had been largely assimilated by 1600. This assimilation therefore coincides with the growth of interest in alchemy, and it will be seen that there are a sufficient number of connections to suggest that Paracelsianism was nurtured within the context of the more generalized alchemical movement. John Dee must have played an active part in this development. The instance recorded in his diary, in which he made a dramatic presentation of 'a copy of Paracelsus twelve letters, written in French in my own hand' to Richard Cavendish, was probably not an isolated event.[60] The alchemical manuscript collections compiled in the later part of the century frequently included long excerpts or translations from Paracelsus and his followers.

The apothecary Edward Barlow's alchemical notes and prescriptions (including many made up for William Gilbert) contain his translation of *De occulta philosophia* dating from about 1590.[61] At the end of his manuscript copy of a translation of *De natura rerum* and *De natura hominis*

[58] R. B. McKerrow, *The Works of Thomas Nashe* (5 vols., London, 1910), III, p.247; IV, pp.259–60. Moore Smith, *Gabriel Harvey's Marginalia*, p.131.
[59] *All's Well that Ends Well* (1603/4), act II, scene iii, 1–22.
[60] *Diary of Dr John Dee*, ed. J. O. Halliwell, Camden Society, XIX (1842), 31 July 1590, p.35.
[61] MS. Ashmole 1487, fols. 40v–52v.

made in 1592, Simon Forman noted that it was taken from an earlier copy produced by William Fallowfield in 1590.[62] Dating from the later sixteenth century, the Sloane collection contains the complete Latin text and a complete English translation of *De natura rerum* and *De natura hominis* made by John Tichborne, both taken from the Forberger edition of 1573, as well as an English translation of texts contained in Bodenstein's 1572 edition of *Metamorphosis, seu, de natura rerum*.[63] Of the numerous shorter excerpts from Paracelsus, and writings by the Paracelsians in the Sloane collection, perhaps the most interesting item is the complete translation of Severinus's *Idea medicinae philosophicae*.[64]

The above manuscript translations of Paracelsus probably represent a small fraction of those produced at the time. This evidence suggests that, contrary to the impression given by Kocher and Debus, English translations of genuine works by Paracelsus were freely available by the 1590s, and that the works which captured most interest were those fundamental to the interpretation of his medical philosophy, rather than those having a rigidly practical bias.

There is no need to repeat Kocher's account of the accumulating references to Paracelsus in vernacular medical writings before 1600. However it is important to re-emphasize the connections between the Paracelsian medical practitioners and the wider alchemical movement, whether in its erudite or mechanical guise.

It has already been noted that alchemists of the fifteenth century placed great faith in chemical medicines. This chemical practice continued among practitioners of all types. The literary attacks on empirics, or prosecutions by the College of Physicians, which occurred even before the first English Paracelsian publication, confirm that medicines based on antimony, mercury or sulphur were in widespread use, that 'metal brewing' was a common practice, and that distillers were becoming a thriving group of London tradesmen. Thus chemical therapy had strong indigenous roots.

Bartholus Sylva, from Turin, was in 1569 the first 'empiric' to be

---

[62] MS. Ashmole 1490, fols. 199v–216r.

[63] MS. Sloane 2193, 320, 3086. John Tichborne became a Fellow of Trinity College, Cambridge, in 1591.

[64] Anthony Bartlet, 'Idea medicinae philosophicae', MS. Sloane 11. See also a collection of transcriptions and translations from Paracelsus, Dorn and Duchesne, MS. Sloane 1627. For a similar sixteenth-century collection including Paracelsus and medieval alchemical writings see MS. 48 in W. T. Wilson, 'Catalogue of Latin and vernacular alchemical manuscripts in the USA and Canada', *Osiris*, VI (1938), 395–403. Petworth House, Leconfield MSS. 95, 96 comprise an English translation (*c.*1575) of Dorn's *Chymisticum artificium* (1568–9), produced for the library of the ninth Earl of Northumberland.

accused by the College of Physicians specifically of using metallic remedies. Before the end of the century more than a dozen practitioners faced accusations relating mainly to the employment of substances like antimony and mercury. The notorious Paul Buck admitted that his major medical authority was Paracelsus. It is likely that many more of the practitioners brought before the College were engaged in similar practices. Indeed, a sufficient number of them are known to have had chemical interests for the assault on empirics to be at least in part construed as an attempt to check the spread of chemical therapy among unlicensed practitioners. Empirics were already difficult enough to contain; identification with the Paracelsian movement would, it was feared, serve to increase further their prestige among the educated public.[65]

The first printed work to reflect extensively the popular interest in chemical therapy was Brunschwig's *Virtuous Book of Distillation* (1527). In the second part of the century the rise of interest in distillation chemistry is indicated by the popularity of Gesner's important handbook *Thesaurus euonymi philiatri* (1552), which was translated into English by Peter Morwyng in 1559, and reissued in 1565. The augmented 1569 edition of Gesner's work was translated by Thomas Hill, being issued after Hill's death by the surgeon George Baker in 1576, and again in 1599. Sensing popular receptivity to works of this kind, John Day, the printer of the original edition of the Gesner translation, announced that he would issue translations of Brunschwig's *De destillandi* and Philip Ulstad's *Coelum philosophorum sive de secretis naturae liber*, a work which was present in Dee's library in both manuscript and printed form.

These projected editions never materialized, although more popular works on distillation were produced, beginning with Thomas Raynalde's *The Virtues of a Lately Invented Oil* (1551) in which the translator openly declared that chemical medicine might become 'a certain and infallible science'. Thereafter specific chemical remedies were discussed by such authors as George Baker (*Oleum magistrale*, 1574; *On the Nature and Properties of Quicksilver*, 1576), Thomas Chaloner (*The Virtues of Nitre*, 1584), Edmund Gardiner (*Trial of Tobacco*, 1610) and Francis Anthony (*Aurum potabile*, 1610). All of these authors had wider Paracelsian or alchemical associations.

---

[65] For details see London, Royal College of Physicians, Annals 1569–1600. Of the authors of popular works on chemical therapy mentioned below, Anthony, Baker, Forester and Gardiner were summoned by the College.

The increasing appeal of chemical therapy is witnessed by the emergence of small handbooks, the first of which seems to have been Francis Cox's *Treatise of the Making and Use of Divers Oils, Unguents, Emplasters, and Distilled Waters* (1575), a work that appears not to have survived, but which was regarded by the College of Physicians as the main source for the chemical practice of Simon Forman.[66] A complement to Cox was *The True and Perfect Order to Distil Oils out of all Manner of Spices, Seeds, Roots and Gums* (1575), derived from various iatrochemists by John Hester.[67] This was the first publication by the leading London chemical practitioner, who between 1579 and 1591 was to issue a spate of Paracelsian translations, including a greatly expanded version of the 1575 text, now entitled the *Key to Philosophy* (1580) and containing a second section specifically attributed to Paracelsus.[68] The *Key to Philosophy* thereby became the second work to be attributed to Paracelsus published in English. Significantly for the wider ramifications of Paracelsian philosophy, and as noted by Sudhoff and Ferguson but overlooked by more recent commentators, the first translation of a definitive work by Paracelsus was the prophetical text *Joyful News out of Helvetia* (1575).[69]

Hester described himself as 'practitioner in the art of distillation' in the catalogue of chemical preparations which he issued in 1588.[70] His wider associations are suggested by the derivation of one of his first translations from Thomas Hill, the dedication of *A Hundred and Fourteen Experiments* (1583) to Walter Ralegh, and the continuation of his chemical practice

---

66 Andrew Maunsell, *Catalogue of English Printed Books* (1595), Pt II, p.6. College of Physicians, Annals, 7 November 1595, where Cox is described by the College as 'an English writer, a very obscure man, absolutely unknown and certainly of no merit'.

67 William Cooper, *Catalogue of Chymicall Books* (1675), sig. C2v. J. Ferguson, *Bibliographia Paracelsica* (5 Pts, Glasgow, 1877–93), Pt I, pp.27–8; Pt V, p.38. STC B, 19181.3. The only recorded copy is preserved in Glasgow University Library. Neither this work by Hester, nor Ferguson's accurate bibliography of books of Paracelsus in English (Part V, pp.31–57), are cited by Kocher and Debus.

68 Maunsell, *English Printed Books*, Pt II, p.12. Ferguson, *Bibliographia Paracelsica*, Pt I, p.28; Pt. V, p.47. STC B, 19181.5. The only complete copies of this work recorded are at Yale and Glasgow University Libraries. For translations of works by Hester, mainly of writings by Fioravanti and Duchesne, see Kocher, 'John Hester, Paracelsian (fl. 1576–93)' in McManaway *et al.* (eds.), *Joseph Quincy Adams Memorial Studies*, pp.621–38.

69 For this work of Paracelsus, see M. Reeves, *The Influence of Prophecy in the Later Middle Ages, A Study of Joachimism* (Oxford, 1969), pp.454–7. This 1575 English translation was not located by Reeves. It is not recorded in STC, but is described in W. Herbert, *Typographical Antiquities* (1786), II, p.891. The translator Stephen Bateman produced other similar prophetic works. For the wider significance of the interest in prophecy, see Webster, *The Great Instauration.*

70 Hester, *These oiles, waters, extractions, or essences, saltes and other compositions* ... [1588]. The only recorded copy, which is in the British Library, belonged to Gabriel Harvey.

by the Puritan minister James Forester.[71] Hester's success as an 'expert artisan' helped to increase the status of alchemical and Paracelsian medical practitioners to that of practical mathematicians and engineers. Gabriel Harvey accordingly included Hester in the select group of English artisans who had raised their arts to an elevated level appropriate to the heroic age in which they lived.[72]

It is easy to appreciate the appeal of Paracelsus to the lower ranks of the medical profession. By following Paracelsus, the traditional practice of these men and women was refined, infused with novelties, and given a sophisticated intellectual basis. This improved their capacity to compete with the organized sections of the medical profession. Neither surgeons nor physicians were in a position so spontaneously to embrace the new medicine. The Barber-Surgeons' Company owed much of its rise in prestige to co-operation with the College of Physicians, and to imitation of the latter's humanistic aspirations. The surgeons believed that by identifying with Galenism they would secure for themselves almost equal status with physicians. Thus surgeons followed the physicians in abusing empirics, and inevitably they came into confrontation with figures such as Valentine Raseworme who had built up successful practices as 'wise alchemists' or 'spagyrists'. Raseworme was attacked by the surgeons Baker, Clowes and Pickering as an empiric and usurper of the name of Paracelsus.[73] But as Kocher has demonstrated, the surgeons were shrewd enough to realize that their area of practice stood most to gain from the selective exploitation of chemical therapy. Accordingly their writings displayed a distinct shift towards Paracelsianism over the period 1570–90. They began with outright censure of Paracelsus, then softened to attacks on Paracelsians, and finally this criticism was itself restricted to abusers of Paracelsianism. Each successive antidotary gave an increased prominence to Paracelsian remedies. Thus George Baker, William Clowes and John Banister, the leaders of their profession, not only advocated chemical therapy but also projected themselves as allies of the Paracelsians. The animosity between Hester and the surgeons was resolved into firm friendship. This reorientation towards Paracelsianism

[71] *A hundred and fourteen experiments of Paracelsus* (1583). *STC* B, 19179.5. The Bodleian copy (Tanner 880) belonged to Roger Cooke, 'laborator' to Dee, Percy and Ralegh. James Forester edited Hester's notes as *The pearle of practise* (1594).

[72] Harvey, *Pierces supererogation* (1595), in A. B. Grosart (ed.), *Works of Harvey* (1884–5), II, p.289.

[73] City of London Record Office, Repertories of the Court of Aldermen, *18*, fols. 196, 211. George Baker, *Oleum magistrale* (1574), sig. Civ, pp.44–5. William Clowes, *Treatise of Morbus Gallicus* (1579), sig. Cii (probably reissue of lost 1576 edn); William Pickering in 1584 edn, sig. Piii.

was associated with a new assertiveness on the part of surgeons about their rights to the general practice of medicine, which occasioned a deterioration in their relations with the physicians. Paracelsianism is probably not irrelevant to the decision of the College to single out John Banister and George Baker as surgeons guilty of illegal medical practice.

One reason for the failure of the College to stem the tide of Paracelsianism was the open support given to unlicensed practitioners and surgeons by the aristocracy and gentry. The College was being driven, out of expediency, to relax its ardent Galenism, and to frame the kind of 'compromise' described by Debus, which would permit greater use of chemical therapy by physicians, but without undermining overall confidence in Galenic pathology, or increasing the tolerance shown to other practitioners. The final seal was set on this compromise by the *Pharmacopoeia* of 1618 which contained a modest section on chemical remedies. But preceding events show that even this degree of accommodation was not easily reached.

The difficulties of the College are underlined by the emergence of a generation of humanistically educated physicians who were openly sympathetic to Paracelsus. The leader of this group was Thomas Mouffet (1553–1604), who is primarily remembered as one of the most distinguished naturalists of the period and as author of *Theatrum insectorum* (1634). This work was published posthumously by Mouffet's Paracelsian ally Sir Theodore de Mayerne.[74] Mouffet became sympathetic to Paracelsus during four years spent studying and practising medicine on the continent (1576–1580). His Paracelsianism was made explicit when he annoyed the academic authorities at Basel by openly criticizing the influential Thomas Erastus, the major opponent of the Paracelsians.[75] However Mouffet enjoyed the support of Felix Platter and Theodor Zwinger at Basel; by the time of his return to England he was regarded as a leading member of the cosmopolitan fraternity of humanistic Paracelsian physicians. Shortly after his return he dedicated to Petrus Severinus an eloquent dialogue in defence of Paracelsus and chemical medicine.[76] He found no difficulty in gaining

---

[74] The main sources on Mouffet are: Heltzel and Hudson, *Nobilis*, pp.xiii–xviii; C. E. Raven, *English Naturalists from Neckam to Ray* (Cambridge, 1947), pp.175–91. See Plate 7.

[75] M. E. Welti, 'Englisch-baslerische Bezeihungen zur Zeit der Renaissance in der Medizin, der Naturwissenschaften und der Naturphilosophie', *Gesnerus*, xx (1963), 105–30. R. H. Blaser, 'Un rare témoignage de fidélité envers Paracelse à Bâle: les "Theses de anodinis medicamentis" du médecin anglais Thomas Moffet (1578)', *Verhandlungen des XIX International Congress für Geschichte der Medizin* (Basel, 1966), pp.502–12.

[76] *De iure et praestantia chymicorum medicamentorum* (Frankfurt-a-M., 1584).

recognition in court circles as a physician. But his relations with the College of Physicians were never more than cool. He was openly hostile while a candidate, and after his eventual election to the fellowship he played virtually no part in college affairs. Mouffet was the leading member of a group of physicians which included Timothie Bright, William Brewer, Thomas Penny, Richard Taylior and Peter Turner, all of whom had distant, or positively troubled relations with the College. Their biographies tend to follow a similar course to that of Mouffet – education at Cambridge, prolonged studies in Germany and Switzerland, interest in natural history, pursuit of non-Galenic strands of medical thought, successful medical careers in England without strong involvement with the College of Physicians, and associations in strongly Protestant circles. Indeed Protestantism was an immediate reason for foreign travel and hence of exposure to Paracelsianism.[77] Not only were the Paracelsians and alchemists influential in medicine, they were also granted public preferment; Bostocke, Gwynn, Mouffet and Turner served as MPs in the parliaments of Elizabeth. Paracelsianism was not construed in a narrow sense, but in the spirit of the broader medical philosophy of Paracelsus. It was therefore easily reconciled with the outlook of such naturalists as Conrad Gesner and William Turner, who, like Paracelsus himself, stressed the medical relevance of the exploration of the animal, plant and mineral kingdoms. The pioneer works on the English flora advocated the demonstration of the medicinal properties of English herbs by chemical means.[78] Full exploitation of the empiricist aspect of Paracelsianism in the latter years of the sixteenth century prepared the way for the emergence of Bacon's natural philosophy.

An important reason for the success of Paracelsianism was its coincidence with the general religious mood of the times. It was therefore fitting that the first general defence of Paracelsian medicine and philosophy was framed in terms of an analogy with the religious

---

[77] This was also the case for the older generation of medical men interested in chemistry, mentioned above; William Turner and Peter Morwyng were exiled on religious grounds, and returned to take up clerical careers.

[78] For emphasis on the importance of 'perfect knowledge' of natural history, see Baker, *Oleum migistrale*, sig. E1r. For criticism of apothecaries' ignorance of botany, see Timothie Bright, *A treatise wherein is declared the sufficiencie of English medicines* (1580), which makes frequent favourable reference to chemical therapy (e.g. p.43), and I.W., *The copie of a letter sent by a learned physician to his friend, wherein are detected the manifold errors used hitherto of the apothecaries* (London, 1587) which is explicitly Paracelsian. Stephen Bredwell composed a prefatory letter to Gerard's *Herbal* (1597) explaining the advantage of a lectureship in chemistry to the College of Physicians. Bredwell and his son were prosecuted by the College over a long period.

reformation.[79] Galenism was dismissed as a decadent heathenish tradition, which authors like Paracelsus were abandoning in the course of their return to a purer tradition inherited from the patriarchs of Israel. Paracelsianism was a manifestation of this true search for wisdom, or *ars sacra, chymia, alchymia,* or *ars spagyrica,* 'which sheweth forth the composition of all manner [of] bodies, and their dissolutions, their natures and properties by labour by the fire, following Nature diligently'.[80] Bostocke placed Hippocrates and the pre-Socratics firmly in this uncorrupted *prisca* tradition which he asserted had achieved its full flowering with Paracelsus. Mouffet presented Paracelsus as the Hippocrates of the new age.[81] Francis Bacon was soon to repeat this line of argument, except for replacing Paracelsus by himself as the restorer of natural philosophy.

The conflict between the Paracelsians and their critics in the later decades of the sixteenth century demonstrated the difficulties of effecting change by compromise. The publication of Mouffet's dialogue in 1584, and Bostocke's apologia in 1585, should not be regarded as isolated expressions of disaffection with Galenism and attraction to Paracelsus, but as signs of a general cultural shift which brought about the revitalization of alchemy and generated new confidence in the capacity of man to cure his ills and attain command over nature. Paracelsianism epitomized this new mood of optimism.

By 1585, then, the works of Paracelsus and his followers were widely disseminated, and actively studied by both laymen and medical practitioners. Practical chemistry was a popular pursuit. In this context it is not surprising that Paracelsianism made a major impact on the vernacular medical literature produced in the last quarter of the sixteenth century. If the evidence from all sources is taken into account it is apparent that in most respects Paracelsianism became as well-entrenched in England as in most Protestant states in Europe. It played a part in eroding the influence of humanistic Galenism, and provided a rehearsal for the full-blooded assault on Galenism which took place

---

[79] R.B., Esq., *The difference betwene the auncient physicke and the latter physicke* (1585). Maunsell (*English Printed Books,* p.4) gives the author as R. Bostocke. This is sometimes without foundation expanded to, Robert Bostocke. Hill, *Intellectual Origins,* p.29, correctly names this author as Richard Bostocke. Bostocke (d. 1606) was a student at St John's College, Cambridge, being admitted to the Middle Temple in 1551: *Venn,* I, p.184.

[80] Bostocke, *Ancient Physic and the Latter Physic,* sig. B1r. Mouffet's *De jure* adopts a similar line of argument. As Donne mentions in *Ignatius his Conclave,* p.25, the source for this *prisca* defence of Paracelsianism is Severino, *Idea medicinae philosophicae.* This scheme was also central to Ralegh's *History.*

[81] Mouffet, *Nosomantica Hippocratea* (Frankfurt-a-M., 1588), sig. A5r–6v.

during the Puritan Revolution. Paracelsian medicine claimed the support of leading figures from all ranks of the medical profession, including some of the most effective medical writers of the age, ranging from the erudite Mouffet to the distiller Hester. These medical practitioners, like their lay supporters, would have subscribed to Bostocke's belief that Paracelsianism represented the culmination of the ancient and sanctified science of alchemy.

Appendix I. A chronological list of published writings by Paracelsus contained in the library of John Dee

The following list of works by Paracelsus, including possibly spurious items, is derived from the catalogue which Dee prepared just before his departure for the continent. It is dated 6 September 1583. The Paracelsian items are grouped together as 'Paracelsici libri'. About two-thirds of these works are attributed to Paracelsus. Authors such as Dorn, Severinus, Duchesne and Suchten are also represented. The two surviving copies of the catalogue (British Library, Harleian MS. 1879, and Trinity College, Cambridge 0.4.20) appear to be similar in content with respect to the Paracelsian items. The present list is derived primarily from the Harleian version. Of the 62 works by Paracelsus 41 are in German (G), 19 in Latin (L), and 2 in Flemish (F). In the following list I have provided the short title of the relevant edition, preceded by the appropriate reference number from K. Sudhoff, *Bibliographia Paracelsica* (Berlin, 1894). Dee's original catalogue adopted Latin short titles for all works; a few of the identifications may be subject to later correction.

13 *Vonn dem Bad Pfeffers* (1535) G
24 *Wund und Leibartzney* (1549) G
29 *Von der Frantzösischen Krankheit* (1553) G
30 *Labyrinthus medicorum errantium* (1553) L
35 *Diė groote Chirurgie* (1556) F
39 *De vita longa libri IV* (1560) L
40 *Wund und Leibartznei* (1561) G
42 *De duplici anatomici* (1561) L
43 *De gradibus, de compositionibus* (1562) L
44 *Spittalbuch* (1562) G
45 *Baderbuchlin* (1562) G
46 *De vita longa libri V* (1562) L
47 *Paramirum* (1562) G
48 *Modus pharmacandi* (1562) G
51 *Der Grossen Wundartzney* (1562) G
52 *Der Grossen Wundartzney* (1562) G
54 *De morborum ex tartaro* (1563) L
56 *Von ersten dreyen principiis* (1563) G
57 *Von tartarischen krankenheiten* (1563) G
58 *Labyrinthus medicinis* (1563) F

63 *Vom podagra* (1564) G
64 *Defensiones, labyrinthus medicorum* (1564) G
65 *Philosophia ad Athenienses* (1564) G
66 *Paramirum* (1565) G
67 *Paragranum* (1565) G
70 *De causa et origine morborum* (1565) G
73 *Liber meteoris* (1566) G
75 *Opus chyrurgicum* (1566) G
85 *Astronomica et astrologia* (1567) G
86 *Philosophia magna* (1567) G
87 *Physionomica morborum* (1567) G
88 *Von der Bergsucht oder Bergkrankheiten* (1567) G
90 *Pyrophila vexationumque* (1567) G
91 *Melancholia und Unsinnigkeit* (1567) G
96 *De urinarum ac pulsuum judiciis* (1568) L
98 *De gradibus, de compositionibus* (1568) L
99 *De vita longa* (1568) L
101 *Pyrophila vexationumque* (1568) L
109 *Philosophiae magnae* (1569) L
110 *De meteoris* (1569) L
113 *Von offnung der haut, von heylung der Wunde* (1570) G
118 *Archidoxa* (1570) G
120 *De rebus naturalibus* (1570) G
123 *Archidoxorum* (1570) L
124 *Chirurgia minor* (1570) L
126 *De tartaro* (1570) L
129 *Archidoxa* (1570) G
130 *Paragraphorum libri XIII* (1571) G
133 *Eines volkomnen Wundartzets* (1571) G
134 *De spiritibus planetarum* (1571) G
136 *Vom geist des lebens* (1572) G
142 *Archidoxorum* (1572) G
145 *De natura rerum* (1573) L
152 *Testamentum* (1574) G
158 *Archidoxa* (1574) G
160 *Paragraphorum libri XIV* (1575) L
161 *De secretis creationis* (1575) G
163 *Paramirum* (1575) G
174 *Von den ofnen schaden* (1577) G
176 *Von der Wundartzney* (1577) G
177 *Aurora, thesaurusque philosophorum* (1577) L
190 *Centum quindecim curationes experimentaque* (1582) L

Appendix II. Checklist of works by English authors relating to Paracelsian and alchemical medicine published before 1600

In the following chronological list translations or works which are primarily translations (both 'tr.') are given under the names of the translator or editor. Short titles are given with modernized spelling. Works are included only if they relate positively to the growth of Paracelsian or alchemical medicine.

Andrews	*Virtuous Book of Distillation* (1527) tr.
Copland	*Secret of Secrets* (1528) tr.
Raynalde	*Lately Invented Oil* (1551) tr.
Morwyng	*Treasure of Euonymus* (1559) tr.
Morwyng	*Treasure of Euonymus* (1565) tr.
Copland	*Secret of Secrets* (1572) tr.
Baker	*Composition of Oleum Magistrale* (1574) tr.
Bateman	*Joyful News out of Helvetia* (1575) tr.
Coxe	*Making and Use of Oils* (1575)
Hester	*True Order to Distil Oils* (1575)
Baker	*New Jewel of Health* (1576) tr.
Clowes–Baker	*Marbus Gallicus . . . Nature of Quicksilver* (1576)
Mouffet	*De anodinis medicamentis* (1578)
Clowes–Baker	*Morbus Gallicus* etc. (1579)
Hester	*Joyful Jewel* (1579) tr.
Hester	*Short Discourse upon Chirurgie* (1580) tr.
Hester	*Key of Philosophy* (1580)
Hester	*Compendium of Rational Secrets* (1582) tr.
Hester	*Hundred and Fourteen Cures* (1583) tr.
Chaloner	*Virtues of Nitre* (1584)
Mouffet	*De iure et praestantia chymicorum medicamentorum* (1584)
Banister	*Compendious Chirurgerie* (1585)
Clowes–Baker	*Morbus Gallicus* etc. (1585)
Bostocke	*Discourse between Ancient and Latter Physic* (1585)
	A Brief Discourse of the Virtue of Balsam (1585)
I.W.	*Copy of a Letter on Abuses of Apothecaries* (1587)
B.G.	*Virtues of Terra Sigillata* (1587)
Clowes	*Proved Practice for young Chirurgions* (1588)
Mouffet	*Nosomantica Hippocratea* (1588)
Banister	*Antidotary* (1589)
Bacon	*De retardandis senectutis* (1590)
Hester	*Treatise of French Pox* (1590) tr.
Hester	*Quercetanus Sclopotary* (1590) tr.
Hester	*Quercetanus Answer* (1590) tr.
Ripley	*Compound of Alchemy* (1591)
Forester	*Pearl of Practice* (1594) tr.
Plat	*Chemical Conclusions* (1594)

Plat	*Jewel House of Nature* (1594)
Clowes–Baker	*Morbus Gallicus* etc. (1596)
Hester	*Key of Philosophy* (1596)
Hester	*Hundred and Fourteen Cures* (1596) tr.
Bacon etc.	*Mirror of Alchemy* (1597)
Baker	*Practice of the New and Old Physic* (1599) tr.

10

The School of Padua: humanistic medicine in the sixteenth century

JEROME J. BYLEBYL

In a volume on medicine in sixteenth-century England it is relevant to give some consideration to the contemporary Italian medical universities, because these were the places to which ambitious English medical students would most likely turn for the advanced training that was not available in their native land. The University of Padua was especially favoured by English as by other non-Italian students, apparently for two major reasons: first, it was generally regarded as the best medical school in Europe, and second, the religious divisions of Europe had not been allowed to prevent Protestant students from studying and taking degrees at this nominally Catholic university.[1]

However, before turning to some of the major characteristics of

---

[1] R. J. Mitchell, 'English students at Padua, 1460–75', *Transactions of the Royal Historical Society*, 4th ser., xix (1936), 100–17; E. Morpurgo, 'English physicians – "doctorati" – at the University of Padua in the "Collegio Veneto Artista" (1617–1771)', *Proceedings of the Royal Society of Medicine*, xx (1927), 1369–80.

In preparing this study, I have relied heavily on A. Favaro (ed.), *Atti della nazione Germanica artista nello studio di Padova*, vols. i and ii (Venice, 1911–12), and L. Rosseti (ed.), *Acta nationis Germanicae artistarum (1616–1636)* (Padua, 1967), cited below as *ANGAP* i, ii, iii; *Statuta almae universitatis d. artistarum, et medicorum Patavini gymnasii* (Venice, 1589), which contains the statutes of 1465 together with subsequent additions (cited below as *Stat. Pad.*); C. Malagola (ed.), *Statuti delle università e dei collegi dello studio bolognese* (Bologna, 1887), cited below as *Stat. Bol.*; and U. Dallari (ed.), *I rotuli dei lettori legisti e artisti dello studio bolognese dal 1384 al 1799* (4 vols., Bologna, 1888–1924), cited below as *Rotuli Bol.* Of the extensive secondary literature, the following have been of particular value: J. P. Tomasini, *Gymnasium Patavinum* (Udine, 1654), cited below as *Gym. Pat.* (see Plate 12); J. Facciolati, *Fasti Gymnasii Patavini*, 3 parts in 1 (Padua, 1757); H. Rashdall, *The Universities of Europe in the Middle Ages*, ed. F. M. Powicke and A. B. Emden (3 vols., Oxford, 1936); G. Giomo, 'L'archivio antico della università di Padova', *Nuovo Archivio Veneto*, vi (1893), 377–460; B. Nardi, *Saggi sull'aristotelismo padavano dal secola XIV al XVI* (Florence, 1958); B. Bertolaso, 'Ricerche d'archivio su alcuni aspetti dell'insegnamento medico presso la università de Padova nel cenque- e seicento', *Acta Medicae Historiae Patavina*, vi (1959–60), 17–37; G. Fichtner, 'Padova e Tübingen: la formazione medica nei secoli XVIe XVII', ibid., xix (1972–3), 43–62; G. Whitteridge, *William Harvey and the Circulation of the Blood* (London and New York, 1971), pp.3–40; N. G. Siraisi, *Arts and Sciences at Padua. The Studium of Padua before 1350* (Toronto, 1973). C. B. Schmitt, 'Thomas Linacre and Italy', in F. Maddison, M. Pelling and C. Webster (eds.), *Essays on the Life and Work of Thomas Linacre* (Oxford, 1977), pp.36–75, became available to me only as this article was nearing completion.

Plate 12. The University of Padua
The main entrance of the university building, known as Il Bò. From
J. P. Tomasini, *Gymnasium patavinum* (Udine, 1654). Reproduced by
permission of the Curators of the Bodleian Library, Oxford.

Paduan medicine, it should be observed that the generally high level of
medical education in Italy was directly related to the central place that
the university-educated physician had come to hold in Italian society. As
Carlo Cipolla has recently shown, in northern Italy such highly
educated practitioners were not, as in much of the rest of Europe, an
exotic phenomenon serving only the well-to-do of the large cities, but
were available in relatively large numbers to a wide spectrum of social
classes, and in the small towns as well as in the major urban centres.[2] As

[2] C. M. Cipolla, *Public Health and the Medical Profession in the Renaissance* (Cambridge, 1976),
    pp.67–124, especially pp.77–99. See also L. Thorndike, *Science and Thought in the Fifteenth
    Century* (New York, 1929), p.104, note 88.

elsewhere, the wealthy collegiate physicians of the cities did indeed form the elite of the medical profession, but a combination of lower financial expectations and a highly developed system of publicly-salaried positions meant that the majority of Italian physicians supported themselves at a more modest level, in terms both of income and of clientele.

Of the learned lay professions only lawyers were more ubiquitous in Italian society,[3] and the numerous Italian universities existed primarily to train the personnel which the legal and medical systems required. The typical Italian university, or *Studio*, consisted of two chief divisions, namely a university of jurists and a university of artists.[4] Nominally the arts university included all the subjects other than civil and canon law, but in fact it was almost as much a medical school as the jurist university was a law school. The most prestigious chairs in the arts faculty were those of the theory and the practice of medicine, and the only other subject that came close to these in importance was natural philosophy, which was primarily, though not exclusively, ancillary to medicine.[5] Only these three subjects had major or Ordinary status, and they were clearly superior in other respects as well. Thus at Bologna, which was the oldest and, in the sixteenth century, still by far the largest of the Italian arts universities, the faculty roster in a typical year would include about fifty professors, of whom there would be about ten each for the theory and the practice of medicine, and six or seven for natural philosophy, in addition to several each for surgery and medical astrology.[6] Padua had significantly fewer professors, but the teaching system still required at least five professors each for theory, practice and philosophy.[7]

Furthermore, the chief degree-granting body of the arts university was a College of Physicians and Philosophers, which was much the same as a College of Physicians in a non-university city, except that it might include a few Doctors of Arts alongside a preponderance of Doctors of Arts and Medicine.[8] Its membership consisted chiefly of the elite of the local medical profession, and besides its role in examining the university students and granting their degrees, it usually had the right to license and

---

[3] See L. Martines, *Lawyers and Statecraft in Renaissance Florence* (Princeton, 1968), especially pp.3–6, 78–91.

[4] Rashdall, *Universities of Europe*, I, pp.233–8.

[5] *Stat. Pad.*, pp.34, 40r, 66.

[6] *Rotuli Bol.*, II, passim.

[7] Tomasini, *Gym. Pat.*, pp.291–332.

[8] *Stat. Bol.*, pp.425–93; *Stat. Pad.*, pp.35–45, 69r; Giomo, 'L'Archivio antico', pp.416–18; Rashdall, *Universities of Europe*, I, p.241, note 4; C. Webster, 'Thomas Linacre and the foundation of the College of Physicians', in Maddison *et al.* (eds.), *Thomas Linacre*, pp.213–18.

regulate all medical practitioners of the town, whether they were non-collegiate physicians or belonged to one of several possible categories of surgeon.

There were, of course, some students who came to the arts university primarily to study one of the lesser subjects, or to study natural philosophy as an end in itself, but the typical graduate would take a doctorate in arts (i.e. philosophy) and medicine, would call himself 'philosophus et medicus', and would pursue a career in the practice of medicine. He might also combine this with a teaching position in an arts university, and if so might start out by teaching logic or philosophy, but more likely than not he would sooner or later advance to one of the more prestigious chairs of medical theory or practice.[9] It was also possible for an individual to remain a professor of philosophy throughout his academic career, whether or not he also had a medical degree, but it was not until well into the sixteenth century that the major chairs of philosophy at the University of Padua were routinely held by such 'career' philosophers, as distinct from those on their way to the medical chairs.[10] And even then, the primary teaching responsibility of the philosophers continued to be that of preparing prospective physicians for their medical studies.

As mentioned, the two principal subjects taught to the medical candidates were the theory and the practice of medicine. These designations are somewhat misleading, however, since both dealt with a combination of theoretical and practical issues, and neither was practical in the sense of 'clinical'.[11] The professor of theory would instruct the students in the general explanatory principles of health and disease (physiology and general pathology), as well as introducing them to the major elements of medical practice, including semeiology, hygiene and therapy. The professor of practice would go over much the same ground, but in relation to a survey of particular diseases; thus his subject matter included special pathology and nosology as well as therapeutics. Both subjects, theory and practice, were taught through a three-year cycle of lectures: the professor of theory would comment, in turn, on

---

9   Nardi, *Aristotelismo*, pp.157–8.

10   For example in 1436 Gaetano Tiene, a Doctor of Arts and Medicine and Ordinary Professor of Philosophy, refused to be a candidate for a chair of medical theory (Tomasini, *Gym. Pat.*, pp.157, 158); around 1520 Girolamo Bagolino did transfer from an Ordinary chair of philosophy to one of medical practice (ibid., p.306), but he seems to have been one of the last of the Ordinary philosophy professors at Padua to follow this route (see ibid., pp.306–9).

11   For a complaint about the inappropriateness of the inherited distinction between theory and practice, see Santorio Santorio, *Commentaria in primam fen primi libri Canonis Avicennae* (Venice, 1626), cols. 4–6, 37–9. Santorio was First Ordinary of Theory at Padua.

three basic introductory texts – the first *fen* of the *Canon* of Avicenna, the *Aphorisms* of Hippocrates and Galen's *Ars medica* – while the professor of practice would lecture, in turn, on diseases from head to thorax, diseases from abdomen to toe, and diseases of the whole body (i.e. fevers).[12] In addition, these general 'public' lectures would be supplemented by an extensive array of 'private' courses dealing with more specialized topics.[13]

Despite the prominence given to the formal lecture and commentary in the official medical curriculum, the training was far from wholly theoretical in character, since it was expected that all students would be exposed to fairly extensive bedside precepting, carried out by the professors of both theory and practice as well as other prominent but non-lecturing physicians.[14] This aspect of medical education received only scant attention in the statutes of the arts universities and colleges, which might create the impression that little importance was attached to it relative to the more theoretical training. However, I would suggest that just the opposite was probably true: all of the professors were routinely engaged in the practice of medicine, and most students would eventually have to make their living in this way, so that this aspect of their training was the least likely to be neglected by either side and therefore required least regulation. At all events, such bedside precepting was carried on very extensively in Italy throughout the sixteenth century, so that it was quite usual for prominent physicians to visit their patients with groups of students in tow. Indeed, it appears that it was primarily such opportunities, rather than the lectures and disputations, that drew the foreign medical students to Italy in such large numbers.[15]

Italian medical universities had taken on the characteristics just described by the fourteenth century, but in the early sixteenth century they were significantly transformed by a movement that was at once both conservative and reforming in its aims: conservative because its guiding assumption was that medical theory and practice had reached unparalleled heights among the ancient Greeks, especially through the work of Hippocrates and Galen, and reforming because its proponents

---

[12] Bertolaso, 'Ricerche d'archivio', pp.22–4.
[13] *Stat. Pad.*, p.38.
[14] *Stat. Pad.*, p.44v: 'In medicina vero promovendus studuerit ad minus per ann. 3. & lectiones omnes ordinarias audierit, & cum aliquo famoso doctore per annum ad minus practicasse, & infirmos visitasse constet'.
[15] See below, and also T. Puschmann, *History of Medical Education*, trans. and ed. by E. H. Hare (1891), pp.251–6; and Cipolla, *Public Health*, p.4.

took a careful look at medicine as taught and practised by contemporary physicians and found it to be distressingly corrupt and incomplete in relation to the surviving monuments of ancient Greek medicine. These medical humanists, led by such men as Nicolao Leoniceno of Ferrara, therefore called for a thorough reform of the arts universities, to be based on an ambitious programme of recovering, editing, translating, and above all studying, the texts of the ancient Greek physicians.[16]

In retrospect it seems that the success of this movement was almost inevitable, since it conformed to the ideal of a classical revival that had become widely diffused in Italian culture by the fifteenth century. Many physicians had long shared the enthusiasm for ancient literature and learning and therefore were probably well prepared for the message that their own profession had much to gain by a return to its ancient sources.[17] At all events, by the 1530s the supporters of the movement had grown from a small handful, centred chiefly at the University of Ferrara, to an ever-increasing majority of the medical profession, and were rapidly achieving dominance in the various medical faculties, first of Italy and then of other parts of Europe.[18] Printed editions and Latin translations of the required texts either had appeared or were about to do so, and they were being discussed and analysed in academic lectures as well as in a growing body of new literature. Of course, Galen also found his critics, and they would eventually have their day, but in medical terms the sixteenth century was predominantly the golden age of Galenism – thanks to the work of the scholars, translators and book publishers Galen's works were more widely available, and in a more complete and accurate form, than previously, and thanks to the dedication of his followers they were also more highly admired, more thoroughly studied, and probably better understood, than at any time before or since.

Despite its avowedly conservative intentions, medical humanism ushered in some of the most significant innovations in Renaissance

[16] On medical humanism, see R. J. Durling's introduction to his 'A chronological census of Renaissance editions and translations of Galen', *Journal of the Warburg and Courtauld Institutes,* XXIV (1961), 230–305; L. Samoggia, *Le repercussioni in Germania dell'indirizzo filologico-medico leoniceniano della scuola Ferrarese per opera di Leonardo Fuchs,* Quaderni de Storia Della Scienza e Della Medicina, IV (Ferrara, 1964); and anon., *Atti del Convegno internazionale per la celebrazione del V Centenario della nascita di Giovanni Manardo 1462–1536* (Ferrara, 1963).

[17] P. Burke, *Culture and Society in Renaissance Italy* (London, 1972), pp.23–5; E. Garin, in the introduction to his edition of Coluccio Salutati, *De nobilitate legum et medicinae* (Florence, 1947), pp.xlv–xlvi; and D. P. Lockwood, *Ugo Benzi, Medieval Philosopher and Physician, 1396–1439* (Chicago, 1951), pp.11, 20, 25.

[18] See, for example, C. D. O'Malley, *Andreas Vesalius of Brussels 1514–1564* (Berkeley and Los Angeles, 1964), pp.65–9.

medicine, both in didactic technique and substantive content.[19] From the beginning its leaders had insisted that it was not enough simply to read Galen rather than Avicenna, but that one must go on to arrive at a true understanding of Galen's words in relation to the phenomena of health and disease. The ultimate goal was to be able to practise medicine in the manner of the ancient physicians. The message had a ring of urgency to it precisely because in medicine a failure to establish the proper relationship between words and things could have dire consequences for human life and health.[20] Leoniceno, the founding father of the movement, had singled out three areas of particular concern in this regard, namely medicinal herbs, specific diseases and anatomical structures.[21] Thus it is not surprising that his disciples should have played leading roles in introducing new forms of botanical, anatomical and clinical teaching into the medical curriculum, along with their efforts to reform the content of the existing lecture courses.[22] Moreover, from teaching these subjects through demonstration of the phenomena themselves it was a relatively short though crucial step to the beginnings of substantial new observations. And while in retrospect the latter may seem to mark the beginning of the decline of ancient authority, originality and innovation within certain limits were readily construed as emulating the spirit of the ancients, and therefore proved quite compatible with the ideals of medical humanism.[23]

[19] Burke, *Culture and Society in Italy*, pp.23–5, points out that innovation in the name of reviving the past was a common phenomenon in this period. With regard to Venetian politics of the late sixteenth century, W. J. Bowsma notes that 'although in an exact sense the *giovani* were reactionaries, they looked to the past as a model in the manner of other reformers in an age when all salutary change was regarded as a return to the better condition of a former time': *Venice and the Defense of Republican Liberty. Renaissance Values in the Age of the Counter Reformation* (Berkeley and Los Angeles, 1968), p.194. C. M. Leslie has pointed out that innovation under the guise of a traditional revival is not unique to Western medicine during the Renaissance, but is going on in other parts of the world today: 'The modernization of Asian medical systems', in J. J. Poggie and R. N. Lynch (eds.), *Rethinking Modernization* (Westport, Conn., 1974), pp.69–108.

[20] Nicolao Leoniceno, *Opuscula* (Basel, 1532), pp.5v, 13, 31r, 42v, 45v, 47v, 53v.

[21] Leoniceno discussed the problems of identifying diseases in *Libellus de epidemia, quam vulgo morbum gallicum vocant* (Venice, 1497); of plants and anatomical structures in *De Plinii, & plurimum aliorum medicorum in medicina erroribus* (Ferrara, 1509). In the latter work (p.85r) he chastises contemporary physicians who, unlike the ancients, do not go out into the field to study herbs for themselves, but 'sedissent in scholis, potius de rebus nullius ad vitam momenti diserentes, & fata hominum, non sua, sed aliena fiducia gubernantes'. On the botanical and nosological achievements of Manardo, Leoniceno's most important student, see E. Pifferi, 'Giovanni Manardo e la botanica', and L. Samoggia, 'Manardo e la scuola umanistica filologica tedesca', both in *Atti ... Giovanni Manardo*, pp.217–23, 241–4.

[22] See below.

[23] In the realm of anatomy, Vesalius and Falloppio both reflect this attitude, though in rather contrasting ways. See the preface to *De humani corporis fabrica* (Basel, 1543), and Falloppio, *Observationes anatomicae* (Venice, 1561), pp.1–6.

As noted, this movement originally took coherent form at the University of Ferrara, but it was at Padua that it achieved its greatest success, especially in the more innovative areas just mentioned. It was within a relatively short period, from the mid 1530s to the mid 1540s, that several of the most fundamental changes occurred, including the transformation of anatomical teaching from a short annual event into a permanent major subject, the institution of a botanic garden under university auspices for the express purpose of teaching medical botany, and the systematic use of the hospital to teach nosology and therapy.[24] In varying degree all three changes involved the upgrading of existing practices rather than creation *ex nihilo*, but all represented distinct innovations, brought about quite deliberately through the action of senior members of the medical faculty who were motivated by the aims of the humanistic programme. Similar developments were occurring at other universities at about the same time, but it was at Padua that they occurred most decisively and effectively.

There were quite definite reasons why the most capable men tended to teach at Padua, and why, once there, they were able to realize their goals, and these reasons lay not so much in Padua itself as in the nearby city of Venice, to which Padua had been subject since the early fifteenth century.[25] Venice and her subject territories were controlled by a hereditary oligarchy of about two thousand male Venetian patricians, who effectively excluded all others from political power, while managing to keep it fairly well diffused among themselves. Padua is only about fifteen miles from Venice and had probably been her chief source of lawyers and doctors even before the subjugation of 1405, so that making her the official state university of the Veneto was simply the formalization of an existing relationship. However, by the middle of the fifteenth century the Venetian nobility had another strong reason for interest in the university, namely that they had begun sending their sons there for a period of study before their entry into political life.[26] Some young Venetians would study law, which would be of direct relevance to their careers in government, while others pursued studies within the arts university for more purely intellectual reasons. In particular the

[24] See below, and also Fichtner, 'Padova e Tübingen', pp.52–4.
[25] On Venice and her relations with Padua, see Rashdall, *Universities of Europe*, II, pp.19–21; Bowsma, *Venice*, pp.58–60; O. Logan, *Culture and Society in Venice 1470–1790* (London, 1972), pp.20–1, 46–7; Burke, *Culture and Society in Italy*, p.47.
[26] Nardi, *Aristotelismo*, pp.115–16, 167–9; Bowsma, *Venice*, pp.85, 123–5, 135–6, 163–6, 199–200, 235; Logan, *Culture and Society in Venice*, pp.17, 27, 50–1, 52, 59, 64; F. C. Lane, *Venice, A Maritime Republic* (Baltimore, 1973), pp.215–16.

Venetian patriciate acquired a decided taste for the Aristotelian natural philosophy which, at Padua as elsewhere, was intimately related to medicine. Thus by the late fifteenth century it was not uncommon for Venetian nobles to take formal doctorates in philosophy and to maintain their philosophical interests throughout their lives. These men would then take their places within the Venetian government, which thus always included a sizeable group which not only had personal and familial, as well as civic, reasons for taking an interest in the university, but which knew its affairs intimately as a result of previous attendance and continuing ties with the faculty. Thus increasingly during the course of the fifteenth century the Venetian Senate began assuming a direct voice not just in overall policy questions regarding the university, but in such things as faculty appointments and promotions, and membership of the Paduan College of Physicians.[27] To prevent these matters from becoming overly politicized the Venetian patriciate barred their own members from the major lectureships, a rule which took for granted that many of them would have the necessary academic credentials.[28]

However, it was another statutory provision which, in the long term, probably did more than anything else to ensure the quality of the senior academic appointments, namely that none of the First Ordinary chairs in the major subjects could be held by native citizens of Padua.[29] Of course, there was nothing wrong with Paduans *per se* – Padua produced more than her share of the best teachers – and the probable intent of the rule was to achieve a balance between local and imported talent. To appreciate this, one must know that for each of the major subjects there were at least five positions, ranked, in descending order, First and Second Ordinary, and First, Second and Third Extraordinary.[30] The two Ordinary professors formed a pair of *concurrentes*, that is they lectured on the same subject at the same hour of the day, and were therefore in direct competition with each other for students. The first two Extraordinary professors formed a similar pair, but they lectured at a different hour from the Ordinaries, and lagged one year behind the

[27] P. Kibre, *Scholarly Privileges in the Middle Ages* (Cambridge, Mass., 1962), pp.69–80; and, for example, Nardi, *Aristotelismo*, pp.117–24.

[28] B. Bertolaso, 'I "terzi luoghi" nello studio padovano', *Acta Medicae Historiae Patavina*, VI (1959–60), 8. Contrast this with ecclesiastical offices: Logan, *Culture and Society in Venice*, pp.31–2; see also ibid., pp.50, 54.

[29] Bertolaso, 'I "terzi luoghi"', pp.2–6; see also Rashdall, *Universities of Europe*, I, p.215, and II, p.17; and Siraisi, *Arts and Sciences*, p.28.

[30] *Stat. Pad.*, pp.34r, 37v–38r, 46v; Tomasini, *Gym. Pat.*, pp.291–332; G. Sterzi, *Giulio Casseri, anatomico e chirurgo* (Venice, 1909), pp.131–2, 150–2. There were also a number of other lesser chairs in medicine.

latter in the three-year cycle of prescribed lecture topics. The third Extraordinary professor lectured either concurrently with the other two, or on the many feast days that dotted the academic calendar. With the acquiescence, indeed the encouragement, of the Venetian government, native Paduans tended to monopolize the lower chairs, including the Second Ordinary positions; these were of considerable importance in their own right,[31] and indeed the Venetians sometimes rewarded unusual Paduan talent by declaring the two Ordinary chairs equal in dignity and salary.[32] However, by preventing such men from occupying the First Ordinary chairs, they ensured that these chairs could rarely be filled by routine promotion from below, because nearly all of those below were ineligible by reason of Paduan citizenship. Instead, the routine way of filling a First Ordinary chair was by trying to identify the most capable candidate outside the university and then making an all-out effort to attract him to Padua.[33] He might be a professor at some other university, but in the case of the senior medical chairs he might also be a famous practitioner who had had a varied career outside the academic world. Thus the University of Padua was continually infused with new blood at the very head, and in this respect stands in some contrast to her larger rival at Bologna, where most positions, including the highest, tended to be filled by promotion from within the ranks of the existing faculty.[34]

As noted, the involvement of the Venetian Senate in the affairs of the university increased steadily during the fifteenth century, but in the early sixteenth century these controls were both formalized and strengthened. From 1509 to 1517, as a result of the War of the League of the Cambrai, the university largely ceased to function and her students and faculty were dispersed to other institutions.[35] Thus, following the war the university had practically to be refounded, and it was at this time that the Venetian government took over the formal reins of power: the native Paduan Moderators of the university were replaced by a magistracy of three Venetian Senators, and the Venetian Senate officially took control of major appointments to the faculty, a control that was gradually extended over the next several decades to include all faculty

31   Bertolaso, 'I "terzi luoghi"', pp.1–15; Tomasini, *Gym. Pat.*, pp.294–6, 300–1.
32   E.g., Tomasini, *Gym. Pat.*, p.301.
33   Ibid., pp.291–4, 297–9.
34   *Rotuli Bol.*, II, passim. Sporadic efforts were made to overcome this pronounced localism at Bologna, but with only modest success. See H. B. Adelmann, *Marcello Malpighi and the Evolution of Embryology* (5 vols., Ithaca, N.Y., 1966), I, pp.15–50.
35   Nardi, *Aristotelismo*, pp.171–4, 331–41.

positions.[36] In the immediate aftermath of the war the rule against Paduans in the first chairs was temporarily ignored, but for well over a century, beginning around 1540, it was quite rigorously enforced, thus ensuring a steady succession of such men as Giambatista da Monte, Vittore Trincavella, Girolamo Mercuriale, Alessandro Massaria, Eustachio Rudio and Santorio Santorio in the top medical chairs.

However, while the Venetians had provided themselves with a virtual monopoly of power in the affairs of the university, they usually did not exercise it without regard for student and faculty opinion. Those members of the Venetian patriciate who took the greatest interest in the university often had close personal and intellectual ties with the faculty, and in addition the foreign students were a privileged group whose favour was actively cultivated by the faculty and at least treated with respect by the Venetians.[37] The major decisions regarding the university usually involved a process of advocacy by various student or faculty factions, working either through the Moderators or directly through their contacts within the Venetian Senate.[38] Nevertheless, the Venetian Senators did have the final say, and as one contemporary observed, they went about the selection of the Paduan teachers in the way that they did almost everything, with great care and deliberation, 'so that only men of demonstrated excellence in their profession are given charge over the education of the young'.[39]

Apart from providing the occasion for a formal restructuring of the relationship between the university and the Venetian Senate, the disruptions of 1509–17 probably did much to facilitate the early ascendancy of medical humanism at Padua, since few of the pre-war medical professors were brought back, and the new men who took their places were generally of the humanist persuasion. It is not clear that this was the result of deliberate Venetian policy, at least initially, since one of the first men appointed in 1517 was Ludovico Carensio, an opponent of Leoniceno and defender of the medieval authorities.[40] By 1522, however, Leoniceno could claim that his supporters outnumbered his opponents at Padua,[41] and when Carensio died in 1539 he seems to have

---

[36] Tomasini, *Gym. Pat.*, pp.25–6, 136, 137; *Stat. Pad.*, p.71v; *ANGAP* I, p.33.

[37] Bowsma, *Venice*, pp.235–6, 253–4; Logan, *Culture and Society in Venice*, pp.13, 36, 46–7, 50–4, 59, 63–4.

[38] *ANGAP* is replete with such instances – e.g. I, pp.33–4, 40–1, 50; II, pp.6, 18.

[39] Johann Jessen in the dedication to Ercole Sassonia, *Prognoseon practicarum libri duo* (Frankfurt, 1610).

[40] Nardi, *Aristotelismo*, p.331; Leoniceno, *Opuscula*, pp.146–75, especially p.158v. See also Bowsma, *Venice*, pp.84–6, 88.

[41] Leoniceno, *Opuscula*, p.137v; see also 145r, 174r.

been the last of the old guard in the medical faculty. He was replaced as First Professor of Practice by da Monte, a self-proclaimed disciple of Leoniceno's who had defended the latter in his fight with Carensio.[42]

Da Monte's appointment was of more than symbolic importance, since he was the most admired physician of his age, and his coming to Padua did much to assure her position as the foremost medical university of Europe.[43] Typical of contemporary opinion was the statement of Girolamo Fracastoro that 'if I may speak like a Pythagorean, the soul of Galen seems to have migrated into [da Monte]'.[44] While at Padua he served as the chief architect of the definitive Giunta edition of the Latin Galen,[45] but it was above all as a teacher of Galenic medicine that da Monte made his mark. Indeed, he could have named his price to serve as physician at any number of royal and princely courts, so that his acceptance of the position at Padua is testimony of his deep concern for medical education, especially for the proper 'method' of inculcating medical doctrine.[46] Moreover, his interest in the principles of pedagogy was translated into great success as a teacher; as one of his students put it, 'of the public teachers at Padua, the school of schools, he was the greatest contemplator of the theory of medicine, and the greatest executor of its practice'.[47] The statement perhaps refers to the fact that after publicly lecturing on the practice of medicine for three years da Monte transferred to the first chair of theory, but quite probably it also alludes to something else, namely that in addition to his public and private lecturing on nearly all aspects of medicine, da Monte was also highly regarded for his bedside discourses on particular cases, both in private homes and in the hospital.[48]

---

[42] See da Monte's letter of 1519 in ibid., p.175.

[43] The only full length study of da Monte seems to be G. Cervetto, *Di Giambatista da Monte e della medicina italiana nel secolo XVI* (Verona, 1839), which I have not seen. See N. F. J. Eloy, *Dictionnaire historique de la médecine*, III (Mons, 1778), pp.326–9; G. Tirabosci, *Storia della letteratura italiana*, new edn, VII, Pt 3 (Venice, 1824), pp.888–90; and L. Münster, 'Die Anfänge eines klinischen Unterrichts an der Universität Padua im 16. Jahrhundert', *Medizinische Monatsschrift*, XXIII (1969), 173.

[44] Girolamo Fracastoro, *De contagione et contagiosis morbis et eorum curatione, libri. III*, ed. and trans. by W. C. Wright (New York, 1930), pp.76–8.

[45] O'Malley, *Vesalius*, p.102.

[46] W. P. D. Wightman, 'Quid sit methodus? "Method" in sixteenth century medical teaching and "discovery"', *Journal of the History of Medicine*, XIX (1964), 360–76.

[47] Giano Matteo Durastante, in the dedication to his edition of da Monte, *In primi lib. Canonis Avicennae primam fen, profundissima commentaria* (Venice, 1557).

[48] Girolamo Donzellini, preface to his edition of da Monte, *Consilia medica omnia* (Nuremberg, 1559), refers to his 'sermones, in Nosocomiis aut alibi ab eo habiti: ut quod Galenus praecepit ac valde necessarium dixit: universalia praecepta, quae e sugesto luculenter explicabat, ad particularia applicaret, ac sui studiosos ea ratione exerceret'. See also Münster, 'Die Anfange eines klinischen Unterrichts', p.171, and Wightman, 'Method', p.373.

So greatly prized were da Monte's bedside discourses that some of his students took down transcripts of them, just as they did his lectures, and following his death these transcripts were published in considerable number, together with his formal written *consilia*.[49] Thus da Monte is the first great physician whose bedside teaching is known to us in some detail, and this has tended to create the impression that he was the first to introduce this method. In fact, though, his approach cannot be sharply differentiated from such longstanding practices as routine practical precepting, both in private homes and in hospitals, formal bedside consultations of two or more physicians, the summoning of colleagues and students to view unusual cases, and the formal discussion of such unusual cases by collegiate bodies.[50] As a result, da Monte's contemporaries seem to have regarded his bedside discourses as superb examples of a common teaching method, rather than as fundamental innovations. Thus Girolamo Donzellini, one of the early editors of da Monte's *Consilia*, said that those based on *viva voce* discussions would provide the rest of the world with an idea of how medicine was taught at Venice and Padua, and he correctly pointed out that the transcripts themselves showed the participation of many other physicians besides da Monte.[51] And a German editor, Reiner Solenander, put them in an even broader context, noting that they exemplified 'the conversations about the patients which customarily take place between the physician and his disciples while visiting the sick. Whoever has visited Italy will be familiar with this highly praiseworthy custom, by reason of which [Italy] excels over all other nations in medical education.'[52] Solenander was an excellent witness both to the commonness of the practice and its uniqueness to Italy, since he had spent seven years around the middle of the sixteenth century studying at Bologna, Pisa, Rome and Naples, and had studied at various Belgian and French universities as well.[53]

---

49 See, e.g. Donzellini's edition of da Monte's *Consilia medica omnia*; and Johann Crato von Krafftheim's edition of his *Consultationum medicarum opus absolutissimum* (Basel, 1565).

50 Puschmann, *History of Medical Education*, pp.251–6; Thorndike, *Science and Thought*, pp.71–6, 84, 104–5; Tomasini, *Gym. Pat.*, p.73. In 1368 the Greater Council of Venice ordered that all of the physicians of the city 'teneantur semel in mense convenire... ad conferendum et disputandum in scienta medicinae, specialiter sub casibus dubiis sibi occurrentibus vel qui ocurrere possent.': document printed in L. Premuda and G. Ongaro, 'I primordi della dissezione anatomica in Padova', *Acta Medicae Historiae Patavina*, XII (1965–6), 140–1. Compare, e.g. da Monte, *Consultationum* (1565), cols. 1000–1, where da Monte analyses a case in consultation with other physicians, with cols. 901–7, where he does so alone.

51 Preface to Donzellini's edition of da Monte, *Consilia* (1559), [p.10].

52 Reiner Solenander, *Consiliorum medicinalium* (Hanover, 1609), preface. The first edition appeared in 1596.

53 Ibid., dedication.

Nevertheless, it seems clear that da Monte did appreciate the unique potentialities of the hospital for clinical instruction, and that by exploiting the Hospital of St Francis at Padua for this purpose he endowed the method with a new and lasting importance.[54] Thus he began one of his bedside discourses with the assertion that 'In the hospital two things can be seen and practised, namely diseases and their symptoms', which suggests that he was deliberately using the hospital to teach practice not just in the sense of therapy, but in its more formal academic sense of a survey of particular diseases.[55] Indeed, one might conjecture that da Monte's transfer in 1543 from the chair of practice to that of theory actually reflected a conscious determination that individual diseases, in contrast to general principles, could more appropriately be demonstrated in the hospital than described in the lecture hall. At any rate, the transfer coincided with two other events, namely the move of the arts university to its new quarters, which were almost next door to the Hospital of St Francis,[56] and the first clear evidence of da Monte's teaching in the hospital on a regular basis. Thus in one of the transcripts, dating from April 1543, the anonymous student noted an event which took place 'at Padua, in the Hospital of St Francis, where da Monte was exercising his students in practice', and further that 'this was the seventeenth visit to the hospital'.[57] And it is interesting to note that on this particular visit da Monte not only gave a lengthy bedside commentary on an especially interesting case of syphilis, but took the occasion to begin a more formal course of lectures on the subject, also delivered within the hospital.[58]

Hence while hospital precepting was by no means without precedent, it does seem clear that in da Monte's hands the method was raised to a new level of sophistication and importance. It is worth noting that this was apparently made possible simply by allowing one man to hold two existing positions, that of university professor and that of Ordinary

---

54 On the Hospital of St Francis, see A. Antonelli, *Cenni storici sull'origine e sulle vicende dello Spedale Civile di Padova* (Padua, 1885); and L. Premuda and B. Bertolaso, 'La prima sede dell'insegnamento clinico nel mondo: l'ospedale de S. Francesco grande in Padova', *Acta Medicae Historiae Patavina*, VII (1960–1), 61–92.

55 Da Monte, *Consultationum* (1565), col. 905. This occurred on the third of four visits to the same patient.

56 O'Malley, *Vesalius*, pp.78–9; Premuda and Bertolaso, 'L'ospedale de S. Francesco', p.87.

57 Da Monte, *Explicatio eorum, quae pertinent, tum ad qualitates simplicium medicamentorum, tum ad eorundem compositione*, ed. V. Casali, second pagination in da Monte, *Explicatio locorum medicinae* (Paris, 1554), pp.237v, 238v. See also Giovanni Rasori, *Opere complete* (Florence, 1837), pp.295–6.

58 Da Monte, *Explicatio eorum*, pp.210–37.

hospital physician.[59] However, the combination was unlikely to have been casual or fortuitous. For one thing, as a busy professor and consultant da Monte would probably have had little need for the hospital appointment had he not been attracted by its teaching potentialities. And, for another, the mid–sixteenth century was a period of intense concern over hospitals in Italy, and in particular da Monte's activities coincided with a vigorous effort by the Venetian and Paduan civil authorities to establish that they, and not the clergy, had the final word in hospital affairs.[60] However, da Monte's clinical teaching was not limited to the hospital, since he continued to take his students on numerous private visits as well. Indeed, it appears that almost anyone, of whatever social class, who engaged his services had to be prepared to be used as teaching material.[61]

It seems quite likely that the hospital teaching was continued following da Monte's death in 1551 since, as mentioned, the Hospital of St Francis was adjacent to the university, and the one or two Ordinary hospital physicians were required to make their rounds every morning.[62] Moreover, the names of the incumbents from 1569 onward are known, and in most cases they doubled as members of the university medical faculty, as had da Monte.[63] However, it was not until 1578, perhaps due to the disruptions of the immediately preceding plague years, that hospital teaching was officially sanctioned by a decree of the Venetian Senate. The initiative in securing this action seems to have been taken by the German students, working in consort with Marco degli Oddi and Albertino Bottoni, the two members of the faculty who took responsibility for the hospital teaching at this time.[64]

From the Annals of the German Nation we learn that the programme as conducted by Bottoni and Oddi encompassed several different elements. First, during the regular school term Bottoni would deliver his public lecture on medical practice (he was First Extraordinary professor), and immediately following this would take the students to the hospital, apparently with the primary objective of demonstrating, if possible, the particular diseases on which he had just lectured.[65] Second,

---

[59] Münster, 'Die Anfänge eines klinischen Unterrichts', pp.171, 173.
[60] B. Pullan, *Rich and Poor in Renaissance Venice* (Cambridge, Mass., 1971), pp.216–38, and especially pp.331–5, and p.332, note 17.
[61] Da Monte, *Consultationum* (1565), passim.
[62] Premuda and Bertolaso, 'L'ospedale di S. Francesco', p.72; Antonelli, *Cenni storici*, pp.31, 38.
[63] Antonelli, *Cenni storici*, pp.156ff.
[64] Tomasini, *Gym. Pat.*, pp.420–1; Facciolati, *Fasti*, p.215; *ANGAP* I, pp.138–9. See also Münster, 'Die Anfänge eines klinischen Unterrichts', p.172.
[65] *ANGAP* I, p.138.

during the summer holidays, when no lectures were given, Oddi and Bottoni would visit the hospital every morning at a certain hour, and take turns in discussing 'some important case [*insigniorem aliquem casum*]'.[66] It is this conception of hospital teaching, rather than the first, that was embodied in the Senate decree, which stated that 'two of the professors of practice will visit the hospital at established times, there to hold forth about the diseases presented by the occasion, for the utility of the students'.[67] It appears that Bottoni emerged as the dominant figure in this process of analysing individual cases, while Oddi's particular speciality was the teaching of uroscopy in the hospital on the winter feast days.[68] Finally, we read of an effort to incorporate post-mortem dissections into the hospital teaching in 1578, but this was forbidden by the hospital officials because of a jurisdictional dispute which called attention to the practice, and in turn provoked fear among the patients.[69] However, it seems unlikely that this was more than a temporary setback for the use of the autopsy in connection with hospital teaching, since there are persistent reports of the practice and, as we shall see, the Ordinary surgeons of the hospital seem usually to have been full physician-surgeons who were also involved in the private teaching of normal anatomy to the medical students.[70]

During the late sixteenth and on into the seventeenth century, at least the last three aspects of the programme – daily hospital rounds with formal discussion of major cases, systematic teaching of urines (and pulses), and autopsies of fatal cases – seem to have persisted as more or less standard parts of the clinical teaching at Padua, though it is not clear whether the aim of using the hospital to illustrate the public lectures on practice ever really succeeded.[71] It is worth noting, though, that by the beginning of the seventeenth century the public lectures of the leading professor of practice, Ercole Sassonia, had come to incorporate large amounts of data drawn from his own current and past cases, whereas his predecessors had tended to focus much more exclusively on evaluating

---

[66] Ibid.
[67] Facciolati, *Fasti*, p.215.
[68] *ANGAP* i, pp.143–4, 235. Oddi's activities continued until his death in 1591 (ii, pp.3, 8), and Bottoni's until shortly before his death in 1596 (ii, pp.76, 80, 88).
[69] *ANGAP* i, p.44.
[70] See below.
[71] Tomasini, *Gym. Pat.*, p.73; Facciolati, *Fasti*, p.364; Münster, 'Die Anfänge eines klinischen Unterrichts', p.172; Fichtner, 'Padova e Tübingen', pp.46–54. See also Pietro Marchetti, *Observationum medico-chirurgicarum rariorum sylloge* (Padua, 1664), pp.1, 27–8, 30, 46, 51, 85, 87, 90–6. On Marchetti, see below.

the varying opinions of the authorities.[72] However, Sassonia's own reputation depended primarily on his heavy involvement in practical precepting, based on discussing individual cases with the students.[73]

By the late sixteenth century the excellence and the ready availability of such bedside teaching were still unparalleled outside Italy, and it was primarily for this reason that foreign medical students continued to come there in such large numbers. Many would come for only a year or two, having completed their studies of natural philosophy and medical theory at a university in their native country and therefore needing only to learn practice, in part by attending the formal lectures on the subject, but especially by accompanying the most respected preceptors on their house visits and hospital rounds. A clear indication of these priorities is provided by an incident that occurred at Padua in 1597.[74] The Moderators of the university, apparently concerned that the students were neglecting their attendance at the formal public lectures, proposed severe restrictions on all outside activities, including the visiting of the sick. The foreign students saw this as being especially inimical to their interests, for, as the annalist of the German Nation put it, 'how few among us are there who, putting aside all the rest, have not come to this famous university for the sake of practical training alone? But how can we gain knowledge and experience of this [i.e. medical practice] without constant inspection of the sick, and careful observation of the daily changes of diseases and their symptoms?' The student representatives went to the Syndic of the university and put it to him bluntly: 'Few or none of us have come here only for the sake of lectures, and all of us have come to learn practice. We do not lack for lecturers in our own country or elsewhere, and we also have books at home which we can just as well read there as here. It is the study of practice that has led us to cross so many mountains, and at such great expense.' The student annalist also noted that the move had provoked unusual unanimity among the foreign students, who continued their practical precepting in defiance of the ruling. Eventually a compromise was worked out whereby those who had completed their philosophy and medical theory could pursue their practical training as before, a ruling which tacitly assumed that it

---

[72] E.g. Ercole Sassonia, *Prognoseon practicarum libri duo* (Frankfurt, 1610), passim, which compare with, for example, Girolamo Mercuriale, *Medicina practica* (Leyden, 1623), passim. Both these works were derived from Paduan lectures.

[73] *ANGAP* I, p.139; II, pp.78, 108; Peter Uffenbach, dedication to his edition of Sassonia, *Pantheon medicinae* (Frankfurt, 1603); Johann Jessen, dedication to Leander Vailatus's edition of *Prognoseon* (1610).

[74] *ANGAP* II, pp.77–8. See also I, p.235.

was acceptable for the advanced students to neglect the formal lectures on practice in favour of the bedside precepting.[75] It was also made clear that professors of both theory and practice could participate in the practical teaching without distinction.

As we have seen, the upgrading of such bedside teaching by the medical humanists required little in the way of formal institutional innovation, since the various ingredients – the professorship of practice, practical precepting, hospitals and the position of hospital physician – already existed and needed only to be exploited in new ways. However, this was by no means true of another major plank of the humanist programme, that of introducing the students to medical 'simples', that is the many substances, mostly botanical, that made up the materia medica of the time. The medieval medical curriculum had made no formal provision for this, although this does not mean that it was not taught at all, but only that such teaching was necessarily of a private, and probably somewhat haphazard, nature. Thus when Francesco Bonafede was named to a lectureship on simples in 1533 it marked a significant innovation, although Bonafede had been a professor of medicine at the university since 1524, so that his new title may have been simply a formal recognition and encouragement of something that he had already been doing.[76] However, with official recognition came the right to seek further provision for teaching the subject adequately. In the case of simples this meant the establishment of a botanical garden, since many of the important medicinal plants were not native to Italy and therefore could be exhibited only in their dried commercial form. Bonafede, da Monte and others on the faculty took up the cause, and with the help of interested Venetian patricians such as Daniel Barbaro they won Senate approval in 1545 for the construction of a fairly elaborate facility.[77] This was the first such garden in Europe expressly designed for teaching purposes, and it was opened in 1546 under the direction of Luigi Anguillara. The spring botanical demonstrations thus became a regular event in the academic year, and eventually, in 1594, the

---

[75]   *ANGAB* II, pp.78–9, 80.

[76]   V. Giacomini, 'Francesco Bonafede' in *Dizionario biografico degli italiani*, XI (Rome, 1969), pp.491–2.

[77]   Ibid., and also Tomasini, *Gym. Pat.*, p.84; E. Meyer, *Geschichte der Botanik* (4 vols., Königsberg, 1854–7), IV, p.256; Bertolaso, 'Ricerche d'Archirio', pp.31–2; J. Stannard, 'Luigi Anguillara' in *Dictionary of Scientific Biography*, I (New York, 1970), p.167. However, a rival claim has been made for the University of Pisa as the site of the first such teaching garden. See E. Chiovenda, 'Note sulla fondazione degli orti Medici di Padova e di Pisa', in *Atti dell' VIII° congresso internazionale di storia della medicina Rome 1930*, ed. P. Capparoni (Pisa, 1931), pp.488–509; and A. G. Keller, 'Luca Ghini' in *Dictionary of Scientific Biography*, V (New York, 1972), pp.383–4.

professorship of materia medica was raised to Ordinary status.[78]

The appointment of Vesalius to the Paduan faculty in 1537 probably represented a similar policy decision to upgrade the teaching of anatomy, again under the inspiration of the ideals of medical humanism. However, there was this difference, that anatomy, unlike botany, had had a modest place in the official curriculum since the Middle Ages, so that Vesalius's appointment involved the adaptation of existing procedures rather than the establishment of a distinct new lectureship. Moreover, the improvisation involved in Vesalius's appointment was to have some important long-term effects for surgery as well as for anatomy, and therefore it is important that we give some consideration to the previously existing situation before seeing what transpired in 1537 and subsequently.[79]

The fifteenth-century Paduan statute governing the public teaching of anatomy treats the latter not as a distinct subject for which one might appoint a permanent teacher or group of teachers, but rather as a special annual event, to be carried out during the winter break in the lecture schedule, and requiring the co-operation of several individuals temporarily delegated for this purpose.[80] The first participant was to be chosen from among the Extraordinary (i.e. more junior) professors, and his office was simply to read the *Anatomy* of Mondino (*legat textum*) bit by bit as the dissection proceeded. The second was to be one of the four Ordinary professors of medicine (theory or practice), and he had two rather important tasks, namely to explain (*declarat*) the portion of Mondino that had just been read, and then to demonstrate (*montret*) the relevant structures in the cadaver. The third person was to do the actual dissection (*incidendum et secandum*), and was to be chosen from among the lecturers on surgery. However, the statute acknowledged that a competent dissector was crucial for the success of the demonstration, and so added that if none of the Lecturers on Surgery was considered suitable, then another person, presumably a surgeon, should be employed for the occasion. Thus in no circumstances could competence

---

[78] Tomasini, *Gym. Pat.*, pp.72, 153; G. Ongaro, 'Contributi alla biografia di Prospero Alpini', *Acta Medicae Historiae Patavina*, VIII–IX (1961–3), 102–7.

[79] O'Malley has to some extent done this in *Vesalius*, pp.79–81, but it seems to me that he has glossed over the differences between the statutory provisions and the actual practice in the period just before Vesalius's appointment.

[80] *Stat. Pad.*, p.42. These provisions are illustrated quite literally in the famous frontispiece to the *Anatomy* of Mondino in the 1493 edition of the *Fasciculo di medicina*. However, it is often wrongly assumed that the presiding doctor is the young man behind the desk reading the book, rather than the older one who is explaining and demonstrating. See, e.g. W. S. Heckscher, *Rembrandt's Anatomy of Dr Nicolaas Tulp* (New York, 1958), p.46.

at dissection by itself qualify an individual for the position of lecturer on surgery, since the statute made explicit provision for the possibility that the incumbents might not have such competence.

Who were these lecturers on surgery? To answer this question something must first be said about the relationship between medicine and surgery at Padua.[81] Here as in other parts of Europe the elite of collegiate physicians generally did not practise surgery, while many of those who did were trained through a craft-apprenticeship system. Before they could practise, these craft-surgeons had to submit to a licensing examination conducted by Doctors of Medicine, and had to promise not to administer internal remedies, and not to treat serious surgical cases except under the supervision of a physician. In addition, however, at Padua as elsewhere in Italy, surgery never ceased to be an academic discipline, which one could pursue through a period of university study followed by the awarding of an academic degree, based upon an examination conducted in Latin. This degree conferred the right to practise all aspects of surgery as an independent agent, including the administration of such internal remedies as might be necessary, as well as to lecture publicly on surgery from an academic chair. However, this degree in surgery was a less prestigious one than that in medicine, and therefore the more ambitious surgeons routinely took the full doctorate in arts and medicine, that is the same degree as the physicians.[82] It is a nice question whether such individuals should be considered as physicians who practised surgery or as surgeons who had taken medical degrees, but the fact is that while they were free to practise internal medicine, they functioned essentially as the elite of surgical practitioners and teachers, and were often referred to as 'surgeons'.[83]

Practising surgeons also found their place within the academic

---

[81] For information concerning the official position of surgery at Padua, see *Stat. Pad.*, pp.42v–43; Tomasini, *Gym. Pat.*, pp.201–3; Giomo, 'L'archivio antico', pp.383, 410, 415–16; Sterzi, *Casseri*, pp.16–17; Morpurgo, 'English physicians at Padua', p.65; Kibre, *Scholarly Privileges*, pp.80–3; C. Ferrari, 'L'officio della Sanità in Padova', *Miscellanea di storia veneta*, 3rd ser., I (1910), 30–1; H. B. Adelmann, *The Embryological Treatises of Hieronymous Fabricius of Aquapendente* (Ithaca, N.Y., 1942), pp.7–8.

[82] E.g. Adelmann, *Fabricius*, pp.6–7; E. Gurlt, *Geschichte der Chirurgie*, II, Pt I (Berlin, 1898), pp.487, 545, 553; and see also below.

[83] E.g. Gurlt, *Geschichte der Chirurgie*, p.355; W. R. Shea, *Galileo's Intellectual Revolution* (London, 1972), p.35. An excellent insight into the practice and teaching of such an individual is provided by Pietro Marchetti's rather anecdotal *Observationum medico-chirurgicarum rariorum sylloge* (Padua, 1664). On the title page, Marchetti identifies himself as 'Philosophi ac Medici Patavini, Equitis D. Marci, Et in Patrio Gymnasio Chirurgie olim, nunc vero Anatomes Professoris', and during most of his career he was also Surgeon to the Hospital of St Francis: Antonelli, *Cenni storici*, pp.158–60. Cipolla is quite incorrect in his assertion that such individuals did not actually practise surgery, or did so only under irregular circumstances: *Public Health*, pp.74–5.

hierarchy as the lecturers on surgery mentioned above. They were responsible for a three-year cycle of commentary on surgical works which prepared the surgical students for their examination, and also provided the element of surgical instruction that was important even for those medical students who would not practise surgery.[84] At Bologna during the sixteenth century there were anything from three to seven lecturers on surgery, who had to be full Doctors of Medicine as well as practising surgeons.[85] Surgery at Padua was less well-off: the fifteenth century statutes provided for only two chairs, and since the salaries were rather low, one individual was allowed to hold both.[86] Thus, for example, in 1526 Nicolò de Musicis was appointed to one of the two chairs, but from 1529 to 1535 he held both, receiving both salaries, and was succeeded, in turn, by two incumbents.[87] In contrast to Bologna, the surgical teachers at Padua did not have to be full Doctors of Medicine, though before Vesalius they sometimes were, and afterward they almost always were.[88] They did, however, have to be practising surgeons, and again it seems that this statutory provision was indeed followed right up to Vesalius's time; for example, de Musicis doubled as Surgeon to the Hospital of St Francis during at least part of his tenure at the university.[89]

Returning to the annual anatomies, we may first note that the options allowed by the statute as regards the dissector were both in use in the immediate pre-Vesalian period. It is reported that in 1529 de Musicis performed the annual dissection 'in accordance with his office', while in 1536 the dissection was performed by neither of the two lecturers on surgery, but by an outside surgeon who was engaged specially for this purpose, as permitted by the statute.[90] The surgeon thus employed was the Paduan Giovanni Antonio Lonigo, who had been trained by Domenicus Sennus, the leading Paduan surgeon of the early sixteenth century, and had established his own surgical practice in the capital city

[84] Tomasini, *Gym. Pat.*, p.84.
[85] *Rotuli Bol.*, ii, passim; *Stat. Bol.*, p.471. For information on various incumbents during the sixteenth century, see M. T. Gnudi and J. P. Webster, *The Life and Times of Gaspare Tagliacozzi, Surgeon of Bologna* (New York, 1950), pp.32–3, 62–3, 83, 97–8; 271, note 43.
[86] *Stat. Pad.*, pp.33–4.
[87] Facciolati, *Fasti*, p.385.
[88] *Stat. Pad.*, pp.33–4. See, e.g. Thorndike, *Science and Thought*, pp.76–7 for one fifteenth-century incumbent who was not a Doctor of Medicine, and Tomasini, *Gym. Pat.*, pp.155–7 for two who were. On the post-Vesalians, see below.
[89] Premuda and Bertolaso, 'L'ospedale de S. Francesco', p.72. I have been unable to determine whether de Musicis was a Doctor of Medicine.
[90] Facciolati, *Fasti*, p.385; Moritz Roth, *Andreas Vesalius Bruxellensis* (Berlin, 1892), p.454.

of Venice.[91] It is not known what formal qualifications Lonigo possessed, but he seems to have been a man of some standing in the Venetian–Paduan medical community,[92] and in 1536 his own most important student, Realdo Colombo, apparently was given the second chair of surgery at Padua, only to lose it the following year to Vesalius.[93]

On the other hand, by the late 1520s the other parts of the Paduan anatomy statute, those pertaining to participation by physicians, were no longer being strictly followed. The statutory requirement that the text of Mondino be read and explained was indeed being carried out, but through a lecture course called the 'Anatomical doctrine' that was quite separate from the actual dissection.[94] This commentary on Mondino was usually given by one of the Ordinary professors of medicine, as provided by the statute, but since he was no longer involved in the dissection at the time of the commentary he could also read the text for himself, instead of having it done by the Extraordinary professor, as called for by the statute. In exchange, the latter was given the other half of the duty originally assigned to the senior professor, that of serving as demonstrator at the dissection, which had thus become a two-man operation, conducted by a physician 'ostensor' and a surgeon 'sector'.[95] That the senior medical professor should withdraw from the actual dissection and devote himself to an elaborate theoretical commentary might seem at first glance like a typical scholastic aberration, but I would suggest that it should be viewed in a more positive light. For one thing, the commentary on Mondino provided the forum for a much more extensive treatment of the functional aspects of anatomy than could conveniently be included at the actual dissection.[96] For another, with the

91   On Lonigo and Sennus, see B. Scardeone, *Historiae de urbis Patavii antiquitate*, in J. G. Graevius (ed.), *Thesaurus antiquitatum et historiarum Italiae* (9 vols in 31 pts, Leyden, 1704–25), VI, Pt 3, col. 248. Scardeone notes that his own brother Vincenzo was a student of both men.

92   See the prefatory letter 'Ioanni Antonio Leonico' from Bassiano Landi in his edition of Jean Tagault's *De chirurgica institutione* (Venice, 1544). Landi was a medical professor at Padua.

93   Antonio Riccoboni, *De gymnasio patavino* (Padua, 1598), p.25r, lists one 'Paullus Columbus Cremensis' for this year, but Bertolaso, 'Ricerche d'archivio', identifies the incumbent as Realdo Colombo. Colombo, *De re anatomica* (Venice, 1559), p.24, refers to 'prudentissimo, ac doctissimo aetatis nostri chirurgo Ioanni Antonio Plato cognomenta Lonigo, quo praeceptore septennium usus sum, adeo ut quantum in hac medendi arte profecerim: me nunquam poenitere possit'. See also pp.60, 122.

94   Facciolati, *Fasti*, pp.385, 386; and R. Eriksson (ed.), *Andreas Vesalius' First Public Anatomy at Bologna* (Uppsala and Stockholm, 1959), passim, and pp.37–41.

95   Facciolati, *Fasti*, pp.385, 386. From the account of Alessandro Benedetti, it would seem that this evolution was already well advanced by the 1490s, since the Paduan anatomies as he describes them are essentially bipartite operations, with no reference at all to the reading of Mondino. See L. R. Lind, *Studies in Pre-Vesalian Anatomy* (Philadelphia, 1975), p.83.

96   Curtius (Matheo Corti), the most celebrated lecturer on Mondino, explicitly conceived of the relationship between lecture and dissection in this way: Eriksson, *Vesalius' First Public Anatomy*, pp.44–6.

separation of the reading and commentary on Mondino from the dissection, the latter was free to develop into a substantive procedure in its own right, with the dissector as the dominant participant. The course of dissections conducted by Lonigo in 1536, the year before Vesalius's arrival, is known to have lasted for a month, and from an eye-witness account it appears that Lonigo was regarded as the major protagonist in the proceedings.[97]

That the annual anatomy at Padua had developed from a cursory illustration of the text of Mondino into so substantial an affair was probably due in no small measure to the influence of the medical humanists. Galen's many anatomical treatises embodied the results of centuries of research, including his own considerable contributions, but most of these works were unknown to European physicians before the 1520s and 1530s, when all of them appeared in Latin translation within a matter of a few years.[98] By this time the revival of interest in anatomy, especially in Italy, had reached the point where significant original observations were being made, but Galen's anatomy was so much more sophisticated, in terms of both detailed content and dissection technique, that it effectively rendered obsolete even the best of what are usually called the pre-Vesalian anatomists. Moreover, the recovery of the Galenic treatises also gave anatomy a whole new significance in academic medicine, since these works showed by deed as well as word just how serious Galen had been when he insisted upon the crucial importance of anatomy, including involvement in dissection, for the physician.[99]

For a short period during the early 1530s the main focus of the Galenic anatomical revival was at the University of Paris.[100] In contrast to Italy, there had been little previous anatomical activity at Paris, so that what took place was almost purely an outgrowth of the newly available Galenic treatises. Thus the Parisian Galenists not only busied themselves with the translation and publication of Galen's anatomical writings, they also quickly sought to make them the basis for a teaching programme based on dissections. Of particular importance in this regard was Jacobus Sylvius, whose private course was based on animal dissections which he carried out himself, while Johann Guinter of Andernach sought similarly to upgrade the annual public human anatomies through

[97] Roth, *Vesalius Bruxellensis*, p.454.
[98] Durling, 'A chronological census', pp.281–95, nos. 7, 17, 42, 43, 44, 49, 51, 68, 70, 79.
[99] O. Temkin, *Galenism. Rise and Decline of a Medical Philosophy* (Ithaca, N.Y., 1973), pp.12–14, 40–2.
[100] O'Malley, *Vesalius*, pp.45–61.

reliance on Galenic sources, though he continued to call on others to do the actual dissections.

Into this environment came Andreas Vesalius, a young Belgian who had completed his preliminary studies at Louvain and in 1533 went on to study medicine under the newly triumphant Galenists of Paris.[101] He was quickly caught up in the anatomical activity of the Paris School, mastering the contents of the Galenic writings, learning dissection technique from Sylvius, and eventually performing the human dissections at Guinter's public course. On the basis of this common experience Guinter published in 1536 his *Institutiones anatomicae*, the first important dissection manual avowedly based on purely Galenic sources, and in this work he praised Vesalius as 'a young man, by Hercules, of great promise, possessing an extraordinary knowledge of medicine, learned in both languages, and very skilled in the dissection of bodies' – in other words, the very model of a humanistic anatomist.[102] However, political developments forced this promising young man to leave Paris before taking his degree. He returned temporarily to Louvain, where the low level of anatomical teaching again made it possible for him, as a medical student, to take control of the annual public dissection, thereby further sharpening his talents in this regard.[103] However, his ambition to enter the imperial service as a physician clearly required a medical degree more prestigious than that of Louvain, and so at some time in the middle or latter part of 1537 he set out for the University of Padua.

In the meantime the new Galenic anatomy had already made an impact at Venice and Padua, where it merged with and heightened the previously existing interest in anatomical studies.[104] Moreover, there is clear evidence of a particular concern for anatomy along humanistic lines among the very men that Vesalius was coming to study under, namely the professors of medical practice at Padua, especially Francesco Frigimelica and Giunio Paolo Crasso.[105] And they must have had at least some prior knowledge of Vesalius's talents, since Guinter's *Institutes*, with its words of praise for Vesalius, was already being consulted at Lonigo's dissections of 1536–7.[106] When Vesalius appeared on the scene

---

[101]   Ibid.
[102]   Ibid, p.56.
[103]   Ibid., pp.62–72, especially p.69.
[104]   See, e.g., Nicolò Massa, *Liber introductorius anatomiae* (Venice, 1536), pp.3–5.
[105]   In the dedication to his translation of Theophilus Protospatarius, *De corporis humani fabrica* (Venice, 1537), Crasso discussed his own and Frigimelica's interest in anatomy. On Frigimelica and anatomy, see also Colombo, *De re anatomica*, p.111; and Gabriele Falloppio, *Opera quae adhuc extant omnia* (Frankfurt, 1584), p.598.
[106]   Roth, *Vesalius Bruxellensis*, pp.16–17, note 6.

and turned out to be as good as Guinter had said, his medical professors probably became convinced of the desirability of having him take over the dissection, as he had previously done at both Paris and Louvain.

However, it was one thing for Vesalius, as a mere medical student, to take charge of the anatomies at places where the previous interest had been slight or non-existent, but quite another for him to do so at Padua, where the level of interest was already quite high and where the actual conduct of the anatomy was governed by well-defined statutory and customary prerogatives and procedures. The events of early December 1537 seem to have been aimed at overcoming the technical obstacles in the way of Vesalius's conduct of the winter anatomy.[107] On the first, third and fifth of this month, less than two months after the beginning of his first academic term at Padua, Vesalius was rushed through the various stages to his medical doctorate, with the greatest possible remission of fees. His chief *promotor* was Frigimelica, and his other *promotores* included Crasso and three other prominent Paduan physicians. He was immediately given both lectureships on surgery, although strictly speaking the simple possession of a medical degree did not qualify him for these positions. Until this time he was clearly headed for a career in internal medicine, and had no known competence either to teach or to practise surgery.[108] Thus the obvious intent of the appointment was to give him undisputed priority over all others in the conduct of the annual dissections, which he began on 6 December.

Moreover, Vesalius was given sole responsibility for the dissections, that is he had the office of *ostensor* as well as *sector*, although this may have been of more symbolic than real importance. The same student who left an account of Lonigo's demonstrations of 1536–7 also attended Vesalius's the following year, and he evidently thought that the two men had performed more or less equivalent functions.[109] In addition, however, Vesalius was allowed to carry out the separate lecture course on anatomy, something which had been a substantial prerogative of the four Ordinary medical professors, although this must have been done

---

[107] The relevant documents are provided by Roth, *Vesalius Bruxellensis*, pp.425–33. See also O'Malley, *Vesalius*, pp.76–81.

[108] Vesalius's first publication was a *Paraphrasis in nonum librum Rhazae ... ad Regem Almansorem de affectuum singularum corporis partium curatione* (Basel, 1537); this work by Rhazes was still the prescribed textbook of internal medicine. On Vesalius's lack of competence for his surgical duties, see O'Malley, *Vesalius*, pp.80, 205–6.

[109] Roth, *Vesalius Bruxellensis*, pp.454–5. The student used the words 'Secante Jo. Antonio Leonico' and 'Secante ... Andraea Vesalio' to describe their respective roles. In the preface to the *Fabrica* (fol. 3r) Vesalius stated that at the Paduan anatomies, 'administraverim ... ostenderim atque docuerim'.

with their agreement since two of the four had served as *promotores* for his medical degree.[110] Thus instead of there being instituted a whole new lectureship, as had been done for simples, the existing lectureships in surgery were transformed into a *de facto* chair of anatomy by disregarding Vesalius's lack of credentials for the surgical parts of the teaching and delegating to him all three previously separate aspects of the anatomical teaching. Unfortunately the explicit terms of his appointment of 1537 are not known, but in his reappointment of 1541 (when his salary was raised from forty to seventy florins) he was expressly designated as 'lector, ostensor and incisor of anatomy', in addition to being lecturer on surgery.[111] To the medical professors, who would have seen in Vesalius a young humanist physician like themselves, this arrangement must have seemed quite satisfactory, although one might well imagine that the local surgeons were not exactly pleased at being displaced from their only slot within the academic hierarchy.

Whatever may have been the underlying politics, the immediate effect of Vesalius's appointment was the significant upgrading of the teaching of anatomy, both from the pedagogical point of view, since Vesalius clearly had a great flair for conducting the demonstrations, and from the point of view of medical humanism, as the substantive content of what Vesalius conveyed through his demonstrations was solidly Galenic in origin.[112] Moreover, the latter was true not only for the anatomical demonstrations but also for the separate lectures, since during his years at Padua Vesalius routinely commented not on the *Anatomy* of Mondino, but on Galen's *De ossibus ad tyrones*, the first Latin translation of which had been published as recently as 1535.[113] Of course, after several years of teaching at Padua Vesalius gradually turned from a skilled teacher of Galenic anatomy into an increasingly harsh critic of it, as he came to realize that Galen's descriptions, based upon the dissection of animals, differ significantly from what is observed in the human cadaver. However, it is important that we see the essential relationship between these two stages in Vesalius's intellectual evolution, namely that it was only because he had so thoroughly mastered the content of Galenic anatomy for teaching purposes that he

---

110   *Fabrica*, and see also below.
111   Roth, *Vesalius Bruxellensis*, pp.429–30. Compare with Facciolati, *Fasti*, pp.385, 386.
112   Roth, *Vesalius Bruxellensis*, pp.455–7; O'Malley, *Vesalius*, pp.81–4.
113   O'Malley, *Vesalius*, p.120. It appears that in 1549 *De ossibus* was made the official text for the anatomical lectures: Bertolaso, 'Ricerche d'archivio', p.29. Falloppio sometimes lectured on *De ossibus*, but seems to have preferred the 'Similar Parts' as an anatomical lecture topic: G. Favaro, *Gabrielle Falloppia Modenese* (Modena, 1928), pp.5–7.

could go on to become the effective founder of modern anatomy.[114]

In retrospect it may be said that Vesalius's tenure at Padua, brief though it was, set the precedent for transforming the lectureship in surgery into a chair of anatomy first, and of surgery second, but it was to take some time before this emerged as the standard procedure. Thus in his absence from the anatomy of 1542–3, the university reverted to earlier practice, with Realdo Colombo being appointed as *incisor* and Crasso as *ostensor*, while Pamphilo Monti, the newly-appointed First Ordinary of Medical Theory, carried out the 'anatomical doctrine', or commentary on Mondino.[115] Likewise in 1544–5, when Colombo had succeeded Vesalius as lecturer on surgery, he was charged only with the dissecting portion of the anatomy, with Crasso again appointed as *ostensor* and Giambatista da Monte as lecturer. Perhaps Vesalius's situation had been seen as only a temporary suspension of the rules, but the reversion to the pre-Vesalian anatomical regime may also reflect the fact that Colombo, for all his talents as an anatomist, was the very kind of person that Vesalius had displaced, namely a true surgeon whose roots were in the local surgical community. Colombo had trained for seven years with Lonigo, and it was apparently on the basis of this practical training that he was named to the second chair of surgery in 1536, only to lose it to Vesalius the following year.[116] In 1541 an effort was made to restore the second chair to Colombo but when this was vetoed by the Venetian government he returned to Venice to assist Lonigo in his surgical practice.[117] By this time he seems to have acquired a Paduan degree, but perhaps in surgery rather than in arts and medicine,[118] and in any case he did not have the polish of humanistic education or the thorough mastery of Galen's anatomical writings that had made Vesalius so attractive to the physicians at Padua.

Thus it was perhaps with mixed feelings that Colombo left Padua for Pisa in 1545, to accept the new chair of anatomy and surgery which

---

[114] I have discussed this point in 'C. D. O'Malley's *Vesalius*: an appreciation', *Journal of the History of Medicine*, XXVI (1971), 87–92.

[115] Facciolati, *Fasti*, p.386.

[116] See above, note 93.

[117] Roth, *Vesalius Bruxellensis*, p.429; Colombo, *De re anatomica*, p.60.

[118] A Paduan document of 1539 refers to Colombo as 'spectabili chyrurgie scholare': cited by F. Lucchetta, *Il medico e filosofo bellunese Andrea Alpago* (Padua, 1964), p.60, note 6. A document of 1544 refers to him as 'perito et bon dottore' (Roth, *Vesalius Bruxellensis*, p.432), but those having a degree in surgery were sometimes so designated. See, e.g. Antonelli, *Cenni storici*, p.31, 'Un dottor di cirogia'. However, the whole question of the 'Doctor of Surgery' requires further investigation.

Cosimo de'Medici had just established at his university.[119] Anatomical teachers who could meet the new standards set by Vesalius were rare creatures in those early days, and Colombo's departure left a gap in the Paduan faculty that was not filled until 1551, when Gabriele Falloppio was named lecturer on surgery, and given sole responsibility for the teaching of anatomy: as was spelled out in his reappointment of 1552, he was to 'dissect, lecture, and demonstrate the anatomy'.[120] However, the very need to stipulate all three activities shows that they were still regarded as potentially separable, and even Falloppio, with his doctorate in medicine and philosophy and his impeccable humanistic credentials, was not immune to efforts to reactivate the custom of divided responsibility in 1554.[121] The prime instigator of this development seems to have been Vittore Trincavella, the influential First Professor of Medical Practice, who had asserted his statutory prerogative to play the dominant role of speaking and demonstrating at the dissection, with Falloppio simply doing the cutting. Falloppio was apparently willing to acquiesce in this arrangement, but on the second day of the demonstrations the students raised such a howl of protest that the anatomical course was cancelled for the year. The next year the whole responsibility was restored to Falloppio, and this can probably be said to mark the point from which the Lecturer on Surgery at Padua was unquestionably the Professor of Anatomy as well.[122]

Falloppio's premature death in 1562 ushered in a new period of uncertainty in the anatomical teaching, but this was resolved in 1565 by the appointment of his most important student, Hieronymus Fabricius. This turned out to be as decisive a resolution as such things can be, since Fabricius held the chair for nearly fifty-five years, until his death in 1619, and for all but the last seven took primary responsibility for the public teaching of anatomy through dissections and lectures. Moreover, throughout this period the level of student interest in anatomy steadily mounted, to the point where the annual winter demonstrations were second only, if at all, to the opportunities for practical precepting in drawing foreign students to Padua.[123] Indeed, numerous incidents

[119] E. D. Coppola, 'The discovery of the pulmonary circulation: a new approach', *Bulletin of the History of Medicine*, XXXI (1957), 51–4.

[120] Tomasini, *Gym. Pat.*, p.96; Favaro, *Falloppia*, pp.216–17.

[121] Favaro, *Falloppia*, pp.90–1, 223–5.

[122] However, as late as 1626 the practice of divided responsibility was still resorted to as a stop-gap when the chair of anatomy was empty: see *ANGAP* III, pp.213–14.

[123] *ANGAP* II, pp.109–10: 'Quis nostrum est, qui Patavium non tam exactissimarum anatomiarum quam fori tantummodo practici caussa adveniat?'

similar to the Trincavella affair demonstrate just how much importance the students themselves attached to thorough and competent anatomical teaching.[124]

On the other hand, Trincavella was not alone among the major medical professors in possessing this enthusiasm for anatomy. Others, such as Bassiano Landi, Mercuriale, Capodivacca and Rudio, manifested their own interests in one way or another.[125] Giovanni Tommaso Minadoi, who eventually became First Professor of Practice, published a treatise in 1590 in which he sought to establish the crucial importance of anatomy to internal medicine as well as to surgery,[126] while Sassonia's lectures on practice actually bear out this thesis to a considerable degree. That is, they contain fairly numerous references to anatomical data, both to establish the normal structural bases for physiological and pathological processes and to illustrate the internal effects of disease as observed *post mortem*.[127]

Support for anatomy was not unanimous within the Paduan arts faculty, however, for in the 1620s the leading professor of philosophy, Cesare Cremonini, addressed a course of lectures to the medical students in which he treated the pursuit of anatomical investigations with withering scorn.[128] It is a sign of death, he said, and of weakness of the brain, when a sick person begins gathering straws, and so also Galen and his followers can be called 'sick' for gathering the myriad details about the human body that are of no use or intrinsic value whatsoever.[129] Anatomy does have its limited role as an 'instrument' for other arts and sciences, especially for surgery, but once it has reached the stage where it can satisfactorily fulfil those ends it is pointless to pursue it any further. To say that anatomy is 'perfected' by the discovery of one more minute muscle or some previously unobserved little gland is absurd, because no good, either intellectual or practical, can possibly result from such

[124] G. Favaro, 'L'insegnamento anatomico di Girolamo Fabrici d'Acquapendente', in *Monografie storiche sullo Studio di Padova* (Venice, 1922), pp.107–35; Adelmann, *Fabricius*, pp.8–22.

[125] Bassiano Landi, *De humana historia vel singularum hominis partium cognitione libri duo* (Basel, 1542); Mercuriale was involved both in Costanzo Varoli's *De nervis opticis* (Padua, 1573) and in his *Anatomiae* (Frankfurt, 1591); Capodivacca, *De methodo anatomica liber* (Venice, 1594); Rudio, *De naturali & morbosa cordis constitutione* (Venice, 1600).

[126] Minadoi, 'De adaequato subiecto facultatis anatomicae', pp.107–25 in his *Medicarum disputationum liber primus* (Treviso, 1610 [for 1590]).

[127] Sassonia, *Prognoseon*, e.g. pp.59, 88, 176, 177, 192, 221, 252, 263, 264, 279.

[128] Cesare Cremonini, *Apologia dictòrum Aristotelis de origine, et principatu membrorum adversus Galenum* (Venice, 1627). From the opening remarks (p.2) it is clear that this work is a transcript of academic lectures addressed primarily to medical students. The principal critique of anatomy begins on p.50.

[129] Ibid., p.61.

knowledge. 'It is for the fool to collect trivia', declared Cremonini, 'not for the philosophical genius'.[130]

The reasons why Cremonini, a die-hard Aristotelian of the old school, should take such a jaundiced view of anatomy are not difficult to discover. For one thing, among the previously unavailable Galenic treatises that had come to light in the 1530s was one of fundamental importance for the whole Galenic system, called *On the teachings of Hippocrates and Plato (De placitis)*. In this work Galen had brought to bear numerous anatomical and vivisectional demonstrations to refute some of the central tenets of Aristotle's biology and psychology, above all his doctrine of the primacy of the heart.[131] Before this time physicians and philosophers alike, under the influence of Averroes, had tended to side with Aristotle on these issues, but the availability of *De placitis* coupled with the growing respect for both Galen and anatomy tended to polarize opinion within the arts faculties of Italy, with the medical professors, who were both more numerous and more influential, generally coming down on Galen's side.[132] The Paduan medical faculty in particular was solidly Galenic in this regard,[133] and by the early seventeenth century anatomy and Galenism were still so closely linked that Cremonini found it expedient to attack the one to get at the other.

However, the fact that anatomical observations could threaten Aristotle's authority on certain specific issues was symptomatic of a more profound change within the arts university, namely that anatomy had, to a significant degree, displaced Aristotelian natural philosophy from its traditional position as the basis for medicine. 'Anatomy, the foundation of all of medicine' had become a byword at Padua,[134] and it was this notion that Cremonini particularly sought to discredit. Anatomy is the 'foundation' of nothing, he declared, and many of the errors of Galen and his followers stem from the fact that they have ignored the 'fundamenta naturalia', that is the rational, natural philosophical foundations of all true knowledge.[135] The physicians make the error of basing their opinions on sense data alone, whereas the

130 Ibid., p.406.
131 Temkin, *Galenism*, pp.53–5.
132 An excellent insight into the role of *De placitis* in this regard is provided by the account of a disputation that occurred at Bologna in 1544, in Francesco dal Pozzo, *Apologia in anatome pro Galeno* (Venice, 1562), pp.116–36.
133 Caspar Hofmann, in the preface to *De usu lienis secundum Aristotelis* (Leipzig, 1615) so characterizes the Paduan medical faculty as he had known it in 1605.
134 For example, the Paduan students invoked this maxim in 1613 in support of their nominee for the chair of anatomy: Sterzi, *Casseri*, p.155.
135 Cremonini, *De origine*, pp.52, 365, 405.

true excellence of medicine depends upon its being subordinate to natural philosophy, that is, upon accepting from the philosopher those universal principles at which he has arrived through rational contemplation, and making them the basis of medical theory and practice. Of course, Cremonini exaggerated the extent to which the medical profession had abandoned philosophy, since all medical students still received a generous dose of Aristotelian doctrine, and Cremonini was himself one of the most influential members of the arts faculty. However, anatomy was there to stay, so that even such medical graduates of Padua as William Harvey and Caspar Hofmann, who shared Cremonini's preference for Aristotelian over Galenic physiology, combined this with the anatomical approach that they had inherited from their Galenist medical professors.[136]

Moreover, institutional realities had long since come to reflect the secure place of anatomy in the Paduan curriculum, alongside the more traditional subjects. In 1584 the *de facto* change that had occurred with the appointment of Vesalius was made official, as Fabricius and his successors were declared to be professors of anatomy with Ordinary status, ranked below the professors of theory and practice, but above the natural philosophers.[137] With this also came a substantially increased salary and *ex officio* membership in the College of Physicians and Philosophers. Fabricius's official duties were declared to be, 'throughout the whole winter to dissect cadavers, and to propound the anatomical doctrine [i.e. the separate lectures on anatomical subjects], and in the remaining months to conduct surgical instruction'.[138] A further symbol of the central importance of anatomy was the construction of a permanent anatomical theatre within the main university building in 1594, while to Fabricius personally there eventually came the designation of Supraordinary professor for life, carrying with it the highest salary of any arts professor.[139]

With advancing age Fabricius was gradually persuaded to give up first some and then all of his teaching responsibilities, first to Giulio Casseri, and then to Adriaan van den Spieghel, and following Fabricius's death in 1619 Spieghel was joined by an active colleague in anatomy and surgery, namely Francesco Piazzoni, who was given the rank of Second Ordinary.[140] Now there were to be two courses of public dissections

---

[136] W. Pagel, *William Harvey's Biological Ideas* (New York, 1967), pp.19–20, 190, 198–9.
[137] Facciolati, *Fasti*, p.388; Adelmann, *Fabricius*, p.7; Ongaro, 'Prospero Alpino', pp.102–7.
[138] Facciolati, *Fasti*, p.388.
[139] Adelmann, *Fabricius*, pp.8–11.
[140] Sterzi, *Casseri*, pp.145–60; Tomasini, *Gym. Pat.*, p.80.

every winter, though given successively rather than simultaneously, and both men are known to have been engaged in extensive private anatomical teaching as well, for those students wishing to gain personal competence at dissection.[141] However, this luxurious situation was soon ended by the premature deaths of both Piazzoni and Spieghel in 1624 and 1625 respectively, and the hiatus was prolonged by the terrible plague that ravaged Italy from 1629 to 1631. It was not until 1632 that Johann Vesling was called to the first chair of anatomy and surgery, and only in 1640 was he joined by a colleague, Pietro Marchetti. Thereafter both chairs seem to have been filled more or less continuously throughout the rest of the century. Furthermore, in 1662 the two incumbents were made professors of anatomy alone, with two new appointees taking over the teaching of surgery.[142]

Thus, 124 years after the time of Vesalius's appointment, the two chairs of surgery were at last restored, although surgery can hardly be said to have suffered in the interval. For the long-term effect of grafting the responsibility for anatomy onto the existing lectureship in surgery was to raise surgery itself to a new level of prestige within the Paduan medical world, at a time when the status of surgery elsewhere in Europe was on the decline.[143] Indeed, the process began with Vesalius himself, for by the time he left Padua he was prepared to begin the Preface to the *Fabrica* with a ringing denunciation of the split between medicine and surgery, and a call for physicians to take up the practice of surgery and thereby restore the medical art to its pristine unity. Moreover, from around this time Vesalius actually followed his own precept by engaging in the practice of major surgery, though apparently not with any degree of competence, at least initially.[144] It seems unlikely that he would have imported such attitudes from the Paris *Faculté*, and so it would appear that Vesalius was as much changed by his occupancy of a chair traditionally held by practising surgeons as his occupancy had itself expanded the qualifications for the chair to include competence at anatomy. This personal synthesis symbolizes the whole subsequent history of the chair, for the occupants from Falloppio onward were, to a

141 Tomasini, *Gym. Pat.*, pp.152, 444; *ANGAP* I, p.xxxvi; Fichtner, 'Padova e Tübingen', p.53; Francesco Piazzoni, preface to his *De partibus generationi inservientibus* (Leyden, 1644); Facciolati, *Fasti*, p.390.

142 Bertolaso, 'Ricerche d'archivio', pp.30–1.

143 For example, in 1660 the surgeons of Paris were officially stripped of all academic status. See Toby Gelfand, 'The training of surgeons in eighteenth century Paris and its influence on medical education' (The Johns Hopkins University Ph.D. dissertation, 1973), pp.18–19.

144 O'Malley, *Vesalius*, pp.205–6.

man, Doctors of Arts and Medicine, highly respected anatomists, and practitioners as well as teachers of major surgery.[145] Some effort was made to keep the two subjects distinct, for example, by giving Fabricius Ordinary status *qua* Professor of Anatomy, but not *qua* Lecturer on Surgery, but the dividing line was continually eroded by what happened in practice.[146] Thus Falloppio, Fabricius and their successors freely intermingled the demonstration of surgical procedures with their anatomical dissections, and the students seem to have reciprocated with interest in both aspects.[147] Before long Fabricius was being listed in the university Rotula simply as 'Ordinary Professor of Anatomy and Surgery', and long after the subjects were formally split in 1662 the incumbents of the chairs of anatomy continued to be physician-surgeons.[148]

As we have seen, the physician-surgeon had long had his place in Italy as the elite of the surgical profession, and now, at least at Padua, he acquired a new degree of respectability as the physician-surgeon-anatomist.[149] Fabricius himself made an enormous fortune by combining the prestige of his anatomical achievements with a practice in major surgery, and so it is not surprising that others should wish to do likewise.[150] Authors of anatomical treatises such as Michele Gavasetti and Casseri identified themselves as 'philosopher and physician, practising both parts of medicine [i.e. medicine and surgery]'.[151] Nor were such individuals strictly academic types, or at least no more so than were the elite physicians; Gavasetti seems never to have held a university post, while Casseri used the designation long before obtaining his official appointment. Moreover, from at least the later sixteenth century

[145] Gurlt, *Geschichte der Chirurgie*, II, Pt I, pp.361–403, 445–81, 486–7, 575–80; III, p.339. See also on Marchetti, note 83 above.

[146] *ANGAP* II, p.108. See also Tomasini, *Gym. Pat.*, p.302, 'Ad anatomen cum Ordinariis, & ad chirurgiam'.

[147] Falloppio, *Opera* (Venice, 1584), pp.596–600; *ANGAP* II, pp.178, 180; Adelmann, *Fabricius*, p.22; Sterzi, *Casseri*, pp.132–3.

[148] See the Rotula for 1601, reproduced in Whitteridge, *Harvey and the Circulation*, facing p.2. When Morgagni, a non-surgeon, was appointed to the chair of anatomy in 1715, it was still necessary to point out that the two subjects had been formally split: Morgagni, *Opera postuma*, I (Rome, 1964), p.43.

[149] O. Temkin, 'The role of surgery in the rise of modern medical thought', *Bulletin of the History of Medicine*, XXV (1951), 249–50, points out that in the Netherlands during the seventeenth and eighteenth centuries the position of surgery with respect to anatomy and medicine was similar to that which obtained in Italy.

[150] Adelmann, *Fabricius*, pp.28–30.

[151] Gurlt, *Geschichte der Chirurgie*, II, Pt I, pp.487, 545; see also p.575. In Harvey's Paduan diploma, Casseri was described as 'Anatomen, Physicam, & Chyrurgiam exercentem': William Harvey, *Opera* (1766), p.639.

onward the position of Surgeon to the Hospital of St Francis at Padua was regularly held by full Doctors of Arts and Medicine, who were engaged in private anatomical and surgical teaching in addition to their surgical practice.[152] And while most of the Paduan medical professors seem to have restricted their practice to internal medicine, they generally were very much interested in surgical problems, and on the whole seem to have had a quite positive attitude toward both surgery and surgeons.[153]

Throughout the period we have been considering the dominant ideology of the Paduan school continued to be that of staunch loyalty to the Galenic tradition, although as we have seen this ostensibly conservative outlook proved to be quite compatible with a fairly dynamic process of evolutionary change. Medicine as taught at Padua in the early seventeenth century was significantly different from that of a century before. Not surprisingly, however, there was one aspect of the curriculum in which the conservative attitude did make for a relatively static condition, namely the teaching of medical theory. Indeed, for upwards of five hundred years, from the thirteenth century to 1767, theory continued to be taught at Padua through a three-year cycle of commentary on the first *fen* of Avicenna, the *Aphorisms* of Hippocrates, and Galen's *Ars medica*.[154] However, in assessing this remarkable continuity one should distinguish between the lectures on Avicenna, on the one hand, and those on Hippocrates and Galen, on the other. The *Aphorisms* and the *Ars medica* were the only two authentic Hippocratic and Galenic works in the official curriculum, so that the teaching based upon them symbolized the commitment of the Paduan school to the classical tradition. Moreover, the canonical status of these texts was greatly reinforced by the fact that the formal examination for a medical

---

[152]   The list of hospital surgeons from 1569 is given in Antonelli, *Cenni storici*, pp.156ff. On Nicolao Bucella, see *ANGAP* I, pp.70, 75–6 (where he is called 'physices tum chirurgiae Doctor') and pp.85, 89, 92 (where he is called 'Medicus et Chyrurgus'). Tiberio Bolognese is probably the individual referred to in *ANGAP* II, p.113, as 'Doctor Tiberius Phialetus Bononiensis Chirurgus et Anatomicus' and by Sassonia, *Prognoseon*, p.85, as 'Tiberius Phialetus Philosophus, Medicus, ac Chirurgus Excellentissimus'. Francesco Barbero is apparently the same as 'D. Franciscus . . . Campana Nosodochii Chirurgus et Medicus Ordinarius', *ANGAP* II, p.274; see also pp.211, 225, 227, 261. On Giulio Cesare Sala, see *ANGAP* II, pp.357–8, 360 (where he is called 'physicus'), 368. On Marchetti, see note 83 above. See also Sterzi, *Casseri*, pp.15–16.

[153]   Gurlt, *Geschichte der Chirurgie*, II, Pt 2, pp.313–14, 417–21, 427–32, 483–5, 522–5, 558–65. See also, e.g., Rudio's discussion of the 'praestantia' of surgery relative to internal medicine in the dedication of his *De affectibus externarum corporis humani partium libri septem . . . utrisque et chirurgis, et Physicis communes, & utilissimi* (Venice, 1606). However, for a somewhat negative view of surgery see Shea, *Galileo's Intellectual Revolution*, p.35.

[154]   B. Bertolaso, 'Ricerche d'Archivio su alcuni aspetti dell'insegnamento medico presso l'università di Padova nelle sette- e ottocento', *Acta Medicae Historiae Patavina*, v (1958–9), 7–8.

degree consisted essentially in expounding a randomly chosen passage from each of these two works. Consequently, to the extent that the professors of theory had the duty of preparing the students for this examination, they could not ignore the texts themselves in favour of straightforward lectures, as the professors of other subjects tended to do. Thus in the early eighteenth century Giovanni Battista Morgagni assured his students that his primary objective in his lectures on theory was to see to it that they were well prepared for their examination on the prescribed texts.[155]

Avicenna had once enjoyed somewhat comparable status as an authority, but he had largely lost it as a consequence of the humanist movement. In fact, he was probably more the butt of criticism for having corrupted ancient medicine than any other single author. He did, however, retain his place in the official curriculum, perhaps because there was no single work by an ancient physician that was comparable in scope to Book I, *fen* 1 of the *Canon*; this is essentially a survey of medical physiology, that is, the natural philosophical principles of human life: elements, temperaments, humours, organs and faculties. However, by the mid-sixteenth century the thrust of the commentary on this work had become, not to expound Avicenna's views but to show what the ancients had taught on these subjects and how Avicenna had distorted their doctrines.[156] Moreover, as interests evolved beyond strict classical orthodoxy, the commentary on Avicenna continued to serve as a fairly flexible format for discussing whatever the lecturer wished. Thus in the early seventeenth century Santorio included rather lengthy discussions of his statical method and of his various other measuring devices and surgical instruments, as well as such things as the Copernican system and the cause of the tides.[157] A century later Morgagni confined his lectures on Avicenna more strictly to the assigned subject of physiology, but the detailed content of what he conveyed was derived primarily from the anatomists and physiologists of the seventeenth and early eighteenth centuries, rather than from the ancients.[158]

However, at the beginning of these lectures Morgagni acknowledged that few Paduan medical students bothered to attend any of the public lectures, whether they were more traditional or more up-to-date in

[155] Morgagni, *Opera postuma*, IV (Rome, 1969), pp.5 and 6.
[156] Oddi degli Oddi, *In primam fen primi libri canonis Avicennae dilucidissima & expectatissima expositio* (Venice, 1575), p.1, and, e.g., pp.402, 406, 416, 477–8.
[157] Santorio Santorio, *Commentaria in primam fen primi libri canonis Avicennae* (Venice, 1626), e.g. cols. 7, 21–4, 27–8, 118–24, 133–5, 302, 405–6, 512–13.
[158] Morgagni, *Opera postuma*, IV and V (Rome, 1969 and 1975), passim.

content.[159] It would seem therefore that such measures as that of 1597, discussed above, had been relatively ineffective in arresting this tendency to neglect the lectures. On the other hand, we have seen that there is abundant evidence that the students cared deeply about the practical precepting that would prepare them for their careers as medical practitioners, and further, that they looked primarily to the anatomists to satisfy their interests in more basic scientific questions. Thus Morgagni showed excellent judgment when, in 1715, he transferred from the chair of medical theory to that of anatomy, thereby helping to cement a relationship between anatomy and internal medicine analogous to that which had long obtained between anatomy and surgery at the School of Padua.[160]

159 Ibid., IV, p.6.
160 See note 148. The classic embodiment of this relationship is, of course, Morgagni's *De sedibus et causis morborum per anatomen indagatis* (Venice, 1761).

Sanford Vincent Larkey (1898–1969)

MARGARET PELLING

Sanford Larkey belonged for most of his working life to the set of institutions developed around the Johns Hopkins Hospital and Medical School by William Welch. Welch had his later medical training in Europe under teachers who included Karl Ludwig, Julius Cohnheim, Robert Koch and Max von Pettenkofer. On his return to America, Welch provided in the Johns Hopkins School an exemplar of his views on medical education. William Osler was among those he selected to join the staff. During the First World War Welch's own interests moved from pathology to public health, and, in 1926, he resigned from the School in order to pursue research into the history of medicine. Both these phases were successively embodied in new institutions at the School. The Institute of the History of Medicine, and the William H. Welch Medical Library, were inaugurated in 1929, the participants in the ceremony including Simon Flexner, Harvey Cushing, and Karl Sudhoff, the first incumbent of the Leipzig chair in the history of medicine, which was unique when it was founded in 1905. When Larkey moved to the Institute in 1935, it was headed by Henry Sigerist, the pupil but not the follower of Sudhoff, who had come there from Leipzig and remained as director, and professor of the history of medicine until 1947.

Larkey's biography reflects some of the same interests and values.[1] Born in California, the son of a physician, Alonzo Sanford Larkey, he graduated MD at the University of California in 1925. His humanist bias expressed itself in the form of a lifelong taste for the history and literature of England, and in particular the Tudor period. He matriculated in 1925 from Pembroke College, Oxford, and took out a

---

[1] See O. Temkin, 'Sanford Vincent Larkey, 1898–1969' [with a bibliography by J. B. Koudelka], *Bulletin of the History of Medicine*, XLIV (1970), 80–5; [obituary], *Bulletin of the Medical Library Association*, LVII (1969), 321; W. B. McDaniel II, 'Sanford V. Larkey MD', ibid., XXXVII (1949), 257–60; [biography], *National Cyclopedia of American Biography* (James T. White & Co., forthcoming). I am grateful to Mrs Pearson Henderson for a copy of the last of these.

BA in English literature in 1928. On his return to California, his first posts formally represented the combination of bibliographical and historical interests which characterized him. He was assistant professor of the history of medicine and librarian of the Medical School at the University of California from 1930 to 1935, during which period he held an international fellowship in Tudor science at the Huntington Library. In 1935, at the age of 37, he achieved the same combination by being appointed director of the Welch Medical Library and lecturer at the Johns Hopkins Institute, after the precedent set by the previous holder of both posts, Fielding Garrison. He retired from the former post in 1963 but held the lectureship, and with it his connections with the Institute, until his death. His contributions to the course curriculum of the Institute were chiefly in the form of instruction on the use of the library, but he also participated in seminars, gave radio talks, and presented papers, most of which were later published, to such bodies as the Washington Academy of Sciences, the American Association for the History of Medicine (of which Sigerist had been one of the founders), and the History of Science Society.

The Second World War had a long-term effect on the direction of Larkey's work, and could be regarded as the most active and stimulating phase of his life. An early advocate of American participation, he had served in the US Army in the First World War and joined the US Army Medical Corps in the Second, leaving it with the rank of colonel. In this capacity he acted as chief of the school branch of the Training Division, supervising medical training in universities and colleges. From 1940 until the middle 1950s he was involved in work arising out of the national defence programme and aimed at the better co-ordination and effectiveness of research. Larkey deplored and sought to remedy the lack of attention and funds given to communicating the results of research, realizing that, without efficient bibliographical services, the real effect of such research might be negligible. Eventually, in 1949, a contract was settled between the Welch Medical Library and the Armed Forces Medical Library for a project to evaluate the current medical indexes, and medical subject headings and nomenclature, with a view to standardization and the introduction of machine methods if these proved more efficient. This project, which presented its last report in 1955, helped to pioneer the use of IBM machines in indexing and bibliography; it ran in conjunction with international attempts, on the part of such bodies as UNESCO and the Royal Society of London, directed towards the same ends and arising equally from the worldwide expansion in government-sponsored research which had occurred during and after the Second World War. The mode of categorization of subject headings developed by Larkey's group was subsequently adopted by *Index Medicus*, and the Welch Medical Library, the National Library of Medicine and other institutions used this and the group's related mechanized system of punch cards to re-organize their catalogues and their retrieval of serial publications.

Although financial support for bibliographical research was slow in coming, the concerns of Larkey and others aware of the problem of the efficient use of information were partly represented by a 'Committee of Information' of the National Research Council. The Information Committee had various relevant subcommittees, one of which, the Historical Records Subcommittee, included J. F. Fulton, Larkey and Cushing. This body had the intention of writing a history of the United States's involvement in the Second World War, and Larkey was evidently chosen to cover the medical services. He served on the editorial board of the American Medical Association's *War Medicine*, which was involved in the early planning of the medical history of the war, and in 1943 was attached as chief of the Historical Division to the Office of the Chief Surgeon in Europe. Although asked to continue with this work after 1946, he declined on the grounds of the length of his leave of absence from Johns Hopkins, and apparently published nothing under his own name in the official histories. He also refused invitations to produce studies of medical aspects of the war on his own account, feeling that these would be too severely limited by his earlier official commitment and the classified status of much of the relevant material.[2] He did however serve as consultant to the Historical Division, and was still active in that capacity in 1949.

Larkey's work in connection with the national defence programme reduced the time available for his other historical interests; item 27 in the bibliography was published incomplete for this reason. However, there was no real incompatibility of principle between these two types of work. Both were directed by a humanist spirit; both paid attention to education, readership, and thereby to substantive effects. In Larkey's view the development of scientific knowledge had two aspects: scientific thought itself, and the standard sources or textbooks. His own work, especially the products of his life-long interest in Robert Recorde and Thomas Digges, illustrated that, by carefully examining the second

---

[2] Personal communication. For further details of Larkey's work during the war, see *National Cyclopedia of American Biography*.

aspect, distortions could often be discovered in the historical account given of the first. Larkey's respect for apparently minor figures led him to important conclusions about the introduction of the views of Vesalius and Copernicus to England, and the emergence of anti-Aristotelianism before Ramus. The significant contributions of Recorde to mathematics and of Digges to cosmology were also made clear. His approach allowed Larkey to notice the unity of theory and practice in the work of Recorde, and the emphasis on utility of the humanist programme of educational reform. All his articles were characterized by a thorough bibliographical knowledge, and a determination to allow the contemporary writer to speak for himself – a sound precaution in the case of authors almost unread. Consistent with this attitude, Larkey placed considerable emphasis on making available representative texts. He saw the critical bibliography of original works as a means of redeeming from obscurity 'the average scientific worker of the Renaissance', and, more generally, as a pre-requisite for the special studies which were to be done before general histories of science should even be attempted.[3] He noted, and was able to assess, every point of information offered by a printed book, and was also able to show that this information was of far greater usefulness than commonly supposed.

Larkey's chief interests were in the field of medical history, but he saw medical thought, in the fifteenth and sixteenth centuries at least, as an integrated part of the general culture, belonging to anyone who could read.[4] He concentrated on England, but was well aware of the influence of continental sources. He had a special respect for works published in the vernacular, but also knew that the vernacular tradition, like printing itself, propagated both old and new learning. Thus he was able to arrive at a more balanced estimate of contemporary knowledge, and the extent to which prominent figures such as Shakespeare were typical rather than prodigious in their acquaintance with medical and other ideas. The Renaissance and Tudor period (*c.* 1485–1603) attracted him because he saw it as transitional, the first dissemination of printed works preparing the ground for the 'revolutionary' age of Bacon, Harvey and Sydenham, but in a complex and characteristic way. It interested him, for example, to notice that the earliest applications of the methodology which came to be called Baconian, coincided with an increasing susceptibility towards alchemy and astrology.

---

[3] For Larkey's views on current history of science, see items 27 and 35 in the bibliography below.
[4] Larkey accepted the finding of other historians that the level of literacy in sixteenth-century England was high.

For Larkey as for others of his generation, the library was as important as the laboratory, which was beginning in any case to reveal itself as creating problems as well as solving them. Larkey himself, rather unusually, envisaged that fundamental collaboration between bibliographer and scientist should also occur in the laboratory, and he opposed a professionalizing of medical librarianship which led to an emphasis on techniques at the expense of an active knowledge of sources. In spite of his espousal of machine methods, the substance of his position was a warning against present and imminent dangers. A book, to his point of view, was and should be 'the epitome of the age itself'; in the books of the past the sciences were united, theory was allied to practice, and science and humanism were combined.[5] The history of medicine had a role of this kind to play in modern education, but Larkey followed Sigerist and George Sarton in thinking that 'the admission that something *like* the humanities is needed is really an argument for the humanities'.[6] In an appraisal of 1949, he saw the humanistic approach to medical history being increasingly followed in the future, and a close relation developing between the historical and the social sciences. The function of history itself could be seen by demonstrating the debt which innovators such as Harvey and Vesalius bore to their own pasts.[7]

Although a bibliographer, Larkey did not limit his own communications to the medium of publication. He enjoyed discussing his work, and that of others; about a third of his published articles were written in collaboration with a number of other workers, and he probably stimulated as many projects as he completed himself.[8] In many of his articles he can be said to have acted as the collaborator of the author of the original work discussed. His papers were often short or occasional, and he produced no book. However, in addition to his published work he also left a collection of papers, now in the possession of Pembroke College, Oxford.[9] The bulk of this is a series of bibliographical cards and textual extracts from sixteenth-century medical and other literature, which was intended to supply the basis of a volume of 'Tudor Scientific Prose'. There are also ten drafts of historical papers, some of which had

---

[5] Larkey's views on the book were clearly those he himself attributed to Le Roy Crummer, who preceded Larkey in reassessing pre-Vesalian anatomy, and the contribution of Vesalius's editors and translators. See item 13.

[6] The quotation is from item 35.

[7] Ibid.

[8] The bibliography below is based on that first prepared by Miss Helen Field: see McDaniel, 'Sanford Larkey'.

[9] I am indebted to Pembroke College for allowing me to consult the Larkey Papers, for which an excellent handlist has been prepared by Mr M. A. L. Cooke.

been read publicly, on subjects congruent with those of the present volume: medicine and public health in Tudor England, Paracelsian medicine, the medical profession and medical practice in Elizabethan England, the plague in English history and literature, astrology and medicine, 'microcosm and macrocosm'. Larkey had been interested in these subjects since the 1930s.[10] He had hoped to use his retirement to carry out a larger project.[11] The terms of this were evolved in conjunction with the Folger Library, to which Larkey had acted as an adviser since about 1963. His stated aim was to arrive at a complete picture of what the average Elizabethan, medical or lay, knew of the medical thought of his time, and to relate this knowledge to the classical heritage and to newer continental developments. The basis of the project was to be the close study of some 200 primary texts, and it was to consist of four complementary parts: firstly, a number of articles or short monographs, on such areas as public health legislation and practice (including housing), sixteenth-century English versions of Galen and Hippocrates, and the translators of medical classics into English; secondly, a small book for the general reader, probably called *Medicine in Shakespeare's England*, to appear in the Folger Booklets series; thirdly, a series of modern reprints, for which he provisionally selected works by Thomas Cogan and Thomas Lodge, and translations of Levinus Lemnius (by Thomas Newton), Roesslin (by Jonas), Dodoens (by Henry Lyte) and William Fulke (by William Painter). These last were to be produced in a form comparable with that of his earlier editions of *An Herbal* and Turner on wines, as items in the Folger Documents series.[12] The editing of the text of Cogan only had been completed, although he had planned an edition of Fulke's *Antiprognosticon* as early as 1934. The fourth and last part of the project was to be a 'definitive monograph', to fill a gap still remaining in spite of work done on sixteenth- and fifteenth-century medicine since 1945. Of the booklet and the monograph, only the former is represented in Larkey's papers in a recognizable form. It is interesting to note the degree to which Larkey's uncompleted project highlights areas of persistent neglect in the historical treatment of the late Renaissance and Tudor periods.

[10] Among the relevant unpublished items in the Larkey Papers is the typescript of an adaptation for the stage by Larkey of Bullein's *Dialogue Against the Fever Pestilence*. This was performed by medical students at Johns Hopkins in 1939, following a successful precedent of the previous year in which talks by Sigerist were combined with the performance of contemporary music associated with syphilis, tarantism and plague.

[11] The following account is based on drafts of successive research proposals in the Larkey Papers. Larkey's work after 1963 was supported by a grant from the National Institutes of Health.

[12] See for example items 20, 28, and 30.

Regarded by his contemporaries as energetic, outspoken and perhaps impulsive, Larkey was active politically as a member of the Baltimore Democratic Club, and the Maryland State Board of Public Welfare (1951–63). He had been a Republican but altered his allegiance to work for the election of Franklin Roosevelt. His articles on public health in Elizabethan England show, in passing, his concern for the lack of progress or even the regression which had taken place in the field of 'socialized medicine'. For Larkey, as for Sigerist in greater degree, 'scholarship and public activities ... belonged to the substance of life'.[13] Larkey died in Baltimore on 16 April 1969, after a long illness.

Bibliography of Sanford Larkey

1. [with W. J. Kerr and A. E. Larsen] 'Coronary occlusion and myocardial degenerations; some clinical and pathological considerations', *California and Western Medicine*, XXIII (1925), 46–51.
2. 'Galen: Greek, medievalist and modern', *California and Western Medicine*, XXXIV (1931), 271–5, 366–9.
3. *Medical Knowledge in Tudor England, as Displayed in an Exhibition of Books and Manuscripts*, Henry E. Huntington Library and Art Gallery (San Marino, Calif., 1932).
4. 'A critical bibliography of English medicine and biology, 1477–1603' [Second International Congress of the History of Science, London, 1931], *Archeion*, XIV (1932), 533–4.
5. 'The Vesalian compendium of Geminus and Nicholas Udall's translation: their relation to Vesalius, Caius, Vicary, and de Mondeville', *The Library*, XIII(1933), 367–94. Repr. London, 1933.
6. 'Childbirth in the days of Queen Elizabeth', *American Journal of Obstetrics and Gynecology*, XXVII (1934), 303–8. Repr. *The Centaur of Alpha Kappa Kappa*, XLI (1936), 243–7; also [St Louis, 1934].
7. [with L. Tum Suden] 'Jackson's English translation of Berengarius of Carpi's "Isogogae Breves", 1660 and 1664', *Isis*, XXI (1934), 57–70. Repr. Bruges [1934].
8. [with Francis R. Johnson] 'Thomas Digges, the Copernican system, and the idea of the infinity of the universe in 1576', *Huntington Library Bulletin*, V (1934), 69–117. Containing Thomas Digges, 'A perfit description of the caelestiall orbes'. Repr. [1934].
9. 'Public health in Tudor England', *American Journal of Public Health*, XXIV (1934), 912–13.
10. 'Public health in Tudor England', *American Journal of Public Health*, XXIV (1934), 1099–102. Repr. in *The Medical Officer*, LII (1934), 233–4, and [New York, 1934].

---

13 Temkin, 'Sanford Larkey'.

11. 'Astrology and politics in the first years of Elizabeth's reign', *Bulletin of the Institute of the History of Medicine*, III (1935), 171–86. Repr. [Berkeley, Calif., 1935].

12. [with F. R. Johnson] 'Robert Recorde's mathematical teaching and the anti-Aristotelian movement', *Huntington Library Bulletin*, VII (1935), 59–87. Repr. [n.pl. 1935].

13. '[Le Roy Crummer] the writer', in A. G. Beaman (ed.), *A Doctor's Odyssey, a Sentimental Record of Le Roy Crummer* (Baltimore, 1935), pp. 169–79.

14. 'Rare books in the Welch Medical Library. I. Conrad Gesner's copy of the Aphorisms of Hippocrates, Basel, 1547', *Bulletin of the Institute of the History of Medicine*, IV (1936), 61–4.

15. 'The Hippocratic Oath in Elizabethan England', *Bulletin of the Institute of the History of Medicine*, IV (1936), 201–9.

16. 'Scientific glossaries in sixteenth century English books', *Bulletin of the Institute of the History of Medicine*, V (1937), 105–14.

17. 'John Shaw Billings and the history of medicine', *Bulletin of the Institute of the History of Medicine*, VI (1938), 360–76. Also in *Bulletin of the Johns Hopkins Hospital*, LXII (1938), 272–88.

18. 'Two letters by John Shaw Billings on the history of medicine, with a Foreword by Sanford V. Larkey', *Bulletin of the Institute of the History of Medicine*, VI (1938), 394–8.

19. [with G. Miller] 'An exhibit of the works of Claude Bernard', *Bulletin of the Institute of the History of Medicine*, VI (1938), 649–68.

20. Introduction to M. Andreas Laurentius [du Laurens], *A Discourse of the Preservation of the Sight: of Melancholike Diseases; of Rheumes, and of Old Age*, trans. Richard Surphlet, 1599 edn, Shakespeare Association Facsimiles no. 15 (London, 1938).

21. 'Health in Elizabethan England', in *The March of Medicine*, ed. by the Committee on Lectures to the Laity of the New York Academy of Medicine (New York, 1940), pp. 18–45.

22. 'The National Research Council and medical preparedness', *Journal of the American Medical Association*, CXV (1940), 1640–3.

23. 'The National Research Council and medical preparedness', *War Medicine*, I (1941), 77–94.

24. 'The division of medical sciences of the National Research Council and national defense', *Science*, XCIII (1941), 241–4.

25. 'Medical research for defense', *Talks: a Quarterly Digest of Addresses of Diversified Interests Broadcast over the Columbia Network*, VI (1941), 53.

26. '... Renaissance to Restoration. VII. Science and pseudo-science', in *Cambridge Bibliography of English Literature*, I (Cambridge, 1941), pp. 879–94.

27. [with F. R. Johnson] 'Science [in the Renaissance]', *Modern Language Quarterly*, II (1941), 363–401.

28. Introduction to *A Book of Wines, by William Turner, together with a Modern English Version of the Text by the Editors* [Larkey and Wagner] ... *and an Oenological Note by Philip M. Wagner*, Scholars' Facsimiles and Reprints (New York, 1941).

29. 'Organization for medical defense', *Bulletin of the Medical Library Association*, xxx (1941), 56–62.

30. [with T. Pyles] *An Herbal [1525], Edited and Transcribed into Modern English with an Introduction*, Scholars' Facsimiles and Reprints (New York, 1941).

31. [with O. Temkin] 'John Banister and the pulmonary circulation', *Essays in Biology. In Honor of Herbert M. Evans. Written by his Friends* (Berkeley and Los Angeles, 1943), pp.287–92.

32. 'Medicine in 1847 – Great Britain' [Symposium: One Hundred Years Ago], *Bulletin of the History of Medicine*, xxi (1947), 478–84.

33. 'Introduction to the problems of medical subject headings', *Bulletin of the Medical Library Association*, xxxvi (1948), 70–81.

34. 'The Army Medical Library research project at the Welch Medical Library', *Bulletin of the Medical Library Association*, xxxvii (1949), 121–4.

35. 'Thoughts on medical history and libraries – 1847 and 1947', *Bulletin of the New York Academy of Medicine*, 2nd ser., xxv (1949), 65–83.

36. 'Report on the Johns Hopkins University research project', *Bulletin of the Medical Library Association*, xxxviii (1950), 113–17.

37. 'The Medical Library Association and medical research', *Bulletin of the Medical Library Association*, xxxviii (1950), 291–5.

38. 'Medical journalism', *World Medical Association Bulletin*, iii (1951), 56–63.

39. 'Report on the research project at the Welch Medical Library, The Johns Hopkins University', *Bulletin of the Medical Library Association*, xxxix (1951), 87–9.

40. 'Some approaches to the problem of indexing', *Bulletin of the Medical Library Association*, xl (1952), 107–12.

41. 'The Welch Medical Library indexing project', *Bulletin of the Medical Library Association*, xli (1953), 32–40.

42. [with C. D. Leake and H. F. Lutz] 'The management of fractures according to the Hearst papyrus', in E. A. Underwood (ed.), *Science, Medicine and History: Essays on the Evolution of Scientific Thought and Medical Practice Written in Honour of Charles Singer* (2 vols., London, 1953), i, pp.61–74.

43. Introduction to 'Government sponsorship of medical research, a symposium', *Bulletin of the Medical Library Association*, xliii (1955), 17–18.

44. [with W. A. Himwich, H. G. Field, E. E. Garfield and J. M. Whittock, Jr] *Survey of World Medical Serials and Coverage by Indexing and Abstracting Services*, Welch Medical Library/Armed Forces Medical Library Project (Baltimore, 1954).

45. [with H. G. Field, W. A. Himwich, E. E. Garfield and J. M. Whittock, Jr] *Final Report on Subject Headings and on Subject Indexing*, Welch Medical Library/Armed Forces Medical Library Project (Baltimore, 1955).

46. [with W. A. Himwich, H. G. Field, E. E. Garfield, and J. M. Whittock, Jr] *Final Report on Machine Methods for Information Searching*, Welch Medical Library/Armed Forces Medical Library Project (Baltimore, 1955).

47. 'Cooperative information processing – prospectus – medicine', in J. H. Shera, A. Kent & J. W. Perry (eds.), *Documentation in Action* (New York, 1956), pp. 301–6.

48. [with J. M. Whittock, Jr] 'Trends in medical abstracting and indexing tools, a symposium. Abstracting services for medicine and related fields', *Bulletin of the Medical Library Association*, XLIV (1956), 416–23.

49. 'In memory of Henry E. Sigerist', *Bulletin of the History of Medicine*, XXXI (1957), 301–4.

50. 'Leprosy in medieval romance: a note on Robert Henryson's "Testament of Cresseid"', *Bulletin of the History of Medicine*, XXXV (1961), 77–80.

51. [with J. M. Whittock, Jr, and E. Eyzaguirre, E. G. Covert, J. B. Koudelka] *The Welch Medical Library – Subject Catalog* (Baltimore, 1961).

52. [with J. B. Koudelka] 'Medical societies and Civil War politics', *Bulletin of the History of Medicine*, XXXVI (1962), 1–12.

INDEX